SHUT THEM DOWN!

THE G8, GLENEAGLES 2005 AND THE MOVEMENT OF MOVEMENTS

Edited by David Harvie, Keir Milburn,
Ben Trott and David Watts

Jointly published by Dissent! and Autonomedia
December 2005

Dissent!   Autonomedia
23–25 Wharf Street   POB 568 Williamsburgh Station
Leeds LS2 7EQ   Brooklyn
West Yorkshire   New York 11211-0568
UK   USA

www.dissent.org.uk   www.autonomedia.org
                                     info@autonomedia.org

ISBN 0-9552065-0-2
ISBN 978-0-9552065-0-4

Cover photo: © Paul Mattsson (paulmattsson@btopenworld.com)
Printed and bound in Great Britain

"If you go to a demonstration and then go home, that's something. But the people in power can live with that. What they can't live with is sustained pressure that keeps on building, groups that keep on doing things, people that learn from the last time and do it better next time..."

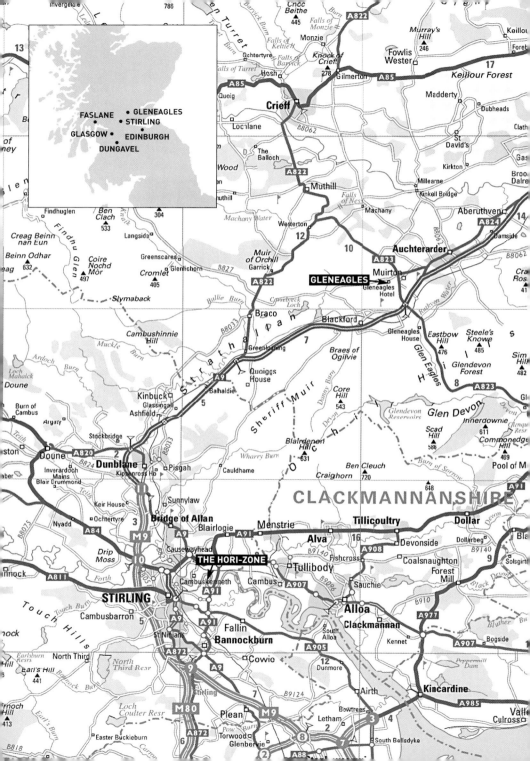

contents

contents

contents

INTRODUCTION

In July 2005, the rulers of the 'Group of Eight' most powerful states – Canada, France, Germany, Italy, Japan, Russia, the UK and the US – came to Gleneagles in Scotland for their annual set-piece summit. As has come to be expected, they were met with counter-summits, protests and blockades. The focus of this book is those attempts to... Shut Them Down!

This book contains some amazing and exciting stories of ordinary people doing extraordinary things but, beyond that, you might wonder why we need to publish anything about the 2005 anti-G8 mobilisation. Was it not just the latest repetition in a series of protests that has already produced many books? This misses the point. Each of these mobilisations is an event within a wider social movement, often called 'the movement of movements,' and the point about social movements is that they *move*. This is how we can best define them: as the shifting or development of social relations. We can see this development by looking at each counter-mobilisation in turn. Each one is different. Each has its specific context. Each presents us with new problems, new lessons to be learnt and prompts particular innovations.

In 1999, the protests against the World Trade Organization in Seattle marked the emergence of a movement into public consciousness. The problem Seattle brought to the surface was the strange new alliances and the startling mix of protesters (trade unions and environmentalists, anarchists and communists, queer activists and church groups). The reflecting and theorising that followed tended to focus on the contradictions in these alliances as they played out in protest tactics, in particular the attitudes towards the window-smashing tactics of the 'black bloc'. A year later, the Prague anti-IMF and World Bank protests saw the development of the principle of 'diversity of tactics,' with the physical sep-aration of the protesters according to their preferred levels of confrontation. This move was then disrupted by an horrific escalation of violence on the part of the police, firstly when three people were shot in Gothenburg, in June 2001, and then with the indiscriminate violence in Genoa five weeks later, which saw beat-ings, torture and the murder of Carlo Giuliani. The reflections that followed focused on this repression, how to deal with it and whether the movement should split or hold together in the face of it.

At Gleneagles[1] the notion of 'violence' versus 'non-violence' did not seem to be such an issue, and the content of this book reflects that. Instead Gleneagles has thrown up its own themes that relate to its specific context. In 2005 the G8 summit was, like most post-Genoa summits, located in a rural area, although Glen-eagles is certainly not as remote as some of the locations our 'leaders' have tried to hide away in. We responded with a strategy that had been developed at the Evian G8 summit two years earlier: our counter-mobilisation was centred on rural camping convergence spaces, enabling multiple blockades of the roads surrounding the summit and the disruption of the delegates and staff that keep the summit running. These tactics proved tremendously effective in facilitating such a deep level of self-organisation that the summit was disrupted, despite a huge security and police operation, which contained the suspension of large swathes of 'civil liberties'.

However, tactics forced on to us also carried their own problems and dangers. We needed, for instance, to maintain a sense of connection across geographically dispersed sites of blockades and protests. And, more fundamen-tally, there was the danger of isolation from the 'general public,' since the conver-gence sites had to be located in such sparsely populated areas. As it turned out, this danger was compounded by one of the more novel aspects of the 2005 G8 summit, the Make Poverty History (MPH) campaign.

For the first time in the G8's history, there was a major campaign to *welcome* the summit. Already pro-G8, MPH itself became overshadowed by Bob Geldof, Richard Curtis and their Live8 concert. A feature of Geldof and Curtis's involve-ment was their activism by press conference: ignoring the wider feeling of MPH's constituent parts, they continually imposed their own agenda and interpretation of events. This was a concerted attempt to capture the energy of the alter-global-isation and anti-capitalist movements, using this energy to fuel a celebrity-led pro-summit and, ultimately, pro-government demonstration. It is hard now to recall the level of hype surrounding Live8 and MPH and the sycophancy accorded Geldof by the media. The effect of MPH-Live8 was to create a situation akin to a surreal

Stalinist state, where the government sets the limits on demonstrators' demands and decrees as illegitimate any protests outside that framework (setting forth a huge security operation to enforce this decree).

This book contains the stories of how people both succeeded and failed to escape this trap. Over seven days, a series of protests and events refused the script that had been provided. The highpoint of this was undoubtedly the road blockades on Wednesday July 6. We brought central Scotland to a standstill, scattering delegates and staff to the four winds and disrupting the summit's opening day. That evening, it seemed we might be able to go on with the disruption and cause the summit to collapse. But even without that, the potential seemed huge. MPH had been almost unopposed in the press, but now, our anti-summit event was impossible to ignore: a new narrative could not possibly be kept out of the media. As the reality of the G8 agreements on debt emerged, our account could only be vindicated, while theirs could only be shown up as spin. The MPH-Live8-New Labour axis was ripe for splintering and might have easily shattered.

But just when it looked like we might possibly shut down the entire summit, and turn all that media hype against its very orchestrators, history shifted again. Bombs exploded in central London and sucked all media attention away from Gleneagles. Without mass media attention, MPH, being almost purely media- and celebrity-driven, dissolved away. The movement that had wanted to shut down the G8 was in a different position, however. In the days which immediately followed the July 7 bombings, we became paralysed by the speed of events – unable to offer much in the way of a collective response to the bombings, or to begin evaluating the meaning or the impact of the mobilisation in light of the events which had just unfolded. It was only in the weeks and months which followed that we have been able to realise the singular nature of the Gleneagles events – of a major success for our movement, deprived of the subsequent media attention which has traditionally followed such events.

Episodes of media attention are always dangerous for social movements, which are, on the whole, ignored. Firstly, the media may cheer-lead state repression. Individuals can be arbitrarily picked out, held up as leaders and hounded. More fundamentally, media hysteria tends to cause social movements to inflate uncontrollably based upon a simplified and flattened representation of the complex dynamics the movement originally consisted of. There is no telling which direction things will go in after such uncontrolled inflation: such flattened representations may form the basis for a whole new burst of movement, for better or ill, or they may not.

Instead of this, our movement now occupies a weird nether-world. Energy has been injected into the movement because we acted successfully, yet it has been neither amplified nor distorted by media attention. There was movement but no inflation. This is not a state of affairs that we planned or hoped for, but it still has tremendous potential. For starters, there is no mass media-written first draft of history we have to escape from before we can learn our own lessons. (After all, if the movement had expanded based on the media representation of the event it would be hard not to attempt to simply repeat it in a simplified fashion.) Instead, we have space and we can harness the energy created to move in productive directions.

That is why we[2] have rushed to get this book out as soon as possible. We see it as part of the movement against the G8. Such mobilisations do not just last a week. For many months before July 2005, people were meeting, discussing, thinking, laughing, emailing, negotiating, learning and inventing new structures. Making the counter-mobilisation possible. And now, stretching out into the months after the G8, people are still meeting, still discussing (and still laughing). This is all part of a simultaneous process of reflection and (re-)invention, which includes *Shut Them Down!* And just as the G8 summit acted as a moment of focus for the week of protests, allowing us to channel our energies and hold together our diverse actions and preparations, so the summit is also the focus that holds the diverse contributions to this book together.

When we were organising to get to Scotland, trying to assemble all the materials and physical infrastructure we needed to create the Hori-Zone, the eco-village on the outskirts of Stirling, we got a profound sense of how deep into wider society our networks reach (in many ways, of course, it is not even possible to define where 'the movement' ends and 'society' begins). It might take ten phone calls to track down a marquee to borrow, but each phone call would land on a pair of sympathetic ears. How far levels of sympathy for our actions penetrate determines our ability to beg, borrow, build and create impressive physical structures. This book shows the intellectual resources we can draw on when it comes to reflecting upon and thinking through our activities. The movement's dynamism – its *movement* – draws in all these resources, attracting contributions from people who did not physically participate in the protests, as well as many of those who did, and making the book's reflections relevant way beyond the specific event from which it arose.

Some of *Shut Them Down!*'s chapters are adventure stories that convey some of the energy the events carried. Other pieces reflect strategically on Gleneagles and the issues it threw up. For instance: which factors allowed this event to be so diverse and flexible?; what are the possible limits of openness and horizontality? Some authors consider the problems of isolation from other movements and our failure to critique the G8 on its own terms. Others explore the ways in which this counter-mobilisation *is* connected to other social movements, or rather is *part* of a wider network of social relations. The book also includes some more general reflections on the meaning of such events and the possibilities of moving beyond them.

Some chapters are more specific and reflect on particular aspects of the mobilisation. Here there is an emphasis on innovations from previous campaigns and struggles. In the UK, for example, a radical perspective on legal support dates back to the work of the Trafalgar Square Defendants' Campaign (TSDC), set up in the face of state repression following the 1990 Trafalgar Square poll tax riot. The TSDC innovators dealt with severe criticism from some other activists, but now it is pretty much accepted that this work is necessary and consequently there is nothing written about it here. Similarly, Indymedia is now fairly well established (since Seattle, in fact), so we have included nothing about the role they played, either. On the other hand, we have included a chapter on the work of communicating with the mainstream media, where there is little consensus. Again, militant protest tactics played a very important role in the Genoa events and much was written about them afterwards, but today they appear to be less controversial. In 2005, other novel groups emerged: the clowns (CIRCA), the 'brat bloc' and the Activist-Trauma Support group are three examples.

It is possible to weave different themes from the contributions in this book. The clowns, for instance, can be seen as a clever attempt to increase the flexibility of the protesters by moving beyond the dichotomous roles of 'violent' and 'legitimate' protester. From another angle they be can understood as part of an attempt, along with the innovative work of Activist-Trauma Support and the creation of the Hori-Zone, to recognise our vulnerability as human beings and to meet the needs which spring from this. The clowns might also be understood as part of a theme that both emphasises the spread of politics throughout the whole of life and attempts to escape the specialist role of the 'activist'.

To take another example, the Hori-Zone can be understood in a number of different – though not necessarily contradictory – ways. First, as a physical base from which to plan the highly effective actions which disrupted the summit's opening day. Second, as an example of low-impact, ecologically sustainable living. And finally, as an experiment in and demonstration of new ways of living and new types of social relations – non-hierarchical, consensus-based decision-making and so on.

But the narratives we have woven from the contributions in the book are just one way of reading it. We hope that you will recognise different themes and narratives leaping out at you. Indeed the story we have told in this introduction is just one story among many that could be told about the Gleneagles counter-mobilisation. Similarly, the contributions here should not be taken as an 'official' representation of the movements and networks protesting against the summit, not even of the Dissent! network. It is not possible to *represent* a network: a network can only be *sampled*, and the place from which we sample will of course influence our results. We are writing from within the hurly-burly of these move-ments and we, along with the authors of individual chapters, make no claim to objectivity. Each contribution reflects merely the opinions of its respective author(s).

As the book's subtitle suggests we (appear to) start with the G8, but the G8 is just our moment of focus. The themes in the book, like our thinking, move through the specifics of Gleneagles to reach the real subject: us, the movement of movements and society at large! The effect of our protests on the G8's policies is secondary really. The G8 is not where the real power lies. Real power lies with us: they merely respond, trying to capture, limit and harness the ferment, sheer unrest and movement of society. When we say *Shut Them Down!* we also mean *Let Us Be!* Reflection on the protests is just a point around which we think we can see an emergent politics cohere, a politics which will allow us to move on and tackle the last and perhaps most important theme of the book: how do we take those new worlds that felt so possible during the week of protests and generalise them so that they make sense in the rest of our lives?

The Editors
Brighton & Leeds, December 2005

1   *'Gleneagles' is shorthand, of course. We do not just mean just mean the actions which took place in the immediate vicinity of the Gleneagles Hotel in the few days surrounding the summit. Protests took place across central Scotland and the period of counter-mobilisation spanned many months (and is ongoing).*

2   *This book was conceived in the fields of the Hori-Zone on July 7. Since then, the editorial collective coalesced into a group of four individuals.*

1

ON THE ROAD
The Free Association

We all realized we were leaving confusion and nonsense behind and performing our one and noble function of the time, move. And we moved!

Jack Kerouac, On the Road

It's 3am. We're midge-bitten and piss-wet through, hiding out in some woods two miles above the A9 in Scotland. We've spent the last few hours like extras from the *Great Escape*, stumbling through the countryside, dodging police cars and helicopters with searchlights. Now we're trying to get a couple of hours kip in the open air, worrying about how we're going to manage that last yomp to the road and how we're going to block it when we get there. In the back of our minds is that conversation we had discussing the possibility that the police will send dogs into the woods to flush us out. We're tired, hungry, and nervous. One of us starts to giggle. It's infectious. Before long we're all shaking hysterically, cracking up at the sheer insanity of the situation. 'What the fuck are we doing? How did we get here? This is madness!'

It's what alcoholics call 'a moment of clarity'. After being caught up in the logic of the situation you get a flash of objectivity and a sense of its ridiculousness. Hang on a minute, perhaps we ought to reverse that. Capitalism is organised in an entirely rational way. The only irrational thing about it is the whole thing: capital itself, which exists only to increase its own value. The bottom line for the whole system is the expansion of zeros on an accounting sheet. From that point of madness a delirium sweeps through the whole of society making our lives seem out of control. Just as a sailor who returns from months at sea can feel dry land swaying, it's capital's delirium that you perceive in a moment of clarity. It's not us that's insane. In fact we, our movement, are the realists. Of all the organisations, groups and actors circulating around the G8 summit, we were the only honest ones. We were the only ones not offering 'pie in the sky' solutions it's obvious wouldn't be tried and wouldn't work anyway. The only ones not asking our 'leaders' to do things we know they can't and won't. Anything we want to happen we do ourselves, here and now. You end up in some mad situations when you try and act sane in an insane world but it's a different kind of delirium we're after.

+ + +

It's the intensity of it that makes you feel so alive. In the Hori-Zone, in the couple of days running up to the blockades, everywhere you looked there were groups of people gathered in intense and passionate discussion. Talking, thinking, planning, arguing, agreeing, cooperating. Intense communication permeated the whole camp like an electric charge. It comes from that realisation that no one's in charge, that there's no secret committee with a secret plan who are going to come and save us. If this summit is going to be blockaded it's down to us, collectively. We were all moving so fast. One evening we emerged from one meeting at 11.30 and realised we needed to rush to grab something to eat as we had to be at another in half an hour. Who on earth arranges meetings at midnight? We had to, time was tight. It all made perfect sense. Meetings are normally painful exercises in frustration, but here it was different. There was such an intense concentration of effort, such focus, that creativity, wit, imagination, flexibility and good sense seemed to come naturally. You could stagger out of a meeting drunk on the sense of connection with the other people. Vibrating with it. It was that visceral. Then, on the Wednesday of the blockades, in the fields next to the road that intensity was ten-fold. Decisions were made so quickly you barely had time to think. Look! that lot in the next field are trying to get on the road, the police are going to block them. Let's charge down here and draw the police off. Great idea, I'll join in. Next time, hey, the police aren't falling for it. They don't believe our fake charges any more. That means we're unopposed. Here we go. Over the fence. On the road. Block the traffic. Yeh, this is actually working. We're running rings around them. We're too smart for them. We're thinking too fast.

+ + +

Of course it wasn't all like that. There are different speeds to decision-making and for a long time the Dissent! network moved slowly. There are times when we need to pick things apart, think critically about the aims of what we're doing. Prise out the underlying assumptions of the way we see things. This tortoise work is what makes it possible for us to go light-speed when we need to. Similarly it's important not to elevate openness into some abstract principle. Openness on its own is not an answer. At Gleneagles, we were alive to all possibilities, but only as long as they were aimed at shutting down the summit. In fact, there had been a debate about whether we should even go to Scotland at all: if capitalism is global and ongoing, shouldn't we just attack it everywhere and every day? Wouldn't decentralised actions all over the UK avoid the concentrations of police? These critiques miss the point that capitalist summits such as Gleneagles (or Seattle or Genoa or Evian) can also be moments of concentration for us, where we can feel our collective strength and achieve together things that we can't achieve apart. Once we had decided to go to Scotland and disrupt the summit we were able to be more open about how people did that. It's similar to how open source software licences allow others to remix and build upon your work, as long as they license their new creations under the same terms: on the road blockades people could come and be as 'militant' or as 'fluffy' as they liked, as long as they didn't restrict the ability of others to do the same. With that focus, we had a commonality that allowed diversity. It was a moment of productive stratification, of closing down some possibilities in order to open up others.

After that virtually every other organisational move helped to keep options open. Everything we organised in advance was about creating the preconditions of spontaneity. We organised the infrastructure to allow people to be in the right areas with the space and time to organise themselves to do what they wanted. At the Hori-Zone, in meeting after meeting we made decisions to defer final decisions, or rather, we made decisions that maximised our degrees of freedom. Our bottom line seemed to be: how do we keep things open? It would have been easy to go for a single set-piece battle in an attempt to shut down the summit. But that would have flattened all of our compositional efforts (creating and maintaining multiple convergence spaces, each containing a whole range of subjectivities) into one spectacular moment of opposition. Instead, we planned multiple blockades and actions wherever and however we wanted to. At a site-wide meeting on the Monday evening, we decided to focus on the blockade of the A9, rather than the M9 – blockading the A9 simply provided more options for individual groups to maintain their autonomy and express their imagination and creativity.[1] And once we'd decided on the A9, some people floated the idea of crashing a car on this road as way of initiating a blockade; but in the end that too was rejected because it would have re-introduced hierarchical coordination and a single location, moving us back from a multi-pointed attack into something more traditional and easy to control. Instead the decision was a repeat of ones we'd made in the run-up to the summit: get ourselves, our bodies, in the right general area, at the same time with useful tools and a shared affect, a group feeling of collective purpose. With those preconditions met we all had to trust that a spontaneously generated collective intelligence would ignite as groups formed, split up and re-formed in a rolling blockade that was impossible to control. When there's no conspiracy, no back-room leaders pulling our strings or marking up maps, it's up to all of us to join the dots. When this happens successfully there is immense creativity with the emergence of new and unexpected properties and capacities.

+ + +

This isn't a new non-linear Leninism; we're not in control. Even when all the right preconditions are in place there's no guarantee that things will gel and cohere. And even if they do there's no guarantee that what emerges will work. In fact our movement only works by fucking up, by our learning from our mistakes and daring to try new things. If we look at the movement in the UK over the past decade, there's been a pragmatic strain running through it and setting the pace. Deeply intelligent, but not hung up on ideology and led off down the many dead ends that can bring. We can chart this movement by observing it breaking the surface of visibility from one event to the next, constantly searching to move on by solving the problems thrown up by the last one. Each event opening up its own problematic. One of the issues being worked through over the last ten years or more is how can we give up activism? Or rather, how can we give up the tran-scendent role of the activist? How can we act without being controlling and prescriptive? When Reclaim the Streets (RTS) emerged after the anti-Criminal Justice Bill protests it was an audacious switch from opposition to composition. Instead of simply protesting against cars and capital, we recomposed reality, creating car-free common space in the here and now. We started with the ques-tion of what we're *for*, rather than what we're *against*. But RTS actions always walked a fine line between the open and the secret: street parties need a clan-destine layer of organisation to ensure that the crowds, sound systems and blockading equipment arrived at the right place at the same time. One of the prob-lems with this was that people could just passively receive these events and the experience of collective intelligence could be hard to ignite. The J18 Carnival Against Capital can be seen, among other things, as an attempt to solve this problem. The May Day Guerrilla Gardening was another attempt to solve it by making passive reception less likely, but the preconditions for spontaneous action weren't there. You need time and space to self-organise and this is the real value of convergence centres – the Hori-Zone in Stirling, the VAAAG at the Evian G8 counter-summit, the 'no borders' camps.

The state has also unwittingly accelerated this drive towards more and more horizontal forms of organising. It has acted as a hostile evolutionary envir-onment forcing immanence – a horizontality and openness – on the movement. Communication is a good example: after the EU summit in Gothenburg in June 2001, eight people were found guilty of 'coordinating and inciting riots', and sentenced to varying terms of imprisonment, for running an info-line during the protests (they'd collected information from scouts and scanners and then used it to tell activists where they were most needed). Faced with this sort of extreme repression, there are two options. The first is to organise even more secretively,

making sure, for example, that the info-line's location is known to only a handful of people and utilising a range of technologies to keep transmissions hidden. The problem with this approach is that ultimately we can never beat the state at its own game: we will always be militarily defeated. The alternative strategy is to remove any remaining layers of direction and control, and effectively create a peer-to-peer network. When we rang the info-line this year, we were told 'There have been reports that...' or 'The BBC is saying that...' The info-lines were a sounding board, bouncing facts and figures back to people in the field. Information was shared, but no one was told what to do or where to go: a critical difference. During the morning of the blockades they were a means of maintaining the collective affect when many people were physically split up and wanted reassurance that they weren't the only people about to rush onto the road.

   This horizontal approach allowed diversity, flexibility and mobility to feed off each other, and this intoxicating mix was fundamental to our success. On the opening day of the summit people switched seamlessly from one tactic to another without slowing down. As we made our first foray onto the A9 a few of us immediately started assembling the makings of a barricade – a few rocks and a large plastic wheelie bin. But, outnumbered by rapidly approaching cops... *switch!*... sit down on the road and all link arms. Our action immediately becomes 'Peaceful protest! Peaceful protest!' For years, the state and media have attempted to label us as 'good' protesters or 'bad'. 'Peaceful' or 'violent'. 'Legal' or 'illegal'. Dissent! or Make

Poverty History. And we've often been complicit in this process of definition. While constituted parties, organisations and their spokespeople have denounced 'violent protesters' and 'trouble-makers', militants have just as frequently revelled in their distance from more constitutional forms of protest. And the police have always used the good cop/bad cop routine as a further way to divide and confuse us. This time around, however, it was us who shifted the roles, both individually and collectively: masked-up militant; pink and fluffy fairy; obliging bystander; outraged citizen. Most of the time the police simply didn't know whether they were going to be hit with a stick or a barrage of legal jargon (or even a dollop of baby sick!); whether we'd be surly or happy to share a smile and a joke; whether we'd ask friendly questions regarding their own accommodation or mock them with kisses and feather dusters... Quite simply, for long periods we wrong-footed the state with our versatility. The advantage we have is that we're quicker to respond, more flexible and far more dynamic than they can ever be. Faced with an obstacle, we can re-route, while they have to refer to their officer in charge. Another moment sticks in our memory: two people blocking the A9 dual carriageway simply by holding up a wagon alongside a van; trapped at the back, with no room to squeeze past, the police could only rev their own minibus in frustration.

This diversity of approaches and tactics, far from making us feel weak or divided, only seemed to strengthen the incredible feeling of connection. When we heard about the successful blockade of the M9, we felt as if we had been there too (even though we were 20 miles away on the A9). When we heard that the Gleneagles fence had been breached, we felt it was us who'd torn it down. Those people who had chosen to be medics or to stay in the convergence centres and cook reported the same feelings of connection, of having done it all. Everyone felt a part of everything. Again this was one of the crucial roles of the Stirling rural convergence. There are times and places when we need to ground ourselves, to take stock, re-focus and re-connect. The Hori-Zone wasn't just a low-impact self-sufficient eco-friendly experiment. Like social centres across the world, whether permanent or temporary, it offered a base camp, a safe space to retreat to.[2] Without that common place, it would be impossible for different velocities, different movements to compose together. It allowed a space for people to go off in different directions (sometimes literally!) or come in from different places, all moving at different but consistent speeds.

Seen in this light, the whole process was a great example of collective intelligence. No single person or group had total knowledge. Instead there were countless overlapping zones of skills, experience and information, and the only entity which had the bigger picture was the living, breathing movement itself. Of course, it's a hard thing to deal with. Some people never quite cottoned on to the No Plan idea and kept on waiting for it to be 'revealed'. As late as Wednesday lunchtime, when we were still playing cat and mouse with the police on the A9, we were asked by some other protesters: 'What d'you want us to do?' All we could reply was 'Do what you want!' But the day before, on Tuesday morning, even we were starting to have doubts about the approach. We couldn't see how we could manage to get thousands of people out of the camp and into the hills. But we were asking the wrong question: as individuals, the task seemed daunting because it was hard to see the collective intelligence at work. But in a mass meeting of 300-plus, the strategy made sense because we could feel our collective power: across the site, people were already self-organising, starting to make their own plans. One of us spent several hours on Tuesday afternoon and early evening driving a minibus. No Plan. Groups simply consulted a map and worked out their own plan: 'There's 11 of us. We're planning to walk somewhere up in the hills. Can you drop us off here?' 'We're going to camp at this spot. We want you to drive us there. Can you do it?' Drivers are important, of course, but they're frequently seen as having a certain authority too. Not this time and it was fantastic.

+ + +

As we've already said, flexibility and a collective being don't arrive by magic. It's a question of creating the right conditions and the right space in which they can emerge. And once established, they have to be guarded and defended. There's always a temptation to revert to old, more established ways of being and doing. On the Wednesday morning we were part of a meeting on a hillside in the rain at 5.30am. As well as being nervous and wet, we were all more than a little confused. It was hard to see any collectivity emerging, even though there were at least 100 of us. A few scouts reported back and told us that a 20 minute walk would take us down to the closest section of the A9... and into the arms of the waiting police. Isolated from other groups, and not really knowing what was going on, the mood of the meeting drifted quickly towards this option. Luckily, a few people refused to accept this, and argued we should stick to the original idea, to hit the A9 at multiple points north east of the Greenloaning junction, even though it meant a much longer hike into uncertain territory. The meeting swung back again and we became a collective body, focusing instead on the practical: which road to take, how to meet up with other groups, etc. In situations like this, it takes more than confidence or bravado to make that leap of faith; we need to feel that connection with others. Solidarity. The scenario was re-played as we reached the road for the first time: faced with police screaming orders, there was a moment's hesitation before, as one body, we vaulted the barbed wire.

This connects to another point. We don't just need the space and the conditions, we need the tools. This might be something as simple as a physical infrastructure: marquees, kitchens and common meeting spaces were central to the working of the barrios in the Hori-Zone, even more so than at Evian. But we can widen the idea of tools to include the whole notion of consensus decision-making and spokes-councils. They seem to have taken root quickly but, to us at least, are still relatively new. Without them, we would have been lost. Consensus allows

us to create collective bodies and establish collective intelligence. It might seem insane now, but in the space of six frantic hours on Wednesday morning we took part in at least three spokes-councils in the hills and fields around the A9, each involving more than 100 people. And each time we managed to arrive at brave and imaginative decisions. It was a way of slowing things down to reassess. Of course all constituted forms can become empty and institutionalised. What they rest on are affects held in common, the right collective feeling – which allows us to cohere, allowing the range of velocities consistent with each other to be widened.[3]

+ + +

Commonality is always precarious. The success of our actions in the first few days couldn't be sustained indefinitely, and the forces that worked to our advantage for the first day of the summit turned against us when news of the July 7 London bombings filtered through. In Stirling, we experienced them as a moment of vertical power which effectively de-mobilised many of us. Earlier in the week at the site-wide meeting to discuss strategies for the opening day, there was an amazing fluidity, and a clear willingness to engage and to find common ground. But by Thursday morning many people had reverted to a default mode of either partying or party politics: there was another massive site-wide meeting, but this time it was dominated by ideology and old-style politics. We came up against a widespread feeling that we had to 'take a position', and there was an energy-sapping effort to draft a press release. In fact, 'taking a position' was the last thing we should have done. We should have dealt with this external event in the same way a crowd of 200 of us dealt with an oncoming police car which attempted to block our path early on Wednesday morning: we literally flowed around it. 'Taking a position' means standing still and losing the initiative. It also means that it's hard to reconcile the different speeds and directions people are travelling in. After Thursday the mood, affect, feeling, buzz – call it what you like – was defensive and closed, compared to previous days: the desire had gone, and with it the energy.

Of course, it's easy to over-state the impact or significance of the bombings. They were simply the flip-side of the liberating processes we'd enjoyed over the previous days: there's always a comedown, even though this was a particularly intense and accelerated one. When we were on the move, all the affects of precarity were exhilarating and empowering. But as soon as things stopped moving, those same affects became disadvantageous – flexibility became precariousness and all those attitudes and techniques we'd developed suddenly became obstacles to liberation. On top of that, we experienced these bombings as an entirely mediated event. The TV, radio and press had a field day, sucking everything into the black hole of endless speculation. For a time we were tempted to see the bombings as proof that there are far wider forces at work, making our mobilisations at Gleneagles and elsewhere pale into insignificance. This is the deflationary effect of all mediation. But in fact the opposite is true. Our week in Gleneagles, just like all the weeks before and since, makes it even clearer that there is no 'wider' field of play, no 'real world' outside of what we do. There is one power, and it's ours.

The whole idea of the counter-summit wasn't really about protesting against the G8. For us, it wasn't even directly about abolishing global poverty. It was about life. It was about being and becoming human. It was about our desire. No matter how 'well-paid' or 'secure' our employment, as we shuffle pieces of paper, as we gaze out of the window in a meeting, as we trudge around the supermarket, we think 'there must be more to life than this...' We never felt this in Scotland, no matter how frustrated we became in one or two meetings, however pissed off we got with a few individuals or angry at the state. This was living; this was being human. This 'ragged and ecstatic joy of pure being'. Of course, it's easy to dismiss this as if it's simply about a 'feeling' or an obsession with 'process'. But doing stuff for ourselves, making decisions, running our own lives... this process of creation, invention and becoming isn't a 'feeling', it's a material reality. The new capacities we experience at these events don't just disappear. They are there to be accessed during the rest of our lives... if we can work out how to reach them again.

Fundamental change starts with small, localised, material innovations, perhaps the introduction of new tools, technologies or ways of thinking. But every now and then these incremental changes build up into an event, a moment of excess, where so much life is produced that it overflows existing social forms. We spend most of our political lives developing such tools but we never quite know when an event will arise or what the effect of it will be. Nevertheless, 'we lean forward to the next crazy venture beneath the skies.'[4]

1   As it happens even the decision to focus on the A9 wasn't prescriptive, nobody was bound by the decision, it was simply a way of focusing energy and assessing what others were going to do. Those who didn't want to target the A9 or thought they couldn't get there simply organised a blockade of the M9 which was fantastically successful and creative. Instead of energy being split, it was amplified.
2   An affinity group can also act as a safe space. During chaotic mass actions you often act with whoever is next to you. If someone makes a suggestion and it sounds like a good idea you join together. Affinity groups are just the people you know better, in whom you have a greater level of trust and with whom you have talked a few things over. During such events you need to keep checking back with your friends and then make the big decisions together, like when to go home.
3   As we start to explore affective activism just think of all the experience and resources we have to draw on. Our movements have always included cultural activism. Punk, rave, free parties, gigs. All based on the creation of shared affect.
4   Quotations in the final two paragraphs are from Kerouac's On the Road.

2

'THIS IS HOW WE DO IT'

Kara N. Tina

From the beginning there was no well-thought-out master plan for shutting down the G8 summit at Gleneagles. In fact, some of us even dubbed the march we were about to embark on the 'Suicide March'. At three in the morning, a large group of militants dressed in black slipped into the darkness of the night as the first rain of many days dumped down on them. The air was thick with the eerie presence of a thousand determined individuals beginning to walk along the deathly still road. Besides the occasional attempt at a chant the group was quiet, perhaps reconsidering the slim probability of success. Five miles and a heavy police presence stretched before us and our only destination in sight: the M9 motorway. This motorway was one of the crucial roads that delegates and support staff to the G8 summit expected to travel down in a few hours.

Wednesday July 6 was determined to be the day of blockading the G8 by calls to action from Peoples' Global Action (PGA), the same loose network that had called for the day of action against the World Trade Organization in Seattle six years ago. The idea of blockading was ratified at the five-hundred person inter-national anarchist assembly in the ancient halls of our convergence space at Edin-burgh University on Sunday. The next day a street party called the Carnival for Full Enjoyment (as opposed to full employment) took to the streets of wealthy downtown Edinburgh in order to protest wage-slavery and the G8. Any doubts about the no-compromise nature of the militants, who had converged here in

southern Scotland, dissipated rapidly on Monday when police attempted to stop the Carnival only to be met by quick-moving breakaway marches and a frontline that refused to be intimidated. And this was only the beginning, a taste of what was to come.

We left Edinburgh for Stirling. Our destination was the Hori-Zone, the point of strategic coordination, encampment and support for the vast network of anarchists and other activists who had come to Scotland in order to halt the G8 summit meeting on its opening day in Gleneagles. The camp was organised by Dissent!, an international anti-authoritarian network of resistance against the G8. The small town of Stirling is practically equidistant from Glasgow, Edinburgh and Gleneagles, and historically has been the major cross-roads upon which all battles for control of Scotland had been fought. Gleneagles, a ridiculously luxurious golf course and hotel, became the heavily fortified home to the G8 meetings but it has very limited facilities. Thus, most of the delegates and support staff for the G8 were staying in Glasgow and Edinburgh, the two major cities in Scotland.

Since Stirling nestles between these three sites, the eco-village provided the perfect location for launching the rolling blockades against the G8 on Wednesday, especially along the crucial M9, the motorway that eventually reaches the front door of the Gleneagles Hotel itself. The Wallace monument stood silently against the gentle skyline on a hill above the eco-village as we prepared to blockade a total of thirty miles of highway. Built in 1869, this 220 foot monument is said to be where the legendary Scottish rebel William Wallace observed the English coming across Stirling Bridge in 1297 before descending into a fierce battle with them. One cannot help but notice the parallel between the ancient anti-colonial battles of Scotland and the battle against the G8 that was being waged in the rolling green hills of Scotland.

At the eco-village we assembled at the very last minute to determine how we were actually going to blockade the G8. As the deadline for the action came closer and closer it was decided that the initiative to carry out the blockades should be left to autonomous affinity groups and each departed to find their own route to the motorway and blockade it by whatever tactics they chose. A major factor in this decision was the unfortunate location of the eco-village. The campsite was surrounded by the River Forth and had only one exit, which could be easily sealed off by police. To avoid such an entrapment, affinity groups began leaving the site around twelve hours ahead of time to situate themselves in the forests or small towns along the motorways that fed Gleneagles from all sides, allowing them to spring into action as the delegates arrived in the morning. While groups were streaming out of the site, about two hundred people were meeting to determine whether or not to have a large mass march leaving the camp, and if so, how it would be organised. This is how the suicide march came about.

'Suicide' was not a word chosen hastily. How could such a group possibly make it to the distant M9 without being stopped and contained by a ten thousand strong police force assigned to the protests? However, even if the march had failed, it would have provided a crucial cover for the clandestine groups to launch their siege on the various junctions of the motorways. The group decided against all odds that the risk was worth it, and the march would begin shortly. At 2.00am it finally felt like it was on.

The march leaving from the eco-village in the early morning was an international contingent with its members coming from the UK, Spain, Germany, Ireland, France, Denmark, Italy, Switzerland, Turkey and the United States. Morale was high as the rain poured down steadily, but little did we know that this thousand-strong militant group would have to battle through five police lines to reach its destination. The determination of the anarchists was heavy, and as we swelled in numbers a small group with thick pieces of wood around seven feet long moved to the front with the purpose of clearing the way for the march to proceed. Another group, clad in shields made from trash can lids and with foam padding taped onto their clothes, bore an ironic banner declaring 'Peace and Love'.

The police force, mobilised from around the UK to protect the G8 summit, was completely incompetent. Poorly assembled police lines were sometimes composed of front-line officers who, instead of arriving in riot gear, came wearing fluorescent yellow jackets to face protesters. The police were often armed only with batons and tried their best not to use them. Perhaps this was a de-escalating tactic, considering that the police seemed to be primarily set on avoiding violent engagement with protesters and instead sought to simply contain them and apply their infuriating Section 60 orders that allowed them to stop, surround and search any suspects for weapons. Had this been any other G8 country, many of the plans implemented on the day of the blockades, especially the Suicide March, would not have accomplished their goals.

The quick-moving group proceeded uninterrupted for fifteen minutes until the Scottish police finally got their act together and moved a line of cops into the group's path. This happened at a roundabout surrounded on all sides by car dealerships, though at this point the group was not distracted by damaging corporate property. We had set our eyes on the prize: to disrupt the roads leading to the G8 summit. The determination was there, but there was no back-up plan. After a quick assessment of the situation, it was decided that the line of police was too deep to take on, and the group began moving back in the direction it came from.

Retreating in order to find another path to the M9 meant building barricades on the way out of the previous path. We found a big stack of pallets in a nearby construction site and piled them into the street. During the somewhat chaotic process of finding another road leading to the highway, the crowd stumbled upon a suburban mall area which included a branch of the Bank of Scotland, and franchises of Burger King, Pizza Hut and Enterprise Car Rental. Some members wanted to keep on moving and not be distracted by the corporate property, but

the sheer rage against the corporations could barely be contained and windows were smashed and walls were spray-painted with slogans.

When the bloc left the corporate oasis we found a sign to a road leading to the M9 and the march surged. A couple of shopping trolleys were taken from the shopping district and were filled with fist-sized rocks from the sides of the road; perfect ammunition for the class war. A German comrade with a bicycle was amongst the group and able to ride ahead as our scout and alert the rest of us of intersections and police movements. He came back and told us of a police line forming in our path. A few people moved into the field on the left to outwit the police. The rest decided that this was the moment when it was necessary to throw down.

The police line was weak and did not have any riot gear apart from their shields. Those with big sticks moved to the front lines and the militants behind picked up stones from the shopping trolley. We marched right up to the lines and began smashing through with stones and sticks. The police were not prepared at all for such determination and after thirty seconds they scurried away. When their retreat was obvious, I heard a thick German accent scream, 'DEESS ISS HOW VE DO IT!'

The road was wide open as we marched the long distances from one round-about to the next, following the road signs to the M9. We came across four people wrapped in trash-bags, who peeked their heads out from the side of the road in

amazement at the march passing by. They were part of the hundreds that had left early to hide among the trees, completely drenched by the continual rainfall.

Our crew had a significant number of locals who were eager to represent their own culture of resistance. One middle-aged Scottish member of the group from Glasgow carried a *bodhran*, the traditional Celtic drum historically used in battles and parades. Another Scottish youth had a didgeridoo that was blown at crucial moments of battle to build up the energy. In the face of such a crowd, it looked as though the police had given up. We had made it to the onramp of the M9. This was it: victory. After trekking five miles in the rain and through police lines, we only had 70 feet to make to the highway. But these things are never so easy. Scores of police vans appeared from around the corner and unloaded hundreds of riot police. It seemed to be too much to take on and we moved back. This time the police seemed as determined as we were and brought another line of riot police to block our only exit.

There was one option left: to battle our way out. The re-stocked trolleys rolled to the front and stones began raining down onto the police, thumping against their shields to the steady battle beat of the *bodhran*. In one of the most creative uses of local resources, even the shrubbery was turned upon the police. This area of Scotland is known for a poisonous plant called Giant Hogweed that causes huge welts and blisters when touched. At one point the bloke from Glasgow grabbed one of these plants from the stalk and beat the police with it. After five minutes the police lines were pushed back fifty feet and a small path leading into a suburban residential area was revealed to one side. As we walked down the path into suburbia only 250 people remained. Most of the initial crowd had separated at various police lines to disappear into fields or return to camp. Though we were few, we had demonstrated our determination and open defiance.

A woman in a white bathrobe walked out of her house, baffled at the march going through her community at 4.00am. The police would later report that damage was done to people's homes, cars and satellite dishes. However, the only property damaged was corporate and police property and the police eventually had to retract their statement. In fact, the woman in the white bathrobe was friendly and she waved at us. We even asked her for directions towards the M9 and she showed us the way.

We had been thrown off our original route and now had to find a new way to the motorway. The police had mobilised a much larger force and were coming toward us from multiple intersections. As we rambled through the unfamiliar suburban streets police would appear from one side, retreat under the force of the bloc, and appear again from a new direction. The sun, which only sets for about four hours between midnight and 4am in Scotland during summertime, was now peeping up over the horizon. We were feeling wet, cornered and lost. Another resident of the area stopped while passing in his pickup and pointed us toward the highway. His directions weren't the most conventional: 'Go down that road and climb down the valley, across the fields, through the trees and that's where the motorway is.'

We had come this far, there was no way we were going to turn back, even if it meant hiking through the fields.

Standing on the edge of the hill, next to a golf course, one could see the trucks travelling on the highway far away. We quickly referred to a topographical map, concerned that there might have been a big drop to the side of the highway that couldn't be climbed. Those of us remaining of the international anti-capitalist black bloc, tired from hours of breaching police lines and soaked to the bone, began a journey towards the motorway we knew we had to blockade to prevent the G8 from meeting.

In a moment of bizarre humour, one of the Scottish blokes amongst us was understandably concerned about marching on the golf course and warned the rest of us: 'Don't walk on the green!' I turned back to observe how many of us were left and was confronted with the surreal scene of hundreds of comrades dressed in black hiking in single file through the luscious green landscape of Scotland. Seeing us there, hours and miles later and still on the move, I realised that most likely the Scottish rebels fighting the English had also passed through these fields centuries ago.

We continued on like this, passing through scenes of another history, through a golf course, three different cattle pastures and knee-high grass as we walked towards a quickly approaching future of our own. Under a pale blue sky we finally reached the motorway. We were the first group to make it on to the highway, but definitely not the last. At that moment the rain stopped.

Delirious from walking and drunken with success we all began to assemble anything and everything we could find on the side of the road – tree trunks, rocks, branches. It was 6am and both directions on the M9 were blockaded.

Walking back to the campsite later we passed the residents of Stirling trying to go to work on the backed-up roads. The reactions we got were varied but at the same time clearly split into two different groups. People who were in private vehicles were upset at the delay and called us many things, most notably 'Bastards!' Those who were in buses and vans and could be identified as construction or roadside workers by their bright yellow vests were fully supportive. We were greeted by raised fists, cheering, and others shouting 'Power to the People!' out their windows.

We returned to the eco-village. At the entrance to the camp there were two permanent flags strung high to identify the political nature of the inhabitants: the red and black flag of social anarchism and the rebel skull and crossbones of piracy. Inside was a vast space of camps, organised by either the geographic origin of the inhabitants (e.g. the Irish 'barrio' – or neighbourhood) or by clusters of affinity groups working together (e.g. the Clandestine Insurgent Rebel Clown Army, CIRCA). A central corridor was lined with different activist support tents, eight different kitchens, medical services, an independent media centre, trauma support, action trainings, and huge tents for the periodic spokes-council meetings. Beyond this central corridor was the multi-coloured sea of hundreds of personal tents. Many of the tents had one version or another of black and red flags with the anarchist circled 'A' flying above. We had arrived home.

The eco-village was buzzing with activity. The intricate communications network that had been set up was functioning in full force. Bicycle scouts, who were situated at major cities where delegates were staying, along the side of the highways, and at major junctions, were providing up to date information on motorcade movements and alerting the affinity groups hiding along the highway about when and where to strike. An information tent at the entrance had a detailed large scale tactical map, providing up to date information on the different blockades of the summit. As the day progressed one note after another appeared on the map marking the points of the blockades '7.00am – Spanish bloc on M9, 7 arrested', '8.00am – 4 protesters with ropes dangling off a bridge on M9', '12.00pm – Group of 50 including CIRCA and the Kids' Bloc having picnic on the motorway with massive amounts of riot cops looking confused', 'All railroads leading north have been halted by activists locking themselves to the tracks.' This was only the beginning and the notes continued appearing throughout the day: a bicycle contingent took over the A9 at 4.00pm, the Belgian and Dutch bloc locked down on Kincardine Bridge at 4.20pm, etc.

The eco-village was the epicentre of brilliant tactical coordination. This was a result of months of reconnaissance work and a chaotic yet functional plan of blockading that provided both fluidity and agility. As soon as a report came in that one blockade was breaking or being threatened by the police, the transportation team would have vehicles ready to take people to the location and reinforce the blockade. The BBC Scotland radio station was reporting that all roads leading north to Gleneagles were backed up with no traffic passing through. Naturally, they did not mention the reason for this, and tried to hide the successful blockades behind a regular traffic update.

Everyone at the campsite was ecstatic and it felt like it was time to start upping the ante, which meant taking on the perimeter fence around the G8 summit. The legal march scheduled for the afternoon by the G8Alternatives, who were largely controlled by the Socialist Workers Party, had been called off by the police due to the disruption caused to the transportation system of Scotland. To their credit they decided to move forward and go ahead with the march at Auchterarder, the town nearest to Gleneagles Hotel.

Now that the stakes were raised, vans from the eco-village began to head straight to Auchterarder rather than to reinforce the blockades. Two hours later the news of the perimeter fence being breached at two different points reached the camp. Anarchists and Scottish socialists were tearing apart the fence and throwing pieces of it at the riot police. Some groups entered the G8 summit area

and were being confronted by Chinook helicopters unloading hundreds of riot police equipped with dogs. At 12.30 in the afternoon it appeared that the group of the eight most powerful men in the world were still unable to begin their meeting in Gleneagles.

There are many lessons to be learned from the victories won at this most recent mass action of the young anti-capitalist movement. Tactically, having decentralised actions coordinated with the same infrastructure, all given the targeted locations in the same area, was an incredible strength for activists attempting to disrupt the summit. Previous mass mobilisations have failed when calls were made for affinity groups to do autonomous direct action without a strategic frame in which to act. On the night of July 5 and into the early hours of July 6, groups in Scotland were able to scatter themselves along a geographical network of points; working together to assess the need for numbers and actions, people dispatched themselves between a multitude of different motorways and byways surrounding Gleneagles and around hotels in Edinburgh. There were threats to blockade not only the roads around Gleneagles but the roads out of the major cities of Edinburgh and Glasgow. This meant the police forces were stretched thin, having to be at Glasgow, Edinburgh, Stirling and Gleneagles at the same time. The state was forced to provide dozens of officers to contain each small group of activists and, as affinity group after affinity group spontaneously hit the transportation corridor, the police simply could not maintain their own coordination or mass their numbers. The Suicide March was a strong challenge to state control and proved impossible to contain, even with the strongest police effort. According to friends inside the summit, the blockades were a throbbing migraine for the G8 and it took some delegates up to seven hours to get to Gleneagles. Suffocating their critical control with a continual barrage of activity and exhausting police numbers by using quick-moving affinity groups to the best possible advantage are tactics that allow us to call the shots, whether it be Gleneagles, Buenos Aires or La Paz. The rabble-rousing group behind the blockades was extremely international in character and the links formed are going to be a major pain for global capital for the years to come. As if this wasn't enough, it was reported that while Bush was riding his bicycle at Gleneagles he ran into a police officer, sending him to hospital.

September 11 reminds most of the world of New York and some of us of Santiago. There was another September 11 more then 700 years ago. On September 11 1297 William Wallace observed the English coming in to impose their enclosure of the Scottish land. This was the day of the Battle of Stirling Bridge where the 60,000 strong English army suffered a terrible defeat at the hands of the Scottish who numbered around 10,000. The English sent two messengers to Wallace to ask for his surrender. Wallace's reply was similar to that given to the G8 by the street fighters in Stirling.

'Return to thy friends and tell them we come here with no peaceful intent, but ready for battle, determined to avenge our wrongs... Let thy masters come and attack us; we are ready to meet them.'

Originally published at Counter Punch (www.counterpunch.org)

3

GLENEAGLES: BREAKING TIME
John Holloway[1]

A scream of fury. More than that, a flash of hope.

Did it make poverty history? Of course not. Capitalism generates poverty: to get rid of poverty, we must get rid of capitalism. Did Gleneagles get rid of capitalism? Perhaps, for a moment, for some people.

We have to talk of revolution, not just anti-capitalist protest, not just rebellion, not just of fighting against the G8. We have to talk of revolution because it is clear that capitalism is destroying our lives, destroying humanity in every sense of the word, destroying nature and the preconditions for human existence. Not a revolution from above, with leaders who take control of the state and keep control of the state, but a radical social change that comes from below.

But how can we possibly talk of revolution now, after the failure (and worse than failure) of so many revolutions?

Only as cracks. Each rebellion creates a crack in capitalist domination. Capitalism is a system of command, a form of social organisation that subordinates our lives to the rule of money (with its various masks of value, profit, capital, and so on). Each time we say No, we tear a rent in the texture of domination, create a crack in the system of command. We do it all the time, often without noticing it. We say, 'No, we shall not shape our lives according to the requirements of capital, we shall do what we consider necessary or desirable.' It does not always work out: sometimes we end up submitting. But now in this moment we rebel, and even if we submit later, we know that many more are taking our place, refusing to submit.

Sometimes these cracks are so tiny that we hardly notice them. But often they are collective, often they lead to a collective and conscious determination to do things differently. And sometimes the cracks are so big that they stand there and radiate their glory through all the world: the Zapatista uprising, for example, or the *argentinazo* of a few years ago,[2] or the recent events in Bolivia.[3] And other times they come as collective explosions of refusal and rage like Seattle or Genoa or Gleneagles.

Each of these cracks may seem hopeless, like banging our heads on a stone wall. But it is not so: if we bang our heads hard enough, even a stone wall begins to crack.

How can we think of these cracks?

Traditional revolutionary theory thinks of the cracks as states. According to Leninist theory, a crack in capitalist domination acquires real significance only when it leads to the taking of state power; for revolution to be complete, the taking of power in one state should lead on to the taking of power in another and so on, until capitalism is abolished in all the world. However, if one thinks in terms of cracks, there is no reason to limit such cracks to states, and many reasons why it is better not to think of them as states. To name just two:

Firstly, the state is a specific form of organisation and of behaviour developed historically to exclude people from the possibility of determining their own lives. Our insubordination is a push towards social self-determination and this implies the development of different forms of organisation and behaviour, forms that include rather than exclude, forms such as councils or assemblies, which aim at the real articulation of struggle as a process of social self-determination.

And secondly, the state as a form of organisation imposes a temporality of waiting upon our struggle: wait until the next election, wait until we build the party or the revolutionary army and seize control of the state. The intensity of the capitalist attack against humanity is so great that we can no longer wait: revolution is here and now or it is not.

But if we do not think of the cracks as states, then how? Perhaps it helps to think of them in various dimensions:

a) As spatial cracks, territories in which the people say 'we do not accept capital's rule here, we shall shape society as we think fit.' Such areas can be small (like a social centre) or big (like the Zapatista region of Chiapas).

b) As cracks related to certain activities or resources: 'in this aspect of our activity or social intercourse, we shall not accept the rule of capital; we shall create or organise as we think fit.' Examples of this would be the struggle in all the world against the privatisation of water and other basic resources, or the struggles against the direct subordination of health care to capital, or the struggle against the imposition of private property on software and music.

c) As temporal cracks: 'in this moment, in this event, capital does not rule; we shall decide the rules and shape the social relations, we shall do what we consider necessary or desirable.' Such temporal cracks can be seen in anti-capitalist events of all sorts, and in outbursts of revolutionary activity such as December 19/20 2001 in Argentina or the recent upheavals in Bolivia. Gleneagles, then, is that: a temporal crack in capitalist domination.

Normally, when we think of revolution, we think in spatial terms, even if we do not put the state in the centre of our thinking. The Zapatista uprising, for example, fits into this way of thinking. But the Zapatistas are in the countryside and there the spatial concept works. The problem posed by the Zapatistas' Sixth Declaration and their decision to come out of Chiapas is whether the same concept can apply in an urban context.[4] Perhaps it can: we would all like the city or neighbourhood in which we live to be a city or neighbourhood in rebellion. But for many of us this is difficult to imagine.

But supposing we change the dimension. Supposing, instead of (or in addition to) thinking in terms of space, we think in terms of time, what happens then? We do not live in the sort of relatively stable community that characterises the Zapatista area of Chiapas, or indeed certain urban areas fifty or a hundred years ago, and we do not own land that we can cultivate in order to sustain ourselves. Our lives are much more unsettled. It is not that our communities do not exist, but they are much more volatile: we come together for a moment, or for a few days, and then we go our own way, until the next time, certainly building friendships and links that last, but the intense sense of community is a temporary one. Perhaps we should take that as a basis and think that the struggle is not so much to conquer spaces as to conquer moments: to conquer moments that belong to us and then try to convert those moments into cracks, cracks that run and spread and multiply.

Thinking of time in this way is an attack on time itself. The importance of such cracks in the time of capitalist domination depends not just on their duration but (perhaps especially) on their intensity. The time of such cracks is not clock time, according to which one minute is the same as another. On the contrary, there is a shooting of clocks, an intensification of time, a 'moment of excess' as our friends from Leeds put it, a pushing towards that moment of complete fulfilment in which time stops still. It opens a perspective in which communism (or whatever we want to call that other world that we say is possible) emerges as a world in which the axis is not duration, but intensity.

This does not mean that I am advocating just a politics of events. I think that events are very important, not so much because of what they achieve in terms of concrete reforms, but above all because they blast apart the dreary tick-tick of capitalist time. But my argument here is not that we should concentrate on events, but rather that perhaps we should focus on time. The explosive, intense time of events needs to be supported by a slower temporality, a temporality of preparation and then of reflection, but also of the patient practice of anti-capitalism in our everyday lives within a capitalist society. The event is not just a hole in capitalist time but at best creates a crack that reaches out, a crack that runs, but runs at a different pace. The event is a brick thrown through a metaphorical window, but the brick does not just make a hole, the hole has fingers or cracks that reach out, cracks that are extended by the determined and unspectacular work of those who dedicate their lives (or, perhaps more realistically, part of their lives, since our lives are always contradictory) to the creation of a different world, the creation of different social relations, the struggle for dignity.

A scream of fury, then, a flash of hope, a brick thrown through the smugness of capitalist clock time, a crack that runs, right across the Atlantic Ocean, to Mexico and beyond, a crack that joins up with other cracks: that is what Gleneagles means to me.

1   *Unfortunately, I was not in Edinburgh or Gleneagles. The present reflection on the events there draws on discussions with Raquel Gutierrez and Sergio Tischler, on the various pamphlets of Leeds May Day Group (in their various appellations) and Ernst Bloch's* Principle of Hope.

2   *The* argentinazo *refers to the uprising of December 19/20 2001 in Argentina, with all that followed: the overthrowing of several presidents, the creation of neighbourhood councils in the biggest cities, the wave of occupations of factories and other places of work, the upsurge of the* piquetero *movement (movement of the unemployed).*

3   *There was an upsurge of revolt in Bolivia in May/June 2005, which forced the resignation of the President: one of the main centres of force was the Juntas Vecinales or Neighbourhood Councils of El Alto, a city on the outskirts of La Paz.*

4   *The Sixth Declaration of the Lacandon Jungle issued by the Zapatistas at the end of June 2005 announces that they are coming out of Chiapas to integrate themselves directly in struggles in the rest of Mexico and beyond, and that they will no longer focus principally on indigenous struggles. This has given rise to an intense period of preparation and discussion throughout Mexico.*

4

REACHING THE
PARTS WHERE
WE FEAR TO GO
AG

August 18 2004, 9.15pm After two hours of inspiring films at the Kebele social centre's monthly film night, some 35 people stay on to discuss forming an anti-G8 group in Bristol. The meeting agrees to go for it. Bristol Dissent! is born.

July 6 2005, 5.30pm Around 400 people attend the Bristol 'NO G8' protest. Naturally, it's organised without any negotiation with the state, so Bristol's cops are out in force. They can't stop the march, but they thwart other plans. Meanwhile, up in Scotland, Bristolians are making a nuisance of themselves. Six have been nicked whilst locking on under a van on the A9, others are dispersed by the police. Bristol's clown platoon are taking the piss somewhere, while a few Bristolians have remained in the eco-village. Bristolians are also active in various Dissent! support groups. In Auchterarder, after the G8Alternatives march, one of Bristol's legal volunteers gets pulled by the police 'Forward Intelligence Team' (FIT) and their support heavies, and accused of organising the fence trashing. Asks one boiler-suited goon of the concerned legal volunteer: 'What would you say to the farmer whose field you have just ruined?' Officer, we couldn't make it up if we tried!

PUNCHING ABOVE ITS WEIGHT
Bristol has a proud and bloody history of resistance to capitalism and the state. From the 18th century onwards, the local working class regularly revolted and were

sometimes met with Dragoons and gunfire. In the 1970s and 80s, it was the turn of the oppressed black minority, supported by disadvantaged whites and the alternative scene, to riot back. The latter part of the 20th century saw Bristol's radical milieu provide many willing activists for a huge variety of campaigns, produce a wealth of alternative media, set-up numerous workers' and land and food co-ops, embrace the rave and free party scene, and put on seven Reclaim the Streets events in five years. Many groups continue today, as the listings inside *Bristle* magazine show.

For a city of just 350,000 people, Bristol's activists consistently punch above their weight. This enthusiasm and wealth of local initiatives have given Bristol's groups and networks the strength to act quite independently, not reliant on the alternative nation-wide political scene and movements. This has continued on into the 21st century with local May Day 2000 actions, the 2001 'Vote Nobody' campaign, and more recently the fiercely independent Stop the War group that facilitated up to 5,000 hitting the streets when the war started. But it had been a few years since activists took an explicitly anti-capitalist and anti-authoritarian message out beyond the activist ghetto: could we do it this time?

LET'S GO TO WORK

Inevitably, at early Bristol Dissent! meetings, most people knew each other. It was more of a network, with individuals from many local campaigns and groups. Over time, this evolved. Some activists already had heavy commitments. Some felt the group was going OK and left it to evolve. Some felt its activities were boring: not enough 'action'. Some were anti-organisation, while others perhaps questioned the whole focus on the G8 and the summits.

But new people got involved. Some (shock! horror!) were new to political activity and/or Bristol; some clearly came from a more liberal, NGO-type background; some were students. Over the ten month period, I'd estimate that 200 to 250 people attended at least one regular organising meeting. Some never returned, but at least we'd made contact. Others came back, again and again, and became integral to the group and its activities. Ace! On average, even when meeting bi-weekly, we attracted 20 to 25 people. Ages ranged from late teens to 50 year olds. There was a good gender mix, but the group was still 99% white. Without doubt, a lot of useful contacts were made, networks were enlarged, and information distributed. The group tried hard to be non-hierarchical, collectivist and autonomous; anyone could come along, have their say, make a proposal, go off and do something, facilitate the meeting, etc. There was no formal membership/affiliation.

From its inception, the Bristol group was clear that it would focus on local out-reach and bringing the G8 home to Bristol. After all, at the first meeting no one was entirely sure who was in the G8, never mind what it did! By its third monthly meeting, the group adopted eleven aims, of which three had a strong

local focus. 1: to educate ourselves, and the wider public, about the G8 – how it works, how it influences the global economy and worldwide events. 2: to identify how the G8 affects us in Bristol on a day-to-day basis – to make it locally relevant. 3: To encourage and promote local resistance and alternatives to the G8, globalisation and capitalism. The remaining eight were more predictable, and the group also adopted the spirit of the PGA hallmarks[1].

And so to work. Kebele kindly provided a free meeting venue and space to store resources. Meetings were open to all. All meetings, events and info/propaganda produced were widely publicised on various e-lists, on Bristol Indymedia, by poster and flyer, and anywhere else we could think of. Two sub-groups were set up. 'Events' worked on benefit gigs (around ten benefit socials were held), outreach activities, producing tat and banners (there was also an 'artivists' group making stencils and similar). We were self-funded through benefits and collections, raising and spending (or donating) over £3,000 before the end of June. The 'Info' sub-group spent several months producing seven 'Briefing papers'. Each was double-sided A4 and all attempted to make the issues covered relevant in a local context.[2] We produced two generic posters and three basic leaflets for general publicity, with other propaganda for specific events. With access to cheap/free photocopying, we produced thousands of these and the briefing papers for pasting up, handing out, and leaving in pubs, shops, clubs, cafes, etc. Persons unknown used spray paint to help get the message out.

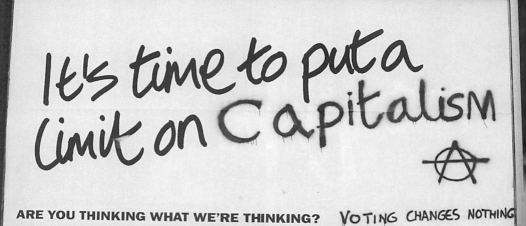

INFO AND ACTION

In recent years, much of Bristol's radical scene has been based in and around northern-central and eastern-central Bristol, and this is where Dissent! drew much of its initial support from. Conscious of this, we tried to go beyond this core, taking street stalls into the town centre and south Bristol, taking info into both Bristol University, in posher Clifton, and to the University of the West of England (UWE) in north Bristol. We also sent propaganda to contacts in Bath (although no active group was formed there), and further afield to the wider South West. These efforts did bear some fruit. However, half-hearted efforts to garner main-stream media attention were unsuccessful.

Bristol's out-reach crescendoed in April 2005. On April 9, we held our own heavily publicised 'Info for Action' conference, with speeches, workshops, art and training. One thousand households near the venue were leafleted, as were some local mosques. 130 people came, although 99% were white. Typically, more attended the evening benefit! On April 16, we ran a stall and workshop at a 'Don't agonise, organise' event, put on by a local charity, African Initiatives, that brought us into contact with the local NGO and charitable types. Typical question from us to them: 'Will you make poverty history in 2005?' Answer: 'Probably not.' Next question: 'Why not?' Great fun! On April 30 we ran another stall and workshop at the launch conference for a local Social Forum, again with good discussions.

It was in May, after the elections, that a local Make Poverty History group became openly active, supported by the NGOs and the left. The left had stayed away from us, and MPH continued the trend. They held a few high profile, photogenic public events, which we went along to leaflet, but the political gap was now enormous. A highlight was their mid-June march and rally on College Green, where they formed a white human wristband, and were greeted by the newly formed South Bristol Anarchists banner 'Make Poverty History – Kill The Rich'. Oh how the liberals tittered... nervously! Our last major out-reach activity was 'Anarchy Bear's Grrr8 picnic', on June 4, on College Green, reclaiming the space outside the town hall in the city centre, without permission of course. A windy day of fun and games, with food from the Kebele Kafe. Well attended, with barely a cop or journo or white wristband in sight, and the first public outing for Bristol's platoon of clowns!

Alongside this out-reach, the group was also turning its attentions to the upcoming summit. Training sessions were publicly organised: direct action training, including a session for UWE's People and Planet group; first aid; legal advice; and a training session for legal volunteers in the South West. After April, propaganda was increasingly centred on calls to action, and in the last month on promoting the late decision to hold a Bristol protest. A few people went off early to help with the pre-summit preparations. The group's funds, always cash-only, were liberally distributed. Benficiaries were central Dissent! and support groups, the Bristol kitchen and space at the eco-village, a number of locally-based affinity groups.

CONSIDERATIONS AND CRITICISMS

It's debatable whether we ever really got beyond the activist ghetto, although we certainly tried. We did come into contact with a lot of new people, and with groups we may not previously have gone near, but on occasions we seemed to be held back by our old mind-sets and ways of doing things. Certainly we could have been bolder in holding public meetings, approaching other communities, and groups and the labour movement. But we lacked both the time and the willing volunteers to do this – at the end of the day, you do what you can within the limits of your resources, and hope to learn for the next time.

A second criticism is that we never had enough political discussion. Although we adopted some specific political aims, as time progressed they were not discussed with newcomers, and in an effort to be inclusive, political differences were often overlooked. Of course, it's possible that those differences were simply differences in knowledge, experience and understanding, but we never got to find out. The open group meetings had packed business-orientated agendas, leaving any political discussion as largely incidental. The 'Info' sub-group did have some heated discussion, and the 'Info for Action' day saw differences aired. Perhaps the apparent unwillingness to read, think and discuss politically is part of a wider political malaise?

There were also problems with the make-up of the group. Someone said at one point that we'd formed a non-hierarchical collective, but not really discussed what that phrase means. Undoubtedly, informal hierarchies emerged at times, based on knowledge, experience and an ability or willingness to speak up (not on a specific desire by anyone to be a 'leader'). What is the greater problem? The people who are perceived as leaders, or the apparent willingness to follow? And how do we resolve it? The answer seems to lie in discussion, support, skill- and knowledge-sharing, education, patience and a desire for change. Of course, we also suffered from the related problem of not having enough people prepared to 'get their hands dirty' – to do the unglamorous, day-to-day campaigning and admin. Much of the group's work was done by a small core of 10–15 people, or at least appeared to be – in fact, over time many in that group changed. Maybe we need to consider organisational structures in more depth if we want to involve more people in a group's core work.

In terms of action, the Bristol group organised little obvious 'direct action', beyond the picnic and July 6 protest. But, like national Dissent!, it facilitated the coming together of networks and individuals, who went off and acted independently of the group (this helped keep cops off our backs). There was plenty of obvious direct action going on in Bristol throughout the period, including blockades, solidarity actions, subvertising, anti-election campaigning and much more. Perhaps the problem lies more in the narrow conception of 'direct action': it's often seen as a (semi)clandestine, usually illegal, activity, when in fact the act of voluntarily coming together to meet and self-organise is direct action too.

Finally, there's a sense that Bristol didn't engage enough nationally. It's a criticism that's true in comparison with some other groups, but Bristol's specific dynamics and its geographical location seemed to mitigate a wider involvement. Perhaps it also relates to how we understand organisations and networks: Dissent! formed nationally and then invited local groups to align themselves autonomously with it... which is exactly what Bristol did. I suspect that, comparatively, more local people were made aware of Dissent!, and the G8, than in many other places.

POSTSCRIPT

Currently, the group continues, with a focus on discussion and support for those arrested during G8 protests and over £1,300 raised for local G8 defendants.

1   The PGA hallmarks are reproduced in note 3 on page 161.
2   They can be found at http://dissent.org.uk/content/view/181/101/ under 'Information on the G8'.

5

DR. SACHS, LIVE8 AND NEOLIBERALISM'S 'PLAN B'

George Caffentzis

At length the term-day, the fatal Martinmas, arrived, and violent measures of ejection were resorted to. A strong posse of peace-officers, sufficient to render all resistance vain, charged the inhabitants to depart by noon; and as they did not obey, the officers, in terms of their warrant, proceeded to unroof the cottages, and pull down the wretched doors and windows – a summary and effectual mode of ejection, still practised in some remote parts of Scotland, when a tenant proves refractory.

Sir Walter Scott, Guy Mannering or The Astrologer (1829)

Neoliberal globalisation entered into its first major crisis seven summers ago, with the so-called 'Asian Financial Crisis'. Since then the ideological power of this form of capitalism has been slowly ebbing. The once attractive image of the creative powers of humanity finally being brought together in the process of globalisation for the 'common good' by borderless transfers of money, capital and labour at the speed of light now seems to be a nostalgic relic. Since 1997, along with the continuing economic crises and stagnation of Europe, South America, and Africa, neoliberal globalisation has faced two major ideological reversals. The first reversal is associated with a city (Seattle) and the second with a date (September 11 2001).

The street blockades that temporarily halted the World Trade Organization meetings in Seattle at the end of November 1999, brought to planetary consciousness the existence of a global movement of resistance to neoliberal globalisation. This movement had been growing through the thousands of 'IMF riots', general strikes and guerrilla wars in the Third World since the mid-1980s against structural adjustment programmes (SAPs – the 'wedges' that opened economies previously resistant to complete control by international capital). But the sudden appearance on the streets of a movement capable of stopping the apparently unstoppable locomotive of globalisation made it clear that there was another reality not buying a future whose only aim was to put the world up for sale to the highest bidder. On the contrary, the movement was able to demonstrate that globalisation will result in the unprecedented immiseration of people throughout the planet unless it is stopped.

The September 11 2001 destruction of the World Trade Center towers and the killing of three thousand people were followed by a 'war on terrorism' that revealed the military aspect of globalisation: *globalisation's invisible hand required an equally global iron fist*. Instead of dealing with 9/11 as a crime whose perpetrators were to be apprehended, tried and convicted on the basis of international law, it was seen by the Bush administration as a symbolic attack on the US's status as the hegemonic power guaranteeing the operation of the rules of the world market. Soon after 9/11, George W. Bush expressed this vision when he identified the real enemy as nation states comprising 'the axis of evil' – Iraq, Iran and North Korea – and any of the other unnamed 30 or 40 other 'rogue', or potentially 'terrorist-harbouring' nation states throughout the planet. Indeed, Osama bin Laden and his project for founding a new Caliphate was all but forgotten in the rush to discipline nation states that for one reason or another were not completely open to global capital flows (Iraq in particular). But this image of globalisation as requiring a literally 'infinite' war against recalcitrant states and populations (branded by Bush's neoconservative advisors as 'anti-democratic') was the sign of a crisis, especially since it undermined globalisation's promise of a closer, more interdependent world where it was in everyone's interest to 'just get along'.

Globalisation's ideological crisis had deepened to the point that by the end of 2004 all the major efforts to extend the 'globalisation' agenda (Central American Free Trade Agreement, Free Trade Area of the Americas, the Doha Round of WTO negotiations, etc.) were being stalled on both the street and the diplomatic levels. This was the time for neoliberal globalisation to explore another option, which I will call, for want of a better term, 'Plan B'. The doctrinaire neoliberalism of the past was clearly failing and the need for alternative means to a neoliberal end was dawning in the British Foreign Office, in the UN, in parts of the World Bank and in the organs of 'global civil society'. If this group's slogan was not 'another world is possible', it was 'another path is necessary'. Indeed, one of the most important features of this 'Plan B' is its ability to use the energies of the anti-globalisation movement for its realisation.

Jeffrey Sachs wrote and published his book, *The End of Poverty: How We Can*

Make It Happen in Our Lifetime (as well as a series of related op-ed articles in the *New York Times*), in early 2005 to respond to this ideological and political crisis. It is one of the first books to proselytise for 'Plan B'. For Sachs represents those who are convinced that neoliberal globalisation, if properly managed, is the only path to a future without abject poverty and misery for billions of people (and the only alternative for the survival of capitalism). The book's publication was timed to reach its greatest audience in early July when the G8 leaders would meet in Gleneagles to consider a new 'anti-poverty package' for African nations that was developed by a variety of agencies from the British Foreign Office, to the UN, to academic centres like the Earth Institute that Sachs heads in New York, to the organisers of the Live8 concerts like Bob Geldof and Bono (who wrote the preface of the book). It clearly sets out the ideology and strategy of the supporters of 'Plan B'.

There is much that is unattractive about the book, besides its ideological purpose. *The End of Poverty* is one part self-congratulatory memoir of Sachs' roles as advisor to the governments of Bolivia, Russia, Poland, India and China, and part world-historical tract justifying the ultimate rationality of neoliberal capitalism (if it is properly applied to 'sick' countries by 'clinical economists' like himself). In the first part of the book Sachs tells us what he advised these governments to do during the time of his involvement, but invariably he adds an upbeat note, even when the results were patently catastrophic. For example, it is estimated that millions of Russians, especially men, died prematurely because of the collapse of wages and the public health system during the time that Sachs was advising the Yeltsin government – perhaps equal to the death rate of a 'moderate' nuclear war! But Sachs' panglossian comment on this episode is: 'Looking back, would I have advised Russia differently knowing what I know today?... To a large extent, the answer is no... Most of the bad things that happened – such as the massive theft of state assets under the rubric of privatisation – were directly contrary to the advice that I gave and to the principles of honesty and equity I hold dear'.[1]

You protest too much, Dr. Sachs. Is it possible to be so nice in our discriminations of the 'good' versus the 'bad' when involved in a process of the primitive accumulation of capital? Can Sachs have forgotten the 'fire and blood' that set the stage for the triumph of the Scottish Enlightenment thinkers like David Hume and Adam Smith he so admires: the massacres of the Highlanders at the end of the 1745 rebellion and the clearances that followed throughout the end of the 18th and 19th centuries (so deftly described by Scott in the epigraph of this piece). The ghosts of those dead greeted the G8 leaders in Gleneagles and spoke a truth that was not drowned out by the fairy tale of Pacific capitalist development told by economists from Adam Smith's day. These ghosts evoked a more sober assessment of the bloody process of introducing neoliberal globalisation. They warned of the collapsing incomes and increasing 'poverty' in countries that have given over the direction of their economies to the 'experts' like Sachs.

The main point of this article, however, is not to slay once again the ailing

dragon of neoliberal globalisation theory. It is to interrogate the definition of Sachs' overt project and then to delineate its covert political purpose.

Sachs claims not be a doctrinaire neoliberal economist, but a *clinical* economist who *uses* the tools of neoliberal theory to diagnose the causes of economic diseases and to provide appropriate *therapies*.[2] The disease he is attacking in this book is 'poverty', and the last part of his book is a plan to end poverty by 2025 (an attractive date since the bulk of his readers have a relatively good chance of reaching it alive!). For Sachs the economic disease is 'extreme poverty' and its cure is a goal only the most doctrinaire neoliberal or fanatic neoconservative would openly find fault with (although some have objected to Dr. Sachs' prescription). Yes, the ending of 'extreme poverty' (after creating so much of it) in twenty years would be a triumph of neoliberal capitalism. But with one plan after another to 'end poverty' since Robert McNamara's World Bank years in the 1970s, launched by the usual suspects – the UN, the World Bank, the development BINGOs (Big International NGOs) – leading to the intensification of 'misery' in Africa, and a political rejection of neoliberal economics in South and Central America (including the violent expulsion of one of Sachs' coworkers, Sachez de Lozada, from the presidency of Bolivia by thousands of indigenous protesters in the period of the 'gas wars') there is much justifiable suspicion of Sachs' claims.

Why is Dr. Sachs so sure he understands the poverty that he claims his plan can end? Should we trust that he and his Live8 colleagues will, at least, do

no harm? A major source for suspicion are the two different, conflicting definitions of 'extreme poverty' he offers: (a) 'extreme poverty means that households
cannot meet basic needs', and (b) extreme poverty means an 'income of $1 per day
per person, measured at purchasing power parity'. Many African or South American villagers can testify on the basis of their own experience that these definitions
do not have the same meaning. There are many villages where the 'basic needs'
of their residents (as they conceive them) are satisfied, but whose collective
income is less than $365 a year per person. This is possible because the villagers
have access to land, forests and water that has not been privatised.

Technically, (a) is a 'use value' definition while (b) is an 'exchange value'
definition. Such definitions, however, are non-synonymous (as the famous
'water/diamonds' parable has illustrated since Adam Smith's day, although now,
with the privatisation of water, it has become less salient!).[3]

For example, in many villages in Africa adults (including, in certain areas,
women) have access to (although *not ownership of*) land that they can use for their
families' subsistence. This is an enormous wealth ('use value') that cannot be alienated and hence does not have an 'exchange value'. But if each adult has land enough
to satisfy his/her basic needs but does not earn more than a dollar a day, then surely
that person is poor according to Sachs' definition (b), but not poor according to
definition (a). Things get even more complicated when we consider the fact that
these villagers' access to similar land in a part of the country that has a real estate
market might be 'worth' a few hundred or a few thousand dollars. Is the imputed
value of the common land, divided by the number of commoners, part of the
annual income of the villagers? Similar questions can be asked about children.
In many parts of Africa, children are 'shared' by villages or extended families and
their actual income is below $1 a day per person. These children often have their
'basic needs' satisfied. Are these children extremely poor, even though the caring
hands they pass through on their way to adulthood satisfy their basic needs?

After all, what does the 'exchange value' measure of extreme poverty – the
quantity $1 a day when considered from the point of view of purchasing power
parity (PPP) – come to? The definition of PPP Sachs and the World Bank use is 'the
number of units of a country's currency needed to buy in the country the same
amount of goods and services as, say, one US dollar could buy in the US'. Consequently, according to the definition, an extremely poor person is someone who
'lives' on the 'goods and services' that one can buy for $1 a day in the US. It is clear
that definition (b) implies definition (a), in that surely one cannot satisfy one's
basic needs on a dollar a day in the US alone, but even that statement is too weak,
for according to the common understanding of what can be bought in the US for
$1 a day, the people that fall under this definition ought all to be dead. *But they are
not.* How is this possible? There must be *non-monetary ways* that the 1.1 billion-plus
people who fit the definition of 'extremely poor', according to Sachs, have organised to reproduce their and their families' lives.

It is notoriously 'difficult' for economists to determine the value of unwaged reproductive 'services' even in a fully monetarised society. It certainly is even more so in a form of life where the unwaged portion overwhelms the waged. Consequently, the surveys that are used to determine the monetary value of 'goods and services' the so-called poor consume are so unreliable they can add or subtract hundreds of millions from the category of extreme poverty on the basis of an arbitrary accounting change (see, for example, the internal World Bank debate between Angus Deaton, who finds no change in the number of 'extremely poor' since the early 1980s, and Shaohua Chan and Martin Ravillion, who find a 400 million decline in the number of extremely poor people on the planet, mostly in China).[4]

This 'difficulty', arbitrariness and evasion is an old story as far as the notion of poverty is concerned, since the *real* definition of being poor is that of one who ought not to be alive... according to the rules of the capitalist system... but is! That is, someone who is wageless and propertyless in a monetary society. From the historical moment (some time in the nineteenth century in Europe) when the wage stopped being the badge of the poor (and the stigma of a lack of independence) and began to guarantee the capacity to reproduce the worker within the system, the wageless were logically doomed. Indeed, the categories of 'poor' and wageless merged then, leading to enormous confusion in both capitalist and anti-capitalist thinking.

Yet, though the wageless were not supposed to be reproduced by the capitalist system, *still they survive*. To generations of capitalists their 'irrational' existence has meant that they were *a priori* criminals (often violating yet undreamed of statutes!). To many Marxists, these wageless ones – the urban 'lumpen proletariat' or the reactionary peasant 'rural idiots' – being undisciplined by the wage, were to be treated with suspicion until they too could be brought into the waged working class proper. But to many other anti-capitalists the poor became the evidence of the existence of a communal continent that existed below the surface of capitalist reality waiting to emerge, both in the planet's countryside and its cities. This continent has been the object of many studies made by anthropologists and political activists as well as intelligence agents (often shifting identities in the course of a career). Though its existence has been debated at times, its earthquakes have certainly created political tsunamis across the planet. After all, the major revolutionary movements of the twentieth century – from Emiliano Zapata's peasant column entering Mexico City, through the nomadic Chinese Red Army, and the Vietnamese NLF fighters, to the EZLN cadres' insurrection against NAFTA on January 1 1994 – arose out of these wageless ones' power to shake the world.

Consequently, capitalism has carefully produced wagelessness, but capitalists remain ambivalently anxious about the wageless, for capitalism, as Prospero said of Caliban, cannot do without them. After all, the existence of the vast continent of the wageless is *the* basic disciplinary threat to be used against the

waged workers of the world. On the one side, they are to be the 'horrific' image of what could happen to a waged working class, if it refuses to accept the dictates of neoliberal capitalism and, on the other side, they are to be a standing 'reserve army' in case capital decides to pick some subset of them for 'development'. Finally, of course, the wageless, especially women, are the basic reproducers of the waged working class.

But the world does not wait on capital. The 'extremely poor' (in Sachs' terminology) necessarily have created non-monetary reproductive systems that have demonstrated the power of communal relations to resist enclosures and provide subsistence in ways that the Scottish Highlanders could never have imagined. On the basis of these systems the wageless are beginning to set off new political earthquakes (especially in South America). Or, in the face of increasing demonetarisation, their reliance on communal relations is creating a situation where they stop being credible potential competitors on the international labour market (especially in Africa).

The 'poor' (in Sachs' terminology) or the 'wageless', therefore, constitute contemporary capital's Scylla and Charybdis. Wageless people's attacks on and exits from globalisation must both be quelled to give neoliberalism a new impulse according to Dr. Sachs' diagnosis. Therefore, it is important to see why it is that Sachs is so insistent on only attacking 'extreme poverty' and assisting the billion-plus people in this category to break out of the 'poverty trap' that keeps them from grasping 'the first rung of the development ladder'. The poverty he wants eliminated by 2025 is one that makes it difficult for a wageless person to become a waged worker, even potentially. It used to be said that in a capitalist society the only thing worse for a worker than being exploited, is not being exploited at all. But Sachs recognises the adage cuts both ways, the only thing worse for the capitalist system than a reduction of exploitation is the reduction of the exploitable! Putting aside Sachs' moral imperatives and his appeals to the heritage of the Enlightenment, the practical consequence of Sachs' medicine is that the pool of potential competitors in the world's wage labour market will be dramatically enlarged once again.

Dr. Sachs is committed to saving capitalism from a catastrophe that all but blind doctrinaire neoliberals (with their neoconservative allies) see approaching. These neoliberals simply assume that if the world labour market consigns billions to death, the condemned will automatically disappear. Or, as the neoconservatives aver, if the condemned resist, they can be isolated, bombed and starved out. Sachs knows that these are just pipe dreams. For the inability to keep expanding the world labour market, and the increasing refusal of many of the peoples of the former colonised regions to be profitably exploited by capital, will create a dramatic reduction in the average rate of profit. In his role as the early 21st century John Maynard Keynes, Sachs like Keynes is not interested in debating the justice (and even the ultimate fate) of capitalism. But he is not as sanguine as Keynes was that capitalists would be willing to accept a couple of per cent as a profit rate just to keep their interesting game going. Sachs is anxious, as a clinician to capitalism (his other, more troublesome patient!), that the world labour market (not the world population) grows in the future, providing the control rods on the demands of the rest of the working class. This aspect of his argument gives his proposals a logic that can appeal to capitalists.

The confusing, non-synonymous definitions of 'extreme poverty' Sachs uses are essential to the political project he and his allies are embarked upon: (1) to sell to the world capitalist class (represented by the club of G8 'leaders') the proposition that a small investment in the reproduction of the wageless of the world in order to transform them into credible competitors in the world wage labour market will be crucial to save the capitalist system in the 21st century and (2) to convince the militants of the anti-globalisation movement to eschew their pessimism 'about the possibilities of capitalism with a human face, in which the remarkable power of trade and investment can be harnessed while acknowledging and addressing limitations through compensatory collective actions'.[5] For if the PPP definition is taken as identical to the 'humanistic' 'basic needs' definition, then it would appear that the most efficient path to end extreme poverty (hence presumably satisfying the anti-globalisation militants) is to create the conditions for introducing wage labour at a rate greater than, say, 10 cents an hour (hence satisfying his capitalist audience).

But if the 'basic needs'/'use value' definition is clearly distinguished from the '$1 a day' one, then the most efficient way to eliminate poverty is to decommodify people's necessities while returning all available resources (land, natural resources, etc.) to communal control. It is exactly this path of decommodification in the *long-run* that Sachs wishes to avoid, even though his plan requires it in the *short-run* (i.e. until at least 2025) by providing to the poor free education, free nutrition programmes, free anti-malarial equipment, free drinking water, sanitation and cooking fuels. But it is exactly this tension between the short-run and long-run (which is the source of Keynes' famous cynical epigram, 'in the long run we are all dead') that Sachs evades. For there is no automatic reason why a people who have 'escaped the poverty trap' through decommodification of basic needs and the development of their commons will necessarily rush to sell their labour-power to the first capitalist offering a wage.

In conclusion, Sachs' prescription for the recovery of his unacknowledged patient, the capitalist class, is to invest in bringing more than a billion of the 'extremely poor' into the planetary labour market by 2025. The sugar coating on this pill is to make this effort appear as an altruistic act (and hence potentially attractive to some of the militants of the anti-globalisation movement). But if the response of the G8 'leaders' at Gleneagles is any indication, the patient is still suspicious of the Dr. Sachs' prescription. And well it should be, for *The End of Poverty* marks a 'return' to Keynesian 'short-term' medicine, now applied on a global scale to save neoliberal globalisation in the long-run. But this is exactly what the neoliberal 'revolution' has turned the world upside down to avoid. Are the capitalists desperate enough to go back to their own vomit?

What impact Dr. Sachs' medicine might have on the anti-globalisation movement is more ambiguous. It cannot be assessed by comparing the number of viewers of the Live8 concerts with the number of anti-G8 demonstrators in Scotland. Its political fate will be decided by the ultimate source of the anti-globalisation movement: in the thousands of sites of confrontations around the control of natural gas and petroleum in Bolivia and Niger Delta, against the drug company super-profits in South Africa and Brazil, for the preservation of the commons in Columbia and Kenya as well as in the streets of the next venue of the G8's meeting.

1   *Jeffrey Sachs*, The End of Poverty: How We Can Make It Happen in our Lifetime *(London: Penguin Books, 2005) pp. 146–47.*

2   ibid., *pp. 71–89.*

3   *The water/diamonds parable or paradox concerns the relative values of these two substances. While water is essential to life (has a high use-value), it is (usually) very cheap (has a low exchange-value). On the other hand, the utility (use-value) of diamonds is much less, yet they are extremely expensive (have a high exchange-value).*

4   *Angus Deaton, 'Is World Poverty Falling?',* Finance and Development 39 (2), 2002; Shaohua Chan and Martin Ravallion, *'How have the World's Poor Fared since the early 1980s?',* World Bank Policy Research Working Paper 3341 (June), 2004.

5   *Sachs,* The End of Poverty, p. 357.

6

REINVENTING DISSENT! AN UNABRIDGED STORY OF RESISTANCE

Alex Trocchi, Giles Redwolf and Petrus Alamire

Has there ever been a society which has died of dissent? Several have died of conformity in our lifetime.

Jacob Bronowski

Everyone knows that the odds are stacked overwhelmingly against us at summit mobilisations. Yet the 2005 G8 mobilisation in Scotland proved that disrupting a summit is not beyond our grasp, and that, if anything, we underestimate our own capabilities.

It is all too easy to state that 'Another World is Possible' – actually creating another world is far more difficult. For a week, an unlikely field near Stirling became the 'Hori-Zone', a model of large-scale horizontal and autonomous decision-making. To create a long-lasting and effective anarchist network is looked upon as a fantasy. However, the G8 mobilisation turned a scattered and divided activist scene into a well-organised network of resistance, capable not only of hosting an explicitly anti-capitalist and anti-authoritarian mobilisation, but also of continuing beyond the G8. As for the inevitable action, anarchists confronted the meeting of the eight most powerful men in the industrial world directly, right outside the G8 summit venue, shutting down their highways and tearing down their fences. The attacks of the fundamentalist Islamic bombers in London the same week look cowardly in comparison. One cannot help but feel that there

is something hopeful back in the air in Britain, even as the dark repression of the police state inevitably kicks into motion after the London bombings.

Britain was the nation in which industrial capitalism first took root, and accordingly it has often remained ahead of its time in the art of protest. The British anti-roads movement of the early 1990s was a harbinger of the 'anti-glob-alisation' movement, featuring a wild and eclectic focus on direct action and cultural resistance, in contrast to the notoriously boring politics of the institutional left. The model was moved with much success into the cities, in the form of Reclaim the Streets, capitalising on the fact that in Britain hordes of ravers will show up anywhere, anytime for a good party in the middle of a street. Within a few years, cities from Brisbane to Bratislava were reclaiming their streets. Coin-ciding with the G8 summit in Cologne, the June 18 1999 Global Day of Action against Capitalism paralysed London's financial centre, prefiguring the shut-down of the WTO in Seattle a few months later.

As Britain's turn came to host the G8 in 2005, things looked grim. There had been successful mass mobilisations, particularly in London for May Day 2000 and 2001, and anarchists had taken part in direct action against the war in Iraq. However, there had not been a 'Global Day of Action' in Britain in six years, and many anarchists in Britain were simply not interested, as they were convinced that mass mobilisations were no longer an effective means of resistance. The early meetings consisted of arguments about whether a truly anti-authoritarian mobilisation was even theoretically possible!

Nearly two years before the G8 summit, an anti-capitalist network called Dissent! was founded in Britain to mobilise against the G8. Its purpose was to bring an explicitly anti-authoritarian and anti-capitalist analysis of the G8 and global capitalism to the forefront of the protests, and to promote direct action against the G8 itself through raising the level of social struggle across Britain in general and directly organising infrastructure for the G8 protests. The questions we want to look at in this piece are whether Dissent! and the 2005 G8 mobilis-ation actually succeeded, and whether they can serve as a model for actions and networks elsewhere. We will begin with an analysis of the formation and func-tioning of the Dissent! network. We will then give an overview of the myriad actions that took place before the blockades around Gleneagles. Finally, we will analyse the blockades and the response of the anarchists to the bombings in London.

THE DISSENT! NETWORK FORMS...

Before beginning, there are two brief disclaimers. First, the participants in the Dissent! network studiously avoid the word 'anarchist', and prefer to call them-selves 'anti-capitalist' and 'anti-authoritarian'. One reason behind this is that the word 'anarchist' might be seen to exclude our comrades in the autonomist communist movement (especially from Germany) and the occasional post-Situationist council communist. A more pressing reason is that in the last decade, just like a century ago, the public in all Western countries has been subjected to a media scare campaign around the word 'anarchist', so the word 'anti-capitalist' is seen as more friendly. Nevertheless, we will just call all the people who participated in Dissent! 'anarchists' since we believe most of them (minus our autonomist and council communist friends, to whom we must just apologise!) would not object to using 'anarchist' to describe their politics, and since the word 'anti-capitalist' could also be seen to include retrograde Marxist-Leninist sects like the Socialist Workers' Party (SWP) who were by design not part of the Dissent! network. Second, we indeed often use the words 'Dissent! network' or just 'Dissent!' to describe the actions of particular working groups and people, and the general feelings of people, in order not to have to specify individual names. Though a useful shorthand for saying 'anti-authoritarian and anti-capitalist' every time we wish to speak of the protesters (many of whom may have had only the slightest of contact with Dissent!), this stands against the official policy of Dissent!, since only consensus decisions at network-wide gatherings can carry the weight of being cited in the name of 'Dissent!', and 'anyone who claims to be speaking on behalf of the Dissent! network is lying'.

Dissent! as a network began after meetings at the UK Earth First! gathering and London Anarchist Bookfair in 2003. More than their North-American counterparts, British eco-activists always tended to have little patience with the notion that the Earth coming 'first' means that its human inhabitants are somehow 'second'. The original plan for Dissent! was to loosely unite the various strands of British anti-capitalism in the run-up to the G8, a grab bag of everything from ecology to insurrection, and to show that it was something that could stand on its own as an anti-authoritarian UK-wide network. The main problem is that there was actually no clearly defined or unified agreement on anything at all, except a hatred of capitalism and hierarchy combined with a love of humanity and the planet. Turning that particular weakness into a strength, Dissent! adopted the most minimal points of agreement: the hallmarks of the Peoples' Global Action (PGA) network[1]. This had the effect of maximising the number and diversity of people who would be interested in participating, while maintaining some political parameters. In particular, these hallmarks feature 'a very clear rejection of capitalism', just in case people thought the network was reformist; 'a confrontational attitude' with a 'call to direct action and civil disobedience', to focus the network on concrete action over bureaucracy; and 'an organisational philosophy based on decentralisation and autonomy', which conveniently excluded authoritarians like the SWP. Some groups participating in Dissent! originally seemed to want only to network on a model similar to Earth First!, so that there would be local collectives such as Edinburgh Dissent!, Brighton Dissent! and so on. Early on, many people seemed to want to dispose of the idea of a mass action altogether, and instead focus on decentralised local actions.

The initial meetings involved endless discussions on the question: what exactly is a network anyway? These involved both very long-winded arguments and a real discussion of how a UK-wide network could enable local groups to join something larger without sacrificing their autonomy. A strategy based on maximising the autonomy of the participants in Dissent! emerged. First, it was decided that all local groups should adopt their own names – Edinburgh Dissent!, for instance, became Reshape Edinburgh! – as a first step toward becoming a network of autonomous groups in practice and not just in theory. Local groups were expected to take care of their own internal finances, have regular meetings, and hold local events. In addition, a Dissent! network gathering was used to donate generous amounts of cash to start social centres throughout Britain. The purpose of these centres was to increase the general level of social struggle, and many local groups coalesced around them.

Dissent! incarnated itself most clearly at its more-or-less monthly 'gatherings', where the local groups came together to discuss network-wide issues and form working groups, the latter ranging from the normal Publicity'and Legal working groups to innovative ones such as the Trauma Support Group, which aimed to reduce burn-out and post-traumatic stress disorder in the wake of police repression, and the Working Group Against Work, which formed to highlight issues of wage-slavery and precarious labour during the G8 protests. The Education Working Group became Trapese, a travelling roadshow that educated people about the G8 through everything from pub quizzes to workshops. Importantly, these working groups allowed individuals from different geographical locations to get to know each other and work together, building bonds of friendship and trust across the network. The network adopted the fairly standard consensus and working-group model, so that during network-wide Dissent! gatherings the often unmanageable number of people at the meeting would break up into their working groups. They would report back to the entire network on the results of their actions (or lack thereof) in between gatherings, and ask for input from the wider network. If any decision was expected to actually affect the entire network, it was decided via consensus in the dreaded but useful plenary meetings.

Dissent! as an anti-capitalist network was a self-fulfilling prophecy. The Dissent! gatherings went on for nearly two years before the mobilisation and two-day long meetings nearly led many participants to a state of heavy drinking. For the first few Dissent! gatherings, the network seemed more like a dis-organisation than an organisation. Many of the original proponents either moved on or dropped the torch for others to carry. From that chaos, however, evolved a sort of flexible order as groups organically came together. Often the first real point of action for a local group was to successfully host a Dissent! gathering. While some of the 'local groups' and 'working groups' were in reality a single individual (or, worse, just an email address from which no one would reply!), some groups formed into solid affinity groups where none had been before. There was no small number of problems, as many groups managed to meet for nearly a year without being able to focus their energies and accomplish anything of note, and frequently individuals were stretched among what appeared to be a never-ending cast of bureaucratic meetings. However, where before there had been almost no activity, new local groups inspired by Dissent! and the possibility of taking down the G8 began to be taken seriously. When weak spots were identified such as finances (after all, no one ever wants to sign their name to the paradoxical bank account of an anti-capitalist network), individuals stood up and took responsibility.

The Dissent! network also jumped through hoops to remain inclusive, albeit with mixed results. At almost every gathering there was a discussion of who should be allowed to participate in the Dissent! network. Could Christians, who might be proselytising an authoritarian religion? How about members of organised political parties? What exactly were the limits and nature of the PGA hallmarks, and who did they include and exclude? By adopting the most minimal radical guiding hallmarks, and by agreeing to disagree on many issues, the Dissent! network succeeded in attracting participation from more than the 'usual suspects' in such scenarios. Novel and accessible projects like the Cre8 Summat community garden in Glasgow and the Clandestine Insurgent Rebel Clown Army further contributed to making the network more diverse and open. Although anarchists are often used to meeting and planning in a clandestine manner, Dissent! tried its best to be entirely open and public, both to avoid the stereotyping of anarchists as secretive and to allow more people to get involved. In a country like Britain where it sometimes feels like every square inch of the ground is under CCTV surveillance, this strategy makes certain sense. The network published all its meeting minutes on its admittedly labyrinthine website, and was remarkably accessible – at least if one were on the email list and read the website regularly, since the communications of the network in between meetings were nearly all digital. Despite this openness, reporters often 'revealed' 'secret anarchist plans to take action against the G8' after visiting the website and discovering among the piles of meeting minutes a juicy tit-bit that had been, after all, publicly announced. Not that there weren't secret plans, but more on this later.

Some aspects of Dissent!, such as its focus on local groups and decision-making structure, were clearly hallmarks of a genuine network. Others, such as the bank account and the mostly centralised production of propaganda, definitely seemed to be the work of something resembling an actual organisation. An informal leadership developed within Dissent!, as individuals and groups put things in motion behind the scenes or overtly set the agenda via the process group and proposals, resulting in much gnashing of teeth at meetings. Yet the informal leadership was flexible, with individuals moving in and out of various levels of activity, and often political manoeuvrings at meetings resulted in issues that were being foolishly ignored being addressed. The 'process group' respon-

sible for creating the Dissent! gathering agenda was in theory supposed to rotate every gathering, although often it did not due to lack of volunteers. At the beginning many processes were heavily criticised. To Dissent!'s credit, the network learned by its mistakes and sorted out many problems, though there is still much room for improvement.

Also, Dissent! had substantial amounts of funding, combining online donations with extensive fund-raising, and the total budget for the protest ran into the tens of thousands of pounds – nothing compared to the multi-million pound budget of Make Poverty History, but substantial for anti-capitalists. People need to think about the issues behind anti-capitalists using money to destroy capitalism. Are we being corrupted or just 'bio-degrading' money out of capitalist circulation?

WHO'S DOWN FOR CIVIL UNREST?

After almost a year of perpetual meetings, the location of the 2005 G8 summit was announced: the Gleneagles Hotel in rural Scotland. This posed a dilemma: commit either to a centralised action around the summit location or to decentralised actions across all of the UK. Earlier at Dissent! gatherings, many shared the implicit assumption that mass mobilisations around summits were a dead-end. Serious thought had been put into what went wrong and what went right at previous mobilisations, as shown by the still useful magazine *Days of Dissent: Reflections on Summit Mobilisations*.[2] The rural location of the Gleneagles Hotel presented added difficulties, since many found it hard to imagine primarily urban activists tromping through the woods and glens of Scotland. On the other hand, the idea of decentralised actions, which had every local working group doing direct action in its home town instead of coming to Scotland, was not appealing. First, just issuing a vague call for action and hoping that every group would do something, even if focused around a theme like climate change, was uninspiring. While days of action where activists had confronted capitalism in their own country or city as opposed to travelling to the summit location itself, such as J18 in 1999, had been successful in the past, recent decentralised actions had failed to accomplish much of anything. No one even remembers the 'Insurrection Night' proposal for decentralised actions across the United States for G8 2004, which was accompanied by an equally ineffective call for solidarity actions in the UK put forward by the Dissent! network. At the urging of many members, especially those in Scotland who were thrilled a mass summit was coming near to their town, Dissent! finally did reach a consensus that it would indeed take on hosting a mass mobilisation in Scotland.

One lurking question was: could anyone organise direct action and not be held accountable by the powers of the state? The repercussions of this nebulous and even dangerous position lent an atmosphere of paranoia to Dissent! gatherings. The year-long operation to round up activists after J18 set a worrying precedent, and often crippled the ability of newer activists to even discuss what they actually wanted to do. Dissent! at first determined it would take as its prime duty the organising of infrastructure for protests. This meant organising a convergence centre open to everyone (except cops, journalists and fascists, of course). However, upon closer inspection of the actual location of the summit, confusion set in even over infrastructure. The location of the summit was north of Stirling, about an hour's drive from both Edinburgh and Glasgow, the two largest Scottish cities. The large reformist coalitions such as Make Poverty History were basing their huge marches in Edinburgh, while cities like Glasgow had a much stronger tradition of working-class resistance, and the nearest towns to the summit itself, Perth and Stirling, had only a very small number of sympathetic activists. As for action, after Genoa many militant anti-capitalists were not excited by the prospect of 'storming the red zone' through a traditional attack on the perimeter fence, which was likely to be heavily guarded. The simple spatial layout of the protest was a nightmare, and if Dissent! was too paranoid to organise any actions, who would?

Due to possible post-summit repression and the inherent stifling of creativity that comes with centrally-organised actions, there was originally a movement for Dissent! to remain neutral towards action, except insofar as it would publicise whatever events other groups organised. This was contradicted by others who were heavily focused on actions, which they thought formed the very heart of the mobilisation. Despite this uncertainty about actions, even the most cursory inspection of a map would give anyone with an inkling of tactical ability reason for hope. Gleneagles was not nearly as remote as many other previous summit locations. In fact, it was extremely vulnerable by virtue of being accessible largely off a single trunk road, the A9. A number of small side-roads led to the G8 venue through the idyllic resort town of Crieff and the Ochil Hills. Since the Gleneagles Hotel only held a few hundred people, and since the entourage of bureaucrats, translators, caterers and other assorted servants of capital for the G8 numbered in the thousands, the vast majority of participants in the summit would have to be driven in from nearby towns and cities.

The idea captured the Dissent! network: well-placed blockades on the highways could paralyse the summit. A large-scale blockade scenario, involving not city streets but rural main roads, had already been experimented with earlier around the 2003 G8 summit in Evian. Now, this idea could be revisited in the Scottish countryside, with far better preparation. It was a difficult concept even to formulate, and somewhat doubtful at times, but it made sense: if delegates, staff and media coming in from hotels could be physically stopped from getting to the G8, the meeting would be shut down. Even if many eventually made it through, a blockade would at least disrupt the meeting and send a message to the G8 that it could not ignore. The sheer number of places the delegates could be staying was confusing, but it seemed likely that a mixture of urban and rural convergence centres located in major cities, with at least one near the A9, would be best. To top it all off, the Gleneagles Hotel was surrounded by hills. One group formed to promote the ancient pastime of 'hill-walking', a time-honoured occupation and hard-fought-for legal right in Scotland. Its plan was to meet at the Gathering Stone in Stirling and walk right over the Ochil Hills. Once on the hills they would light 'Beacons of Dissent', fires on the top of the hills that could be seen by the G8 leaders below in their hotel, and then descend upon the hotel, not stopping until they were having a whisky at the hotel bar in Gleneagles.

The impasse over whether or not actions should be organised by Dissent! was overcome organically as people simply started forming autonomous action groups and hatching plans around blockading and hill-walking. Since the action groups were autonomous and not representing anyone but themselves, and their decisions did not need to be ratified by the rest of the network, anyone was allowed to join in any legally-risky action-planning. On the other hand, people who didn't agree with a particular action or who were not in a position to suffer legal repercussions could still participate in the Dissent! network. The combination of hill-walking and blockades around the roads to Gleneagles would be hard for any centralised police force to deal with, and was nearly guaranteed to disrupt the summit as long as people showed up ready for action.

CONVINCING PEOPLE OF THE IMPOSSIBLE

Would people actually show up for action against the G8? There had been some activity in Europe: many considered the prior anti-G8 mobilisation in Evian, France to be a success since blockades did manage to substantially delay the G8 meetings, but Scotland was considerably further away than Lake Geneva for most of Europe. And many anarchists and assorted anti-capitalists in England were probably more familiar with the hotspots of Barcelona than they were with Scotland. Nearly two years ahead of the protest, the Dissent! Publicity Group began producing ludicrous quantities of stickers, posters and pamphlets to announce the summit mobilisation against the G8. These texts went through an often painful but rewarding group-writing process; many did end up sounding like the voice of the genuinely new spirit many of us were feeling in the heyday of the 'anti-globalisation' movement before the vultures like Globalise Resistance moved in. An International Networking working group formed, and hosted a packed meeting in Tübingen, Germany five months before the G8. This made it much easier to get the word out in Germany and for people from overseas to arrange their travel. In outreach it is often the small things, like helping to pay the travel costs of anarchists from Ukraine and Russia (where the G8 will be in 2006) that build true international solidarity. When it appeared there might not be many Mediterranean activists at the mobilisation, a series of workshops was organised in Spain and another International Networking Gathering took place at Thessaloniki in Greece. In Britain itself, at every major and minor activist event, from the autonomous spaces around the European Social Forum in November 2004 to an anarchist ballroom dance in Cambridge, the word spread that something big was going to happen in Scotland during the summer. Towards the end, thousands of small stickers were printed, and these proved to be an immensely effective tool in spreading the word about the G8, as they were easier to put up than large posters, which need to be fly-posted, and stayed up longer.

The Dissent! network made an effort to ensure its media policy did not create leading spokespeople. Too often in anarchist groups one person, usually a white male, gets labelled as the 'leader' by the media, usually through talking to the media about the message of the protest. One of the earliest decisions by Dissent! was that 'anyone who claims to be speaking on behalf of the Dissent! network is lying', in order to prevent any self-proclaimed media spokespeople from arising. Only decisions and statements approved by the plenary meeting of a Dissent! gathering could be cited in the name of Dissent! However, local groups, working groups and individuals could make as many statements and do as much media work as they wanted to, as long as they were clear about who they were and spoke in their own name. As a tool for preventing the media from creating leaders, this policy was excellent. The policy was misunderstood by many participants in Dissent! as explicitly forbidding all media work, and confounded by so many anarchists' overt opinion that all media coverage was inherently negative. Local and working groups did not for the most part deal with the media at all, with only a few of them occasionally communicating to the media through a collectively-written press-statement. In turn this led the media to more or less make up whatever they wanted to about the 'sinister' Dissent! network, and ironically ended up with a situation where the cops and corporate media were the only ones speaking for Dissent! to the media. While the corporate media are, with a few notable exceptions, scumbags who are interested in making anti-capitalists look like deranged axe murderers, this media policy didn't make it easy for anyone outside the anti-capitalist scene to feel sympathy towards or even understand Dissent! or the radical anti-capitalist analysis of the G8. In the final few months before the summit, a media-group called the CounterSpin Collective emerged. The CounterSpin participants sent letters to newspaper editors regarding the sensationalist British media's outright lies about the 'dangerous anarchists', and helped individuals who were prepared to be interviewed as individuals. Members of this group acted as a go-between for mainstream journalists through a 'media phone number' that they advertised. A group within Dissent! even managed to get an opinion piece published in *The Guardian* newspaper, where the efforts of Make Poverty History and Live8 were called the world's first 'embedded protest', pointing to how they allowed Blair to co-opt, domesticate and diffuse the struggle for global justice.[3]

EVEN THE ROCK STARS MOBILISE

Throughout the two years leading up to the Gleneagles summit, other groups and networks against the G8 started organising their own large-scale activities. The Southeast Assembly, an anti-authoritarian network around London, took on the ambitious plan of hiring trains to transport protesters from London to Edinburgh for the mobilisation. This was viewed as a way to increase the level of anarchists' organisational capacity by taking care of some of the necessary but unglamorous and expensive work, such as booking transport, which is normally left to the traditional Left and socialists. One interesting point to note is that instead of organising exclusively in large cities, Dissent! made it a priority to organise in smaller towns that were in need of more momentum and conveniently had less police surveillance.

At the same time as Dissent! was forming, two years before the G8, large NGOs such as Oxfam launched a massive media campaign and strategic alliance to 'Make Poverty History', a campaign centred around asking the G8 to cancel Third World debt, enforce 'trade justice', increase aid to developing countries and – in a very radical gesture – not let privatisation be the condition for any aid or debt relief. While the agenda seemed far-reaching, in practice the campaign consisted of wearing white wristbands manufactured in a Chinese sweatshop and pinning all hope upon the G8. Many anarchists in Britain, and many NGOs actually composed of Africans, saw Make Poverty History (MPH) as a literal whitewash of the power held by the G8 by the largest British NGOs. Even within MPH, many of the more radical NGOs, like War on Want, began heavily criticising the endless praise being heaped upon Blair and his chief economic wizard Gordon Brown, as well as the fact that Oxfam, Comic Relief and the more conservative NGOs were effectively ditching their own goals in their attempts to cuddle up to the G8. It appeared some of the NGOs might even be sympathetic to Dissent!

At the mobilisation against the G8 in 1998 in Birmingham, many of these very same NGOs, under the banner 'Jubilee 2000', formed a human chain around the G8 during its meetings. This was tactically useful and provided a great counterbalance to the direct action that took place in the city centre. This time around the NGOs did a massive media campaign that took 'marching in circles' to a whole new level: Make Poverty History hoped to mobilise two hundred thousand people dressed in white to form a white armband around a non-existent target in central Edinburgh an hour away from Gleneagles and on the weekend before the G8 actually met. Whilst there is something to be said for bringing so many thousands to Scotland for issues of social justice, this was a massive mobilisation on the wrong date and in the wrong place.

Later in the day, the Trotskyist SWP quickly put together its own coalition, G8Alternatives. In what can only be called a remarkably bad idea, some SWP members proposed holding a corporate rock concert in order to sell people newspapers and distract them from direct action, but after the Scottish Parliament denied them funding, the plan fizzled. G8Alternatives, with a remarkably anti-authoritarian constitution, began gathering steam, and in a much more sensible move decided on hosting an 'alternative summit' to discuss alternatives to capitalist globalisation in Edinburgh. While Dissent! was based primarily in anti-globalisation networks south of the Scottish border, G8Alternatives attracted many more Scottish people due to the widespread socialist tendencies of Scotland and good old-fashioned regular and well-advertised meetings in that country. However, the grassroots constituents were more feisty than the leadership bargained for and, after Dissent! revealed its plans for blockading the G8, leading SWP member Gill Hubbard attempted to prevent a defection of more direct-action oriented types by announcing that G8Alternatives would host a peaceful march to Gleneagles regardless of whether they got a permit or not.

A few months before the summit Bob Geldof, who had been a singer in the mediocre band The Boomtown Rats in the 1980s and organiser of the massive Band-Aid record and Live Aid concert, announced simultaneous Live8 concerts which would be held in various locations around the world on the same day as the Make Poverty History march. His invitation was for everyone from the Pope to rapper 50 Cent to join in his call for the G8 leaders to 'do something' about poverty in Africa. The politics of Live8 were murky and unclear at best, with no set agenda besides celebrities grandstanding and legitimising the G8, holding them up as potential saviours who, under the pressure of a few rock concerts, would use their powers for good instead of evil. In what could only be termed a truly bewildering turn of events, Geldof then announced a concert on July 6 in Edinburgh – the same day as the blockades – and called for everyone and anybody to bunk off school, take the day off work or whatever in order to flood Scotland. The police panicked as visions of half a million confused pop fans wreaking havoc in the city began troubling their sleep. Some anarchists viewed this as a potential opportunity to expose hordes of well-meaning and previously depoliticised people to radical politics. The government was likely simply pleased there would be a giant rock concert to show on the evening news rather than protesters. Geldof's second-in-command, Midge Ure, admitted that instead of worrying about anarchists hijacking Live8, Live8 was in fact hijacking the anarchists' event.

The Dissent! network steered clear of sectarian warfare with reformist groups by being friendly, while making no promises and being openly critical of their politics. The Blair spin-machine was using anti-globalisation rhetoric to posit the British leader as a responsible world statesman, portraying him as the saviour of Africa and pitting him against the Bush regime, in its refusal to admit that climate change was real and caused by humanity. In contrast to many previous anti-globalisation protests where the public seemed unaware and apathetic to the issues, it became positively hip to talk about the G8 and anti-globalisation, and the forces of state and capital seemed to be positively aping some early Naomi Klein article in their rhetoric. Even Gordon Brown, the Chancellor of the Exchequer, was spotted wearing a Make Poverty History wristband. It was like some anarchist dream: people knew the world was going to hell in a hand basket due to poverty and climate change and were looking for solutions. The main problem was that instead of relying on their own ability to take action, people were petitioning the G8 leaders, the very ones responsible for the problems, to solve them. As one leaked document after another showed, the G8 was not even going to agree climate change was a 'problem', and poverty in Africa was only going to be worsened through further devastating privatisation, even though a few small debts might be written off. Not a big surprise since, as the radical research group Corporate Watch had already revealed, the G8 agenda had been stitched up ahead of the summit in collaboration with the very corporations destroying Africa and the global climate – from Shell and Rio Tinto to Monsanto. One could almost feel the disillusionment in the air: and now, as the dreaded anarchists took the stage, this could have been the historic moment when many people finally understood that solutions to the problems of the world could only come through direct action.

HISTORY SPEEDS UP!

Even though there was a strong feeling about doing 'something' at the Global Day of Action on the opening day of the G8 summit, it was felt by many that just another spectacular protest was not enough. Instead, as one group after another began formulating plans for actions around the G8, the Dissent! network publicised and connected the diverse range of actions of many groups, from a demonstration in front of the Dungavel Detention Centre, where asylum seekers are imprisoned on arrival or pending deportation, to the blockade of the Faslane nuclear submarine base, where Britain's fleet of Trident nuclear submarines is based, organised by Trident Ploughshares and Scottish CND. These alliances were crucially important: while the local anti-G8 Reshape! groups were only just starting in Scotland, Scottish CND had a decades-long history of blockading and pacifist direct action, and was widely applauded by everyone who disliked the storage of all of Britain's nuclear weapons in Scotland. The idea of focusing all energy on a single day of action gave way to the idea that a diverse tapestry of actions should be woven together, starting months before the day of action itself.

THE MONTH BEFORE JULY 6: CRE8 SUMMAT

From the beginning, the Dissent! network tried make its radical politics accessible to people of all sorts. Anarchists in the UK were inspired by the 'Fix Shit Up!' community outreach actions in the previous G8 summit in Georgia, which connected the G8 mobilisation with local struggles. Tired of being seen as merely destructive, anarchists saw it as crucial to demonstrate how direct action was also 'positive' and constructive. It became a clear agenda for many anarchists not only to attack the existing system, but to begin to construct and demonstrate what the

better world might look like. As the sensationalist media were bound to tell everyone that senseless anarchist thugs were coming to burn down their homes, and as Scotland had no previous exposure to such a large anti-globalisation protest, some form of community outreach was vital. The idea of a 'Cre8 Summat' ('summat' being slang for 'something') finally took flesh when a group of permaculture activists hooked up with campaigners in Glasgow to create a community garden in a desolate patch of urban wasteland, in one of the city's poorest neighbourhoods. Although community gardens and social services were usually supported by the Scottish government, in this case they wanted nothing less than to wipe whole sections of the neighbourhood of Govanhill off the map, in order to build the M74 motorway extension. In order to do this, Glasgow Council had begun to shut down one social service after another. Now, residents had responded, even mounting a militant occupation in order to reclaim their Victorian swimming baths.

Early in June, after a few planning meetings with some of the local residents, anarchists arrived in Govanhill armed with spades and with plants carefully propagated months beforehand. Since the land was unsuitable for growing edible plants, having been a wasteland and dump for years, truckloads of soil were brought in as locals watched, interested but wary of the outsiders. One by one people walking their dogs and kids riding their bikes came through the garden and were soon gardening hand-in-hand with the anarchists. In this wasteland on which the state was planning to construct a supporting-column for the massive road, there soon stood a garden with sculptures, paintings, flowers and herb beds. The Cre8 Summat ended with an all-day celebration at which the entire neighbourhood showed up to party and local newspapers published encouraging stories about this 'new way of protesting'. While the Cre8 Summat was going on, it was announced that the M74 motorway extension would be delayed by at least two years following citizens' legal challenges. To its credit, the Cre8 Summat helped to empower people in the neighbourhood around the project and demonstrated that people do have the ability to bring about positive change without waiting for the 'sympathy' and 'aid' of any politician. Some of these people who would otherwise not have been interested in the G8 got involved in Cre8, and went on to participate in the rest of the G8 mobilisation.

THE MONTH BEFORE JULY 6: NOT ONE, BUT THREE CONVERGENCES

One problem with mass mobilisations is that no one knows exactly how many people are going to show up. When a member of the Edinburgh Council asked someone from Dissent! exactly how many people were in their 'organisation', the only response was somewhere between a thousand and twenty thousand. While not everyone coming in from afar needed full 'bed and breakfast' treatment, some legal autonomous space near both major transport centres and within spitting distance of Gleneagles was crucial. The Dissent! network decided on the ambitious policy of opening multiple convergence centres: urban convergence centres in both Edinburgh and Glasgow, and a rural convergence centre somewhere near Gleneagles itself. Since there was a whole week of actions planned in or near the cities of Glasgow and Edinburgh in the run-up to the G8, it made sense to have a base in both cities. Most people would come directly to either Edinburgh or Glasgow rather than to a rural convergence centre near Gleneagles. With Glasgow having a large and historically volatile working class and Edinburgh hosting the massive Live8 and Make Poverty History events, it was reasoned that some of these people could be tempted to join in more radical politics once they were actually exposed to them.

The Dissent! network formed convergence working groups six months before the protest and they began to look for someone insane enough to rent a piece of land or a building to anarchists. In Glasgow local activists found a nearly derelict warehouse that could be rented for hard cash and no questions asked and, after a Herculean clean-up of pigeon-shit, the Glasgow convergence space was up and running, with funds allocated to help get a new permanent social centre off the ground.

Edinburgh was another story. The tight housing market in the expensive capital of Scotland made finding space for a full-scale convergence centre impossible, so a shop-front opened as the 'Dissent! Infopoint' to offer free Zapatista coffee and G8 information to interested parties. After what was either a naïve or an insane plan by the Scottish government to house both the anarchists and police in a single football stadium in Edinburgh (!), pressure from everyone from the Dissent! network to the Green Party prompted the city to provide state-sanctioned protest camping in the Jack Kane Centre, miles away from the city centre. The protest site was revealed to have a price-tag and to come complete with security and surveillance. On July 1, everyone already in Edinburgh took the decision to meet those newly arriving in Edinburgh on the train from London, and together they set up a squatted campsite more to their liking in Pilrig Park. This horrified the authorities, who proceeded to drop the cameras and lower security, and even let Dissent! set up its own tent and food facilities.

In order to bring in more people from the streets, the Dissent! network, in cooperation with the reformist yet very effective People and Planet student group, set up a free 'Days of Dissent' conference of workshops and films in Edinburgh University. Around the corner, in the remains of a former church, Indymedia set up dozens of computers to serve as the media communications centre for the G8 protest.

Inspired by the VAAAG – *Village alternatif, anti-capitaliste et anti-guerres* – set up in Annemasse, France at the 2003 protests against the Evian G8 summit,[4] the rural convergence centre was designed to be both a demonstration of the world we want and a base for action against the G8. The amount of energy spent in specifying exactly how the world we want would function was intense and the original idea for a campsite was transformed into an idea for an eco-village to demonstrate sustainable alternatives to life under capitalism. With the protest just a few weeks away there was still no eco-village in sight, despite six months of intense searching, forming a non-profit company, planning the details down to the plumbing and allying with much more publicly respectable groups such as People and Planet and Scottish CND. Two sites on which tentative agreements had already been reached fell through. Rumour had it the owners received menacing visits from agents of the state. In an emergency manoeuvre, the rural convergence working group approached the City Council in Stirling (the city due south of Gleneagles and on the A9 trunk road to Gleneagles) and made a simple statement: it was fundamentally better for everybody, including the residents of Stirling, if the protesters had a legal place to camp with proper food and toilets than to have them squatting buildings and rampaging throughout the countryside. One Member of Parliament from the region reported concern from his constituents that Italian anarchists would be camping in their backyard with their sheep. After considerable debate, and even interest from Stirling Council in greywater systems, a cattle field behind the Stirling football stadium was offered to Dissent! It was unfortunately bounded by the swift-flowing River Forth on all sides except the entrance. For actions it appeared to be a certain trap, but it was still far better than having no place to hatch plans and organise within walking distance of Gleneagles. The chessboard was finally set.

THE WEEK BEFORE JULY 6: THE ECO-VILLAGE OPENS

Within days of the deal being struck, the cattle were cleared off the land and the rural convergence site was ready to roll. Somehow a giant lorry had been 'captured' by anarchists and went around the whole country collecting all the needed wood and other bits needed for the eco-village. The eco-village was divided into two main sections, a small one for People and Planet to hold their festival, and the other the much larger Hori-Zone initiated through the Dissent! network. As a week of intense set-up began, volunteers worked day and night to get everything sorted out, anarchists from outside Britain began pouring in and the eco-village started to take shape. Against all odds, it actually was a genuine eco-village: thousands of anarchists managed to live for a week in an ecological fashion, including a vast 'diversity of toilets' (as Starhawk put it) ranging from composting toilets to the immensely non-ecological but legally necessary portaloos. Water was dealt with via greywater systems which were meant to filter the water through woodchips inoculated with beneficial water-cleansing bacteria (although the clay soil of the site made this difficult!), and an alternative energy collective had varying levels of success in getting wind and solar energy working to help power mobile phones and an Indymedia centre. As for ecological living, even the BBC noted that it 'could be a model for us all'. The eco-village was criticised for not being ecological enough, since many non-recyclable materials were used in its construction and a lot went to landfill afterwards. However, if more time had been available for set-up instead of waiting for Stirling Council to commit to giving the site to the protesters, better planning could have made the eco-village even more ecologically sound. Some felt excluded by the often haphazard decision-making process at the eco-village, including the so-called 'bureaucracy bloc', an *ad hoc* group which ended up dealing with infrastructure and all manner of troubleshooting.

The camp was organised around 'barrios' or neighbourhoods, usually centred around a kitchen, since a kitchen provided a natural place for everyone to be together for breakfast and dinner. Each neighbourhood had its own consensus meetings and would self-organise in order to deal with its own problems, and each neighbourhood would send representatives to the site-wide consensus decision-meetings that met every day to deal with village-wide issues. The Dissent! network emerged from the realm of bureaucratic meetings and ethereal cyberspace to become concrete and real, as each local group and social centre became a neighbourhood within the eco-village. Food was bought from local organic farms and elsewhere, and distributed through the network of neighbourhood kitchens. Medics provided rations and supplies to take care of people's possible medical needs both in the eco-village and for the blockades. Whole neighbourhoods took care of children, and a loving and caring spirit made the eco-village a surprisingly relaxing hive of activity.

It was a kaleidoscope of resistance: a death metal band raging against capitalism, pagan healers helping anarchists deal with emotional trauma and Celtic

fiddle keeping everyone's spirits high. A number of Stirling residents visited and came away impressed both by the welcome they received and by just how together it was. Many others, nervous about communicating with us, drove up to the entrance to have a look and turned back. Corporate journalists were kept corralled in a media tent outside. The occasional noisy drunk would be dealt with by a 'tranquillity team' of mediators who maintained security on site, while others watched the horizon for approaching police. Many people, when confronted with the idea of a world without government, quickly retort that without government we would just rob, loot and kill each other off. Instead, without any state, thousands of people lived, loved and actually made decisions together by consensus, often agreeing to disagree and respecting the wide array of diverse opinions there. For those in the eco-village, it was like living the revolution.

SATURDAY JULY 2: MAKE POVERTY HISTORY

The Make Poverty History march began in the Meadows of Edinburgh – sort of. While many people had imagined an actual march from one point in the city to another, the organisers had set it up so people would literally march in a circle, for the sole purpose of a media stunt: a white band around central Edinburgh, just like their 'Make Poverty History' wristbands that had been distributed throughout Britain. As hordes of people showed up, the event became one big traffic jam. People were standing around for hours waiting to begin marching, while others milled around on the large lawn of the Meadows, listened to speakers and paid money for bottled water and food from corporate stalls. It was, in short, a 'happening' rather than a march, and a very disempowering one at that, although many of the speakers did have a surprisingly radical flavour and questioned the legitimacy of the G8, the IMF and, even occasionally, capitalism itself. Despite threats by certain members of Make Poverty History that those not wearing white would be removed from the march, a horde of clowns showed up to add colour and humour to the event. Dissent! had printed 80,000 leaflets carefully subverting Make Poverty History's logo to 'Make History: Shut Down the G8', in order to encourage everyone at the march to stay on in Scotland and take direct action; everyone from old Scottish ladies and young children from council estates took the flyers, often resulting in confused questions and engaging debates about social change. While the message of anti-capitalism was spread, few of those people seemed to actually come to the eco-village, showing not surprisingly that it takes more than handing out a leaflet to get people to act.

Anarchists met in a disorderly fashion in front of the 'Days of Dissent' conference. There had been debate about whether anarchists should split up into small affinity groups for the day or march as one large contingent in order to radic-alise it, but as the moment approached the crowd simply split into two main groups, with one sizeable black bloc running off early and the clowns and others making their own way later to the march. After a good deal of pointless milling about, the colourful anarchist contingents mostly dispersed into the crowd, but the black bloc tried to lead a breakaway march. It was a bit too late, for by then the police had had enough time to prepare their own forces: the black bloc was surrounded with heavily armoured riot police, sending a message to all that no unauthorised demonstrations would be allowed. Using the particularly British policing tactic of 'frustrate and disperse', they managed to isolate and eventually split-up the bloc. For better or for worse, the rest of the march seemed to pass without incident. Nobody knows if they actually managed to create the giant white wristband of people circling Edinburgh, although there were thousands upon thousands there.

MONDAY JULY 4: BLOCKADING FASLANE NUCLEAR BASE

On the Monday before the days of action, two actions of differing natures happened in Edinburgh and the Faslane Nuclear Base. For seven years before the G8, Scottish CND and Trident Ploughshares had organised large non-violent blockades at Faslane, home to Britain's infamous Trident nuclear submarines. This year they moved the date of the protest close to the G8 summit in order to remind people that the G8's domination of the world was backed up by murderous wars, not by handing out debt relief to poor countries. This long and proud tradition of civil disobedience was only strengthened by the energy and numbers brought in by the anti-G8 mobilisation, and for most of the day the entire base was shut

down. The police, long-accustomed to this sort of thing, actually were rather kind and accommodating to the protesters. It's unclear how much of a cross-over took place between the peace activists and anarchists. Many were no doubt distracted by events in Edinburgh, where a different story was taking place.

MONDAY JULY 4: CARNIVAL FOR FULL ENJOYMENT

In Edinburgh, the Carnival for Full Enjoyment took to the financial and tourist district of Edinburgh, in order to connect the mobilisation against the G8 to the everyday struggles of people in the city. The Carnival encouraged everyone to take a day off work in protest against low wages, lack of job security, over-working and dole slavery. In the city that played such a key part in the birth of the anti-poll tax campaign, this definitely hit a chord: thousands of locals showed up for the Carnival and Princes Street was lined with ordinary people waiting for something – anything – to happen.

The state and the media had promised everyone a riot in central Edinburgh, and they were hell-bent on making it transpire. Hordes of cops were everywhere and they went out of their way to harass, as the newspapers put it, the 'most militant anarchists': the clowns. They also quickly trapped the black bloc again and targeted medics for arrest. However, the Infernal Noise Brigade, the Seattle-based marching band, made it to downtown Princes Street and then courageously took the streets. The police reacted by blocking them in too. However, as one older Scottish gentleman noted, while from their limited perspective the police thought they had won the day, the anarchists did a classic pincer around Princes Street, as there was not one but three gathering spots for the Carnival. As these other groups arrived, the police found themselves surrounded by people on every side and proceeded to panic.

The Carnival then began in full force. Police attempted to block one unit of the Carnival with a line of horses, but the hilarious movements of a black Industrial Workers of the World sabotage cat puppet terrified the horses. Police from Manchester attempted to arrest a man and anarchists were outdone by angry locals who shouted for the English cops to get the hell out of their town, and backed up their threats by throwing uprooted flowers, rubbish and even benches at the police! The Carnival sought to move people to targets like the Social Security head office, home of dole fraud investigator Joan Kirk. Sturdy banners made from large bits of carpet with handles were used to help reclaim some of the streets and a sound system was pulled out at the last minute.

Many locals were disgusted with police behaviour and enjoyed the Carnival because of, not despite, the chaos: people roaming the streets, cars trapped, music playing, clowns mocking police officers, the houses of the corrupt and wealthy targeted for payback. It was anarchy in its most pure and undistilled form, and it felt a hell of a lot better to everyone involved than the zombie-like shopping that dominates Princes Street every other day of the week.

WEDNESDAY JULY 6: THE DAY OF ACTION

'Violent extremists come to Gleneagles: And we're going to try to stop them!' the web-page of Dissent! proclaimed. And against all odds this is exactly what happened. The hill-walkers met at the historic Gathering Stone inside the grounds of Stirling University and began their long walk through the Ochil Hills. On the top of the breath-taking Scottish hills and within viewing distance of the wine-glasses at Gleneagles, the hill-walkers lit their 'Beacons of Dissent!': fires which traditionally signalled an impending invasion. The day before July 6, the day of action, the eco-village was abuzz with last-minute talk of blockades. Likewise, a series of difficult meetings was taking place in the Glasgow warehouse, and anarchists were busy hatching a scheme in Edinburgh as well. To say that communication between the various convergence centres was difficult would be an understatement: people for the most part had little or no idea what other groups were doing. Although last-minute guides to blockading the G8 had been produced by the notorious Deconstructionist Institute for Surreal Topology, to almost everyone the plan seemed vague and informal: find friends, exit the convergence centre and stop the delegates on the roads by whatever means you can. There was a method to the madness.

Scotland is home to an insect called the midge. The midge is like a mosquito, but terrifyingly tiny, and they travel in hordes, making them even more ferocious and unstoppable. Due to their small size and speed, you cannot even slap them to kill them, but can only resist by literally running away from them. In retrospect, the entire plan seemed to be based on 'The Midge Principle': hundreds of irritating and determined small groups moving in and out of critical road junctions would be impossible for a centralised police force to cope with. This contrasted with the Make Poverty History march, which seemed to be based on the behaviour of another common Scottish animal also known to wear white: the sheep. The police, much like a shepherd, can easily control vast numbers of people if they are docile and scared of confrontation. In contrast, the 'midge' action was based on confront-ation through swarming, so that even when facing a vastly superior force, smaller groups could overcome it by surprise and speed, just so long as they were highly mobile, coordinated and had numbers at the critical point of engagement equiv-alent to that of the 'superior' force.

Although the plan sounded dodgy, autonomy worked: groups had met in their eco-village neighbourhoods and decided together how far they were willing to go to stop the G8. The answer was pretty damn far: the highway to Gleneagles was many hours' hike from the eco-village and rain clouds were gathering. Since the eco-village was surrounded by a deep river and had only one exit, it would be ludicrously simple for the police to simply block the exit and trap everyone inside. To counter this, affinity groups began leaving the camp *en masse* the evening before the day of action, often with nothing but a plastic trash-bag for a raincoat and no supplies to block the road but their bodies. Hordes of affinity groups scattered to the four winds, each trekking to find their own way to the A9. The police set an emergency Section 60 order that let them stop and search anyone in Scotland for weapons, a technique used mainly to separate activists and even arrest them. But as the groups slipped out one by one, the police seemed to be sleeping on the job.

THE BLACK BLOC STRIKES BACK
As nightfall approached, roars could be heard from the campfire. Over a thousand people, including a large black bloc contingent, had stayed behind in the camp, preparing themselves to march straight from the eco-village to the M9 motorway (which becomes the A9 a little further north). This courageous plan was dubbed the 'suicide march' since it likely meant a direct confrontation with the police. For the inevitable throw-down with police the black bloc prepared by fashioning some impromptu padded armour, a 'battering ram' made of a line of lorry tyres attached to a banner which bore the semi-ironic slogan 'Peace and Love' and some very big sticks. Since it was assumed that the police would attempt to block the camp early in the morning, the mass walk-out set its leaving time for 3.00am. As the black bloc gathered in front of the entrance as it readied to leave, the heavens opened and a giant torrent of rain came down, soaking the bloc and all the affinity groups already massing outside of the eco-village.

Resolute, the mass walk-out departed – only to discover that in an act of shocking incompetence the police had not blockaded the camp's exit. While the police did eventually move in to stop the black bloc, it was too little and too late as much of the bloc had already left the eco-village unchallenged. When the Scottish police finally managed to stop the bloc *en masse*, they attempted to trap them in a nearby industrial estate. The police learned all too soon this was a mistake, as in a controversial but tactical move the bloc began to wreck corporate outfits like Burger King and Pizza Hut. This was exactly the type of behaviour the police were trying to stop, and they had just caused it by trapping the bloc in a chain-store shopping district. The police backed off and the bloc managed to find a road out. As it approached the M9, the state finally pulled out the riot cops who formed a line blocking the bloc's route.

But to the shock of the police, the bloc reacted with a full frontal charge on its lines. *Ya Basta!*-style armoured members took the initial charge – and then, in a very non-pacifist move, turned on the police and attacked them from behind! The front line of the bloc was armed with the now infamous big sticks, and managed to beat the police at their own game by giving them a shocking beat down, while rocks were thrown at the police from behind. Overwhelmed by the ferocity of the bloc, the police line collapsed and the impossible was accomplished: the black bloc and others involved in the mass walk-out victoriously took the M9, shutting down traffic going to Gleneagles. In a panic, the police sent hundreds of riot cops to surround the bloc, but again the bloc battled their way out, and eventually dispersed and escaped through the Scottish countryside to return victorious to the eco-village. The 'suicide march' was a momentous victory, and the taking of the M9 by the bloc would turn out to be the largest and most public of a series of blockades.

GLENEAGLES SURROUNDED

Earlier, it had generally been thought that affinity groups would never leave the camp the day before and move into position to take the roads. It was simply too much to ask of activists from all over the world who had just come to Scotland and had little experience with rural actions and the topography of the Scottish landscape. But that is exactly what happened.

No doubt bringing much planning to a crescendo, affinity groups spent the evening and night before the day of actions scattering around the roads surrounding Gleneagles in a radius of several miles, waiting to stomp on their targets. A vacation in the Scottish countryside this was not: it rained heavily during the evening and vicious midges attacked the activists. As the morning traffic started, the groups mobilised and took the roads – creating an almost impossible policing situation. Suddenly, as if from nowhere, the activists were everywhere. A handful of affinity groups made sure the first wave of actions to halt traffic at all crucial junctions leading to Gleneagles was successful. One of the first blockades to hit was an innovative five-person lock-on in Muthill near Crieff, a small village immediately north of Gleneagles that had never been

discussed openly as a site for protest. Thinking themselves safe, the American delegation to the G8 had located in Crieff, and then had to spend hours waiting for the police to disable the complex lock-on.

At the same time, another blockade, this time using a car with lock-ons inside and underneath, hit the small road south-east of Gleneagles at the village of Yetts o' Muckhart. Because the police had to spend so much time dismantling the Crieff blockade, this one was up most of the day. Just in case the delegates were re-routed around the A9, another large blockade hit the exit from Perth, with two smaller ones south-west of Perth, near Forteviot and on Kinkell Bridge. Even earlier, the train-tracks going to Gleneagles were disabled using a compressor, tyres set ablaze on both sides as a warning. With the black bloc taking the M9 west of Gleneagles, the Gleneagles Hotel was completely surrounded by blockades for most of the morning. The Canadian delegation never even made it to Gleneagles. Mission accomplished!

The original plan was to coordinate these blockades with disruption at the hotels where the delegates were staying in Edinburgh and Glasgow. This made sense given the convergence spaces present in both cities. While most of the anarchists had gone to the eco-village, the blockades guide released on the internet somehow got garbled by the media, who announced that the anarchists' main plan was to blockade Edinburgh and riot in Glasgow, and in response more of the police seemed to be based in Edinburgh and Glasgow than in Stirling. Disinformation, whether intended or not, helped to confuse both the police and ourselves.

There was, however, an element of truth in the reports. Instead of going to the eco-village, a substantial group of anarchists stayed in Edinburgh. In the early morning, they went to the Sheraton Hotel where the Japanese delegation was staying: despite the presence of hordes of police officers who prevented any mass action, affinity groups blocked the road using a bin and surrounded the delegates' bus just as they were climbing on. Then, as these delegates left the hotel with the help of the police and made their way north to the Forth Bridge, a giant steel construction connecting Edinburgh to central Scotland, anarchists crashed two cars into each other on the road to blockade these delegates, in a literally death-defying action.

In Glasgow, many of the anarchists had felt out of the loop of the action plans, and were getting ready to head up to the eco-village, when another wave of anarchists, including the Wombles, showed up in order to blockade delegates' hotels in Glasgow. However, by then the anarchists already in Glasgow were demoralised and in the process of leaving, so the blockade organising in Glasgow broke down and the Glasgow plans fell through.

To add to the confusion, on the afternoon of the day of action the police mounted a huge operation against the Wombles. This group had been a major anti-authoritarian organising force within London for years and had bested the London Metropolitan Police before; their social centres had been the main hubs of organising everything from Indymedia to medic trainings in London in preparation for the G8. The police were sure they were the ring-leaders behind the G8 blockades, guided perhaps by the blind assumption that the UK anarchist movement works, like the police, as an operation commanded from London. As the Wombles were in a van leaving Glasgow, hundreds of police proceeded to surround them and arrest eleven of them for 'conspiracy to breach the peace': charges so ridiculous they were dropped almost immediately. The next day Wombles were even harassed by the police in a pub! The Wombles did have two strengths which doubled as weaknesses: their open organising meetings allowed the police to discover their identities and plans easily, and their support of militant direct action (as well as many of them dressing in all black) made them the anarchist targets the police were looking for. The amount of repression the Wombles were dealt was due to their previously effective anti-capitalist activity, yet the strength of a network lies in the fact that no matter what happens to one individual component, the network still functions. In an ironic twist, the focus of corporate media on 'urban riots' and the Wombles led the police to ignore the activity in the eco-village and the many other groups preparing for blockades.

SWARMING THE A9

One by one, all the early morning blockades began to be cleared off, but these were only the beginning. Lock-on blockades are by nature troublesome and difficult for the police to deal with initially, but once they were removed and the participants arrested, it was easy to get the delegates through. While the groups committed to lock-ons around the perimeter of Gleneagles made sure the traffic got snarled, many affinity groups which didn't have pre-decided targets proceeded to get as close as they could to the hotel itself and literally jump in the road. These affinity groups, after many hikes, played a sort of cat-and-mouse game with the cops, capitalising on two obvious principles. The first is that drivers tend to stop when they see someone in the road to avoid running them over, even if said driver is transporting G8 delegates. The second is that the police are by nature terrified of leaving their comfortable vehicles to run into some countryside field to chase an anarchist. The combination made the blockades around Gleneagles almost impossible for the police to deal with, as their reliance on vans and cars often led the police themselves to be blockaded. A typical blockade struck first early in the morning, and simply strolled around the highway: a few people doing this was enough to bring traffic to a standstill. If there were any available materials, such as orange traffic cones, they were re-arranged (and there are even reports of burning tyres being thrown into the road).

The vast majority clearly had no plan but to cause disruption, and groups would appear on the road, blocking it by just walking around until the police could mobilise and get near them, or dragging branches and dislodged paving stones onto the tarmac. Then, they would simply exit the road and go into the nearest field, walking away in order to get to another part of the road. The police almost never followed them, and would eventually disperse to go deal with another blockade – and at that moment, the affinity group would reappear at another nearby location in the road, blocking traffic yet again till the police re-mobilised. This effect was multiplied exponentially by the number of affinity groups doing it. Just as the police would mobilise to stop one group, another group would appear and blockade their way!

The clowns were present all over the place, aggravating the police and keeping everyone in good cheer. At a certain point there was even a 'kids' blockade' of children blocking the road. A car blockade left the eco-village, and they gleefully thanked the police every time they were stopped and searched, as this delayed traffic even more. Cyclists, who had arrived in Scotland on a bike-tour against the G8, also lent their mobile support. At the eco-village people kept flooding back in and out, and a transport group kept in touch with information from Indymedia, a Dissent! info-line and various bike-scouts and affinity groups in order to attempt to re-route groups to critical junctions. The police were simply unable to keep track of the movements of so many small groups taking the highway, such that even after the lock-ons were eliminated and the black bloc returned to the eco-village, the highway remained closed to G8 traffic. Delegates, media and other assorted staff simply could not make it to Gleneagles, and inside the hotel the meetings tottered close to collapse, with nothing of any substance happening.

The BBC announced that the roads were closed by the anarchists and the police sent announcements urging everyone to avoid the A9, stating that traffic all over central Scotland was a mess. The Scottish police were caught with their pants down. The news reported that a member of the Scottish government announced that 'Dissent! was both organised and dangerous'. At the eco-village, one person stood up at a consensus meeting and announced: 'We have successfully defeated 10,000 of Britain's best police.'

TAKING THE FENCE DOWN

Humiliated, the police announced that they would stop G8Alternatives' noon march to Gleneagles, which had previously been permitted. G8Alternatives did all they could to get thousands of people to Gleneagles. In one humorous incident a few days earlier, G8Alternatives' leadership demonstrated its single-minded resolve by sending out a press-release blaming the anarchist blockades for jeopardising their march. They obviously failed to understand the point that directly disrupting the G8 summit was more important to many than yet another round of marching in circles. Still, G8Alternatives pledged to hold the march, legally or otherwise, and, if stopped, they threatened to march on the US Embassy in Edinburgh. When the police disallowed their demonstration, people undertook a spontaneous march through Edinburgh to demonstrate their right to peaceful protest. The police backed off and allowed the march to go on. Later in the afternoon, when the trains were functioning again and the roads were less of a mess, several thousand people showed up to march on Gleneagles, including many people from the Dissent! network, Scottish CND and beyond. As usual a fence had been erected, marking a large outer security zone around the hotel, yet instead of being large and intimidating, the fence was barely taller than your average anarchist. One could climb over it. Inside that fence was another fence, the inner security fence. As the march left the village of Auchterarder and went down one suburban street towards Gleneagles, it was blocked by part of an outer fence. Spontaneous anger at the arrogance of the G8 rose from the crowd, and groups such as the Dundee Trades Council went to the fence and put their banners on it. One contingent got right next to a fence and simply pushed and kicked it right off the ground, breaking the fence!

Police managed to corral the crowd back onto the march path, aided by panicking G8Alternatives stewards who were absolutely terrified that an ounce of direct action might interfere with the well-scripted peaceful protest. However, the grass-roots of G8Alternatives was much more feisty and ready for action than their Trotskyist leadership. On the road back to the park there was an open field, and in what can only be explained as remarkably poor security, at the far end of the field was the inner perimeter fence surrounding Gleneagles Hotel itself! Climbing over a smaller fence to access the field, spirits raised by the Infernal Noise Brigade and a host of red 'Revolution' flags, a trickle and then a storm of people approached this inner security fence through a field. Hundreds of people ranging

from clowns to Congolese drummers were in the 'red zone'! The police were caught off guard and didn't even have enough riot cops to defend the inner fence. Just as a police officer would try to arrest the black bloc kid who threw a rock at them, he would nearly trip over a rainbow-draped hippie and then from out of nowhere a Scottish trade unionist would jump in front of the confused officer and in outrage demand his right to peaceful protest! Soon, the mechanical buzzing of choppers could be heard overhead, as hundreds of riot cops were flown in on Chinook helicopters, formed a giant line, and eventually cleared the field. They had to literally send in the helicopters to stop the red zone from being breached!

Tactically, the blockades were a tremendous success, for nearly the same reason the Dissent! network was a success: instead of homogenising everyone into a single course of action, the blockades provided a structure that gave people just enough to hang on to, while encouraging creativity and a diversity of actions. Everyone felt they could do something to stop the G8, and a vast diversity of tactics was employed. With a common goal, everyone knew they were going to disagree on specific tactics, but managed to get along anyway. The most controversial tactic by far was the black bloc's physical confrontation with police as it left the eco-village. Some of the pacifists, who often were facilitating the meetings, were shocked by the relatively minor property destruction and this physical confrontation, feeling that it betrayed the understanding they had reached with some of the residents of Stirling and the local council. Others felt that since the bloc had been one of the first to shut down the M9, the action was a stunning success, and that for the most part the confrontation had been well-timed and tactical. There was no consensus reached, but in the framework set up by Dissent! autonomy was the secret weapon. Unlike many other protests in which a vast centralised plan keeps everyone in check until the moment of chaos actually hits, the Dissent! plan was to have no 'plan' but to facilitate the creation of many plans. This created real autonomy, allowing everyone to self-organise around their own particular style and concerns.

On the other end of the spectrum from the black bloc was the Clandestine Insurgent Rebel Clown Army, who aimed to protest the G8 by using their arsenal of three – wait, four! – secret weapons of humour: ridicule, red noses, face paint and silly army costumes. Nobody expected the clowns! But the clowns had held trainings for many months leading up to the G8, helping staid activists to release their 'inner clowns'. The results were fantastic and the police absolutely baffled at how to deal with them. Because the uptight British police knew they would look ludicrous if they beat or even arrested a clown, they appeared powerless to prevent the clowns blockading the road and making fun of them at the same time! The clowns were one of the most organised contingents and, when organised but disparate groups ranging from the clowns to the black bloc could sit together in one meeting and work together to shut down the G8, the phrase 'diversity of tactics' really meant something. One could also speculate that the process of actually living together and having to cooperate on more mundane matters such as keeping the toilets working helped everyone get along.

The blockades' success was not entirely the anarchists' doing; it must also be attributed to the utter incompetence of the police. Due to their mistaken belief that anarchists wanted a Genoa-style riot in Edinburgh, they put an incredibly large concentration of their force in the city and, no doubt because of requests from the London Met, obsessively focused their efforts on following and arresting the Wombles. The police force was a bizarre composite of English police in full riot gear and Scottish police in bright yellow jackets; with so many different police forces called in to help in Scotland, the police sometimes appeared to have even worse communications than the protesters. The police would let themselves be isolated, would not apply force until it was too late and, in general, seemed to have no idea how to cope with protesters who were even a little bit disorderly. We should not kid ourselves into thinking that it was our tactical genius that won the day. It was about half tactically sound ideas and about half sheer police incompetence. In the end, the day of action had proved to be a victory for the global movement against capitalism and everyone wondered what the next day of action would bring.

THURSDAY JULY 7: THE MOMENT OF TERROR

Under the cover of darkness early on Thursday, the police finally did what everyone had feared they would: in revenge for the blockade of the G8, they blockaded the camp. They formed a large line outside the camp's main entrance point, searching everyone coming in and out and even arresting people. Most people coming back after a hard day of blockading and marching found themselves trapped. As discussions on how to deal with this new development began on Thursday morning, everyone was still exhausted but elated by the success of the blockades the day before. Still, tensions soon became felt. The more insurrectionary anarchists argued that the police blockade around the eco-village had to be disposed of in order to continue the success of the previous day. With the police so obviously weak and the fence easily toppled, they believed that one more coordinated action could shut the summit down. The more pacifist wing felt that any attempt to force through the police lines, especially now that the police would not be caught off-guard as they had been on the previous morning, would be a disaster, but they couldn't propose a way to deal with the police blockade.

Before discussions about the next few days of action could really commence, news came of the terrorist attack in London. It hit everyone like a physical punch in the stomach, and the whole meeting came to an eerie standstill. A tremendous wave of shock and sorrow swept over the meetings; many people had friends and family in London who could be dead. The news continued to worsen: one bomb had gone off on a bus full of Londoners going to work, and more bombs had gone off on Underground trains across the city. These bombings were clearly targeting civilians whose only crime was to live in London and their one and only intention was to spread fear. Rumours spread that the G8 summit itself had been cancelled – although it later turned out that it was just interrupted while Blair flew down to London to make a statement. The bombings were quickly said to be the work of Islamic fundamentalists enraged by Britain's complicity in the war on Iraq. The timing was almost too convenient: it shattered any dreams about refocusing the debate on climate change and poverty, inescapably pulling the focus onto George Bush's rusty refrain on war and terror and, most importantly, sending everyone fleeing for protection into the arms of the state. The net effect of the terrorist attacks was complete paralysis. The spectacular bombings simply fed into the image of the G8 as the defenders of western civilisation from anarchy and Islam. The response of activists was half-hearted to say the least: there was a plan for some sort of press release. Various anarcho-communist and anarcho-syndicalist groups outside of the Dissent! process put together a very solid and inspiring 'Statement against London Bombings'. Another faction at the eco-village didn't see how the bombings really changed anything and aggressively pushed to continue the blockade of the G8. The fatal flaw of this proposal was the police blockade around the eco-village. It was going to be hard to mount an escape without a united front and most people were physically – and now emotionally – exhausted. Finally an agreement was reached to do a vigil for the victims in both London and Iraq through a peaceful march out of the eco-village.

Predictably, the vigil was stopped by the police before leaving the eco-village, and in a very strange moment the anarchists and the police seemed to share a moment of grief together. There was a ceremony at the gates of the eco-village, where a procession of anarchists with candles sang to the shift of cops while a few others verbally raged at them. Many of the police seemed disenchanted with their job of 'containing the anarchist menace', but at this critical juncture the police were unable to break from their roles as defenders of the G8 and stood their ground to prevent any direct action, despite the fact that it was these very same leaders that had moved the entire police force of London to deal with the Wombles instead of doing their supposed job of guarding London. The energy left the eco-village and people eventually began leaving in small groups. The police, in a style of policing no doubt learned after decades of successful empire, would act as kindly as possible up to the moment they searched someone leaving the eco-village using the now infamous Section 60, then make an arrest if they had any suspicion they were part of the black bloc or were otherwise wanted. Things continued like this for days until finally almost everyone had escaped the eco-village.

In our stunned silence we could not even enunciate clearly that the enemy of our enemy is not our friend. The religious fundamentalists behind the attacks in London hold beliefs and carry out actions which are just as antithetical to anti-capitalism as those of the G8. In all respects, both the G8 and Islamic fundamentalist terrorists share the aim of disempowering people through the media spectacle they create and their ability to murder at will. This brings us to an important point: the difference between the terrorists and anarchists is precisely in the effect that their action has upon both the participants and the observers. Fundamentalist terrorists want to see people disempowered, to provoke fear in the average person on the street. Unlike terrorists, anarchists want to see people empowered to take control of their own lives, to inspire hope rather than fear. The alternative represented, however imperfectly, by the eco-village, Dissent!, and anarchists everywhere is the real alternative to terror and capital.

A media blackout of course fell on the anarchists after the bombings – but is what we are doing merely a spectacle for the media to report on? For their own part, the anarchists had very little to say. One does not use the word 'racist' lightly, but it is hard to explain this lack of response. People were very naturally shocked and horrified by the events in London, but the same number of people have been dying frequently in Iraq due to the depravity of the US and their twin puppets the British and Iraqi governments. Just because it happens in Britain, is it 'different'? In one obvious manner it is different, since it is more likely our own families and friends in London that could have been killed, and so some loss of momentum for everyone to check on the safety of their loved ones is both to be expected and is an expression of our humanity. To the credit of the anarchists, the G8 protests did continue onward, with a massive street party against climate change, seizing the M74 in Glasgow on July 8 as part of the international day of action against climate change.

In the final analysis, those responsible for the conditions that lead inevitably to disasters such as the London bombings and the war in Iraq were left unmolested in Gleneagles after the bombings. It can only be called a failure of imagination. People desperately want another option besides Bush and bin Laden, and anarchists could have shown that in their response to the bombings. Although it is tactically unclear what could have worked, one has the feeling that something beautiful and brave could have somehow caught the imagination of the British population. Perhaps we should thank this turn of events for showing us that despite the dreams we made reality, the world is engulfed in a larger nightmare that we must learn how to respond to and eventually banish.

RUTHLESS CRITICISM

We can only move forward if we inspect our mistakes instead of blindly repeating failing stratagems. There are definitely criticisms to be made of the day of action, since the blockades disrupted but did not actually shut down the G8 summit. There are clear reasons for this. Up until the very day before the day of action, most groups were confused about even what city to be in. Dissent! could have done a much better job at communicating the goals and actions of the blockades. Dissent! was on some level too ambitious and stretched its organisational resources too thinly in setting up three convergence centres, one of which was attended by only a few hundred and the other deserted on the day of action. The convergence centres could have simply shut themselves down after their purpose had been served, and moved everyone to the eco-village. Communicating within one consensus meeting is hard enough; communicating among three simultaneous consensus meetings is nearly impossible and serious thought needs to be put into how such a thing could be done realistically. On the other hand, this lack of communication and lack of a central convergence centre may have been a saving grace, as lack of clarity about the blockades was probably one of the deciding factors in the police's failure to focus on the eco-village and the A9 itself.

Second, many groups who were out blockading felt very much alone and isolated from other groups. Dissent! did not establish much of a communications infrastructure, providing only a series of phone numbers one could call for updates and a communications map at the eco-village. The map itself was useful but could have been better managed, as it was usually unclear where to send people to blockade. Most updates spread through rumour, and bike scouts were few and far between, although some affinity groups had put together their own scouting and communication networks. The black bloc that left the eco-village was mostly lost until they ran into a bike scout. Affinity groups who organised through the public process often chose their location and time of blockade almost at random, which led to crucial junctions not having enough people blockading them and other less critical junctions being overstocked with anarchists, so that the G8 was eventually able to re-route its delegates through the blockades. Still, through sheer mass and some clear thinking by certain affinity groups, the plan did succeed up to a point later in the afternoon in literally shutting down the G8. A network is only as powerful as its communications, and something like a text-mobbing server (that was used on a much smaller scale to great effect during the Republican National Convention protests in New York City the summer before) would have allowed groups to use the ubiquitous mobile phone 'text' (SMS message) to communicate where more blockades were needed and where the police and delegates were. On the other hand, once again, reliance upon a centralised text-messaging centre would have had drawbacks: it could easily have been infiltrated or shut down, and it might have turned out to be simply useless in the Scottish countryside where mobile phone service can be dodgy at best. Regardless, the gain should have outweighed the cost, allowing groups to more flexibly coordinate where the blockades were going and when. Not surprisingly, many groups got lost rambling in the sheep fields around Gleneagles, and a topographic map was worth its weight in gold on the day of action, so obviously a much better job of briefing people about the geography around Gleneagles could have been done.

Third, the main reason the G8 summit was not shut down was not because the police managed to break the blockades, but, due to sheer exhaustion and lack of food and water, the various blockading groups simply went home early. Had the level of intensity of blockading been kept up for only a few more hours – which it might have been, if only people had known how effective their seemingly isolated blockades actually were! – the summit would have likely been shut for the entire day. Dissent! had set aside money for extra food and water for the blockaders, but it wasn't enough and it would have been difficult, due to the success of the blockades, to get the food and water to them anyway. Groups should have been made self-sufficient not for a morning and afternoon of blockades but for three full days of non-stop action. While this sounds impossible, many of us have gone camping for at least three days, and carrying that amount of food and water is possible – it just requires time and money for preparation that most of the groups did not have. Provisioning would have allowed the groups to continue their midge-like presence around Gleneagles. It was only a matter of time until the police trapped people who had returned to the eco-village inside. To the extent the blockades were a success, it is proof that we can aim for something that appears impossible, and pull it off! In retrospect, we just need to aim even further and press harder!

SPREADING THE FLAMES OF DISSENT

One of the most important things about Dissent! was its radical anti-capitalist analysis, since this was what served as the concrete framework for organising direct actions. It separated Dissent! from the SWP leaders of G8Alternatives: while in theory they are anti-capitalists, in true Trotskyist tradition they are also absolutely terrified of direct action. What Dissent! accomplished was to unite the various strands of British anti-authoritarianism and anti-capitalism into a mobilisation framework, strengthening the movement in Britain, and generating excitement about the G8 overseas. The anarchists set their own game plan for the G8 and succeeded: we organised our own infrastructure, finances, publicity and even action plans independently of the NGOs and the old Left. While earlier mobilisations like the Free Trade Area of the Americas protests in Quebec city had shown that anarchists could successfully organise their own mobilisation, the Dissent! G8 mobilisation was done by anarchists on a national scale with international participation. One should recognise how few people actually participated in the G8 mobilisation in Scotland and that the total number of people involved in the direct action and self-organisation numbered five thousand or so at most. A few hundred really formed the planning and organisation in the month leading up to the G8, with only dozens working on the mobilisation half a year beforehand. The fact that the protest worked so well was a testament to the power of a fairly small number of people to self-organise, and the superiority of swarming and decentralised networks over centralised hierarchies. However, Dissent! never reached the point of generating a giant mass mobilisation of its own. One could only imagine how much more powerful the protest could have been had more people gone to the eco-village instead of staying home and watching Live8 on television or if even a tenth of the participants at the Make Poverty History march could have been persuaded to join in the direct actions. Interestingly enough, more people who otherwise would not have been involved in the eco-village and the day of action seem to have come from the Cre8 Summit site than the Make Poverty History march, and this shows that concrete activity is always a better way to get allies than just flyers. As the ruckus at the G8Alternatives march proved, more people are up for direct action than anarchists tend to give them credit for, but for first-timers this often requires the context of a mass action where even a clear affinity group is not a prerequisite. Public opinion was in favour of doing something about climate change and poverty in Africa, and in retrospect Dissent! to a large extent was simply outmanoeuvred by Make Poverty History and (in Scotland) by G8Alternatives, as far as involving masses of people was concerned. This was primarily due to two factors: first, Make Poverty History had a well-oiled media machine and contacts in Scotland. Second, they had paid employees and were virtually endorsed by the government, who knew very well their ineffective approach would not be a threat to the G8. Dissent! did eventually start making leaflets with more popular appeal such as the clever posters that sent up the *Big Brother* TV series, but it was too little, too late.

The moments when global anti-capitalism can truly seize the popular imagination are few, and while the Dissent! media policy obeyed its own principle of preventing the rise of media spokespeople, it followed its policy too well, and, in the words of one frustrated activist: 'When no one speaks to the media, the police just end up speaking for us!' That is exactly what happened as anarchists were routinely vilified, and even sympathisers who were not 'in the know' often found Dissent! and the mobilisation mysterious unless they could actually make it to one of the meetings. One lesson for future mobilisations is to craft a more coherent media policy that can use the media to artfully get the message across without creating the impression of leadership. Something like the media policy used by the masked Zapatistas, in which anonymous spokespeople are carefully selected, might be more effective. Otherwise it could simply be the case that more of us who have sensible things to say to each other should be prepared to say them to the public through the media as well, however much that risks having our message distorted.

Moreover, the best means of promoting anarchy is not abstract analysis or propaganda, but by helping people live it. The connections to local everyday struggles such as those against work in the Carnival and those against the demolition of poor communities at the Cre8 Summit both worked well and were crucial to the success of the G8 mobilisation. It seems that with tactics such as the opening of social centres, the anarchist movement in Britain will slowly yet surely make these connections. On a purely practical note, if the convergence space search had begun in earnest a year before instead of months before the protest, everything would have been easier, since organisers wouldn't have been in a continual state of panic over accommodation!

Big Bother

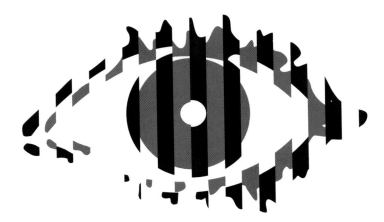

Gleneagles Hotel, 6-8 July.
Evict the G8.

Eight men will be dropped by helicopter and locked in a luxury Scottish hotel. These 'rulers' of eight powerful countries say they will attempt to address the world's most important problems, like global poverty. Few are fooled. Massive resistance to the 2005 G8 Summit and the world it represents is being planned by groups and networks from around the UK, Europe and beyond. The G8 have been meeting for 30 years. The world is still full of poverty, environmental crises and hated jobs. Only we can change this. The G8 and their world have to go. Join the Eviction!

JUNE Convergence centres open Spaces for people to gather, dream and plot will open in a major Scottish city. *www.dissent.org.uk*
11 JUNE Cre8 Summat, Glasgow Cre8 a community garden, and more, until 18 June. *www.dissent.org.uk*
29 JUNE Cre8 Summat community festival Glasgow, until 3 July. *www.dissent.org.uk*

1 JULY First Anti-G8 Train departs from London to Edinburgh. Tickets £50 return. Book well in advance via: *www.resistg8.org.uk*
2 JULY Make Poverty History march in Edinburgh.
3 JULY Make Borders History Tour in Glasgow. *www.makebordershistory.org*

4 JULY Day of Action against Faslane Nuclear Submarine Base *www.faslaneg8.com*
Carnival for Full Enjoyment, with sound systems and samba. Expressing our resistance in and out of work. Meet 12:00 @ Princes St. Edinburgh. *www.nodeal.org.uk*
Second Anti-G8 Train departs from London to Edinburgh. *www.resistg8.org.uk*

5 JULY Beacons of Dissent! Lighting beacons in the hills surrounding the G8 summit the night before the conference begins.
Open Borders, Close Dungavel Asylum Seeker Detention Centre, mass protest, near Glasgow. Shuttle bus from Glasgow.

6 JULY Mass Blockades of G8 Summit on its opening day. *www.g8blockades.org.uk*
Global Day of Action decentralised actions in villages, towns and cities worldwide. *www.agp.org*

6-8 JULY Hill-walking actions Ochil Hills, Gleneagles. *www.dissent.org.uk*
7 JULY Peoples' Golfing Action (PGA) Golf tournament at Gleneagles! *www.dissent.org.uk/pga.html*
8 JULY International day of action against the root causes of climate change *www.dissent.org.uk/ g8climateaction*

Convergence spaces will provide camping accommodation and a place to meet people, while being living examples of leaderless, free and ecological communities.
See **www.dissent.org.uk** for details, email *dissent-enquiries@riseup.net*, call **07913 263515**

As everything from the discovery of the melting permafrost in Siberia to the rapid destruction of the world's carbon sinks in the Amazon shows, however, we may not have time for slowly but surely. Despite the pestering by popstars and NGOs, the G8 managed to give only a paltry sum, far from even debt relief, to developing countries while furthering massive privatisation. The G8 made no substantial agreement on tackling climate change. The ecological collapse caused by climate change is coming, hand in hand with the stark possibility of economic depression and social crisis due to declining oil reserves, and it will take all the collective power we can muster to make sure that humanity survives. Time is of the essence, and the sustainable, decentralised forms of society so briefly glimpsed at these convergences must strengthen now, if the psychotics hiding in comfort in 10 Downing Street and in caves in Pakistan don't do us all in first. Everything depends on this. In fifty years, it will likely be too late.

BEYOND THE G8

It is all true: there are working-class heroes whose hearts are made of gold and villains in business suits who will try to stab us all in the back. The Emperor has no clothes: in Gleneagles, the leaders of the world watched events unfold on the news mutely, wondering why their retinue of sycophants and servants were stopped behind an army of assorted anarchists, clowns and children. As Dissent! mobilised, we proved we actually are more powerful than we can possibly imagine, when we dedicate ourselves to accomplishing otherwise seemingly impossible tasks. In the eco-village, we came to understand that another world is not only possible, it can exist right now: thousands of people can organise their own lives, cook food for each other and even literally handle their own shit without a single boss or policeman. There are thousands of us – at least. We are not alone, and even the most capable of us must join hands with others, forming networks of resistance capable of changing the world. Dissent! is just one such network – there are others and there need to be more. The G8 was just one event, in the tradition of Seattle, Prague and all the other moments where the established order ruptures and something strangely beautiful emerges. The real question is: what next? The lessons of this mobilisation are clear. The Dissent! network was an excellent example of how a nation-wide above-ground anarchist network can successfully organise the infrastructure for a mass mobilisation, and unlike many past protests, design the entire infrastructure to encourage effective actions. Dissent! showed how one can organise without losing autonomy. Large-scale rural actions like the blockades of Gleneagles can be done, and for the next summit that takes place in some remote location, such as the G8 mobilisation in Russia in 2006 and in Germany in 2007, the key point to strike will be the roads leading to the summit. Outside of summits, we must find some way that these model forms of struggle can emerge outside the traditionally conceived arena of 'globalisation' and be put to use against the fundamentalism of both Bush and bin Laden. This mobilisation showed how concerned many ordinary people are with the problems that we anarchists are grappling with, and if anything we just need to do a better job of broadcasting our solutions and, as done in the eco-village, actually demonstrate how anarchist organisation and sustainability can be put into practice. The ability to create autonomous spaces that provide concrete alternatives to capitalism, such as the eco-village and the Cre8 Summat, equals in importance the day of action itself. When the world is screaming for these types of alternatives, anarchists need to become better equipped and proficient at creating them.

The G8 is, if anything, a convenient excuse for us rebels to demonstrate our own power – after all, capitalism and the state exist every day of the year, not just on days of action. The importance of these days lies not in shutting the summit down, but in inspiring people to demonstrate to take action into their own hands. The bombers in London managed to nearly shut the summit down and only caused paralysis and terror among ordinary people, a fact that was quickly exploited by the G8. In contrast, the G8 knows that the real threat to their regime comes from the anarchist and anti-capitalist mobilisations against them. Blockades nearly shutting down summits and anarchists building eco-villages are proof by example of a spreading collective power that is far more dangerous to the G8 than any bomb, for it demonstrates the gathering momentum of a widespread global revolt against all would-be rulers of the world. These days of action are days of celebrating our resistance, strengthening it, and furthering it. During these intense days and nights we remember we are neither alone nor insane, and that our friends and lovers inhabit the entire world. Still, the mobilisation against the G8 was just a glimpse of what a truly organised, diverse and visionary revolutionary movement could be.

1   *The PGA hallmarks are reproduced in note 3 on page 161.*

2   *Available at www.daysofdissent.org*

3   *Kay Summers and Adam Jones, 'The first embedded protest',* The Guardian, *June 18 2005, at http://www.guardian.co.uk/comment/story/0,,1509192,00.html*

4   *See 'The VAAAG: a collective experience of self-organisation', in Days of Dissent, at www.daysofdissent.org.*

7

FREE-WHEELING AND CONTROL-FREAKING
Maff, Bristol

I was out 'hill walking' on the day and night before the start of the summit, with a hastily assembled affinity group. Due to a chronic lack of planning, we ended up blundering around, *Dad's Army* style, from one Section 60 search to another. The exercise was made far from pointless, however, by a chance meeting with two local kids, Paul and Gregor. We approached them for directions, got talking, and they agreed to take us down a lane not on the OS map that the police were not patrolling.

They played it cool and aloof for a while, but then started asking us questions about why we were there, and what we were protesting about. We told them the truth about the eco-village (a different perspective from the 'G-Hate camp' image of the local media), and illustrated how we felt the Western stranglehold on trade affected normal people, like them, on the other side of the world. In turn, they told us of the way the massive police operation in the area had affected their lives.

The day before, Gregor had been freewheeling past the countless riot vans in the village, giving a bit of front as any teenage kid would do. They would give him a hard-stare, he'd give one back. After several lazy fly-pasts, he started to get annoyed – these English 'polis', in his village, on his main street, giving him attitude just for riding his bike? So the next time he went past, Gregor gave them the finger, before wheelying away with his pride restored.

Two minutes further down the road he was flagged down by a riot van, surrounded by eight polis in stormtrooper gear, and subjected to a Section 60 search. Section 60 searches are supposed to be used to search for weapons in order to prevent a terrorist attack. Here they were being used as an excuse to get revenge on a 15-year old kid who hadn't shown the necessary 'respect for law and order'. Gregor was humiliated and furious, as were Paul and the rest of their friends and families. So, when they saw us and heard our story, they were more than happy to help us out in any way they could.

So, to anyone who feels disheartened by having their own plans thwarted in the face of a watertight police operation, take heart from this story: they may have won the battle but every day, in every town, city and village, the control-freaks are losing the war.

8

G8 ON OUR DOORSTEP
Sarah

Local political activists in Stirling started organising for the arrival of the G8 a few weeks after G8Alternatives held an open meeting in January 2004.

I booked a room at the local community centre and the word went out via email lists to the local peace activists, Scottish Socialists and People and Planet at the university. A dozen people arrived representing the full cross section of political activism. Participants ranged from those exclusively tied to lobbying style politics right through to long-time anarchists. There was the potential for immediate arguments and even fall-outs, but we found common ground. We agreed not to affiliate to either G8Alternatives or Dissent! but to keep updated with the activities of both groups and then try to be useful as local people on the ground. We knew that Stirling would likely be central to visiting protesters' activities. We also agreed that counter-information would be necessary. If the G8 had been held in Devon, most of us would not have participated. But it was happening on our doorstep, so we would have to get involved.

And so Stirling G8 Network was initiated.

As the year progressed we were subjected to ongoing police harassment, not as G8 activists, but in other circumstances. The police questioned anyone doing anything political and visible on the streets. This included CND members on their stall in the town centre. Local peace campaigners were filmed by the police whilst protesting against weapons of mass destruction – a road convoy transporting Trident nuclear warheads passes through Stirling every few weeks.

We met regularly. Some weeks later, the caretaker of our meeting place told me that the police had been in touch wanting information about us. Our numbers dwindled to half a dozen faces, so we concentrated on producing a counter-information leaflet. We laboured over this, aiming to produce something official-looking, but without watering down the content. Even then, all the leafleters were questioned by police – who went as far as requesting that they show their faces to street security cameras.

But what we were really waiting for was news about the eco-village. Our group wasn't composed of natural Dissent!ers. Most of our personal political activity didn't orientate around autonomous movements (well, there's not a lot of that ilk going on locally!). By and large we are trades unionists, peace campaigners and socialists. But living in a semi-rural area, we're not bound by the politicking that goes on in Edinburgh or Glasgow and the resulting prejudices. We have a lot of experience between us – we have facilitated direct actions in the peace movement and we have seen the police in action during the 1984–85 miners' strike at local pits. We wanted the anti-G8 activities to be successful, and the idea of a campsite nearby was exciting to say the least, so we wanted to help.

When the eco-village site was eventually confirmed I punched the air with happiness. I was delighted that a mobilisation like this would really be happening near my home. There was only two weeks to get it ready. I put the word out that there were people in Stirling who wanted to help and soon practical requests came our way. Did we know where local skips were? Where could oil drums be found? What about a friendly local farmer? A few of us visited the site when it was being set up and brought beer, a giant CND symbol and a money gift from Stirling CND.

I felt frustrated – I knew that as locals we had more to offer than just practical assistance, especially as most of us are not very practical! We had recced the site before it was set up and could see that it was isolated and how the police could easily blockade it. Originally our group had intended to set up a meeting with people from the camp to discuss outreach work and what we could do to help, including tactics. But there was so little time and everyone was busy getting ready for the G8, both in and out of the campsite. I did talk about the problems of the site's geography to individuals, but generally I felt like a spare part when I visited the camp. On the second day of set-up, I was asked if I wanted to help in the kitchen, which gave me little pleasure. I felt that local political activists should have been treated with importance. Then I experienced self-doubt, perhaps I was just being egocentric? But I have spoken with others who felt the same as me. And I also know that there were isolated individuals from small villages, turning up at the camp, seeking solidarity and not being helped to meet up with other like-minded locals.

So looking back, I know that my gut feeling was correct. We, as local people, should have pushed much harder and *insisted* on inclusion at some of the plan-

ning within the eco-village, regardless of the fact that no formal invitation was extended.

The location of the convergence space wasn't finalised 'til the last minute, but the authorities probably knew all along that it would be in Stirling. It is clear now that the low level police harassment we had experienced over the months was just part of a concerted campaign to frighten off local activists and to drive a wedge between local people and protesters. And other tactics were in operation too. Police advised local employers (including my own) that protesters were dangerous aliens from outside that workers required protection from.

As the G8 week progressed, the media fabricated tales of unprovoked violence and the police swarmed around Stirling with their sirens blaring, deliberately creating a false impression that crimes were happening everywhere, all of the time. The atmosphere became hateful and full of fear. Strangely the massive police presence failed to stop a minority of well-known local young men from becoming increasingly aggressive in their behaviour towards protesters, including myself.

The state worked purposefully to ensure minimal participation by ordinary local people in the protests and for good reason. Imagine if we had been better prepared and more locals had participated in the blockades and demonstrations. Imagine if the police lines outside the eco-village had been met by local people coming from the other direction. As it stood, there was so little organisation,

that even sympathetic people didn't know what was going on in their own town. If the police had invaded the camp, there might not have been locals present to even bear witness, never mind provide support.

Outside of the camp, local activists were isolated, alienated and sometimes fearful of the quasi-police state that was mushrooming around them. I realised that we on the outside needed the solidarity and help from the people in the camp too. We were all in it together.

But it wasn't just me who realised all of this. On Thursday, the second day of the summit, we organised a meeting at the nearby Scottish Centre for Non-Violence where campers and local activists met with purpose for the first time. The discussion was positive and mutually supportive. It wasn't about protesters apologising for damaging Burger King, or explaining themselves to the locals. It was about us joining together, in solidarity, to start countering some of the blows dealt out by the state that week. And the process of attempting to do this was an important feat in itself. We planned what we could in the hours that remained of G8 week. It was too little, too late, but we did our best.

We held stalls in Stirling town centre, where CIRCA participated. Here the power of the clowns' activities became apparent as they created the environment where I felt I could take back control. The fear and paranoia that had built up in me, a direct result of the state repression I had witnessed in my home town, dissipated, as we exerted our presence once again on the streets. And I'm sure that everyone we encountered felt some of this too. A similar response had resulted from Critical Mass's memorable cycle ride through Stirling with the open mic on Tuesday.

Meanwhile, the eco-village had put out an invitation on local radio for all listeners to come to dinner at the camp that night. Some people did come, including members of a local community council. This allowed us to determine the truth about the extent of damage to residents' property and a real dialogue between those affected and protesters took place.

These honest interactions between people were the highlight of the G8 activities for me. The open mic in Stirling, the meeting, the local and visiting activists working together in town, local people eating a meal on the camp. Movements for change are all about people taking action and it was from these small events that I made connections with real people and gained ideas about creative ways of engaging in political activity in the future. For me, that future is in my locality, working to effect changes to the real lives of real people – not the next G8 mobilisation.

The process of mobilising for the G8 was a success in so many ways. The eco-village alone was an impressive and important experiment in self organisation and all the participants, including us locals, have learnt from the experience. But one of the lessons has to be this: change is achieved by ordinary people for themselves. If we don't have the confidence to believe that we (not *they*) can do it, then what are Dissent! mobilisations all about? The good news is that Dissent! is continuing to work and develop as an activists' network. But future mobilisations must include people who live locally and strategies for developing trust and solidarity must be considered as a 'must have', not a 'would like'. Otherwise mobilisations of large numbers of people descending on a small geographical area, for whatever reason, will never be successful.

9

THE CARNIVAL CONTINUES...

Lydia Molyneaux

'The worst street disorder in Edinburgh since the Porteous riots of 1736', trumpeted the Scottish press after the Carnival for Full Enjoyment. For those with little knowledge of 18th century Scottish history, this refers to an event when crowds rioted against the execution of a smuggler and ended up hanging the official who had passed the sentence.

Well, no public officials met their end on July 4 2005. But there are other ways for an event to leave its mark. We were certainly fighting for much more than the right to party – but how much of this came across? Like many others who took part in the anti-G8 mobilisation, we were aiming for more than a flash-in-the-pan spectacle. We were looking for new kinds of action that would inspire continuing resistance wherever we work and live.

LOCAL ACTIONS FOR LOCAL PEOPLE

Inspired by recent activity in Italy and Spain, we wanted to express resistance to increasingly insecure and precarious conditions of work and life; to low pay, pressure and stress for those in employment; forced labour for those who are unwaged. The organisation, control and exploitation of work is central to capitalism, and we aimed to subvert that basis as we took to the streets against wage slavery, benefits slavery, debt slavery and army slavery. We raised the banner for full *enjoyment* as opposed to full *employment*.

After a big demo you often hear people saying 'forget about those spectacular mass actions – we've got to organise in our local community.' Many of us have been active on a local basis for years, and will continue to do so. But lately we've had to ask: what do our local 'communities' consist of? Communities, like work, are increasingly transient and previous approaches to community organising can become just as limited as tired tactics in other spheres. Yes, milling around in a crowd and getting penned in by the cops can be depressing and does nothing to improve our daily lives. But localism by itself can also become a demoralising swamp – ask anyone who's spent time sitting in draughty halls at tenants' association meetings hearing the persistent drone of some council official, or endured rainy afternoons leafleting outside a job centre in the company of two mates and a dog. In organising the Carnival, we hoped to take steps towards bridging the gap between local/workplace struggles and mass actions.

ENJOYMENT ZONE

Some inspiration also came from an action in 2000 in Bristol opposing the introduction of an 'employment zone' – where local unwaged people become guinea-pigs for time–wasting 'pilot' schemes and social engineering attempts to create a desperate and docile workforce. According to the Bristol Benefits Action Group (BBAG), activists 'turned the local Labour Party office into an "Enjoyment Zone" to protest against the introduction of employment zones, the cutting of benefit entitlements to asylum seekers, the extension of the New Deal, the cutting of social security spending in the budget and to have some fun...' The occupation/party lasted half an hour. BBAG then distributed leaflets at the job centre and invited other claimants and action groups to join in the fun and to set up enjoyment zones in their areas.

We decided to do this on a larger scale and mark the beginning of the G8 summit – when leaders meet to discuss how to organise the exploitation of the world's population – with a mobile party 'visiting' institutions that plunge us into poverty, overwork and debt. Targets included organisations implementing the New Deal and workfare, employment agencies, sheriff's officers (bailiffs), shit bosses and army recruitment centres. Many of us were already involved in claimants' and debt resistance, and saw this as a chance to raise these struggles from marginalisation and beleaguered localism to vibrant transnational resistance. We also wanted to link opposition to war with a local campaign against 'economic conscription', where unemployed youth are pressured to sign up for the armed forces.

We saw this as a move away from the moralism encountered in some anti-G8 propaganda. For example, an early statement on the G8 Climate Action website suggested: 'We have a unique opportunity and a global responsibility to take action for the millions of more repressed people, for ecosystems and for future generations.' To be blunt, this sounded too much like a direct-action version of

Geldof's patronising posture. Solidarity is a different thing altogether. We saw resisting the G8 – in the words of one of our leaflets – as 'an opportunity to link everyday struggles against the bosses and politicians here in Edinburgh with the struggles of working class people throughout the world.' If we approach social cuts, privatisation and compulsory work schemes as part of a worldwide enclosure of resources and means of living, we have a concrete basis for connecting our own liberation to struggles of the dispossessed in the 'global south'. Ultimately, the bailiff at your door is a not-so-distant cousin of the cartel forcing peasants off common land elsewhere.

Furthermore, we weren't just trying for a rerun of J18. The 1999 'Carnival Against Capital' in the City of London (marking a G8 summit in Cologne, Germany) was a watershed action and many of us have fond memories of the day. However, J18 was very much focused on finance capital – which was a good place to start. But six years later, it was time to move on and think of how we can subvert and attack the actual *social relations* of capital.

Our interest in Standard Life, the biggest employer in Edinburgh, was not only tied to its role in finance capital. It was also related to the exploitation of temporary staff, with denial of benefits and increased pressure for all workers. Some of us knew people who had worked there, or we had worked in similar companies ourselves. In response to media lies that *carnivalistas* planned to attack staff, we passed out leaflets at Standard Life addressing working conditions. We invited workers to join the Carnival and 'take an extended lunch break... Better still throw a sickie all day and get your own back'.[1] We had a positive response and, in the end, many workers did get a day off!

COPS 'N' CORDONS

We knew there'd be lots of cops in our way. As well as the publicised meeting point, we had other informal meeting places so that people could converge and break through any cordons the police formed. Unfortunately, many people did get 'kettled-in' despite the plan. It was frustrating to be held back by police lines that could have been broken by some basic, well-organised (lightly) padded tactics. As with other situations, better networking with affinity groups could have also brought more people out where they were needed.

Still, the police weren't able to keep total control of the area as mobile crowds circulated around Princes Street, grouping and regrouping. The most inspiring aspect of the day was how 'locals' outside the activist orbit joined in. This went beyond the traditional second shift of 'kids' who appear just as many knackered anarchists are resting in the pub. People of all ages massed on Princes Street from the afternoon onwards. Later, it was local anger at the police that fuelled the most direct resistance.

Many activists were concerned that arrests on the Monday could deplete the ranks for the blockades. Some even said that the Carnival was a diversion. Events proved them wrong. As one Stirling-based participant later wrote: 'The Carnival for Full Enjoyment set the stall out for the hugely successful blockades that were to happen later in the week. The refusal of people to be penned like sheep was a good indication that the state was not going to get everything its own way. Most of all, perhaps, the Carnival helped to cement a bit of solidarity, and that in itself is always inspiring.'

Taking on board the need to stay free for blockades on Wednesday, many activists headed towards safer places around 4–5pm. Meanwhile, 'locals' were going to kick off the action again around Rose Street. It was ironic that many Edinburgh people didn't worry about saving themselves for 'the big day'. Monday's Carnival was *their* day and they were going for it! Maybe this points to the error of putting too much emphasis on the climactic 'big one', when potential disruption of state control and capital (and consequently, the functioning of the G8) can come at unexpected times and places.

But even at its best, was the Carnival primarily a defensive struggle against the police for control of the streets? It made a good showing and had its excellent moments, but did it break any new ground? For some, a lot of the actual politics got lost in the shuffle. As a writer from Irish Indymedia observed: 'There were a few banners the organisers had which made the themes explicit, but these were lost among the corrals.'[2]

The fact is that we didn't get around to 'visiting' most of our political 'targets'!

The big windows of the office where the Benefits Agency 'fraud' squad is based did get flyposted with the name and number of Scotland's chief dole snooper,[3] but the damage was very quickly repaired. We've heard that two sheriff's officers buildings had been hit, but if this is true then the glaziers were too quick for it to be confirmed. If this aspect of the Carnival had been successful, dole snoopers, New Deal apparatchiks and sheriff's officers in Edinburgh and beyond would have got a strong taste of public disgust and resistance. Most important, the message would have spread that we don't need to fear these people if we act together.

In the future, we could think about better networking with affinity groups to prevent cordoning – or to see that important places are visited if larger groups get trapped. In fact, such a back-up plan had been discussed, but it was too late in the day to make the necessary contacts for it to be very effective. It could have also ensured wider distribution of publicity. I suspect that balance and coordination between public and affinity group actions had also been a crucial issue for other actions.

A lot of this discussion could and should have taken place around the anti-authoritarian assembly held in Edinburgh on July 3. The assembly had originally been set up to coordinate anarchist/anti-authoritarian actions over the week. But when the Sunday rolled round there wasn't time left to discuss anything other than the Wednesday blockades. This points to some organisational issues looked at later.

LONG, PAINFUL AND KNACKERING

In the short term, the above problems can be put down to a last-minute rush to get too many things done. But why did we find ourselves in that situation, when we started to meet and talk about the action in late October 2004? On reflection, it goes back to an early mistake: we relied too much on Dissent! and Dissent! gatherings as a point of contact and organising, as well as the Beyond the ESF event (October 2004) and the Anarchist Bookfair (November). At the time, it made sense to meet at events when people from various cities would be in one place. However, the Dissent! gatherings were often long, painful and knackering. Many later gatherings were devoted to infrastructure and didn't leave much time or energy for sorting out actions. Perhaps these gatherings put the cart before the horse – could we have talked first about actions, then decided what support structures we needed to make those actions possible?

The fact that Dissent! was a network that didn't plan actions itself seemed to be an excuse not to deal with them at all. Many of us had supported the initial decision on the role of Dissent! in the interests of diversity, security and avoiding yawn-provoking discussions about violence. But Dissent! meetings were also meant to provide space for facilitating and coordinating actions, and where did that go? At the Newcastle gathering (early December 2004), we did spend a productive afternoon setting out a provisional timetable of actions. But much more typical was a Glasgow gathering in February 2005 that left about 15 minutes at the end for action groups to meet and then report back to the gathering. It was only when we had our own meetings in Edinburgh to organise the Carnival that we got on with some concrete and creative plans. The first public Edinburgh meeting had been in May. Imagine how much we could have achieved if we had started this process in February or even March. Furthermore, people came to our meetings in May and June who had never been to a Dissent! gathering. So rather than focusing so much on Dissent! as our point of contact, we could have held regular meetings in Edinburgh and involved a lot more people locally from the outset.

We need to keep this in mind when participating in future networks. At the same time, you could also ask if a network is serving its purpose when groups must hold a lot of additional meetings. Given limitations in most people's finances and time for travelling, many would have to choose between action planning meetings and taking part in general network gatherings.

It's been suggested that a lot of internationals hadn't been aware of what the Carnival was really about. Our international outreach could have been better. We tried to engage networks organising around precarity such as EuroMayDay – and here there was a strong sentiment that mobilisations at summits were *passé*. Presentations had also been made at international G8 mobilising conferences in Tübingen and Thessaloniki but clearly we need to think about other, less obvious international networks in the future. However, an internationally diverse bunch of comrades eventually showed up for a discussion on precarity on July 3 and we made contacts that could be built on there.

PULLING TEETH

In the bad old days of the 1990s, class-struggle anarchists and eco-direct-actionists in the UK seemed to live on completely separate planets. But later in the decade we saw events and actions (e.g. J18 and the collaboration between Reclaim the Streets and the Liverpool dockers) that challenged the assumptions of both sides, and brought them together in the networks often described as 'anti-capitalist'. During some Dissent! meetings it felt like none of this had ever happened (despite the publication of *Days of Dissent*).[4] Had I been caught in some kind of weird 1990s timewarp? I could almost hear whining strains of 'Wonderwall' as a background to what was passing for 'political' discussion.

It was like pulling teeth to get many (but not *all*) people in Dissent! to contemplate the possibility that class struggle might have anything to do with mobilising against the G8. Struggling over our own living and working conditions is pure selfishness, seemed to be the attitude. No, no, we're for lofty, altruistic things like Saving the Planet and helping those poor souls Over There! Again, there seemed to be confusion over the stark difference between patronising charity – and solidarity. This was symptomatic of an approach that took anti-capitalism as a matter of abstract morality, rather than desire, rebellion and fighting those who keep us down. In fact, some propaganda seemed downright offensive when it appeared to blame climate change on those thick working-class people flying to their holidays in Spain and eating out-of-season satsumas with their Christmas dinners. At times the satirical slogan 'Abolish Capitalism and Replace it with Something Nicer' didn't seem too far from reality.

As the commentary on Irish Indymedia put it, we were aiming to 'push the style of reclaim the streets politics beyond spectacle towards clear class politics.' Not everyone liked that. But when we talked about our project at gatherings, no one really argued against it either. Often, it was just met with sniffy silence, constraining any real political debate and halting the development of ideas for action.

A GREAT BIG DOLLOP OF CHILLI

This inability to discuss politics and action was not limited to Dissent! gatherings, unfortunately. It was present in other groups (Wombles, South East Assembly, etc) though possibly for different reasons – an urge to get to the pub ASAP? When we brought stuff up people nodded or said nothing. There also wasn't much consideration of a proposal put forward by University of London anti-authoritarians for an action in Edinburgh on July 7. This lack of space for dealing with actions may have also led to poor showings at the pre-G8 finance, employment and environment ministerial meetings in London. If comrades thought certain ideas or proposals sucked, fair enough! But let's hear why, let's talk and find something better.

We only heard, well into June, that some people thought the Carnival plans weren't important and we must all save ourselves for our proverbial wedding night on Wednesday. In retrospect, this showed a narrow view of what a 'blockade' could be – couldn't it also be about 'blocking' how capitalism functions and runs? And as we later saw, Monday's action did have a positive knock-on effect for Wednesday.

Despite the odds, the Wednesday blockades around Stirling and Gleneagles turned out to be successful and inspiring. Those of us who'd been emitting grumbles about 'hippies sitting in the middle of a field' had to eat our words – with a huge dollop of chilli. But I'd still say that actions need to hold city centres to achieve a lasting impact beyond symbolic delays. There seemed to be an ambivalence about urban blockades and urban actions like the Carnival. It has even been suggested that the urban convergences should have been shut down at a certain point to concentrate resources in Stirling.

However, stronger actions in the cities could have compounded the disruptive effect of the other blockades. Forward planning and publicity could have mobilised more people to come to urban blockades – those who might not camp out in the rain but would get active on their own city streets. Why did the press and the police have their knickers in such a big twist over the Carnival? While

we don't want to fall into the trap of taking on our enemies' hype, it would be useful to look at the fire behind the smoke. They were worried because the Carnival took place in a city centre, where the major workings of capital and the state are based – and where thousands of people can come together. 'In the streets power is made and dissolved', as the old Reclaim the Streets slogan goes.

The fate of the urban blockades made many of us very glad we didn't shove all our eggs into one basket. In effect, the Carnival turned out to be one of the few big city centre actions, though Glasgow's Boogie on the Bridge on July 7 also had potential. This action sought to link struggle against the imposition of a motorway in a poor area with the root causes of global climate change. It marked a positive shift from finger-wagging moralism to solidarity with community resistance in a truly anti-capitalist approach to climate change, and showed similarities with the Carnival in the connections it made.

ALRIGHT ON THE NIGHT
At the root of some problems was a 'come to an assembly and it'll all be alright on the night' way of thinking. But most successful mass actions (such as J18) had a good year's preparation. That didn't rule out input and self-organisation by people who turned up. The planning worked on providing the groundwork and a framework that encouraged autonomy and flexibility and new initiative as well.

A lot of hard work and planning went into organising the infrastructure, but overall development of actions was very last-minute – almost deliberately so. While some affinity groups did put a lot of preparation into their own plans, what about the larger picture? Shouldn't a network provide an overview and a means to spread resources around? For example, we could have made sure there were more people in Edinburgh and groundwork could have been laid for a Glasgow blockade. When you don't plan ahead, everything gets crammed into a few agonising, dreadful meetings where we've got to re-invent the wheel the night before. That also determined the limits of the anti-authoritarian assemblies.

DRY RUN

While neither the Carnival or the Boogie on the Bridge achieved all their aims, perhaps we should look at them as try-outs for future actions that tie local and workplace struggles to global resistance.

Looking towards 2006, the G8 summit in St Petersburg can be an opportunity for us to forge stronger links in Russia and Eastern Europe. With the current movements of capital and labour around west and east Europe, this will be essential – as shown in recent solidarity actions with Polish casual workers at Tesco's in Ireland. In the past year we've also seen massive street demonstrations in Russia against the restriction of pensions and disabled benefits, which resonate with issues we face in the UK.

Of course, we don't want our horizons to be bound by summits of bosses and politicians. However, these events can still give us openings to highlight and support struggles in a particular area, and additional possibilities for internationalising local resistance. This approach can also extend to the G8 summit in Germany in 2007, and far beyond that.

Meanwhile, a friend who read an earlier draft of this article said: 'You're being too negative and self-critical. It was a *great* day, the best day in the week. Working-class Edinburgh people knew exactly what it was about!'

Who knows? Maybe she's right...

1   See 'Substandard Life' at www.nodeal.org.uk
2   For a good report and discussion see www.indymedia.ie/newswire.php?story_id=70649.
3   Joan Kirk, Castle Terrace office, 0131 222 5089.
4   Available at http://www.daysofdissent.org.uk

10

GETTING OFF THE ACTIVIST BEATEN TRACK
Members of the Trapese Collective

The government says we have weapons here and they are not wrong. Education is a very dangerous weapon; it wakes up minds and consciences.

Zapatista teacher from a school in an autonomous community

WHY WE DID IT

The anti-capitalist movement which has emerged over the past decade is not a sub-cultural one-off or passing phase. It has become part of mainstream awareness and the subject of political rhetoric. Be it the demise of the local shop, the privatisation of essential services, the war in Iraq, 'human rights' suspended for the 'war on terror' or the effects of climate change, the arguments made by those 'in the movement' should resonate more widely with the lived experiences of the 'general public'. However, whether we manage to engage with and relate to this 'general public' is another question. People who are actively resisting the madness around us and building alternatives are still marginalised, vilified and repressed. What this makes clear is that the leap from general agreement about the ills of this world to taking positive action towards radical social change remains a tough one to take. So, where are the possible bridges and connections? How can we escape the cynicism that the overwhelming range of problems and injustices tends to force us into? How do we really achieve social change? And with the G8 summit being hosted in the UK, could we use this moment as a platform for

bringing our politics to a much wider audience rather than being further marked as 'extremists'?

These were some of the issues and questions that we discussed in the first meeting of the Dissent! network's Educate the G8 working group in the summer of 2004. Like many others, we believed that for a successful mobilisation against the G8 summit, we needed to expand our usual circles and tactics and explore ways of developing our political networks. Our motives for educating, information-sharing and outreaching to people went beyond getting the 'masses' up to Scotland in July. The aims of developing the Educate the G8 project were to not only raise awareness about what the G8 is but also to question what that means to people in their daily lives and to provide the space for such debates to take place. Another motivation was to attempt to counteract the (mis-) information from the mainstream media about the issues, the protests and protesters.

WHY POPULAR EDUCATION?

Formal state education presents itself as objective while actually it is designed to socialise us from a young age to accept certain power relations. In contrast, popular education is upfront about its political motivations. It is usually associated with social movements and is traditionally aimed at groups of people excluded from full participation in the political process. Examples abound throughout history, from the Workers' Educational Associations and Labour Colleges of early twentieth century Britain, Civil Rights education in the 1960s in the US, community empowerment groups in the 1970s in the UK and the *Rondas del Pensamiento Autónomo* ['roundtables for autonomous discussion'] in contemporary Argentina, to name a few. Histories of resistance and civil disobedience are hidden from us, and an important part of building popular power to challenge the status quo is to relearn the histories and successes of previous struggles.

One influential theorist of popular education is Paulo Freire. Under Brazil's progressive government of the early 1960s, his methods were used in thousands of cultural circles across the country. These national literacy programmes taught everyone, including those who lived in the *favelas* [slums]. However, reading and writing for the masses was perceived as a communist threat; indeed the government was ousted in 1964 by a CIA-backed military coup and Freire was imprisoned for 70 days as a traitor. Freire's writings, most famously *Pedagogy of the Oppressed*, have inspired many to use education as a 'practice of freedom'. He saw education as a tool with which people could begin to understand the context of their own oppression and to organise to liberate themselves. The focus was on empowerment and starting from people's lived experiences as a basis from which to question their positions in society.

WHAT WE DID

One group that emerged from the Educate the G8 group was Trapese – Take Radical Action through Popular Education and Sustainable Everything – a name which caused some confusion about our lack of circus skills. Trapese's aim was to tour Britain to inform, mobilise and inspire people to take action about the issues related to the G8. The idea of the project was to go beyond talking to the established activist population and offer workshops at an 'introductory' level, on issues such as the G8 and the global economy, climate change, debt, resistance and what we called 'living alternatives' (autonomous spaces, independent media, etc). We aimed to share the information that had inspired us to resist the G8, demystify the protests that were causing so much hysteria and to be open and upfront about our motivations. Despite having 'popular education' in our name we weren't driven by any academic interest in education. When we started, we were responding to a direct need for people to group together for inspiration, motivation and to plan in the run-up to the G8. Perhaps it is in fulfilling this need that our project was so successful.

Another aspect of our tour was to go to social places such as pubs or open mic nights to try and inject some politics into the evening entertainment. By incorporating information on the G8 into a pub quiz format we further widened our net. So on September 16 2004, we nervously hosted our first anti-G8 pub quiz in front of a bemused audience at the Forest Café in Edinburgh. All four of us who took part still cringe at the thought of it. Quite possibly it had no redeeming features whatsoever. But despite the heckling and our immediate thoughts of 'what on earth are we doing?', we ploughed on. From these humble beginnings, by June 2005 Trapese had become a fairly experienced group with over 100 different events under its belt. We realised that very few people were doing this sort of thing and that there was a surprisingly high demand.

Our events ranged from all sorts of venues and from three to 300 participants. We worked with a lot of existing groups, such as university student unions, support groups, theatre groups, or in community centres. We found that working with already established groups was much easier as there was already trust between people and also a greater chance of further workshops and meetings with the groups. Because we usually only had a couple of hours we tried to cram a lot in while we had people as a captive audience, and looked at problems, causes and tried to think about actions and solutions. But we also left leaflets, posters, stickers, films, books and pamphlets.

At times the roadshow provided an excuse for people to get together and talk about what their local response to the G8 summit would be; in some places it acted as a catalyst or launch for forming a local Dissent! group. People told us that it also made going to Scotland seem much more realistic.

The roadshow itself, whilst not always on the road, became our lives full time – something we had not fully anticipated. Two people, who formed a core group, were more or less permanently on tour with about ten other people involved at some point or another. Although it was very rewarding, life on the road was often stressful and distinctly non-glamorous as well as mentally exhausting. But there were many inspiring moments which kept us going. There are always so many websites to click through and emails to send, but it doesn't compare with actually meeting people face-to-face. Reflecting, discussing climate change and other fears, making links between their lives, our lives and how the global economy affects us all, began to generate a sense of solidarity and community against the G8, and for us to really see the diversity of people who share this common belief. Whether or not this sense of community can be maintained when there is no G8 summit in the UK to unite against remains to be seen.

OUR APPROACH TO THE WORKSHOPS

To build a non-hierarchical society, the way we learn is as important as what we learn. We tried to design workshops which would build collective knowledge and try to break down the distinction between teacher and learner. To bring out the knowledge from the groups, the workshops were based on a participatory, interactive methodology and we used lots of activities and games. We always pointed out that we weren't experts and tried to make everyone feel comfortable to contribute. Understanding issues like the G8 and climate change are far too important to remain the concern of the people who read books about them.

We used methods of learning that engage with participants and their ideas – brain-storms, role plays, articulate games, debates and so on. For example, we

shared information about the history of neoliberalism and key moments in the resistance to it by sticking cards up on to a time-line. We used a game with ten chairs to show the inequality of wealth distribution in favour of the G8 countries. Simple but very visual demonstrations can sometimes have more impact than listening to a list of shocking statistics that you can't take in.

TAKING ACTION

Popular education involves a non-dogmatic approach: it does not aim to determine the political action that a person takes, but builds on what emerges from the experiences of the participants. At the same time we didn't want to be a one-off event, but wanted to facilitate action plans, local organising and networking so that we linked people to an ongoing process of resistance. At times people would call us the Dissent! Roadshow. But although we definitely considered ourselves part of the network, we were not a recruitment drive for Dissent! In many of the places we visited, it would have been unrealistic to do anything other than impart the information we knew about the mobilisations against the G8 as a whole. We became aware of the exclusiveness of a 'direct action' focused mobilisation. For refugee groups and others of an insecure legal status, for example, attending the Make Poverty History demonstration was a much more relevant option than forming an affinity group and attempting to blockade the G8, even if they shared our criticisms of the big NGOs.

Other groups we worked with were simply less aware of more radical critiques and this raised other difficulties. Imagine: somebody is for the first time reflecting on the G8 and the system it symbolises, and we then suggest that overthrowing the entire capitalist system is the only viable option – this is possibly quite a disempowering experience!

Of course we had our own beliefs, including fundamental premises – that the G8 and the other assorted acronyms should not exist in the first place, for example – so as workshop facilitators we struggled to be positive about people going off to the G8Alternatives march in Auchterarder or pledging to buy energy-saving light bulbs. But we also felt that by immediately criticising such steps as ineffective, and judging the potential of others' actions, we were discouraging people's own legitimate choices and the realities of the lives they live.

A popular education methodology is about finding the connections you have with people and not judging them for their chosen path. We have surely all been on actions while simultaneously wondering whether we really are changing anything, so why should we give the impression that we are privy to some magical formula when talking to other people? It is vital that we remember that very few of us had an epiphany and suddenly ended up on the front line. We each went through a unique and valuable journey to reach our political views. One of the great challenges of projects like Trapese is to convey the sense of urgency and scope of social change we see is needed, without being dismissed as completely utopian and irrelevant to people's lives. This doesn't mean it isn't worth trying, but it's important to allow people time to process information, to not overwhelm them. To really be effective, popular education has to be rooted in local struggles and form ongoing solidarity.

BUILDING FROM THE EXPERIENCE

Of course, many people came to a workshop who already knew all about it, and we hoped that people would feel inspired to go off into their own communities and give similar workshops, where there was more common ground. Distributing a CD-Rom with all the resources we used, we hoped that there would be nodes of people travelling within an area, and not just us. After all, we had started with very little clue and had adapted many of the resources from people doing similar work around a previous G8 summit in Canada.

Although some other groups were doing outreach, by May 2005 we were inundated with requests for workshops and talks and couldn't do them all. Ideally we could have had an info-mobilisation tour, or speakers and popular education more rooted in people's local areas.

We felt that we had raised our heads above the parapet and consequently ended up doing a large number of public events. We never wanted to become mouthpieces, and were surely criticised for this, but it begs another important question: why won't more people do this sort of thing? Perhaps for fear of criticism or lack of confidence. But we have so much to tell, give, and share, and there is so much we can learn from other groups by sharing our arguments with different people. Maybe it's the idea of being the only focus, when we are used to speaking whilst sittting in circles. But it is possible to subvert the occasion, and the opportunity to reach a large audience makes it worth it. We can be pretty brave in the face of police attacks and other repression by the state: surely we can cope with the odd heckler and a few yawns. For sure, some people are worried about becoming 'speech-makers' or claiming to represent a network, but the more of us give it a go, the less this becomes a problem. And the more people there are expressing radical views and explaining our rejection of capitalism, the G8, lobbying NGOs etc, then the more political space we can occupy.

CONCLUSIONS

It is clear from our experiences within Trapese that popular education has an enormously important role to play in raising awareness, linking campaigns, generating critical thinking and building autonomy. It's an essential tool in helping spontaneous resistance evolve into conscious social movements. As one group we could only reach so many people, but hopefully this was in a way which touched them beyond that of reading a leaflet, and which will encourage them to continue resisting beyond one day of action.

When the summit was over we felt that our project was just beginning, and we will be continuing with Trapese, although we're not clear exactly where, or what topics we'll focus on. We recently co-hosted a popular education seminar in Escanda, Spain, which was attended by around 80 people from projects around Europe and the Middle East, including some planning a tour around the G8 summit in Germany 2007. We would like to continue to share ideas and practise more participatory education that interacts closely with campaign groups and social movements building autonomy. When it develops beyond being a mere mobilising tool we think that this kind of work could become a much more important part of our 'movement'. We are and have been activists and/or campaigners, and we have many useful skills and ideas, but we must not forget that what is right for us won't be right for everyone. Rather than trying to convince people of one course of action or campaign by spewing information, we should all learn to listen. This is popular education, and much more of it is needed.

For more information on Trapese and to access our downloadable material, including a booklet with games and activities, see: www.trapese.org, trapese@riseup.net

11

PRIVATE PARTS IN THE GENERAL MAYHEM
Commodore Koogie

July 7 2005. The news filtered through without significance at first. London was another world – on the outside rather than the centre of everything as it usually is. Four bombs had gone off in London and killed many people. One of the bombs, in Tavistock Square, went off on the number 30 bus right by the statue of Gandhi I loved to talk to when I worked and studied in that part of town. Then the news became significant. After everything we'd done and worked for – after we'd poured love and passion into the world to change the paradigms of coercive power and harm to ones of possibility and creativity – the memory of this summer for the majority of people in the UK would be of a violent and desperate act, an affirmation that it is only violence that really changes anything. So I went to the field of flowers beside a bend in the river, beside a glimpse of another world, our eco-village in Stirling, and lay down in despair to cry.

    The gentle and sympathetic wildflowers of Scotland were willing to lend an ear. But their message of hope was being drowned out by one of those bloody helicopters which the police insisted on flying over the camp morning, noon and night to spy on us and intimidate us. And so I ended up lying in the field looking at the helicopter feeling sorry for myself. Then gradually I started to see the flowers around my body and face, and the sky above me, which was a fresh blue with little clouds scudding by. And I started to look for hope. And while I looked for hope and relished the beauty of the place, the dappled greens and purples of the hills, the oak tree standing in full leaf at the edge of the field... I stopped seeing the helicopter. It was there, I heard it above somewhere – but I'd stopped seeing it. It had dropped outside of my circle of vision because I chose another view.

The previous May I'd walked onto St. Werburgh's – a community farm in Bristol – to find a little green caravan with big flames painted over its wheels and swamped by a large solar panel on its roof. An old, silver van stood nearby with a large tarpaulin sheet and a big bundle of camouflage netting with plastic flowers entwined in it, making it impossible to untangle, sitting nearby. I also found a friendly, somewhat stressed group of people in a state of general mayhem (a clown name if ever there was one) and a couple of sets of old army uniforms which needed pieces of pink and green fur sewing onto them in time for a show which was to start in a couple of hours.

That first show lasted about four hours, and torrential rain tested our tarpaulin shelter to the full (literally – we had to keep emptying rainwater over the sides that had collected in the middle, threatening to drown our audience in a great deluge at any moment). The performers told tales of civil disobedience, reenacted the Fourth World War, drilled a puppet clown army to imperfection and showed videos of beautiful and hilarious acts of rebellion and resistance from around the world. Meanwhile the audience struggled to hear what was being said over the sound of the rain and children and see what was happening in the fading daylight with the aid of little blue fairy lights. And something rather special happened too. The rain made the audience huddle together, and keeping the rain from bursting the roof became something everybody started to participate in. They may have been cold and a bit damp but they stuck with us right to the end and everyone ended up laughing together. There was real warmth in that audience and while we learnt some important lessons about lighting, how to sort out the rain shelter better, making the show shorter and giving it more structure, there were also lessons to be learnt about hope and about good things coming out of seemingly impossible adverse conditions.

Bristol was also the birthplace of my clown. Clown training was a two-day intensive course in the art of rebel clowning and non-violent direct action in a church hall and community theatre space. We learnt to become aware of each other and protect each other as a group; we learnt spontaneity and our 'presence' as performers was nurtured as everybody's confidence started to grow. We started to remember how it felt to play and shape the world to us and this vital skill would go with us into the actions round the G8.

Again and again people's clowns would emerge and we would all love them and learn to recognise them. A clown is not made in a day – or even in two days – or a week or year. It's a changing, intrinsic part of a human being, and cannot be 'finished' any more than any other aspect of a person. I can only describe this from my own experiences, but it seems that my clown is the most vulnerable part

of me, the only human, silly, playful part. It is also a magical, shamanic part that can walk right up to the edge of my ingrained, social limits – where obedience ends and disobedience begins – and dance on that edge until it dissolves or bends or stretches into a different shape. I'll try to explain.

I didn't see how clowning would work on the streets, in the 'front line' of direct action, during the training in Bristol. I wouldn't really understand properly until a moment on July 2 when two clowns stood in front of a line of policemen, who had encircled and contained a group of activists in Edinburgh, all looking stern and grim, but still wearing bright yellow jerkins nonetheless, and started singing the banana song: One banana, two banana, three banana, four...

One by one a larger group of us joined in, the song gathering volume and beautiful harmonies (we started to sound really good) as we went. It took on a life of its own and suddenly we were more clown than not clown and at some point the faces in the line in front of us started to twist and contort in the strangest ways. One guy's eyebrows went into a steep 45-degree angle and his lips pressed together tightly, as his mouth got wider and wider. And then it dawned on me. They were desperately trying not to laugh. They failed, of course, and I finally understood how it was our vulnerability, standing there with nothing but our humanity to protect us, that was our best defence against repression. For a few magical moments, the police were no longer a 'thin blue line', absurdly protecting society against itself, or the rich and powerful few against the mass whose lives have become a poor second place to capital, but fellow human beings with different personalities and, weirdly enough, even a sense of humour. As they started laughing, they stopped being a line – physically stopped standing in a line. They too were vulnerable as they tried not to laugh and embarrass themselves in front of their fellow officers.

Running on biodiesel bought in exchange for the oil used to cook free chips for our audiences, the silver van and little green caravan criss-crossed the country, connecting with people in London, Birmingham, Sheffield, Manchester, Newcastle, Aberdeen, Glasgow and Edinburgh. I was seeing a different UK – one not cast through television or newspapers but seen and felt in the flesh. The Metropolitan Police tried to scare off our London host by saying that we were 'not a normal travelling theatre company'.

Undeniably true and proudly quoted, the real us were and are the best anti-dote to the fear-mongers – whether they be police or corporate media. We pleaded our case with local authorities and landowners again and again just to be able to get the show on in isolated car parks, in town centres, in green spaces. Again and again, hope won over fear.

We spent summer solstice at the northernmost point of the tour in Aberdeen, around a fire by a fast flowing river, flooding and silver in the full moon. We were fast reaching the culmination of all our efforts, the clowns getting fatter and juicier in the belly of our little green caravan. The police must have felt it too as their Forward Intelligence Team filmed our penultimate show for posterity. 'You're nowt but a bunch o' cloons!!', a street alcoholic yelled at one point. If nothing else, we'd got the point across to at least one person.

Our final show took place by the Cre8 Summat community garden. Built on a piece of land destined to have the M74 motorway extension plastered all over it, it was a brave and beautiful design. The clowns were starting to connect with the rest of Dissent! and some of the other projects that had been going on to make links with the local community in Scotland. I think it was our best show – brim full of pleasure from start to finish. It had taken all the problems and difficulties, all the inspiration, everything that had happened between Bristol and Glasgow to reach this point. All the people who'd put us up on their floors, or in their beds, who'd cooked us dinner, who'd helped with the logistics, who'd come to our shows, who'd engaged in debate, who'd asked questions, who'd trained with us, who'd wandered into the infoshop, who'd heckled, who'd decided to trust us... were there in that final show. And it was all of us who played keepy-uppy with a big blow-up beachball of the world to the sound of Louis Armstrong's 'What a Wonderful World' who symbolised the web of connections that is our movement – the one that is counting its blessings as it launches the world, spinning into the air, again and again.

Around two hundred clowns emerged in Edinburgh. They emerged as we

all put on our face paint on the morning of the Make Poverty History march. Everyone's clown was different and special and every clown contributed to make magic happen while the governments of the G8 tried to make everyone forget their illegal wars and open up the way for more thefts – of lives, land and resources. The clowns made magic happen while four suicide bombers planned their final exits. It happened when clowns kissed the perspex shields of the riot police, leaving lipstick kisses. It happened when they bowed down in front of a line of police that just happened to be called away at that moment – making it look like a rapid retreat before the unbearable worshipping of the clowns. It happened whenever a policeman laughed or smiled against his will. It happened when we played grandmother's footsteps with the police in Faslane. It happened when we and some members of the public got a puzzled stare from a member of the marines observing us from the loch through a pair of binoculars as we 'hid' behind small leaves and strands of grass for camouflage on the shore. It happened when the crowd became clowns to support a bloke sitting on the fence of the naval base and embarrassed the police for intending to arrest him by singing and playing games, the rules to which they never seemed to get. It happened with games that the police did become complicit in – turning scenes of confrontation into parties: a game of pontoon to get our big blow-up beachball world back from outside the police line, a game of giants, pixies and wizards – where a line of police and a line of clowns ended up hugging. It happened as we ran helter-skelter down the A9 – the unusually silent road transformed into a giant playground full of fun things like traffic cones.

The clowns fished and socked with love and various other emotions, marched in almost imperfect formation or scattered in all directions to escape containment. And we did it all by consensus, by spokes-council, with no leaders. 'I'm Clown Knickers! No, he is! No, she is!' we responded to police questions of 'Who are the ringleaders?'

And who can deny that clowns are enchanted creatures before the maniacally grinning face of the Clown Castle episode? The day before the main blockade, we still didn't really know what we were going to do or where we were going to go. Rinky Dink, a bicycle-powered sound system, and its attendant eccentrics knew of a place we could stay in for the evening. No one let on but we all put our trust in them and piled into minivans, which took us out of Stirling, across the river and towards Gleneagles and Auchterarder. On a hill in the distance we saw the turrets of a fairytale castle amongst the trees. 'Wouldn't it be funny if we were going there!' we joked. 'Ha ha' said the universe as we pulled open-mouthed into the driveway of Cloan House. As the clown army danced to Rinky Dink in the manicured gardens of our castle and centre of operations, we learnt that a previous owner, one of the Lords Haldane, had been the founder of the modern British army...

By the time we got to July 7, we were exhausted. The tour, the actions, the clowning had taken us to the limit both physically and emotionally. The healers of the eco-village, those who designed and set it up and maintained it and had done all the local outreach and liaised with the council – everybody who found all the tat needed, who kept things clean – all of them prevented us from falling in a big clownish heap and not moving any further. The Healands barrio kept us together, body and soul, with their wonderful food and warm hearth, which was kept burning into the night as we recovered from the actions of the day. They were – the whole thing was – really amazing.

And so why all this palaver? What were we actually doing? Did it really change anything? At least the G8's intentions were good, weren't they? And surely a world with them keeping things under control is not as bad as a world without?

The grand claims of the G8 to bring poverty in Africa to an end and slow down climate change were a con. Make Poverty History and the genuine goodwill of thousands of people was hijacked by the British government and its pet pop stars. The governments of the eight most powerful countries on earth came to the conclusion over those few days that climate change is not an urgent issue. Important, but not urgent. As chunks of ice the size of countries break off from the polar ice caps, as flooding and freak weather conditions spread across the earth, killing thousands, as species disappear and ecosystems are destroyed every day. Not urgent? Surely these people are insane. And make poverty history in Africa by opening up economies to foreign investors who will continue to plunder its rich resources as they have done for centuries and leave nothing but exhausted soils and devastated landscapes for the miners and farmers and their families who were worked to death to facilitate that plunder? This is what privatisation has meant for those in Latin America, those in Asia, those in the Middle East, those invisible unpersons hidden in the cracks of our own nation state. Misery, not happiness is what it has meant for millions over the last few hundred years.

The governments of the G8 and the CEOs of the multinational companies they serve are fools. But we are fools too. We are the kind of fools who can step outside the paradigms of coercive power and laugh at the limitless absurdity of the capitalist system in order to understand it. The amount of debt to be forgiven will be offset by a reduction in aid to the poorest countries, which will be reduced dollar for dollar according to the debt forgiven (which will be paid back by other means to the international financial institutions to which the G8 is accountable). This makes the G8 meeting nothing more than an exercise in spin, a PR opportunity that the global justice movement is seeking to discredit as an exercise in cynicism. This is why we blocked roads, why the clowns conducted Operation HA HA HAA (Helping Authorities House Arrest Half-witted Authoritarian Androids) to keep the ministers of the G8, the eight most dangerous terrorists in the world, behind the fences at Gleneagles, where their brand of insanity can cause no more harm.

I stopped seeing the helicopters in Stirling because they stopped mattering that much to me. There are other things that matter more, that actually deserve my attention, creativity and energy. Those things won't sit in a suit at the other end of a long boardroom table or in the freezing wastes of an opposing political or ideological pole, because they aren't to be found at the extremities of life, but in the thick of things. They can't be fundamentalist because they are part of a web of beneficial relationships where equality is a communal garden, an everyday kind of practice. Those things are sensationalist only in that they taste delicious, or look sexy, or feel gorgeous. Those things are the playthings of the strange, vulnerable, surprising, foolish and imaginative. The infinite pleasure of being clowns may just be able to confuse and distract long enough for that other world – the one that is possible – to be born.

MAKE
Popstars
Politicians
and the Police
History Ⓐ

12

'IT'S THE POLITICS, STUPID'

HOW NEOLIBERAL POLITICIANS, NGOS AND ROCK STARS HIJACKED THE GLOBAL JUSTICE MOVEMENT AT GLENEAGLES... AND HOW WE LET THEM

Paul Hewson

Thanks to Bob, Bono and Make Poverty History's efforts, a more informed debate is happening. ... Bob and Bono are ... making these issues massive and mainstream so power must come to the people, not the other way round.

Jamie Drummond, DATA (Debt, Aids, Trade, Africa), June 2005[1]

What we have been trying to do is put pressure on the leaders of the G8 summit to make a real change in the world, but I don't even know what these people want. ... We are already getting movement from the G8 group on these issues. Anyone who wants to cause trouble on the streets should go home.

Midge Ure, Live Aid veteran, July 2005[2]

Shortly after Bob Geldof called for a million people to converge in Edinburgh for the opening day of the G8 summit, Midge Ure, the co-organiser of Live8, was asked if he was worried about the events being hijacked by anarchists. His response was that Live8 was, in fact, hijacking the anarchists' event.

Kay Summer and Adam Jones, The Guardian[3]

Now that the horse shit has been cleared off the streets of Edinburgh, the travelling anarchist circus has left town and the G8's annual recycled lies already forgotten for another year, it's time for the Dissent! network to face up to the possibility that maybe, just maybe, we blew it. Not the train or the campsites or the legal support; not the convergence and Indymedia centres or the activist trauma support; not even the blockades, which might have been unwelcoming for a mass action but caused far more disruption than first thought. No, where we let ourselves down was actually in relation to the most important aspect of all – the G8 itself.

Despite two years of counter-G8 preparations and a decade of undermining the G8 governments' assumed right to impose their collective will on the rest of the planet, the Gleneagles summit was the most politically legitimised, ideologically uncontested gathering in its grubby little history. One statistic tells it all: in 2001, 300,000 people hit the streets of Genoa to protest against the G8; in 2005, the same number came out in Edinburgh to *welcome* Blair, Bush, Berlusconi and co. to Scotland. As far as most of the people who get their news and views from the mass media were concerned, the G8 summit was a high-level inter-governmental summit at which world leaders in the North were taking historic decisions to help eradicate poverty and needless deaths in Africa. These bastards left Scotland with their reputations enhanced, boosted by a chorus of cheers from everyone from international statesmen and newspaper editorials to those meddling rock stars whose vanity project drowned out the dismay of even Make Poverty History (MPH). In the real world – not the activist ghetto – there was no 'dissent'.

This might sound a bit harsh. After all, the G8 is an illegitimate, undemocratic forum of global governance and taking on the politics of this year's summit would in some ways have simply lent this gang of thugs a credibility and legitimacy they don't really have. The media, the clever co-optation of UK global justice campaigners by New Labour, Oxfam and Geldof, the unfair disparity in the resources available to those NGOs and corporate interests behind the G8 agenda, and, of course, the destructive role of the Socialist Workers Party (SWP) in summit mobilisations, all made our job a lot harder. But ultimately, having good excuses doesn't change the fact that we lost. It doesn't change the fact that because we failed to make any significant inroads into popular opinion, the G8's neocolonial plan for Africa and the rest of the global South will continue unabated and the very neoliberal and authoritarian policies we oppose in the core capitalist countries will also remain largely unchallenged.

The irony and thus tragedy is that it didn't have to be this way. The Gleneagles G8 represented our best opportunity in years to put new momentum into anti-capitalism in the UK and land some telling blows on our enemies. It was also a chance to work out more clearly who we are, take our ideas to a mainstream audience and attract more people into our movement. As Dissent! begins to plan the next big 'action', I believe that now is the time for a sincere discussion within the anti-authoritarian, non-hierarchical wing of the anti-capitalist movement about who we are and what we are trying to achieve. This means learning from our mistakes – and also the strategies of others. This essay is meant as a personal contribution to that self-reflection. It is deliberately provocative – no offence intended, honest!

DOOMED TO FAILURE?

With 12,000 police officers plus army support, a raft of new anti-terror legislation, a relatively remote location, a high level of surveillance, a mid-week
meeting, a hostile mass media, a co-opted trade union and NGO movement, an
international activist no-show and the events of July 7, the odds were stacked
against us winning the politics of the G8 summit. Especially given the dire state
of UK social movements. Gone is much of the energy that infused the anti-capitalist movement in the 1990s and early 2000s, and while there is renewed interest
in 'anti-authoritarian' politics, the fractious, individualised, racially homogeneous
and class-riven nature of the anarchist scene remains a massive barrier. And with
British socialism and trade unionism in serious decline, combined with the
haemorrhaging of the Marxist-Leninist left, the traditional labour movement is
rapidly becoming extinct.

Whatever the weaknesses of their politics and memberships, having the
support of unions and institutional left parties on a clear anti-G8 ticket, as in Genoa
and Evian, would have made an enormous difference at Gleneagles by mobilising greater numbers on the mid-week actions and putting more pressure on
MPH to adopt a more critical and confrontational position. This would have
changed the political dynamic of the summit, altering the media coverage and
closing down some of the space in which the Live8-MPH 'con show' operated. We
can now understand just how disastrous the London European Social Forum

(ESF) was in its failure to allow a meaningful dialogue to take place across a wide spectrum of actors on how to approach the G8.

Another major factor against us was the press. The corporate and state-owned media machine was always going to be a lost cause, but media complicity with the G8 was at an all-time high in terms of its sophisticated 'good protester/ bad protester' strategy. Beginning more than a year away from the summit, rarely would a couple of weeks go by without a series of articles promoting the ominous spectre of potentially 'violent anarchists' planning to disrupt progress on Africa as part of their 'extremist agenda'. Undercover reporters would magically infiltrate open public meetings of Dissent!, lacing their sensationalist reportage with military-style language to describe the use of fairly innocuous protest props. Contrast this with the deification of those celebrities and NGOs 'responsibly' lobbying the G8 on Africa and their commitment to the hungry, needy and helpless. As the summit approached, these black and white stories would become a daily phenomenon. The de-mobilising ideological effect of this kind of media bombardment cannot be underestimated.

Arguably the biggest obstacle of all, however, came from some of the very campaigning organisations and groups that are often – and wrongly – seen as either members or allies of the 'global justice movement'. In contrast to almost all previous G8 summits (except, interestingly, the 1998 Birmingham summit), the major civil society mobilisation for the G8 – MPH – comprising the major trade unions, development NGOs and faith groups with 'political celebrities', shamelessly organised *in favour* of the summit! And what a breathtakingly effective mass disinformation campaign it proved to be. MPH's white wristband mania and star-studded PR succeeded in simultaneously capturing millions of ordinary people's imagination about global poverty and, with the added last-minute support of the Live8 concerts, leading them as far away from the authors of that poverty as possible.

By turning the spectacle of summit-stopping on its head, MPH-Live8 served to grant the G8 and their multi-national corporations a legitimacy they have never previously enjoyed and went a long way to ensuring that Dissent! and G8Alternatives stood little chance of ideologically contesting the summit. But were we really just innocent victims of a cleverly orchestrated hijack? It would be convenient to think so. In reality, however, we played right into the hands of the G8-MPH-Live8 scam.

MAKING ~~POVERTY~~ SOCIAL MOVEMENTS HISTORY

There's no doubt that the rise and rise of global anti-capitalism in the decade or so since the Zapatistas declared war on neoliberalism from the Lacandón jungle of Chiapas has been nothing short of remarkable. Over the past 12 years, millions of us worldwide have been radicalised into political struggle and direct action against an economic system geared to the interests of capital and its ruling class.

We have achieved some great symbolic victories and concrete gains along the way, and at arguably the height of our 'counter-power' between 2001 and 2002, marked by the Genoa G8 and the Argentina popular uprisings, we were challenging almost every assumption, outcome and institution of neoliberal capitalism and corporate globalisation.

Most powerful of all has been the phenomenon of summit-stopping: wherever and whenever the global capitalist institutions meet – the WTO, IMF, World Bank, G8, NATO – we have almost always followed them, bringing chaos to the streets, disruption to the meetings and occasionally succeeding in shutting them down *à la* Seattle and Prague. As throughout history, power has quickly learnt from these experiences by geographically shifting most summits out of major Western cities and into remote mountain ranges or police states. However, for this year's summit, the G8 had limited options to hide away in the UK, and however difficult Gleneagles was to penetrate it still offered the possibility for a more successful repeat of the Evian blockades. If only the huge anti-war feeling in Europe over Iraq could be mobilised to Scotland, the potential for the UK's presidency of the G8 summit to become a political disaster was very real.

Disrupting the G8 would not have simply been a diplomatic embarrassment to the British state. This year's G8 was an absolutely crucial summit for rich countries to get their act together amid the continuing slowdown in the world economy, rising oil prices and dwindling reserves, and the new-found solidarity among Third World countries which have been blocking further liberalisation in the WTO since the 2001 Doha Ministerial. The G8 needed to work together with their business elites to get consensus on how to kick-start the neoliberal globalisation agenda in their interests, as well as try to overcome differences on international terrorism and the future course for Iraq. A protest movement capable of bringing media and public attention to the real nature of the G8 summit and the implications of their agenda for all of us would have been a major victory with powerful repercussions for an anti-capitalist resurgence.

Faced with this scenario, the UK government knew it needed a plan to avoid the battle scenes of previous summits, and a set of powerful and influential allies to carry it off. The first stage was to ensure that the official agenda for the G8 summit took the moral high ground away from the protesters. A summit publicly focused on Iran, nuclear power or free trade – which were all actually discussed at length in Gleneagles – would have been a sitting target for activists and lefty journalists. In the 20th anniversary year of Live Aid, what better *cause célèbre* than Africa. The 'forgotten continent' had long been the centre-piece of Tony Blair and Gordon Brown's 'moral crusade', the cornerstone of their 'liberal internationalism'. They had seen how successful it was as a diversion the last time the G8 had met in the UK when the government and the Jubilee 2000 campaign worked together to make debt cancellation the big public concern of the Birmingham summit and then pull the wool over everyone's eyes afterwards – the

'historic promises' on debt were betrayed within weeks of the summit.

Africa was also one of those issues that would see journalists lose any remaining critical faculties and suddenly be unable to write anything bad about politicians. After all, who could be against a rhetorical agenda apparently aimed at saving dying babies, feeding the poor and malnourished, building new hospitals and schools, allowing poor countries to trade with us on a fairer basis, cancelling debts and promising new drugs to kids with AIDS? In a country where most people's understanding of Africa's history and problems has come from Bob 'give us your fookin' money' Geldof, saving Africa *again* was a perfect instrument to divert public attention away from the disaster in Iraq.

The Africa focus made sense for another, more crucial reason. What we often forget when drowned in what Rotimi Sankore calls the 'pornographic images of poverty in Africa' is that Africa is unimaginably rich.[4] Rich in the natural and human resources capitalism feeds on. Precious stones and metals, energy sources and cheap labour are in abundance with one prize increasingly valued above all others – oil. With the rise of Chavez in oil-rich Venezuela, the instability in Iraq and future uncertainty of Saudi supplies, getting hold of African oil has become a major priority for the G8 powers, not least because China is massively stepping up its presence on the continent and threatening the status quo. The US alone hopes to be importing 25 per cent of its oil from the African Gulf of Guinea region within the next ten years. European powers have of course been stealing and destroying these resources from Africa over the past five centuries, killing more than 100 million Africans in the process. Despite this, the continent remains a largely untapped reserve of profit hence the launch, at the 2002 G8 in Kananaskis, Canada, of the infamous NEPAD (New Partnership for Africa's Development) initiative, which locks African states into a progressive liberalisation of their economies under the tutelage of their former colonial masters.

NEPAD's slow progress and widespread illegitimacy among African civil society gave Blair and Brown the perfect opportunity to give the initiative fresh impetus for Gleneagles. So in February 2004, the government set up the Commission for Africa, fronted by Bob Geldof, to help create the political process of consensus-building between G8 governments, their corporations and Africa's core of neoliberal politicians. It was also a clever PR stunt: by having a majority of Africans on the Commission, its recommendations could be spun as being literally 'out of Africa'. In reality, the African Commissioners had been hand-picked by Blair and Brown, and formed a 'web of bankers, industrialists and political leaders with connections to the IMF and the World Bank, all committed to spreading the gospel of free market capitalism'.[5] Following strong input from Western oil and mining corporations, the Commission's 454-page report was ghost written by Geldof's biographer – Paul Vallely of The Independent – under the close supervision of the Department for International Development (DfID) and former World Bank chief economist, Sir Nicholas Stern.[6] Unsurprisingly, the report's recommendations for more aid, debt cancellation and fairer trade rules came with a rather large catch: African governments had to spend any new resources on turning their continent into a single capitalist market economy fit for foreign investment.

The next stage was to ensure that the major development NGOs were onside, a task made easier by the strong funding relationship between DfID and most NGOs working on international development issues. In 2003, a series of meetings are rumoured to have taken place between government officials and the leadership of Oxfam, which exposés by both New Statesman and Red Pepper have shown has particularly strong links to New Labour.[7] Bringing Oxfam into the G8 inner core was a clever move by the government given its hegemonic role within the global development scene. This power is partly due to its size and wealth. In 2004, Oxfam UK's annual income surpassed £180m, three times more than agencies like Christian Aid. It is also the preferred aid agency of most foreign governments and other public bodies, receiving huge amounts of state funding for its work in developing countries.

The government also developed a strong relationship with a host of mainstream development NGOs, like Comic Relief, CAFOD, World Vision and DATA (Bono and Bill Gates' charity). Comic Relief's support for Blair and Brown's agenda was beneficial given that a large number of smaller, more politically radical NGOs and groups depend on the charity for funding, and its founder, comedy writer turned film director, Richard Curtis, had incredible influence in the entertainment industry. Getting stars of stage and screen behind the government's G8 agenda would be an immense coup.

For their part, Oxfam and Comic Relief's willingness to be the government's junior partners was largely due to their desire to help undermine the growing interest of grassroots campaigners and movements in the global justice movement associated with the World Social Forum process. It is no secret that the reformist bloc of Northern development NGOs led by Oxfam had found itself increasingly marginalised as the poor and exploited of the global South suddenly emerged to represent and speak for themselves and not through the medium of the professional aid worker. And when the poor spoke, they read from a very different script to the Oxfams of this world, talking about 'self-organisation' and 'struggle from below' and the need to mobilise and organise independently of state, capital, party and trade union bureaucracies. This represented an enormous challenge to the traditional interest groups exerting leadership over civil society and left NGOs like Oxfam needing to be re-legitimised as the 'official' representatives of the poor. Working so closely with the government would enable Oxfam to have the means to do this and put social movements back in their box.

To ensure that the UK's 2005 presidency of the G8 was a mutually beneficial political success, New Labour, Oxfam and their celebrity friends hatched the perfect plan. Oxfam would initiate a feel-good, media-oriented NGO campaign for a mainstream audience with a simple concept: that 2005 really could be the year in which this generation could come together and make history by 'making poverty history'. Led by an international cast of stars from the worlds of music and film, the campaign would combine the best of corporate marketing, the obsession with celebrity culture and the enthusiasm of global justice to propel a straightforward message to a global audience: that the problems of the developing world, particularly Africa, could be solved by the richest countries making tiny sacrifices to increase aid, cancel debts and make trade fairer. Britain's presidency of the G8 and EU would increase the chances of this happening given Blair and Brown's 'undoubted commitment to Africa'.

It would be so politically uncontentious that everyone, from Rupert Murdoch to Nelson Mandela to the UK government, could support it. All the public would be asked to do was show its support for the UK government's stance by signing up to the campaign, sending the occasional email to world leaders to remind them of their moral duty to help the poor and wearing a special white wristband. To encourage as many NGOs and charities as possible to get involved, they would be allowed to sell these white wristbands and keep the money for their organisations, an arrangement that turned out to be a lucrative money-spinner for many. Once safely co-opted into the campaign, those NGOs who identified themselves with grassroots movements in the global South, like War on Want, the World Development Movement (WDM) and Friends of the Earth would be

powerless to act as a clever celebrity-fronted spin-machine began to heap praise after praise on Blair and Brown for being ahead of other world leaders on trade, aid and debt.

These two leading neoliberal politicians would in turn be so comfortable with the MPH campaign that both could be publicly identified with its slogans and symbols, wearing the white wristband on the UK election campaign trail. While Iraq would no doubt still play badly on the doorsteps, Blair's promise to 'save Africa' would play well with his own party and help woo back much of middle England. Those critical on the outside would be pushed to the political fringes as the anti-poverty agenda gave no reason to protest against the G8. Anyone who took to the streets intent on causing trouble would just be violent anarchists intent on property damage and not serious about solving world problems. Those who spoke out would be labelled as 'cynics', or 'purists', who put idealistic visions of mass movements before the *realpolitik* of long-term, gradual social change. The idea was brilliant, all it needed was a name. Finally it came to them: they'd call it 'Make Poverty History'.

The success of the strategy was embodied in the July 2 Make Poverty History rally. The UK government had cleverly scheduled the G8 for mid-week to ensure that as few people as possible could turn up, and had got agreement from MPH that the main civil society mobilisation would be held on the Saturday before the mid-week opening of the summit. This was obviously to ensure that the large

numbers of people expected could not be drawn into the counter-summit protests planned by Dissent! and G8Alternatives. In return, MPH had the full cooperation of Edinburgh City Council, the Scottish Executive and the local police. To make sure that the 'wrong people' didn't attend, the Stop the War Coalition's efforts to mobilise a big anti-war presence on the day were thwarted amid a furious spin strategy by MPH press officers to portray their event as a nice day out for middle-class families: '[It is] not a march in the sense of a demonstration, but more of a walk. The emphasis is on fun in the sun. The intention is to welcome the G8 leaders to Scotland and ask them to deliver trade justice, debt cancellation and increased aid to developing countries.'[8]

MPH worked with the Scottish Tourist Board to get cut-price weekend break transport, accommodation and tourist excursion deals for those planning to attend the 'welcome walk for the G8'. MPH's website and literature made absolutely no reference to the planned mid-week protests, counter-summits or blockades, or to the other mobilisations. Everything was geared for people to stay the weekend before the summit and then leave the city. In short, MPH succeeded in simultaneously mobilising hundreds of thousands of people to Scotland but away from the G8. The *coup de grace* came when MPH finally abandoned any semblance of not being run by the Treasury with the announcement that Gordon Brown had been invited to the July 2 rally. And just in case the pressure of MPH's moderate lobbying threatened to embarrass the G8's predictable inability to deliver, Geldof's decision to stage the Live8 concerts diverted all media attention away from the July 2 and 6 demonstrations.

As we now know, the MPH-Live8 axis was almost completely successful. By cleverly focusing the Gleneagles G8 on the issues of Africa and global poverty through the Commission for Africa, the MPH campaign and the Live8 concerts, the G8 set the political agenda of the summit and the media coverage of it. While we will never know what would have happened if the London bombs hadn't turned the G8 summit into an irrelevant sideshow, it is obvious that the end of summit communiqué, which fell far short of even MPH's conservative demands, would still have been euphorically welcomed by Bono and Geldof at the post-summit press conference, ensuring that the next day's media coverage was dominated by heroic praise for Tony Blair and the G8. It therefore seems difficult to pinpoint how we could have really challenged the system in this way. After all, they had the money, the media, the human resources, the celebrities, the issues and the momentum. And they had the music (I'm joking). But surely we could and should have tried harder to resist the hijacking of the global justice movement and the co-optation of progressive forces. The big question is: why didn't we?

DISSENT!'S POLITICAL VACUUM

The G8's bogus agenda, and those civil society forces supporting it, demanded a principled opposition by the anti-capitalist movement. The deliberate silencing of African people, both those on the continent and the *diaspora* living alongside us in Europe, demanded the same solidarity we have shown to the indigenous movement of Chiapas, the landless workers of Rio Grande do Sul, the *piqueteros* of Buenos Aires, the militant trade unionists of Seoul, the Dalits of Mumbai and the Palestinians of Rafah. Sadly, none was forthcoming. Instead, we were complicit in that silence. Where was our solidarity with African people? Where were our booklets and handouts on the history of colonialism and slavery, the debt system, the 'new scramble for Africa'? Where were our critiques of the Commission for Africa and the G8 debt deal? Where were our public meetings about what the G8 was really all about? Where were our attempts to build new networks of struggle with African resistance movements?

To our eternal shame, the only real dissenting voices came not from us but from G8Alternatives – yes, the bloody SWP and fellow travellers! Only they took up the challenge of politics by hosting a genuine counter-summit and helping to produce an alternative Africa Commission report from African social movements themselves. For Dissent!, the fact that the G8 was focusing on Africa appeared irrelevant. For a movement that is so brilliant at bringing the struggles of Latin America and Asia, and the people of those struggles, to a Northern audience, why did we treat Africa so differently? As unpalatable as it may be, are we too suffering from our own form of 'institutional racism'?

Our refusal to confront MPH was also a major mistake. Most of us in Dissent! believed MPH to be a bunch of naïve NGOs whose campaign had been 'co-opted' by the UK government. In hindsight, this was just plain wrong: MPH was in fact the *creation* of the government and there was more than enough evidence around at the time to make this obvious. Instead of treating the NGOs in MPH as misguided allies, we should have taken them on directly. Instead of encouraging people to go and hold hands on their apolitical demonstration, we should have mobilised to cleverly hijack it. For instance, before the G8, there were calls within Dissent! for a multi-colour T-shirt bloc on July 2 with slogans subverting the 'Make Poverty History' brand. Imagine if we had taken a little time to promote this idea, to put out leaflets and stickers, to contact sympathetic groups in MPH and build up a little momentum. Imagine if the 10,000 anti-capitalists in Edinburgh for that rally had formed a giant bloc on the demonstration with a very different message to the white T-shirts of MPH. Instead, we had the rather pathetic spectacle of 300 black-clad activists locked down in an Edinburgh side street.

In my view, Dissent! was simply not able to organise strategically against the politics of the G8 for three main reasons. Firstly, we were constrained by our own dogma and ideology. Our core belief that the G8 is an illegitimate institution and represents a corrupt and undemocratic set of governments led to the logical conclusion that by taking on the G8's agenda we would have been effectively legitimising it and thus selling out. This view was pervasive. Alas, while such a principled stand may warm our hearts, in the context of this year's G8, it was ultimately self-defeating. Rightly rejecting the G8's popular mandate and its suitability for solving the world's problems did not stop us from using the Africa and climate change agenda to make that position more intelligible to a mainstream audience. This is precisely what MPH and Live8 were doing, as the quotation from DATA's Jamie Drummond at the beginning of this piece reveals. Friends who have never shown any prior interest in global justice issues could reel off the slogans 'more aid, trade justice, drop the debt' instantly, some even explaining why the aid was needed, the trade-distorting role of the Common Agricultural Policy and how much money was wasted on debt servicing. The fact that MPH's analyses and solutions were plain wrong gave us a great opportunity to engage a wider public in the kind of debates that can so often get more people on our side and involved in our movement. But Dissent! didn't have a view on these things, apart from in the most general of terms. It was in this vacuum we helped to create that the G8 agenda was legitimised by MPH and the media.

Secondly, in order to create the Dissent! mobilising network, we effectively suspended the issue-based elements of our anti-capitalism. The PGA hallmarks began as the ideological basis for our cooperation and the means by which we could exclude other anti-G8 forces with very different motivations and methods, such as vanguardist Leninist-Trotskyist parties. Yet our politics went no further

than that. Perhaps for this G8 no other path was possible and no one can deny that Dissent! proved essential to the sharing of practical organising information and tasks that enabled the mobilisation to happen. Nor can the difficulties involved in getting Dissent! off the ground be underestimated. But we need to recognise that the PGA hallmarks told people almost nothing about where we stood on the issues of the day or how our broad principles related to the British political context. This led to an over-simplification of our politics and gave too much ground to soundbites and slogans in place of deep and extended debate. For the G8, we needed to go beyond our own rhetoric and make anti-capitalism and horizontality accessible to the people 'out there'. Yet the very politics we were fighting for and the very identities of the different local groups and individuals in the network were suppressed in order to work together. This meant the opportunity for a more fruitful and ongoing dialogue with each other about what we were for, why were mobilising against the G8, where we stood on the G8 agenda, how we could resist it and how we could expand our movement, was lost.

Thirdly, our antipathy towards representative politics and the media led to a rejection of any attempt by groups and individuals within Dissent! to represent our politics to a wider audience. I believe we could have worked out a strategy to enable the network to contest the ideological discourse of the G8 without compromising the network idea and the principle that 'no one can speak on behalf of Dissent!'. This strategy would not have meant having official spokespeople or putting ourselves at the mercy of corporate news reporting that sees every word twisted and deliberately misinterpreted. Nor would it have meant wasting months playing the media game when there were more important things to be done. Instead, we should have worked much more seriously on creating our own propaganda and media – in addition to and beyond Indymedia – to both communicate directly with 'ordinary people' and engage in counter-spinning against the G8. The mainstream media can be useful and thus used in this regard. Don't get me wrong: engaging with the media won't alter 99 per cent of the coverage and always runs risks of backfiring as we are anti-capitalists and the corporate interests behind the media want to destroy us. But journalists are also political players who always want information that will shaft the government, embarrass the local council or pour scorn on the police because, at the end of the day, it's a story and a career made. Taking some time to write a few letters, bombarding journalists with press releases, posting comments on a newspaper or magazine's website or even getting the odd useful news story in the mainstream press through an old friend or contact, can have benefits and at the moment is the only way of directly communicating with a mass audience.

In the same vein, Dissent!'s autonomous groups ought to have done more to actively politicise people through organising events, talks, lectures, stunts, producing literature and flyers with useful information on. The fact that this didn't happen wasn't just due to there being so few of us. Deep down, our ideological rejection of vanguardism and top-down, expert-led politics means that we shudder at the very thought of being an elite grouping, of organising mass meetings with speakers, of trying to get people to think like us – of recruiting! Yet this can go too far the other way and stop us working out innovative ways to have political meetings with people we don't know, who don't necessarily share our way of thinking and speaking without compromising our politics. Another related factor is a profound lack of confidence in our own politics and knowledge. Horizontality has become something to hide behind instead of having an opinion on the state of the world and what to do about it in case we're wrong. As in any movement, some of us are well-read and have formed political opinions and analyses over a long period; others are only just discovering the literature and the legacy of this movement and are unsure of not just what they believe in but the best way to express themselves. Yet it seems that we are all afraid of intellectual confrontation, of talking outside of our own circles. It was pretty clear that during the build-up to the G8, most of us knew very little about Africa and thus didn't feel confident about engaging with the issues, leaving them to the NGOs.

WHERE TO NOW?

It is clear that the Dissent! network proved an incredible success in bringing together like-minded groups, networks and individual activists to mobilise collectively against the G8 summit in Scotland. Let us not undervalue our collective achievements nor waste this opportunity to renew and reinvigorate the network for the struggles that lie ahead. At the same time, we need to realise that the politics of contestation do not start and end in blockades. It is not enough to simply take direct action against summits or, at a wider scale, corporations, governments and the Far Right. We have to explain why we are doing this to people who are not in 'our movement'. Nor is it enough to be just against power and authority. We have to take much more seriously promoting what we are for in ways that do not alienate, or provide our enemies with easy pickings. Otherwise, we will continue to talk to ourselves, engaging in a form of 'radical suicide'.[9] Finally it is not enough to simply see Dissent! as a network to mobilise actions. Actions do not exist in a political vacuum. We can only work out which actions are needed in the context of discussing what our priorities are as a movement. This means thinking and acting strategically, not just spontaneously or emotionally. Now is the time for us to use the opportunity provided by this communication space to discuss how we collectively move forward as a movement. A gathering of UK-based anti-capitalist, anti-authoritarian forces is planned for early in 2006 to do precisely that. Let's not waste it.

1   'Bob, Bono and Africa', letter to The Guardian, June 27 2005. DATA is Bono's charity.
2   'Ure urges anarchists to "go home"', Edinburgh Evening News, July 5 2005.
3   'The first embedded protest', The Guardian, June 18 2005.
4   Rotimi Sankore, 'What are the NGOs doing?', New African, August/September no. 443, 2005, p. 15
5   Paul Cammack, 'Blair's commissioners', Red Pepper 132, July 2005, p.25
6   Commission for Africa, Our Common Interest, 2005. For evidence of corporate involvement in the G8 and the Commission for Africa, see www.corporatewatch.org.uk
7   See Stuart Hodkinson, 'Inside the murky world of Make Poverty History', Focus on Trade (Focus on the Global South/Bangkok), 2005; Katherine Quarmby, 'Why Oxfam is failing Africa', New Statesman, May 30 2005.
8   Bruce Whitehead, spokesperson for Make Poverty History, January 28 2005
9   Rapina Tore and Paglio Ccio, All and nothing: for radical suicide. Towards some notes and confusion on 'You can't rent your way out of a social relationship: a critique of rented social centres'... and to continue the dialogue (2005). At http://www.56a.org.uk/rent.html.

WORLD'S #1 TERRORIST
Socialist Worker
Blair
HANDS OFF IRAN AND SYRIA
WORLD'S #1
Another World Possible
PACE

13

THE INTERNATIONAL MOBILISATION TO GLENEAGLES
Alex Smith

We are the network, all of us who resist.

Subcommandante Insurgent Marcos

News that the 2005 G8 summit would be held somewhere in the UK (at this point none of us knew where) was first discussed in a workshop at the 2003 Earth First! Summer Gathering near Ripon, North Yorkshire. A second meeting, which actually became a series of meetings, took place at the Anarchist Bookfair in London in October later that year. Amongst those who attended each of these events, there was a general feeling that the radical movement in the UK had been in decline since the hugely successful day of action in the City of London on June 18 1999,[1] and that the G8 summit could potentially provide an opportunity to reinvigorate, broaden and develop the movement in the UK, and allow for the development of more meaningful relations with groups and movements elsewhere.

A NETWORK FORMS (SO THAT WE WOULD BE WINNING...)
Around a month after the Bookfair, in November 2003, a UK-wide meeting was held in Nottingham and the Dissent! network was officially born. The meeting was attended by people who had previously been involved in the ecological direct action movement in the 1990s, London Reclaim the Streets, the Wombles, the anti-war movement, a few people who had been active in the anarchist movement in

the 1980s and a few who had been involved in the worldwide Peoples' Global Action (PGA) process and mobilisations around international summits.[2]

It was at this meeting that the PGA hallmarks[3] were adopted by Dissent! as a means of articulating both its organisational principles and its political orientation. In essence, the hallmarks were an expression of a commitment to decentralisation and horizontality, to developing a structure which allowed for and promoted autonomy, to recognising and rejecting a multiplicity of structures and mechanisms of domination, and to direct action and disobedience as a means of resisting the summit. Whilst some of us had been involved with, and were sympathetic to, the PGA process, there were others who were either disinterested in, or sceptical of, Peoples' Global Action as a network. In other words, the adoption of the hallmarks was, from the outset, intended more as means of articulating the politics of the network than as a statement of affiliation to the PGA.

Over the months which followed this meeting, a number of pre-existing locally-based radical groups joined the network, whilst others were established explicitly in response to the G8 summit. By June 2005, there were almost thirty local groups listed on the Dissent! website – although it must be said that the actual existence of these groups was far more real in some cases than in others. Meanwhile, a number of working groups focused on specific aspects of the mobilisation: producing publicity, fundraising, building and maintaining a website, producing an irregular newsletter and so on. As the summit drew closer, action groups were set up to organise specific events (the Carnival for Full Enjoyment, actions around the issue of climate change, the hill-walking actions and so on...), take on practical 'support' roles (legal observation, medics, media 'counter-spin'...), and provide the logistical infrastructure for the 'convergence' spaces which were opened in Glasgow, Edinburgh and Stirling.

Most local groups met on a regular weekly or bi-weekly basis to plan local mobilisations, fundraise and, in some cases, to open social centres – self-managed spaces in which resistance to the summit could be planned and local groups and networks developed and strengthened in the process. Working and action groups generally communicated via email lists and irregular meetings. A generic e-list was used to maintain communication between the various nodes of the network and bi-monthly (and as of January 2005, monthly) Dissent! gatherings served as the network-wide decision-making space, in which budgetary decisions were 'ratified' and an overall strategy developed. The gatherings, as with the various local, working and action groups, were open to all those who subscribed to the PGA hallmarks.

Whilst the concrete objectives of the mobilisation against the G8 were never explicitly articulated by Dissent!, and the level of priority given to certain aspects of the mobilisation in relation to others differed from person to person and group to group, there nevertheless seemed to emerge five distinct objectives that were either worked towards or stated as key motivating factors by those involved in the mobilisation.

First of all, the physical disruption of the summit was for many a high priority. The function of direct action carried out against the summit was generally understood as two-fold: (i) as an expression of 'our' collective power; and (ii) as a means of hindering the expansion and intensification of the neo-liberal project, and the smooth reproduction of the capitalist system as a whole.

Secondly, there was a recognition by some that the mobilisations in Seattle, Genoa and elsewhere had gone some way towards destroying the myth that, following the end of the Cold War, the 'end of history' had been reached, that liberalism had won, that there was no alternative. In this sense, displays of radical, anti-capitalist opposition to the summit made sense to the extent that they could open up a political space in which alternative modes of social organisation could at least begin to be discussed.

Thirdly, there was a desire to develop and articulate a critique of the summit which would go beyond that which we expected to be expressed by the 'mainstream' mobilisation. Of course, in the early stages of the Dissent! mobilisation we had no idea quite how mainstream the mainstream would become. We were expecting Susan George and Caroline Lucas, not Hilary Benn and Bono.

Fourthly, many hoped that the models of self-management and ecological sustainability that we intended to put in place at the convergence centres would provide a means of demonstrating and engaging people in organisational forms and processes radically different from those which we tend to experience in our daily lives. And finally, we hoped to both broaden and strengthen local and global anti-capitalist networks which would last well beyond the summit itself.

THE INTERNATIONAL MOBILISATION TAKES OFF
(SO THAT WE WOULD BE EVERYWHERE...)

From the outset, there seemed to be a consensus within the Dissent! network that the mobilisation against the summit should have an international character. In other words, it was not only hoped that 'internationals' would travel to Scotland and take part in the counter-summit, but that they would get involved in the organisational process itself.

With this end in mind, in Spring 2004, an international call was drawn up, translated and circulated around the world.[4] In effect, the call was an invitation to those involved in social movements elsewhere to discuss in their own groups and networks the means by which they thought the summit could best be resisted. They were invited to feed their discussions back to Dissent!, and to take part in a series of international discussion, networking and planning sessions.

The general sentiment within Dissent! appeared to be that the events in Seattle, Prague, Gothenburg, Genoa and elsewhere had indeed achieved a great deal. Not only had they opened up a space within which an anti-capitalist politics of the post-Cold War era could begin to be articulated, but they had contributed substantially to the development of real and meaningful networks of resistance. In other words, the organisational and networking processes leading up to the various events; the experience of collective action on the streets; and the 'follow-up' work (prisoner support, de-briefings, processes of reflection and discussions about the future) carried out after the events had contributed to the develop-ment of an inter-connected global 'movement of movements' which is in many ways unprecedented.

However, there was a feeling that the response to international summits was becoming increasingly predictable, and that serious critical reflection was needed if we were to move beyond merely fulfilling the roles that were expected of us. This first international call, then, was not intended as a direct call to action, but to reflection, consideration and discussion. It explained, 'This is not a call to action yet because we don't know what action people will choose to take... This is a call to learn from our history and our successes; a call to assess our current pos-ition and our current strengths; a call to debate and strategise; a call to formulate a response to the heads of the world's most powerful states meeting in Europe next year.'

THE INTERNATIONAL NETWORKING GROUP SETS UP (SO THAT OUR
RESISTANCE WOULD BE AS TRANSNATIONAL AS CAPITAL...)

The Dissent! International Networking group was set up shortly after the call was written. As was the case with most of the other working groups, its 'membership'

shifted throughout the mobilisation, and its precise remit was never made explicit. Broadly speaking, however, its function basically became: disseminating Dissent! publicity (posters, leaflets, stickers and so on...), and other information relevant to the mobilisation, to groups and movements around the world; providing a contact point for those outside of the UK involved or interested in the mobilisation; translating and disseminating various texts produced by Dissent!; and attempting to 'internationalise' the mobilisation, primarily by organising a series of workshops at international events which aimed to both share and build upon the collective experience of those in attendance (many of whom had direct experience of mobilisations against international summits), and to provide a space in which those based outside of the UK could begin to integrate themselves into the organisational process.

Efforts towards internationalisation were, to a great extent, successful. The European PGA conference in Belgrade in July 2004 served as an initial catalyst for this process. It was here that a number of us involved with Dissent! met with many of those who would later take on the important role of disseminating information about the counter-summit in their regions and throughout their networks. On top of this: information and publicity was distributed; insightful and inspiring discussions about the function, limits and future(s) of counter-summits were held; a call for a global day of action on the opening day of the summit was drafted and agreed upon by the conference's final plenary;[5] and practical tasks (such as the setting up of an international email list and the hosting of an international planning meeting in the final months before the summit) were taken on.

This process was accelerated at the 'Day of Dissent'[6] held at Beyond ESF, one of the autonomous spaces surrounding the 2004 European Social Forum in London. Here, several hundred people, many from outside the UK, took part in a series of workshops, some of which were designed as educational and informative: discussing, for example, the history of the G8, its food and agricultural policies, its links to climate change, war and oil and so on. Others were intended to provide practical information: legal information, advice about direct action tactics, information about the alternative media mobilisations and so on. And others still were intended as 'purely' networking sessions: in other words, as opportunities to exchange experiences and ideas, and to intensify the international coordination against the summit.

Networking processes continued apace at the World Social Forum (WSF) in Porto Alegre, Brazil, in January 2005. The purpose of a number of people involved in the International Networking group attending the WSF was understood as twofold. Firstly, it provided an opportunity to meet face-to-face with others who were, or had been, involved in similar mobilisations elsewhere (against the APEC meeting in Santiago, Chile in 2004; the 2003 G8 summit in Evian, France; and the forthcoming World Trade Organization Ministerial in Hong Kong, IMF and World Bank Meetings in Washington DC, and the Free Trade Area of the Americas summit in Argentina). A series of workshops, all of which were held in the *Caracol Intergalactika*,[7] provided an opportunity for people involved in each of these mobilisations to exchange ideas and experiences, and to discuss the ways in which we could support one another's mobilisations in the future. And secondly, it provided a forum in which the call for a global day of action against the G8, issued by the European PGA conference, could be distributed and discussed.[8]

Many of us involved in the International Networking group had been tremendously inspired by the displays of international solidarity which had erupted around the early summit mobilisations. The 200,000 farmers who marched through the streets of Hydrabad, India calling for the death of the WTO, and the 50,000 unemployed workers and peasants who took to the streets of Brasilia as riots erupted around the WTO Ministerial in Geneva in May 1998; the London street reclaimers who took over the City of London, laying siege to the Liffe (London International Financial Futures Exchange) building, and the 10,000 protesters who risked serious repression in order to take over and shut down Port Harcourt, Nigeria's oil capital[9] as thousands protested outside the 1999 G8 summit in Cologne, Germany; the saboteurs who cut the power supply to the WTO Headquarters in Geneva, and the striking students from the Autonomous University of Mexico City who attacked the American Embassy in solidarity with those being arrested in Seattle, were not merely expressions of solidarity with the victims of (often brutal) repression elsewhere, but signifiers of an increasing recognition of a common enemy and common struggles – and, importantly, a willingness to express that recognition in terms of concrete action.

The global days of action provided a means by which a huge multiplicity of singular struggles could begin to be woven into one, without the very real differences between them (in terms of political histories, forms of resistance, and the material conditions in which movements found themselves) becoming obscured in the process. However, as mobilisations around international summits appeared to reach their peak in Genoa in July 2001, so too did the international mobilisations which coincided with them. Whilst, to be sure, actions continued to take place in the build-up to, during and (in particular) after summits – perhaps most notably, in terms of the international solidarity with those arrested and held in jail following the EU summit in Thessaloniki, Greece – none of them paralleled either the scale or the extent of the mobilisations which took place in the period from 1998–2001 (the period in which, as some have said, we *were* winning). We hoped that, alongside the call issued at the European PGA Conference and its subsequent distribution around the world via email lists and independent media outlets, our visit to the Forum would contribute to the resurgence of global days of action as a means of further developing global solidarity. To this end, a statement entitled *Global Resistance 2005: A Call to Action* was issued from the final plenary of the *Caracol Intergalactika*, calling for coordination, communication and collaboration amongst those involved in the mobilisations against the international summits coming up later that year (the IMF and World Bank in the US; the G8 in the UK; the FTAA in Argentina; and the WTO in Hong Kong), and for global days of action to be held on the opening days of each of the summits.[10]

The final 'big push' to internationalise the mobilisation against the summit took place early in 2005. For three days in February of that year, around 120 people from 23 different countries gathered in Tübingen, southern Germany, for an international networking and coordination meeting.[11] For many of us from the UK, the meeting was a tremendously inspiring experience and, in many ways, marked the beginning of a *real* international collaboration. To be sure, a number of people based outside the UK had by this point already been working hard for a long time to try and mobilise people from their networks and regions to come to Scotland, to take part in local solidarity actions during the summit, or to provide material support for the Dissent! mobilisation. The Tübingen meeting, however, allowed for a whole number of many-to-many connections to be made between people involved in various aspects of the mobilisation. Medics from the UK, Germany and the Netherlands were able to meet with one another, share ideas and begin to coordinate. Catering collectives joined forces. Action plans were exchanged and new ones were hatched. Pleas for equipment (vehicles, marquees, IT resources...) were both made and answered. Moreover, face-to-face contact allowed for the development of a greater feeling of both trust and common purpose than any amount of communication mediated through anonymous email lists ever could have done.

A number of other, smaller, international events also took place closer to the summit itself, most notably perhaps the Festival of Dissent! (held in Scotland in April 2005) and an international meeting in Thessaloniki (in May 2005).

THE MULTITUDE ARRIVE (SO THAT ANOTHER WORLD COULD BE POSSIBLE...)

Almost a month before the summit began, internationals began arriving in the UK to lend their support to the Dissent! mobilisation and to initiate and develop their own projects. Bringing resources, inspiration and – at this stage, most importantly – energy, the influx of people from outside the UK contributed enormously to developing the material basis upon which the mobilisation could function (helping set up the camp, cleaning out and making habitable the convergence spaces) and adding a sense of possibility to the days and weeks which lay ahead at a time when many of us who had been involved in the organisational process for well over a year were beginning to feel a little shaky.

As the final days before the summit approached, thousands poured into the UK from continental Europe, the US and elsewhere. The international dimension to the mobilisation contributed enormously to the perceived successes of the counter-summit.[12] The gathering of large numbers of people from different backgrounds, with varied social, cultural and political histories, and the experience of organising within a huge breadth of social movements, allows (often unconsciously) for a form of collective intelligence to emerge which is far more potent than a more homogenous event of a similar scale could ever be. The knowledge and experience that people were able to draw upon; the breadth of action forms that people adopted – from explicitly non-violent blockades and clowning, to militant actions and sabotage; and the organisational forms (affinity groups, black blocs, spokescouncils...) that were experimented with meant that people were exposed to – and often became involved with – forms of political action and organising with which they had previously little or no experience. Of course, it's not always easy to adjust to ways of acting, organising or relating to one another which are radically different from those we are used to, and there were certainly problems, conflicts and clashes. However, observing and experimenting with other ways of acting plays an essential role in the development of movements, helping avoid stagnation. As each of us return home from events like Gleneagles, we take with us the experiences and lessons that we have learned from others – of course, sometimes we end up learning what doesn't work at least as much as what does.

THE IMPORTANCE OF THE INTERNATIONAL (SO THAT ONE DAY, WE CAN CHANGE THE WORLD WITHOUT ANYBODY TAKING POWER...)

The history of capitalist development is a history of crisis, rupture and struggle. Capital's greatest crises have, more often than not, been precipitated by a period which can best be described as an international circulation of struggles. It would not be impossible – and indeed some have tried – to chart a history of capitalist development in which the intense circulation of struggles have created periods of crisis, followed by a phase of restructuring and, ultimately, another period of struggle. Recognising this, then, our task is to develop and ferment struggles capable, eventually, of breaking this cycle – of pushing through capital's rule and coming out the other side.

The international circulation of struggles described above has, on occasion, been described as spreading like a virus in which localised revolts contaminate other areas of the globe, spreading both common desires and common practices. The slave revolts which proliferated throughout the Caribbean in the early nineteenth century; the workers' soviets and councils which erupted during the late nineteenth and early twentieth centuries; and the anti-imperialist and anti-colonial struggles and guerrilla movements that blossomed across Africa, Asia, South and Central America, Europe and the US during the mid-twentieth century are all examples of this. Each of these cycles represented, more often than not, not only the recognition of a common enemy – slavery, industrial capitalism, colonialism, imperialism – but common forms of struggle and ways of organising.

Others have described the proliferation of struggles through the analogy of a mole – appearing in one place, in one moment in time; only to disappear, suddenly, out of sight and reappear somewhere else. Of course, the mole doesn't ever really disappear entirely. Rather, she burrows beneath the earth and into a subterranean world – always travelling, making her way from one 'moment' (in place and time) to another, undermining the foundations of the current world in the process.

The hugely successful actions which took place around the WTO Ministerial in Seattle in 1999 have been described, on more than one occasion, as the 'coming out party' for the current global cycle of struggles. Implied in this is a recognition that the event not only inspired a number of similar mobilisations (in Quebec, Prague, Sydney, Gothenburg, Sao Paulo, Genoa, Cancun, Gleneagles…) but that it also 'revealed' a previously hidden past, i.e. the *real* origins of the current cycle – the numerous mobilisations against the projects, institutions and policies of neoliberalism which had already taken place in the 'global South'. The Zapatista rebellion in Chiapas which began on the day in which the North American Free Trade Agreement (NAFTA) was due to come into effect; the 'IMF riots' which by this point had taken place over ten years previous in Sudan and elsewhere; and the popular resistance to World Bank sponsored projects such as the Namada dam in India were (almost instantly) understood as singular elements within a common cycle of struggles to which the Seattle events belonged.

Central to every cycle of struggle has been the ability to communicate news of the uprisings, for this news to be 'translated' so that the struggles could be recognised by others as their own, and another link in the chain added. As processes of globalisation tend towards bringing about a universalised deterritorialisation, the common condition in which we all find ourselves today is far greater, and far clearer, than in previous eras. In other words, despite the continued existence of real and important differences, the neoliberal era of capitalist development has finally enclosed the entire globe within its realm. The peasant driven off her land in Chiapas; the Indian farmer denied a livelihood by the patenting of seeds which have been sown by his family for centuries; the Starbucks worker in New York City fired for attempting to unionise; all occupy different positions of privilege within the global order. But whatever name it is given (neoliberalism, capitalism, Empire…) the root cause of the increasingly precarious existence that we are all tending to lead is clear.

Events such as Gleneagles, then, have a global importance to the extent that they allow for us to both make explicit the common nature of our current condition and, importantly, to take unified, coordinated action: building upon past experiences, creating new ones and working out ways in which we can do it all better in the future.

1   June 18 1999 (J18) was the opening day of that year's G8 summit in Cologne, Germany. It was marked by a global day of action which – in London – involved the occupation of the City of London, Britain's financial centre. For an account of the J18 mobilisation and the events which unfolded see 'J18: Our Resistance is as Transnational as Capital' in Days of Dissent, available at www.daysofdissent.org.uk

2   For information on these groups see their respective websites: http://rts.gn.apc.org/ (London
     RTS), www.wombles.org.uk (Wombles), www.agp.org (PGA).

3   The PGA hallmarks are:
     1) A very clear rejection of capitalism, imperialism and feudalism; all trade agreements,
     institutions and governments that promote destructive globalisation.
     2) We reject all forms and systems of domination and discrimination including, but not
     limited to, patriarchy, racism and religious fundamentalism of all creeds. We embrace the full
     dignity of all human beings.
     3) A confrontational attitude, since we do not think that lobbying can have a major impact in
     such biased and undemocratic organisations, in which transnational capital is the only real
     policy-maker.
     4) A call to direct action and civil disobedience, support for social movements' struggles,
     advocating forms of resistance which maximise respect for life and oppressed peoples' rights, as
     well as the construction of local alternatives to global capitalism.
     5) An organisational philosophy based on decentralisation and autonomy.

4   The call for international participation in the mobilisation against the summit is available
     online at http://www.dissent.org.uk/content/view/19/63/.

5   A copy of this Call is available online at
     http://www.nadir.org/nadir/initiativ/agp/resistg8/index.htm.

6   The invitation to, and agenda of, the Day of Dissent is available at
     http://www.indymedia.org.uk/en/2004/10/298904.html.

7   The Caracol Intergalactika was one of the 'barrios' (or neighbourhoods) inside the
     Intercontinental Youth Camp, an encampment of 50,000 people at the World Social Forum in
     Porto Alegre, Brazil in January 2005. For more about the Youth Camp, see: R. Nunes, 'The
     Intercontinental Youth Camp as the Unthought of the World Social Forum' in ephemera:
     Theory and Politics in Organization Volume 5, Number 2 (May 2005). (Available at.
     http://www.ephemeraweb.org/journal/5-2/5-2nunes1.pdf). For an excellent personal account
     of the 2005 World Social Forum, with particular emphasis on the goings on in the
     Intercontinental Youth Camp, see T. Mueller, 'Notes from the WSF 2005: The Good, the Bad and
     the Ugly' also in ephemera: Theory and Politics in Organization Volume 5, Number 2 (May
     2005). (At http://www.ephemeraweb.org/journal/5-2/5-2mueller.pdf).

8   To this end, the call issued by the European PGA conference was translated and distributed
     alongside 30,000 English, Spanish and Portuguese flyers produced by the Dissent! Publicity
     Group, explaining our motivations for mobilising against the summit and calling for people to
     take coordinated action around the world on the opening day of the conference.

9   A short report from the action in Nigeria, which brought together activists from the Ijaw Youth
     Council and the Ogoni Solidarity Movement with students and environmentalists, is available
     at http://www.nadir.org/nadir/initiativ/agp/free/global/j18nigeria.htm.

10   The call is available online at
     http://www.nadir.org/nadir/initiativ/agp/resistg8/actions/caracol __ en.htm.

11   The original invitation to this meeting is available at:
     http://pl.indymedia.org/pl/2005/01/11268.shtml. The minutes are also available to download

from http://www.nadir.org/nadir/initiativ/agp/resistg8/news/tuebingen_minutes.pdf.

12 *Alongside the actions in Scotland, the various international calls for action were met by events around the world as the world leaders began to gather at Gleneagles. A counter-conference took place in Mali; demonstrations were held in Oxford, Bristol, Berlin, Berne, Minsk, Richmond (Baltimore) and Kansas City; film showings were organised in Buenos Aires; a mini-riot erupted in San Francisco; street theatre was held in Moscow, Cologne, Hanover and Vienna; and Tony Blair's house was paid a visit in South Bristol. For a fuller list, and a number of more detailed accounts of the international actions, see*
https://www3.indymedia.org.uk/en/2005/07/317234.html.

14

THE FEEDING OF THE FIVE THOUSAND
Isy Morgenmuffel

Five loaves, two fishes, 5000 hungry anarchists... OK, it had more to do with sound planning, teamwork and a sense of humour than any supernatural powers, but at times cooking for the anti-G8 mobilisation still felt like a bloody miracle.

Finding supplies for our central food store, sorting out enough money upfront for these supplies (as well as not being out-of-pocket afterwards), communicating amongst ourselves and actually cooking all day for hordes of hungry people was a huge and daunting task – but somehow, it worked out. And at a deeper level, the kitchens weren't just about infrastructure or logistics; they were an integral part of our politics. If we're serious about self-organisation and autonomy, washing spuds is as good a place to start as any. This is the Anarchist Teapot's story of how we did it...

With thanks to: Kaos Café (London) cooking at the Glasgow convergence; Café Clandestino (Brighton) cooking in Edinburgh; Kokkerelen (Belgium/'Lowlands' barrio); the Irish barrio kitchens; the Scottish Healands kitchen; the kitchens from the social centres in Bradford (1in12) and Leeds (Common Place, with some Sheffield people too); Nottingham's Veggies; Why don't you? from Newcastle; the kitchens from Lancaster, Bristol, and Oxford; the Queer barrio cooks; the Purple Penguin bakery; and of course the Dutch Rampenplan with whom we formed the Rampenpot, or Anarchist Plan.

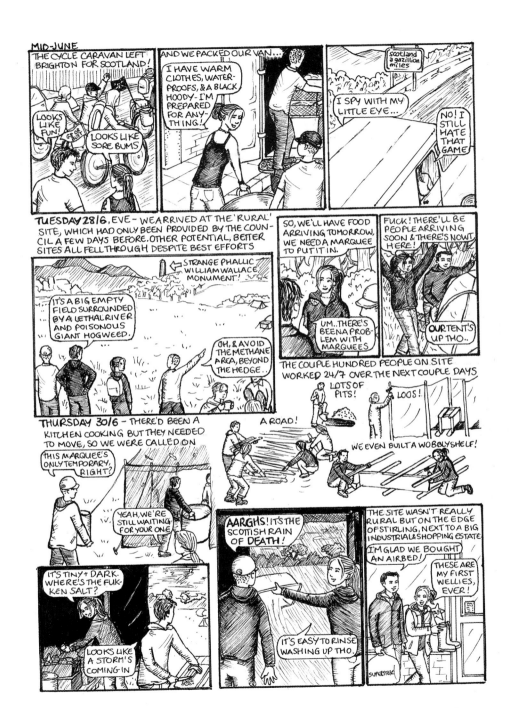

MID-JUNE
THE CYCLE CARAVAN LEFT BRIGHTON FOR SCOTLAND!

LOOKS LIKE FUN!

LOOKS LIKE SORE BUMS

OR OR

AND WE PACKED OUR VAN...

I HAVE WARM CLOTHES, WATER-PROOFS, & A BLACK HOODY - I'M PREPARED FOR ANY-THING!

scotland a gazillion miles

I SPY WITH MY LITTLE EYE...

NO! I STILL HATE THAT GAME

TUESDAY 28/6, EVE – WE ARRIVED AT THE 'RURAL' SITE, WHICH HAD ONLY BEEN PROVIDED BY THE COUN-CIL A FEW DAYS BEFORE. OTHER POTENTIAL, BETTER SITES ALL FELL THROUGH DESPITE BEST EFFORTS

← STRANGE PHALLIC WILLIAM WALLACE MONUMENT!

IT'S A BIG EMPTY FIELD SURROUNDED BY A LETHAL RIVER AND POISONOUS GIANT HOGWEED.

OH, & AVOID THE METHANE AREA, BEYOND THE HEDGE..

SO, WE'LL HAVE FOOD ARRIVING TOMORROW, WE NEED A MARQUEE TO PUT IT IN.

UM..THERE'S BEEN A PROB-LEM WITH MARQUEES

FUCK! THERE'LL BE PEOPLE ARRIVING SOON & THERE'S NOWT HERE!

OUR TENT'S UP THO..

THE COUPLE HUNDRED PEOPLE ON SITE WORKED 24/7 OVER THE NEXT COUPLE DAYS

LOTS OF PITS!

LOOS!

WE EVEN BUILT A WOBBLY SHELF!

A ROAD!

THURSDAY 30/6 – THERE'D BEEN A KITCHEN COOKING BUT THEY NEEDED TO MOVE, SO WE WERE CALLED ON

THIS MARQUEE'S ONLY TEMPORARY, RIGHT?

YEAH, WE'RE STILL WAITING FOR YOUR ONE

IT'S TINY + DARK. WHERE'S THE FUK-KEN SALT?

LOOKS LIKE A STORM'S COMING IN

AARGHS! IT'S THE SCOTTISH RAIN OF DEATH!

IT'S EASY TO RINSE WASHING UP THO.

THE SITE WASN'T REALLY RURAL BUT ON THE EDGE OF STIRLING, NEXT TO A BIG INDUSTRIAL & SHOPPING ESTATE

I'M GLAD WE BOUGHT AN AIRBED!

THESE ARE MY FIRST WELLIES, EVER!

SUPERSTORE

165

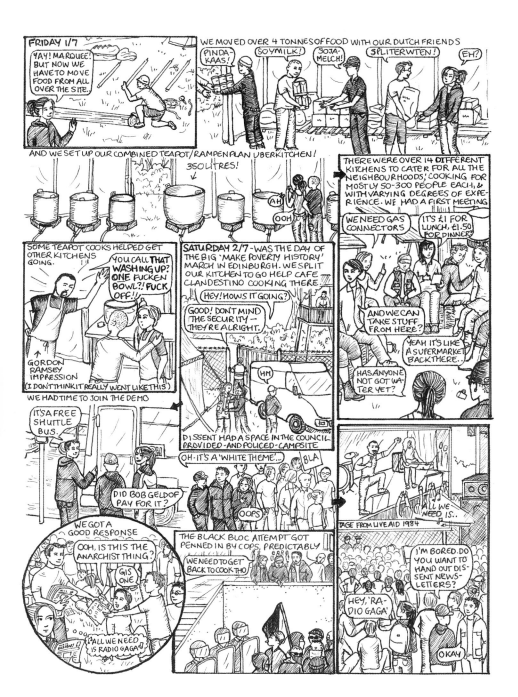

169

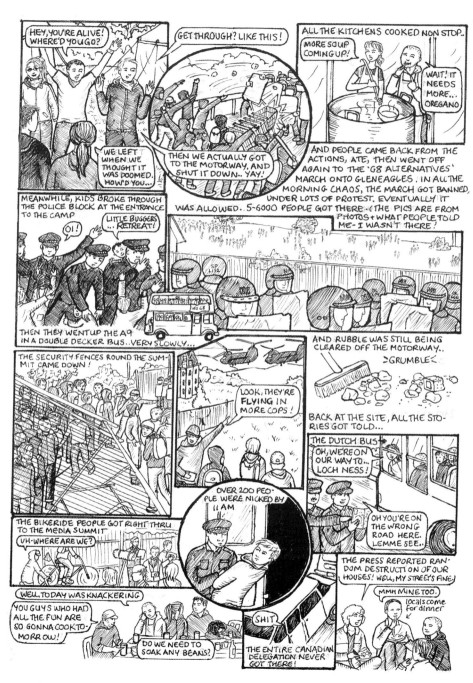

nearly as useful as gaffa tape...
the SHOPPING TROLLEY!

DURING THE G8, RESOURCEFUL PRO-TESTORS DISPLAYED THE MANY USES OF THE HUMBLE SHOPPING TROLLEY...

KIDS' ENTERTAINMENT
YAY!

TRANSPORT FOR KITCHENS
CAREFUL IT'S BUMPY HERE
CAN'T SEE ANYTHING ANYWAY

VEG WASH
OI! GET THE SPUDS, NOT ME!

BRICK TRANSPORT!
ROCKS! ANYONE FOR ROCKS?

INSTANT BARRICADE!

...AND COLLECTION
WE MAKE RE-CYCLING, JA?

SEATING

BARBEQUE
MMMH..
YIKES!
BATTERING RAM
AAAAAH!

(bottom bott-croppered off)

"A kingdom for a trolley!"

15

INSIDE AND OUTSIDE THE G8 PROTESTS[1]

Anonymous

The demonstrations against the G8 summit in Scotland in July 2005 had two distinct aspects. Which one you saw depended largely on whether or not you were involved in the protests and actions around the summit. On the one hand, most of those that were involved seemed to have been inspired by what they had experienced, firstly in mobilising for the summit and then during the actual protests. Many felt that the summit protests had been a great success. On the other hand, for most of the rest of the population, the summit protests meant Bob Geldof, Live8 and lots of people (including the Prime Minister!) wearing white wristbands. This represents a massive hijacking of an anti-summit mobilisation to turn it into an effectively pro-government rally.

These two aspects of the summit protests seem a little contradictory, and yet, to properly assess what happened, we need to take both into account. The two opposing appearances of the mobilisations really didn't connect with each other. Those involved in the actions and demonstrations got on and did their thing and paid little attention to the spectacle all around them. Those on the outside saw little else. The mobilisation against the G8 summit was an *activist* mobilisation and did not really manage to reach beyond this. The impression you have of the summit protests thus probably depends on whether or not you were 'inside' or 'outside' – whether or not you were involved and to what extent you identify as an 'activist'. However, we can attempt to take a critical position apart from both of these aspects, which allows us to see how both realities of the protests are related.[2]

FROM THE INSIDE

People who were involved with the protests against the G8, who generally came away feeling quite inspired, seem mostly to have been impressed on a practical level. The whole process of organising the mobilisation brought a lot of people together, often creating links and connections on a local level that hadn't existed before. Many were struck by the general level of self-organisation, especially in the rural campsite in Stirling: that thousands of people got together without hierarchy and organised themselves, that everyone pulled together to make it happen in such a short time, under such pressure. People felt empowered by the sense of feeling our own collective strength, making links and building a community. Moreover, the actions themselves bettered many people's expectations in that they happened at all and the police didn't totally stop them. Roads were blocked, the opening day of the summit was disrupted, delegates were delayed and the fences surrounding the conference centre were partially torn down as people invaded the 'red zone' surrounding the Gleneagles Hotel.

However, there were definite limitations to what took place. Dissent!'s programme of events appeared to promise a week-long series of actions. However, in reality, Wednesday's blockades day overshadowed everything else, with far greater numbers and a higher level of organisation. This day was collaboratively organised by its participants, but this was not the case with many of the other events and, with these, a distinct lack of organisation began to show through. Moreover, despite our success on Wednesday, we failed to maintain this pressure and, in the end, the G8 protests became about just one day. This was exactly what some people had tried to avoid, but perhaps reflects an inevitable tendency. The numbers involved in actually trying to shut down or disrupt the summit were also quite limited. In the normal run of British activist politics, it was a very big event – but compared to the numbers who participated in Make Poverty History's demonstration-cum-G8 welcome, it was numerically weak. The blockades could clearly have been much more effective with greater numbers of people. And however impressive the eco-village at Stirling was in many respects, it also reflected this. It was inspiring and good for 'us', but didn't really connect with anyone else – its awful location (not the first choice of the organisers, it should be pointed out) certainly didn't help. Stuck just past an industrial estate, down a dead-end road on the outskirts of Stirling, it was not going to attract a lot of interest from those passing by.

Despite a large number people getting involved locally around the UK and the impressive degree of self-organisation of the whole mobilisation, this involvement largely remained inside the activist ghetto and attempts to reach outside of that and to link the protests to the wider concerns of people in the country mostly didn't get very far. For their part, the actions against the G8 stuck pretty closely to the traditional summit-demonstration formula. Despite energy, particularly by some of the mobilisation's organisers, being put into trying to think about this beforehand, we failed to come up with anything really radical and innovative.

Thus, within the activist world, the protests can be counted a real (although limited) success. However, this perspective disregards the whole other aspect of the summit demonstrations: the view from the outside. From this perspective, the mobilisation appeared less successful due to the extent of the hijacking by Make Poverty History, Live8 and the government. So, to assess their overall political impact we need to understand how the summit protests' outward appearance came to be.

FROM THE OUTSIDE

Since the WTO protests of 1999, there have been concerted attempts to bring some selected NGOs into the summit meetings of the international elite in an attempt to break the alliance of NGOs, trade unionists and more radical activists which brought gridlock to the streets of Seattle. However, the Gleneagles G8 summit was perhaps unique in the degree of convergence between the host government and the NGOs supposedly protesting against the summit or, at least, lobbying it. Most people from the outside saw only an extravaganza of backslapping between Blair, Brown, Bono, Geldof and various other film and music megastars. This was the other side to the summit protests, with the sudden last minute media onslaught of the Live8 bandwagon totally swamping everything else.

The Make Poverty History coalition, which organised the G8 'welcome walk' in Edinburgh, is the successor to the Jubilee 2000 campaign and has essentially the same goals – increased aid to the 'Third World', debt relief and 'trade justice'. Blair and Brown have both spoken in favour of some of these goals in the past. So their support now is not totally unexpected.[3] But the wild card in the protests against the 2005 G8 was Live8 – the huge global rock concert event organised by Bob Geldof, which reached quite nauseating depths in its sucking up to the Blair government. Live8 was considerably less radical than even the most right-wing of the NGOs, who at least were asking for something more than they were being offered. Live8 dropped any veneer of 'protest' and became explicitly pro-government – Richard Curtis, one of the main organisers, even said that the point of all the concerts was to support Blair and lend weight to him against the other G8 leaders.

The convergence between the government hosting the G8 summit and the NGOs lobbying it, presided over by the media and proclaimed a done deal, was something that demanded a response from radicals. If the G8 summit deal were to be seen as some unexpected act of benevolence on the part of the G8 leaders, this would undercut any more fundamental critique of the G8. It was thus necessary for radicals to explain what really lay behind the rhetoric and to explain why Blair and Brown particularly were pushing this agenda.

Why, after many years of accumulating debts for some of the world's poorest countries and the governments of the richest seemingly oblivious to calls for debt relief, was everything suddenly now different? It would seem that multilateral institutions and Western governments profited from the debt. So why were they now willing to consider writing it off?

THE LOGIC OF DEBT RELIEF

There are material reasons behind the British government's championing of debt relief. The writing-off of portions of the debt accumulated by some of the world's poorest countries is in underlying British interests. 'Third World' debt has been useful in providing a lever with which to force recalcitrant governments into line with the current global neo-liberal plan, but this has had the side effect that these countries have been permanently trapped in debt-related financial crises, which have tended to rule them out as potential sites of capital accumulation. Debt relief will lift an economic burden from these 'developing' nations so that they can be properly integrated into the global market. Also, much the same 'levering' role can now be played by the conditions attached to the debt relief as was played by the conditions attached to the loans in the first place.

Britain particularly is pushing this agenda as, due to the importance of finance capital in the British economy (financial and business services as a whole account for over 70% of GDP),[4] Britain tends to take on the role of representing finance capital and capital-in-general on a global level. As British Chancellor Gordon Brown told a Chatham House audience, 'For the world economy to prosper and for the companies operating in it to have markets that expand, developing country growth is a necessity.' Without this, rich countries were 'unlikely to maintain the growth rates we have enjoyed over the past 20 years.' Brown talked further of 'bringing the millions who live in these countries into the modern productive economy.'[5]

There is no particular disadvantage for Britain in promoting or allowing the 'development' of some of the world's poorer countries because the UK is one of the world's most 'advanced' capitalist countries. It is de-industrialised and de-agriculturalised to a greater extent than perhaps any other country. If formerly indebted countries do 'develop', then the sectors of the economy that they are 'developing' are unlikely to present any competition to the mainsprings of the British economy. Further to this, there is an actual advantage for Britain in that it has much of the finance capital and the corporations that are going to be doing the 'developing'. Britain stands to economically benefit through the companies that will be doing the investing and consulting and running the privatisation programmes, etc. required by the conditions attached to the debt relief.

What people saw of the G8 summit from the outside was a carefully

managed spectacle, at its worst simply fulfilling the role of a giant PR campaign to polish Blair's tarnished image after the Iraq war. It was a cynical exercise in using the language of the 'global justice movement' to sell the British government's global agenda of privatisation and 'free' trade – an extension of neo-imperialism by another name. Many people involved in the more radical end of the summit mobilisations realised this, but despite some valiant attempts, we were unable to do enough to make a clearly visible stand against it.

RECUPERATION AND REPRESSION

Unlike some other summit mobilisations, there doesn't seem to have been a huge wave of state repression and downturn following the Gleneagles G8 – perhaps because our actions were not as spectacular as on some other occasions. The problem for other movements has sometimes been that when the dust has cleared and everyone has gone home, radicals have been left in a much weaker position than before, with a combination of police repression, imprisoned activists to support and a general atmosphere of clampdown and a lack of public support for radicals.[6] To the contrary, in this situation we *seem* to have been left in a stronger position. This is hard to call of course, but local groups have formed and worked together to organise against the summit, there are new social centres in several towns and cities, and on a national level, there is the new anti-capitalist Dissent! network.

However, the Live8/government hijacking of the protests nullified some of the political impact of the various protests and demonstrations. It was always going to be difficult to make clear our perspective when faced with the massive media onslaught around Live8 and try and prevent ourselves being seen as merely the radical wing of the whole Live8, debt-relief spectacle – different in militancy, but not in essentials.

As much energy needs to be put into combating recuperation[7] as into avoiding repression. But less thought was put into this in advance by those involved in the radical end of the G8 protests. The failure to distinguish ourselves from the positions of the mainstream NGOs was compounded by the decentralised nature of the Dissent! network, in that it included people whose politics were barely distinguishable from Make Poverty History, and there was always a danger of things being produced under the Dissent! banner which read as if they had been written by Christian Aid. This said, however, there were plenty of people who realised the necessity of making our position clear and put effort into doing so, but it was always going to be a very uphill task.

Despite this, the hijacking of the agenda by Live8 and the British government did not totally negate the value of the radical end of the G8 summit demonstrations and the mobilisation to disrupt and blockade the summit. Particularly when the reality of the paucity of the deals done at the G8 summit began to come out in the days following, and it became obvious that it was going to be business as usual, the actions of radicals in attempting to shut down and blockade the summit seemed to make more sense. Even if our *ideas* didn't get out through the media, our *actions* did – and they conveyed a fairly clear message of rejection of the G8. A message which was retrospectively justified by the clear pointlessness of much of the mainstream mobilisation, seeking to ask the very people, institutions and states responsible for world poverty to go against their entire past record to try and end it.

RITUALISATION

Taking a stance apart from both aspects of the summit protests allows us to see how the two realities of the G8 protests were related. As they have become more established, summit demonstrations have become ritualised. They are a known quantity – people know what is supposed to happen. There is therefore a tendency for people to come and fulfil their predetermined roles, to do their thing, like they have done before. The ritualised nature of summit protests leads to a disconnection or a disregard for their overall context. Each one is seen as just another in a series, its context being provided by previous summit protests rather than the particular political circumstances surrounding the mobilisation.

There was a real disconnection between the activist protesters and the whole spectacle of the Make Poverty History demonstrations, Live8, etc. Not that there should have been an active engagement with this by the radicals, but it was as if they were in different worlds. The activists just got on and did their thing, preparing the blockades etc. and Geldof *et al.* carried on with their thing on the level of the media. In some senses, summit demonstrations have become a victim of their own success. They have dogged the leaders of the world wherever they have chosen to meet, forcing them behind giant fences and into more and more remote locations. They have helped extend an opposition to neo-liberal globalisation into the countries of the global North. They have created new links and networks between radicals and given new hope to them, creating new forms of politics and putting 'anti-capitalism' into everyone's heads. But their very success has resulted in them becoming stuck in a ritualised repetition. They have seemingly reached a plateau and their early promise to push beyond this has receded. From being something open, which had the potential to go in any direction, they have settled into a way of being and taken on a form.

But how else could it have been? That is surely the point about so-called 'moments of excess':[8] that they are points at which possibilities open and anything could happen. Yet, it is in the nature of this state that they are brief. These situations cannot last long. Sooner or later they will settle into something. And the very fact of becoming *anything* rather than being a moment of openness, a jumping off point for an unknown future, must in a way feel like a disappointment. So, unable to go further, having reduced all the possibilities open to a new phenomenon into merely one, you repeat. The process of something becoming ritualised is not unexpected. In a way it is in the nature of revolutionary politics. It is like a failed revolution.

In revolutionary politics, everything you do is an attempt to push beyond the world we live in now, to open up new cracks, new paths, to open up as much space to experiment with alternative forms of life as possible. And until we succeed, we are going to keep failing. That means there are going to be a lot of revolutionary moments and openings that have solidified into institutions or rituals: insurrections that have become organisations, uprisings that have given birth to networks, projects and infrastructure that remain when the initial cause is over.

Every little opening in alienation makes us want more. Things almost inevitably disappoint because we are always greedy for more. These summit demonstrations initially excited a lot of people because they seemed to open new possibilities, make new links and connections; they seemed to show a new way of being anti-capitalist. But they obviously could not go on pushing boundaries forever. They were obviously going to settle down into something that was more or less 'ritualised'.

Given that this is the case, the point is to preserve as many of the high points of a phenomenon as possible and to keep as much flexibility and openness as possible – not to completely ossify. We need to defend the gains that we have made and, when there is a wave of a radical upsurge, ride that wave and somehow

allow it to leave us in a better position when it recedes than we were in before, ready and better prepared for the next thing. One way of preserving the gains of a particular innovation is through 'ritualisation'. This obviously has disadvantages, which many of the critics of summit mobilisations have pointed out: things become dull and stale, the authorities know how to deal with them more easily, the element of surprise and unpredictability is lost, and they have less potential to go beyond this – they only promise more repetition of the same. However, if the ritualisation of struggles is to a certain extent inevitable, then maybe we also need to look at the other side of this process.

The repetition of a winning strategy, or a form of action that worked, is one way of maintaining and keeping what you have gained. Given the unlikelihood of some tactic like summit mobilisations being able to push the boundaries endlessly, we are left with the choice of either abandoning this form of action or keeping on. The tendency to establish something, some form of resistance and then after it has been successful, to abandon it and move on to something new is quite strong. Something new, a new issue, a new campaign, a new tactic, because it is new and untried still feels like it has the potential to go further and break the mould. But partly this is just a product of its newness. Rather than always chasing after new things, there might be something to be said for a certain amount of ritual.

Historically, there have been ritualised forms of rebellion – folk customs of attacking the rich and powerful at particular times or in particular ways. These things are not necessarily totally bad – just limited. What's good about such things is also what is limited in them. When forms of rebellion become ritualised it can mean they are repetitive, stale, stagnant. But also that they are ingrained, have become customary, expected – which can be a big pain for those in power, but also simultaneously limiting for radicals. Things can become entrenched – with both the positive and negative sides of that – a position that is firmly held and very difficult for the enemy to shift but also difficult to move forward from.

It is a measure of the success of these summit mobilisations that they have bred both things – both the ritualisation of protest on the part of the activists and the recuperation of protest by pop stars and the government. These two things are connected because a successful movement is more likely to become ritualised and a ritualised, fixed form of protest is easier for those forces seeking to assimilate the movement back into the mainstream to latch on to. This has in turn generated this two-sidedness to the summit mobilisations and the disconnection between their two aspects.

1   An earlier version of this article appeared in Aufheben, 14. See: www.geocities.com/aufheben2

2   I was actively involved in the anti-G8 mobilisations and therefore was obviously very 'inside'. When I talk about taking a 'critical position' in order to think about something, I don't mean that you shouldn't also be practically involved. I just mean that sometimes it is useful, for the purposes of critical reflection, to mentally step outside of your own shoes for a while. Nevertheless, it is still worth noting that this account of the protests against the Gleneagles G8 summit is limited by my experience as someone involved mainly with the Dissent! mobilisation, the rural Stirling camp and the blockades of the summit on July 6.

3   For example, in February 2002, Blair called for a major public campaign on the issue of tackling poverty in Africa, saying he wanted a campaign similar to the Jubilee 2000 one on world debt relief. See news.bbc.co.uk/1/hi/world/africa/1812382.stm

4   Economist Country Briefing: Britain. See: www.economist.com/countries/Britain

5   Speech given by the Chancellor of the Exchequer, Gordon Brown, at the 'Financing Sustainable Development, Poverty Reduction and the Private Sector: Finding Common Ground on the Ground' conference, Chatham House, London, January 22 2003.

6   See Days of Dissent: Reflections on Summit Mobilisations for some examples and discussion. Available at www.daysofdissent.org.uk

7   In Situationist jargon, recuperation is the process whereby a radical phenomenon potentially threatening to the existing order is transformed into something harmless and integrated back into capitalist society. Capitalism assimilates our ideas and actions, dilutes the passion and anger behind them, and then repackages them as something unthreatening or even beneficial to itself.

8   A phrase used by Leeds May Day Group in discussing summit mobilisations. See www.nadir.org.uk

16

DIARY OF A COMPOST TOILET QUEEN
Starhawk

JUNE 8 2005

'The problem is the solution' is a permaculture principle, but today the problem just seems like a problem. I was hoping to start out these updates for the Scotland G8 organizing with something upbeat and optimistic, but it hasn't been that kind of a day. Yesterday I was climbing a beautiful mountain above a clear, calm loch where misty blue mountains rolled away toward the horizon. Today I was sweeping pigeon shit off the floor of a warehouse in inner-city Glasgow. That was actually a good part of the day – it is just these little contrasts, after all, that keep life interesting. The frustrating part was coming back into cell phone range last night to all the messages telling us that the site for the rural convergence space had once again fallen through at the last minute. The farmer who had been very keen on the deal had backed out, unexpectedly, for mysterious reasons.

I was climbing that mountain to recover from the effort of teaching forty-odd students a ten-day crash course in permaculture and ecological design, aimed at creating a resource pool of knowledgeable people who could turn that rural convergence site into a model eco-village, For ten days we wallowed in compost toilets and greywater systems – okay, I'm being metaphorical here – we wallowed in discussion of these things, conceiving of ways in which problems might become solutions, waste be transformed to resources, physical structures support directly democratic social structures and people might be encouraged to wash their hands. How many shits does it take to fill a 55 gallon drum, and what is that in liters? What could you do with it afterwards? How many liters of greywater would 5,000 people produce in a week, and where could it go if the clay soil doesn't drain? And just how did I become the Queen of Compost Toilets at this point in my life, anyway?

...

Overall, I'm phenomenally impressed by the level of care and thought and preparation going into every aspect of the mobilization. Dissent!, the broad network of direct-action oriented groups, has been organizing up and down the land for over a year, and has managed to bring together a wide spectrum of groups. There are convergence spaces in Edinburgh and Glasgow that have been rented and will provide facilities for meetings, trainings, housing and feeding people. There are medics in training and kitchen collectives coming to cook and a two-week long training for trauma workers who will provide counselling and support for anyone suffering post-traumatic stress. A network of nonviolent direct action trainers has been offering trainings for over a year in several regions of England and Scotland. A group of Pagans, the Tribe of Brigid, is coming with a geodesic dome to offer spiritual healing during the actions. Watching this all come together, I feel confident that if we do some day run the world – or rather, facilitate the world's autonomous running of itself – we'll all be fed, housed, educated, and all our physical and emotional needs will be well looked after.

And meanwhile, there's the Cre8 Summat about to happen, an effort of a coalition of local groups here in Glasgow who are resisting the building of a motorway through a low-income community. The plan is to plant a garden, designed by the community, in a vacant lot in the motorway's path, and hold a week of activities, workshops, cultural presentations and celebrations that bring alive something of the world we keep saying is possible. Everyone involved is deeply committed to strengthening the local, long-term organizing around this issue and I'm very excited and honored to be involved – it's just the kind of organizing and strategy that I think can be effective, tying the local issues to the global, planting a garden in the path of the bulldozers, opposing power-over and destruction with creativity and life.

JUNE 10 2005

I feel like a bride jilted twice at the altar who gets a new proposal. We have a site for the rural convergence – maybe! Stirling Council, who to their credit do seem to really want to work with us, have found a big field next to the football stadium, in a bend of the River Forth. Because it is close to an old rubbish dump, they need to test it for methane emissions – so we won't know one hundred per cent for sure until next week sometime at the earliest, which is making us all nervous. However, aside from that it looks good, big enough, on the edge of town so we're looking at fields and a couple of picturesque ruins, with access to the river, and with a faerie hawthorne in its midst. If we really get it, we can create a beautiful eco-village, and because it is slated for development, some of our problems around impact on the land will be much more easily solved.

Yesterday I worked on informational materials as an act of faith that we would eventually need them, then went down to the warehouse to sweep up more pigeon-shit with the masked anarchists – dust-masked, that is. It's really sweet to see how hard everyone is working just to get the space clean enough to use without being a health hazard...

JUNE 14 2005

Cre8 Summat has begun, the community garden built on land where a much-contested motorway is planned through the Gorbals, an historic, low income community in Glasgow. The actions are finally underway. And it went beautifully!

At first the beginning seemed inauspicious. Saturday night the van carrying the kitchen for the garden got stopped by the police south of Glasgow. The driver got into the back of the police car to answer some questions and was whisked off without a word, leaving the van with no one to drive it. Sunday morning, June 12, dawned grey and drizzling. I declined to be on the team that got up at 5am to put up tents, but made my way down around 9.30, wondering what I would find.

The tents were up, and a few people were venturing out into the rain to continue to pick up garbage. The police had come by, and simply wished everybody luck. A seating circle of old tires had been made in a central area – a continuation of an area the neighborhood drinkers had already pioneered informally. Plants had been delivered, and a truckload of soil. We spent some time wandering around, trying to decide what should go where, while Rob drew up a map. We had advertised a 10am time for a community design process, but no one showed up, which didn't actually surprise me. The organizers of the project deeply want to involve the community in the overall design, but my experience with such things has been that people get involved in actually doing things. An overall design seems very conceptual and overwhelming – building a raised bed or planting a flowerbed is fun and creative and that's how people feel a sense of agency and ownership. But around noon we all gathered, looked at the map and what was already on the ground, and came up with a plan that built on what was already there – paths that dog walkers had made, the seating circle, a small beginning of a community garden in a few bathtubs up front. These things were, in fact, the input of the community, writ upon the ground.

As the afternoon wore on, the sun came out, and more people joined in. The bike ride arrived at 2pm, with the JAM74 group who are organizing to stop the motorway scheduled to go through this vacant lot. A reporter from a local paper came out, and a local artist arrived to lead a mosaic workshop. Two young women built an herb spiral out of 'urbanite' – broken up concrete. We filled tires with gravel and planted a few with ornamentals. We made a small vegetable garden in a big tub. A group of energetic men, joined by some of the neighborhood boys, attacked the high bank around the site with pickaxes and spades, and made a flat entranceway. Other neighbors came by to plant things or just to see what was going on.

The mood got brighter and brighter as the sun poked out of the clouds, then scurried back in periodically to let a few bursts of showers rain down. The garden grew! Abi from Talamh came by and showed me how to weave a living willow lattice arch – a skill I've been longing to acquire! And by the end of the day, the missing kitchen had arrived. The piece of barren, toxic, trashed ground we started with had been transformed into the beginnings of the community gathering place the organizers had dreamed of creating. After all their hard work, frustration, overwhelm, and fears, they had done it! And the best news – we got word that the motorway construction has been put back to at least 2007! That gives the community more time to organize, and more time we can be assured that our garden will remain. It's a partial but important victory that contributes to the joyful mood as we continue to plant and beautify the waste ground.

...

JUNE 20 2005

Friday, June 17 was the last formal day of work at the Cre8 Summat... All week long, activists and a steady stream of locals had been building the garden, collecting rubble and building new beds, filling tires with topsoil and planting hazels, berries, fruit trees. The atmosphere was relaxed and happy, the police unobtrusive. We even got some good press.

When anarchist organizing works, it's a beautiful process to behold. Work and play blur, and everyone chips in and does what needs to be done without anyone giving orders or directions. The garden consistently had that feel. People were doing hard, sometimes unpleasant physical work: hauling rubble, digging out banks, picking up garbage – but all of it joyfully, with something of the feeling of kids building a clubhouse or digging a snow fort out of a bank. Addi, the slender, smiling woman from Ao Tearoa (New Zealand), who had been at our training, decided to build a labyrinth, and soon had devoted young men carting bricks. Jo, the magenta-haired videographer I was staying with, along with Flee and others built a Sensory Garden, with raised beds accessible by wheelchair devoted to Smell, Taste, Touch and Sight, with tripods hung with chimes for Hearing. I had offered to lead a cob session, but one day it rained, and the next day the clay was too wet. Finally, on my birthday we had two tons of topsoil delivered, which proved to be a perfect consistency for cob – which is a kind of adobe made of clay, sand and straw. We mixed up a batch by dancing on the clay until it deflocculates – loses its molecular structure and becomes a kind of glue holding the sand particles together in a natural form of concrete. We added straw and rolled up big balls, or 'cobs' then punched and pummelled them into a bench on a base made of chunks of concrete.

Rob and Uri and Harry, some of the Earth Activist Training organizers and former students, joined in and we rolled up balls and discussed anarchist theory.

When we broke for dinner, a young Quebecois woman named Miriam asked me for advice. She'd painted a faerie on the mural at the front of the garden, and wanted it to say something. 'I want a faerie army,' she said, 'for the actions. Like the clown army.'

'Do you realize that, on this land, if you call for a faerie army you will get a real faerie army?' I asked her.

'Yes, that's what I want!'

'A faerie army – let's be a faerie army!' Others started taking up the cry, and suddenly I realized that a faerie army is, of course, exactly what I want to see marching up the road on July 6, bringing alive all the powers of the land and the raging earth to confront the power of the G8. On Miriam's mural, someone had painted, 'Beneath the concrete... the garden!' (A revision of an old Situationist slogan from the sixties: 'Beneath the concrete...the beach!') Miriam added: 'The faerie army rises, Hidden power of earth.'

...

JUNE 23 2005

I spent most of today in Stirling talking to Council members about greywater and compost toilets. We're coming down the home stretch – tomorrow is the final

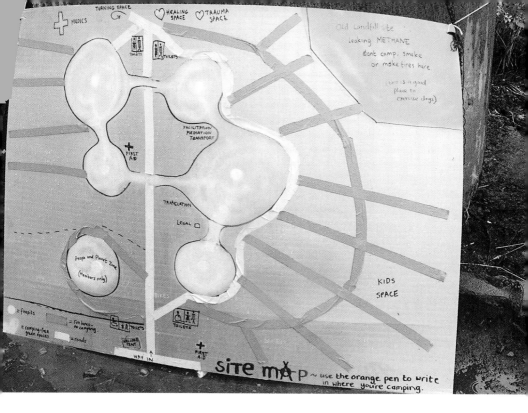

Map labels (as visible):
TURNING SPACE · MEDICS · G · HEALING SPACE · TRAUMA SPACE · TOILETS · TOILETS · Old Landfill Site — leaking METHANE — don't camp, smoke or make fires here. (but is a good place to exercise dogs) · FACILITATION MEDIATION TRANSPORT · FIRST AID · TRANSLATION · LEGAL · People and Planet Zone (Members only) · BIKES · KIDS SPACE · = firepits · = camping-free green spaces · = Fire lanes, no camping. · = roads · TOILETS · TOILETS · WELCOME TENT · WAY IN · FIRST AID · **site map** ~ use the orange pen to write in where you're camping.

licensing meeting, and overall it's looking good. I have to say the Council has been very supportive and are quite genuinely interested in some of the alternatives. But I didn't get much sleep the night before. For some reason, dealing with all the physical realities and the details of these projects throws me into a kind of flashback to high school – staying up late trying to finish a term project – that awful feeling when you don't have enough time to finish and you have to finish anyway, and you can't find the fact or the reference you need and the library is closed. (Okay, I guess that dates me all right!) And while I can stand quite calmly in front of a line of riot cops, I have to fight not to panic about exactly how many tank adaptors we need for greywater tanks – challenging to figure out when we don't know how many kitchens there will be or how many people are coming altogether.

The Council has a composting and recycling officer who had actually read my books and seemed a little surprised at my role in this.

'I can understand how you'd be drawn to the politics and the activism,' he said.

'But how did I become the Queen of Compost Toilets? I wonder that myself,' I admitted. And the answer that came to me is either (1) I am deeply and nobly dedicated to the cause; or (2) I'm not very smart. But seriously, compost toilets are as holy and beautiful as anything else. What could be more magical than the transformation of something hated, feared, and considered a disgusting waste into a valuable resource, a source of fertility? When does it get better than that?

...

JUNE 29 2005

Yes, we have a rural convergence centre for the actions. Finally, after all the setbacks and last-minute disappointments. It's in a bend of the River Forth, with views of Stirling Castle, the Wallace Monument, and the Ochil Hills. We're camping onsite, setting up. I got there Monday, after a weekend of travel so insane I won't even describe it or you will be calling the trauma team to do an intervention. Monday was one of those horrible days when everything falls apart. Sunday night a visitor in some altered state of consciousness tried to swim in the treacherous river and nearly drowned. The Rescue Squad and police had to come out – fortunately, he was saved. Monday morning, the metal tracking for the road didn't come. The big tents, marquees in the language they speak over here, fell through due to storm damage at last weekend's festival in Glastonbury. So did the biodiesel generators, big water tanks, and compost toilet barrels. We lost about a third of the camping area to methane emissions from the former dump. Basically just about everything that could go wrong did. A whole lot of people were standing around eager to do jobs that couldn't be done. Nonetheless, people mostly remained civil to each other, and tried to solve the problems. Emma Magenta, a magical forester woman from the Highlands, came up with the idea of using scrap wood, the half-rounds and shaved-off pieces from milling, to lay a track. Other people with road and truck experience contributed ideas and everyone pitched in to carry wood and lay the track, about two hundred meters of it, lovingly and carefully placed, and eventually covered with chicken wire. It was exhausting carrying heavy batches of wood, but satisfying, and nice to do something that required no thought or analysis. We had a meeting, got organized, and Tuesday was much better. We now have two compost toilets almost built, plus the Scottish Environmental Protection Agency gave permission for pit toilets to one of the local activists, a man named Jim, who has great experience setting up these systems and excellent designs. We have chemical toilets required by the Council as well, giving us a true diversity of toilets. In a day or two, perhaps I can stop obsessing about toilets and start thinking about something else. As important as toilets are, there is more to life, I vaguely recall.

...

JULY 2 2005

Our eco-village is a reality. Those lines that Beth drew on paper weeks ago are now a meandering roadway of boards and chicken wire. Those endless discussions about composting toilets have been translated into small structures complete with curtains and informative signs. The weeks of pondering greywater systems have led to two intense days of building them, one after another after another. I had a moment of realization yesterday – that normally in a two-week permaculture course we might build one demonstration greywater system – in the last few days we've done over a dozen!

...

People are pouring in, tents are going up, some of them amazing structures like the double-hooped, canted I-don't-know-what-to-call-it that looks like a giant covered wagon hoop. Barrios are filling up, kitchens are setting up. Everyone has been working for days, like a happy beehive humming with activity. We've managed to overcome the chaotic moments of panic and a thousand disasters and now it seems that every project attracts the workers that it needs. I have a great crew of people putting in greywater systems and helping with the compost loos. Every morning we check in on the day's work, split into groups and go off and do it. Some skilled carpenters have helped build the structures for the loos, and some less skilled carpenters have gained more skill completing them. We have designed a greywater system to fit the needs and sites of each kitchen. ... We even provided the medics with a biofilter using straw inoculated weeks ago with mushroom mycelium that break down toxins. We've brewed up lactobacillus inoculant to help the compost toilets break down. I think I've found a local community garden – called an allotment over here – to take our kitchen scraps. I've personally tested the composting toilet, and found it very comfortable (although I realized at a crucial moment that it desperately needed screening from the back, which has now been provided).

There have been a thousand frustrating moments and a million irritations, but right now I'm just enjoying the satisfaction of seeing this all come together. There's a hundred times I've asked myself, 'Why do I put up with this?' The answer is the sheer beauty of seeing how this work happens when it happens well: everyone working together for the sheer joy of it, everyone looking for what contribution they can make, what job they can do. For every job, however gruelling or hard – carrying heavy boards or staffing the gate at 3am, there's a willing volunteer. There are people who hold more information and help figure out what to do – Elanor takes on the job of coordinating jobs, for example. If we need workers for something, we tell her. If someone wants to help out, they ask her. But there is no one issuing orders or telling people what to do, no coercion, no bosses. And so, where only a week ago we finally got permission to use the site, today we have a small city in progress that seems to spring magically into being.

...

JULY 3 2005

Yesterday was the big march in Edinburgh. We grabbed a ride on the transport van from the convergence. It's an aspect of this mobilization that someone has thought about every possible support feature – even down to hiring minivans to transport demonstrators. Mark, who has led climbs in the Himalayas, was our driver. 'How long will you be picking people up,' we asked. 'Until everyone gets home,' he replied. I was thinking about how bus driving is one of those unglamorous jobs that aren't high status in ordinary life, and how missing the action in order to drive other people to it is the kind of thing that a hierarchical society reserves for some lesser class – but here it's a job that has plenty of volunteers, because it needs to be done. And how we appreciate it!

Edinburgh was packed with people, and full of the energy of a city when a big demonstration is happening. The organizers of the Make Poverty History march asked everyone to dress in white, and most people did. Not the clowns, the faerie army or the anarchists of course, but the overall impression was a sea of white and those of us who had neglected to pack any white clothes stood out like little dark blots. Lisa, Juniper, Geneva and I cruised through the rally area, then ran directly into a small group of the local Pagans with whom we had a date to have a ritual later. Niall, Louise and Victoria were carrying a banner for the combined Dragon Network – a Pagan activist network in the British Isles – and Scotland Reclaiming. 'Now is the day, Now is the hour, Ours is the Magic, Ours is the Power!' it read.

...

JULY 5 2005

Tonight the camp was all abuzz, people coming in, lots of people going out to avoid the possibility of all being blocked in tomorrow morning. It was full of the excited energy of masses of people preparing for action – once again another tactical nightmare, a few thousand of us up against fifteen thousand police. No one naïvely expects this to be easy – it may not even be possible, but we have to try. So the day is spent in meetings and trainings. The meetings are finally running more smoothly. We have a small collective of direct action trainers and facilitators who have taken on the task of making the meetings happen and finding good facilitators for them. They are also offering trainings and helping affinity groups get together. All over camp, circles of people are meeting, small affinity groups deciding their plans, bigger clumps of people working on action plans. The odds are against us but the energy is sweet.

Yesterday Juniper, Lisa and I went out to Faslane to support the blockade there. There's a longstanding campaign against the nuclear weapons that the British Government keeps in Scotland, the Trident missiles on submarines at the Faslane base. The peace camp at Faslane has been there for something like 25 years, and the annual blockade is something of a ritual, very nonviolent, well-organized and quite peaceful. We went to the south gate, alongside a beautiful sea loch, where a happy crowd was dancing in front of the locked gates. A small group of people were locked down on the road, lying down with their arms in big tubes. Inside, their hands are tied to carabiners clipped to a metal pin, so that the police can't pull them apart. They would have to be carefully cut out of the tubes, taking much time and prolonging the blockade. But no police are trying to evict them: they've closed the base for the day, and people are dancing and celebrating. A group of women dressed in white kimonos, perhaps commemorating Hiroshima and Nagasaki, walk up and stand before the police. Clowns in army fatigues, part of the Clandestine Insurgent Rebel Clown Army, dust the shoes of the cops. We move on to the north gate, where a similar crowd is dancing and drumming.

But we can't stay, because we have responsibilities back at the camp. We're still putting in greywater systems and fixing ones that have gone wrong. The clay soil we're on is clay but no soil and does not drain at all. Every soakaway pit becomes a pond. Juniper, fortunately, is an engineer and hydrologist. Patrick, another engineer, offers to help. We manage to relocate some of the kitchen soakaways to places where they can be piped or drained away, but others need to be redug or enlarged. We've got a digger machine, basically a mini-bulldozer, for a second day, and one of the high points for me was taking a turn on it and learning to work the thing. I can see why every boy in the camp was following the machine and its driver around, begging for a turn. It's a real sense of power. We've got a couple of systems working well; others will become storage ponds and I call a friend to bring down duckweed to float in them! Even the problems have their educational side. I call a small meeting, asking for a representative from each barrio, each neighborhood, to take on responsibility for maintaining the compost toilets and greywater in their area. Because the ditches fill up, people have to watch how much water they use. Because we've built compost toilets, we have to actually think about what happens to our shit, and who is going to deal with it. 'We're spoiled, normally,' a young woman says. 'We don't usually have to think about any of this.' 'It's anarchism in practice,' I tell them. 'Being self-responsible at a very, very basic level.' In that moment, watching the realization dawn on them that water has to go somewhere, and shit has to be dealt with somehow, I feel that all the work and stress of this project has been worth it.

Meanwhile we're getting horrible reports from the Carnival for Full Enjoyment in Edinburgh. Police have attacked demonstrators with horses, people have been injured, there's a riot going on. Finally our friends return and we get the full story. Some of these reports later prove to be rumors, but there have been altercations and injuries, and a few arrests. But the clowns, I'm told by a friend, shifted the energy and helped calm the crowd.

At the end of the day, Catherine and I do a training for an Irish group who are protesting a Shell oil refinery to be built in County Mayo. Five local farmers have refused to sell their land, and been jailed by the Irish government. Some of the contingent has stayed home to support them. The others, who are here, organize a demonstration and possible occupation of the company headquarters. They are a mix of ages – lots of youth but a good sprinkling of the middle-aged. One of

the pleasures of this particular mobilization is that it does span the generations – the average age is probably late twenties and there are many people in their thirties, forties, and even a few of us older than that!

But there's all along been a chaotic, slippery quality to the energy of this project, something that resists plans and timetables and logical organization. Maybe it's the fairies, hanging around the hawthorne tree. By the end of the day, we have plans, multiple plans, plans so complex and overlaid with fallbacks that even if we're infiltrated, I doubt the cops can understand them. We barely do. There are small affinity groups off on secret missions. There are others who want to plan an open blockade, something that everyone can join on to: but they can't quite bring themselves to announce when and where it will be, as the police will undoubtedly shut it down. The mass action sort of devolves into an action of small groups, and someone else plans a truly mass action but still can't bring themselves to announce exactly when and where it is. There are times when I love the camp and everyone in it: it has a sweet energy and is truly a glimpse of a world we could create. There are other moments when I swear I'll never do this or anything like it again. Like late at night when we're all having our pre-action meltdowns. Suddenly all the plans seem completely chaotic – but then, chaos is what we're trying to create, and when chaos is your goal, you've got all the forces of the universe with you. I'm just going to put my trust in some other kind of order, some forces that are working with us, and hope.

JULY 10 2005

... let me back up and describe our day of action. Because I haven't written much fiction in a while, I'm going to write this as a story, about Greywater, 50-ish, grey-haired veteran blockader, and her friends.

WEDNESDAY: THE DAY OF ACTION

Tuesday night most groups headed out from camp, either early to stay elsewhere or in the middle of the night to camp for a while by the highways and be in position to blockade. Greywater's affinity group, however, organized a car caravan to meet at the civilized hour of 6.00am and support the blockades. They were due to meet at an Esso station near Stirling but the scout car who left early called back and said it was full of cops. They got up, dressed, and jumped in the car and went out there anyway. Sure enough, it was full of cops but it takes more than that to daunt their driver Kira, who had been through so many actions that it would take a tank at least to set her back. She drove in, got gas, drove out, and somehow collected most of the caravan. After a slight delay, a caravan of about seven cars headed out to the stretch of road agreed upon for the mass blockades.

When they approached the area, they got a call that there were groups blockading and needing support. The two head cars in the caravan drew up next to each other, taking up both lanes, and slowed down. They drove very, very slowly down the road, slowing all the traffic behind them, and sure enough far ahead they could see a small knot of blockaders on the road. They heard sirens behind them, and held a short conference on the wisdom of blocking the cops, which was interrupted by the cops pulling up beside them on the shoulder of the road, ordering them off, opening doors and reaching through windows and roughly pushing the cars off the road. They did not arrest anyone, however, just pushed the blockade off the road and ordered the cars to move on.

The caravan went on, only to be met by a new blockade up ahead. And so went the day. Every time the police cleared off a small blockade, another appeared somewhere else. The road was blocked, opened up, got blocked again. Larger groups of blockaders were corralled by police and detained, but mostly not arrested. Smaller groups were let go, to walk up and down the roadside and try to regroup. The advantage of the car caravan was mobility – although Greywater's friends had organized many blockades, they themselves actually hate to sit still, and Kira especially likes to move around and see what's happening. They were now getting word that in Edinburgh a hotel had been blockaded and also the M9 motorway, that the early morning walk-out from camp had gotten out and had a battle with the cops, that other roads were blockaded along with the train tracks. What only became apparent after the blockades were over and all the stories were collected was the extent of the action: every route into or around Gleneagles was disrupted with small or large blockades. A critical mass of bicyclists rode very, very slowly from Edinburgh to Gleneagles, delaying all the journalists set to cover the meetings. Independent affinity groups did lockdowns on the smaller roads. None of the blockades lasted terribly long – maybe half an hour at most and some just for a few minutes. 'If you'd blinked, you would have missed our blockade,' one activist said. But as soon as one was cleared, another popped up, and the cumulative effect was to delay and disrupt the beginning of the summit.

After an hour or two, Greywater found herself wanting a change. Hawthorne was riding shotgun and navigating, her daughter Foxglove was crammed into the back seat between Greywater and Lily of the West, the medic from Montana, both big women. Foxglove was getting carsick and Greywater wanted to dance. The police were blocking the road and Kira attempted a U-turn to go back. They stopped her, said the road back was blocked. She argued with them, said we were going to the legal march planned to start at Auchterarder, near Gleneagles, but they kept us halted. Across the road, a busload of marchers was also stopped, and so was the entire line of traffic coming to Gleneagles from the west. A small side road ahead of us led into a village. They all jumped out of the car and Kira parked in the turnaround in the middle of the road. Other demonstrators were hovering nearby when they all noticed a Mercedes full of delegates at the head of the line of cars about to turn into the village. A French affinity group jumped out and sat in the road, blocking them. They gathered around, drumming and dancing and singing. The delegates got out of their car, looking disgusted. The police stood around and radioed for backup. For a good half an hour, they carried on and the carload of delegates eventually gave up and turned around. They tried hard to get the busload of marchers to come out and join us, but they wouldn't. Finally, more police arrived, and the French linked arms, held tight, and made the police drag them away. They used some scary looking pain holds on some of them, but did not arrest them.

One of the qualities of this action is that, while the overall whole was tremendously effective, no one part felt very effective or dramatic in the moment. Some people spent the whole day being followed or corralled by cops. Only later did they realize that, by distracting the cops, they might have opened the road for others to blockade. The action was like an African drum ensemble, where each instrument is playing a simple beat, but the overlays and interactions create a complex and exciting whole. An emergent system, like a beehive or anthill or a flock of birds.

They carried on. There were groups of clowns roaming the side of the road, adding a surreal touch to events. They de-escalate violence by the use of mirth and humor, and they look great, in clown makeup and army fatigues. We never quite found the time or ability to organize a Faery Army as a complement, but we did see a few Faeries appear in the actions, with wings and streamers and bright colors. At one point, the car caravan got blocked by the kids' blockade, which the police had let through the lines only to have them block the bridge to the Gleneagles road. There were kids and clowns and a samba band all drumming and

dancing on the bridge while a big bubble machine spewed rainbow bubbles, and even the cops seemed mostly amused.

Around midday, most of the groups were heading to Gleneagles for the legal march organized by G8Alternatives, which had been called off, on and off again several times that morning. The car caravan joined them, but by the time they were rerouted around Auchterarder, parked and headed toward the march, it was twenty minutes ahead of them. They were cold, wet and tired, so they had lunch. Later they regretted it, as the tail end of the march found a weak spot in the fence around Gleneagles and tore it down, and they would like to have seen that.

Okay, enough of fiction. We got back to camp to find people in a mixed mood – restrained jubilation alternating with attacks of rampant panic. People were very afraid that the camp would be raided by cops in retaliation – for the success of the day, or for the acts of property damage committed during the early morning mass walkout, when a group ran through an industrial estate in Stirling and through the High Street in Bannockburn and smashed up a Pizza Hut and some other businesses. I was personally really saddened to get that news. Whatever the justifications might be for those tactics, doing it right next door to the safe space we had labored so long and hard to create, and antagonizing the community we had worked so hard to establish good relations with, makes as much sense as shitting in your own bed.

In any case, people were afraid of the cops coming in, although many of us thought that highly unlikely. The Scottish police force is simply not like the Italian police in Genoa, who did raid the sleeping quarters of some of the protesters and the Indymedia centre after the 2001 G8 protests and brutally beat demonstrators. But it was clear to me and many others that this situation was politically and tactically very different. Nevertheless, rumors were rampant. They were going to raid. They were going to come in in the middle of the night. They were going to parachute in from helicopters. We eventually agreed on a plan and an approach – that our first response would be to try and de-escalate police violence. We formed a team of de-escalators who took shifts at the gate, and I went to sleep in a friend's van near the front gate to be on call.

The call came at 2.30am, when the police arrived and did exactly what some of the cooler heads expected them to do – they took up a position at the point where our road met the roundabout, and blocked us in. I and about twenty other people spent most of the night de-escalating the drunks and sprinkling of outright psychotics from our own camp who seemed magnetically drawn to the police lines, trying to prevent any incidents that could flare up and spark a larger confrontation. I caught a couple of hours of sleep at the end of the night, and woke up in time for the meeting where we got the news of the London bombings.

...

JULY 11 2005

'Tat' is a word I'd never heard until a few weeks ago, that has dominated my life throughout this action. 'Tat' means 'stuff', material resources, generally of a low but useful quality, and often acquired from 'skips', which at home we call 'dumpsters', by a process known as 'skipping' (tr. 'dumpster diving') or sometimes by 'blagging', which means talking people into or out of something. Hopefully not by 'nicking', that is, stealing, although 'getting nicked' also means 'getting arrested.' We spent weeks tatting, or acquiring tat, in order to create the eco-village – from old bathtubs to plumbing parts to wood, and now we are 'tatting down', or taking the eco-village apart. It's sad to see it go, sad to see all the social fabric deconstruct itself, the coaches turn back into pumpkins. Before it goes away entirely, I want to write something about the last few days.

Thursday was a muted day. The bombings in London and the fact that we were blocked in by lines of riot cops made it impossible to mount any major actions. We focused on cleaning up the camp and on prisoner support. By Friday, the last day of the G8 meetings, the police presence was lessened and many people went off to Glasgow to take over a bridge and protest the extension of the M74 motorway through a low-income neighborhood, where earlier in the month we had built the Cre8 Summat Community Garden. Others went to petrol stations and did climate change actions, the clowns bringing swimming pools and setting up tropical beaches.

In camp, we had an emergency meeting to deal with the toilet crisis. Our diversity of toilets included nine composting toilets built around wheelie bins (wheeled garbage cans) which would be sealed and stored for two years, and the resulting compost then used on trees and ornamentals. It also included many trench toilets dug along the edges of the field, which would simply be filled in and left to compost in peace. And it was supposed to include forty porta-loos (porta-potties, honey huts, chemical toilets), required by the Council for the licence and which we were counting on for capacity. Due to many circumstances beyond anyone's control, we never had more than fifteen, and for days the company had been unable to come in and clean them. First this was due to the police lines, but by Friday, a truck had managed to come through, only to be mounted by an exuberant and possibly drunk crowd who danced on top of it and reputedly threatened the driver. When his boss phoned for help, someone on the phone allegedly swore at him, and now the company was refusing to come back.

The incident illustrated some of the wild contradictions in the camp. While the vast majority of people were there to mount and support actions against the G8, there was a small but significant group of the festival/party crowd, who drank heavily, ingested, I'm sure, other consciousness-altering substances, and caused an immense amount of trouble to the rest of us. Overall Scottish and British culture is much more alcohol-focused than us US puritans are used to, at least in action situations, and even the most serious activists like their beer and some loud disco music to unwind with at night. There were multiple sound systems in camp, and the thundering bass vied with the thrum of helicopters to disturb any possibility of sleeping.

By setting up an encampment, where we all had to live together for a week, we were constantly faced with the real life, practical implications of our politics. Does anarchism simply mean that no one can ever tell me what to do, whatever state of consciousness I'm in or however I'm affecting the good of the whole? How do we respect the individual freedom of those who are in no state to make rational decisions or listen to the needs of others, and who gets to decide? And at what point does the good of the whole override the absolute freedom of the individual? It's one thing to consider these issues in the abstract, another to spend half an hour at 2.30am trying to get a drunk to move back from the police lines.

And there were also many moments of wondrous beauty. At night, before the disco music started, groups would gather in the eddies of the meandering path through camp and play African drums or Scottish pipes. The Irish barrio, each night, would be gathered around the campfire, playing fiddle, singing songs, or listening to each others' poetry as their ancestors have done for centuries. One night the Infernal Noise Brigade, a radical marching band from Seattle, led us all in a procession around camp, joined by a samba band and challenged by the disco bloc. Another night, a midnight candlelit vigil walked from the gate to the police lines, carrying with it a palpable blanket of silence, and placed its candles at the feet of the riot cops. We had rituals around the faerie hawthorne tree at the edge of camp, and deep conversations around the kitchens and campfires. We had meetings where people listened to each other and let their opinions change, where we brought our best collective thinking to a problem and went away heartened by the experience.

Saturday night, we were taking apart our improvised road, made of softboard laid over sticks that were milling waste from a local timber company. There was no practical way to re-use or recycle the sticks, so we pulled the boards off, piled up the sticks into pyramids, and burned them. One by one, bonfires came alight: five, eight, thirteen, seventeen, dancing beacons of flame under a new moon. A woman told me that this was one of the fields where William Wallace, Scotland's great hero, had called people to fight against the English invaders by lighting beacons in the field. We were all feeling sad at the ending of the camp, but the fires cheered our hearts and seemed to burn away any stuck or negative energies. We stood in the centre, playing music, singing, and drumming, with an abundance of fire all around us, beacons calling us all to the ongoing fights for freedom. The faeries were very pleased. And now the camp is gone, the field is bare again, the experiment is done. But because it existed for a short time, in some realm of being it exists for all time, complete with all its problems and promise, a seed of what is possible.

This is an edited version of Starhawk's G8 2005 Journals. The unabridged diaries are available at http://starhawk.org/activism/activism-writings/G8_2005_journals.html
NB. These diaries may be freely posted, forwarded and reprinted, but only for non-commercial purposes. All other rights are reserved.

17

WHEN THE KIDS ARE UNITED, THEY WILL NEVER BE DEFEATED!

Kate Evans

It's a cliché because it's true: your life changes when you have kids. For me, I realised something had changed when I was four months pregnant and I found myself being dragged under a police van on May Day in Trafalgar Square. Up until that point, as an activist, I had made a point of interposing my body into confrontational situations. Now I had something else to protect, a new little life. I was sure that I wanted kids, and could make a case for motherhood as a revolutionary activity – raising the next generation that will be able to sort this mess out. But now I didn't know where I stood as an activist. Where was my place in the direct action movement? Was I just meant to stay home and wash nappies?

Two years on, we travelled to Scotland completely unsure of whether the G8 protests would be a safe environment in which the needs of our child could be met, but determined that the only way to make that happen was to go there and make it happen. It's their future – another cliché, but still true.

My child is still breastfed, so there was no way that I could be arrested. Fortunately, at the camp in Stirling there were a lot of other people in the same position. The kids were having a whale of a time, going mad with paint and making banners or conducting water bomb wars. The adults got together for a lastminute.com discussion of what we were up for. We were nervous. Was this sensible? But then, is anything sensible in this crazy world?

It transpired, amid the nosewiping and breastfeeding and nappysniffing, that we wanted to leave Stirling and travel to the G8 on the Wednesday to demonstrate. That we would travel in vehicles, in convoy, and be able to leave any flashpoints *en masse*. That we would take joint responsibility for any lost or distressed children. That we would be completely open with the media and the police about our aims. That we would all carry food and water. That we would have a good time.

We decided all this on Tuesday July 5 (very lastminute.com). On the Wednesday morning we achieved the logistical near-impossibility of getting everyone into vehicles to leave site by 11am. Someone handed out gold rosettes to identify the parents and their vehicles. A badge of parenthood! We had decided that we were going to join the legal march at Auchterarder, but now the police were saying that the march had been cancelled, and were advising everyone to stay away from the area. We were also expecting the main roads into Gleneagles to be blockaded, so we were unsure of where we would end up. We had very little experience of driving in convoy, the police attempted to split the convoy using low-loader lorries, and we thought we were going to run out of mobile phone signal. This had the potential for utter mayhem.

Road blocks were in place. We proceeded haphazardly, following a double-decker bus with the Make Poverty History brand on the side. We ended up going down some back roads, approaching Gleneagles from the south. The police refused to allow us to proceed to Auchterarder. More fool them. We were now, completely accidentally, at a very strategically important point: a bridge over the motorway where delegates' cars were entering and leaving the Gleneagles site. We unleashed the children from their car seats!

Firstly, most importantly, food. Let's have a picnic. On the riot policemen's shoes. We laid out some blankets in the drizzle immediately in front of the police lines. The kids had fruit and nuts and hummus and oat cakes. The policemen had kittens! I was chatting to one of the boiler-suited mob, he had a little nine-month-old boy. I looked at him and commented, 'They don't train you for this, do they?' They knew and we knew that there was no way that they could advance their line through the toddlers. Could we move? Ooh no, not till we'd finished our picnic. Hungry children are angry children we pointed out. If they insisted we move, then I'm sorry, but they'd have to take responsibility for the children.

The police now informed us through a loudhailer that, 'You can join the march at Auchterarder.' What? They had LIED! They had said there was no march taking place in Auchterarder. What a terrible example to set in front of the kids! We were perfectly happy here in any case: we had a little samba band, there was some clowning around, a couple of small sound systems turned up. A couple of delegates' cars turned around and drove away.

After a while, we did make a not-particularly-coherent decision to leave and join the end of the Auchterarder march. If we could stay on the bridge late into the evening we would restrict the movements of the delegates. But we had

kids, and they would be soggy and whingy by evening time. There were hot chips in Auchterarder. Time to go.

The atmosphere in Auchterarder was much more relaxed. There seemed very little chance of an unforeseen baton charge by riot police, and the brat bloc informally disbanded. Our family ended up in the church hall, drinking coffee and eating scones. Aagh! All that adrenaline! All that worry! All that wondering about whether we were using our children, unnecessarily exposing them to risk! And we end up at a coffee morning, having afternoon tea. So much for revolutionary parenthood. But we, and our kids, did have a good time.

18

THE 'BRAT BLOC' AND THE MAKING OF ANOTHER DIMENSION

Massimo De Angelis and Dagmar Diesner

I

Another dimension! The process of social constitution of a different reality can only be the creation, the production, of another dimension of living, of another mode of doing and relating, valuing and judging. Children are often said to be living in another dimension. In our experience as parents of a 20 month old child, one of the many things that has struck us is Leonardo's praxis of time. He seems to be living in 'phase time' all the time, his attention being enthusiastically taken by new objects which he points at, by new directions to walk the street's walk. This of course means that we must continuously invent new ways to keep him happy while we take him on our daily trivial pursuits rooted in linear time (going to the shops, washing dishes, etc.) and circular time (the alternating of the rhythms of daily life, going to bed, eating and so on). Phase time is the time of emergence of new dimensions and is as much a part of life as linear and circular time. When we scale up this little domestic vignette to the problems of the making of a new world, what becomes clear is that none of these dimensions of time is specifically the time of revolution, the time of new modes of social co-production. Revolution is a mode of their articulation, a re-articulation of phase, linear and circular time.

II

During the anti-G8 actions in Gleneagles, the Stirling camp was a temporary autonomous zone in which these three dimensions of time were re-articulated. The participants were the actors of this re-articulation, and participants were also parents and their children.

As parents, the decision to go to the anti-G8 demonstration and, especially, to stay at the eco-village surrounded by police and by media hungry for pictures of 'violence', was not easy to make. We have both been involved in demonstrations and actions before, although we've luckily escaped, so far, the worst of police brutality as at Genoa in 2001. Other comrades were not so fortunate. We both had stories to tell. But for the first time in our lives we were confronted with the non-theoretical problematic of 'safety' concerning those little creatures who live in phase time all the time, and for whom every experience is formative, every event potentially traumatic or enriching. This is, of course, a risk that many children, their parents, friends and relatives around the world face on a daily basis – the brutality and stupidity unleashed against the needs and desires of a social body that does not regard global markets, financial discipline and 'competitiveness' as gods. We heard one journalist asking a mother whether she was behaving irresponsibly by taking her child to the demonstration. What a photo opportunity that could be – a young mother with two children splashed on the front page of a tabloid next to a picture of a cop beating a black-clad activist in a balaclava. We could imagine the headline – 'Shame!' – and the argument – 'Doesn't she know that being anti-G8 means trouble?' Apart from the fact that the journalist did not understand the function of the G8 and the irresponsible effect it has on the lives of millions of children around the world (you know – snap your fingers, a child has just died of preventable disease, snap your fingers again... and so on), from our perspective as parents with children the Stirling camp offered two other responses to that question. First, it was a place of peace. Second, it was a place from which to launch a peaceful war.

That it was a place of peace was obvious to us as soon as we arrived late in the afternoon. We had spent the previous two nights at the 'prison camp' in Edinburgh, a large green area next to the Jack Kane community centre which was surrounded for the occasion by a two metre high fence. All the way along the perimeter, security guards specially contracted in from Wales were monitoring us 24 hours a day. They must have been briefed to behave very politely towards the colourful activists, thus giving the camp a surreal atmosphere – the vibes of what emerges out of social engineering attempts. By contrast, in Stirling we were in a fully autonomous zone, with the corresponding chaotic order, making it a genuine laboratory of social and relational experimentation. We parked our small van next to a large sandpit and put out our awning so that 'Uncle Olivier' who was travelling with us could stretch out his long legs and sleep.

The sandpit was a bonus. Leonardo began to run up and down, interacting with other children, picking up our neighbour's things and having fun. One of the things that parents gain in getting involved in these events is that the

communal dimension here is not a fantasy or an ideology: it affects the body. You tend to relax your control over the child, giving it up, since you know that around you other eyes and other ears are ready to knit the dangers implicit in phase time with the 'responsibility' of linear time, and act if necessary. It is as if as individuals you amplify your powers and diminish your worries by simple virtue of being closer to others, others who are there not simply as bodies having things to do and directions to follow (as when you are close to others in a Tube carriage), but others with whom you are also together in circular time, the time of norms creation. The eco-village, in other words, was a relational field not only at the 'structural level' (organised into neighbourhoods within which to take decisions and coordinate work ranging from garbage collection to direct actions) but also in terms of a widespread communicational tension, a widespread easiness in talking and relating that overcame fixed images we have of 'the other'. Just a few minutes after we arrived, for example, two young people approached the sandpit and started to throw long darts to see how far they could get. They were the spitting image of what you see on the front page of the *Sun* or *News of the World*, hoods up over their heads and a swaggering walk that says 'don't mess with me'. Massimo carefully grabbed Leonardo's hand, since they were throwing stuff in our direction. They noticed Leonardo, and politely asked whether it was OK to carry on or whether they should perhaps throw in the other direction. A middle-aged intellectual meets the image of a council estate 'yob' (as portrayed by the *Sun* and the

Prime Minister's office) and the funny thing is that they can communicate: they share a common discourse, the safety of children!

III

In mainstream financial and economic disciplines, 'risk assessment' is something that entrepreneurs and business people do all the time. When they talk about 'risk', they generally talk about the probability of losing assets or money, following an investment decision by an individual agent. In our case, 'risk assessment' was not something we could do before taking the decision to join the camp and the actions. Because once you are part of an autonomous zone, together with others you contribute to creating a context in which that risk is not only evaluated from a multiplicity of perspectives and needs, but also constructed. You become an actor together with others with whom you socially constitute 'risk'.

The affinity group with parents and children emerged out the need to be a united front against possible police brutality. Many of the participants (mostly women and mothers) had experiences from previous counter-summits and demonstrations which were directly aimed against economic, military and global power, and hence knew to what extent our governments use police forces to repress social movements and keep popular protest away from the 'red zones' surrounding their meetings. Since many of us have been engaged for many years in the movement, becoming a parent hasn't changed the way we regard the G8 and the institutions of global capitalism. Above all, as a parent the anger intensifies, acquires more concrete depth and mixes with a deeper sense of sorrow as you more readily empathise with the pain of the victims of structural adjustments and understand the extent to which the struggles of our sisters and brothers in other parts of the world for food, water, health and education also acquires the value of preserving the bodies, spirit, dignity and future of children. No – becoming a parent does not mean becoming 'petty-bourgeois', withdrawing into the overwhelming preoccupations of 'private life' and allowing these self-appointed leaders of the world to decide who can survive and who cannot. We are on the streets with our children, to reclaim our powers, so our children are not raised in isolation or as puppets of the current machine, but grow aware of the systems that articulate our lives and develop their relational powers to build communities with others, however they want to use these powers in their lives.

Our determination to be there meant that the fear of police brutality was something that we had to confront, not escape. Many other parents shared this attitude, and so, along with our children, we put together what was initially called the 'babies bloc'. That name was then turned down because the older children could not identify with the young ones. So the 'children's bloc' was born – although we prefer to call it the 'brat bloc'.

At least fifty families were at the first meeting, called in the middle of the camp by word of mouth, and the issue of 'safety' and how to participate in the protest and direct action activities became top priority in our agenda. The first important decision was made through easily achieved consensus. While most other affinity groups were planning to leave the camp in the middle of the night or in the early hours of the morning to avoid being surrounded by the police, we were never in any doubt: we would only leave *after* breakfast! Then there was a series of discussions, decisions, and sound no-nonsense problematisations of the issues, tasks, dangers and opportunities. When children and the problematic of reproduction are centre stage, all nonsense of political talk vaporises and decisions become immediately a matter of common sense.

One of the central questions was, of course, how to deal with police brutality in case another Genoa scenario evolved, either in the streets or if the camp was raided. In both cases we hoped the police would not touch us if we visibly stood our ground as a group. In the event of a raid on the eco-village, we would gather in an open area in the middle of the camp, making our children clearly visible to the police. Since rumours and speculations of such a raid were mounting, we made sure that both the media and the police knew that there were children in the camp, and that they knew our actions and intentions. It's funny how in these cases you rely on what is common between you and the police: they have children too, don't they? They know what it means, don't they? There are even policewomen there, aren't there? We remember having read in some tabloid that demonstrators were opportunistically using children as shields. Far from the truth. When mothers and fathers bring their children on to the streets, it is not to use them as a shield. It is to hold individual members of the police to account for their values: we are forcing them to acknowledge or reject that children's safety is a common issue between the two camps.

The following morning, we left in a convoy and drove to the motorway to support the people who were blocking the roads to Gleneagles. We left after breakfast quite excited, some of us with costumes and music. Our van was painted with a 'Make *Charity* History' sign, and some clowns from the Clown Army cheered Uncle Olivier, Uncle David and Leonardo. A few policemen attempted to prevent us from leaving the camp, but this was soon solved and we finally drove through in a festive mood.

What we hadn't foreseen, however, was that when travelling in a convoy you always have to keep an eye on the vehicle behind you and make sure you are being followed. Somehow, the convoy got a bit split up, with some cars driving too fast, and others allowing the convoy to fall apart at roundabouts. Once we passed the slip-road for the motorway where we wanted to go, something went seriously wrong because the police were blocking the entrance. Fortunately, we ended up in a traffic jam in Stirling where we were able to re-group and make our way back to where we wanted to go in the first place following side roads.

When we got closer to Gleneagles, signs of actions were in sight, especially when we saw the 'hooligan faces' of the 'black bloc' of the day (that is, the riot police) chasing the smiley faces of the 'colourful bloc' (that is, the Rebel Clown Army). It was quite hilarious. One of the many bridges leading to Gleneagles was our demonstration point, and some people stopped there. Others, including us, drifted around the area, following 'road diversion' signs. In the end, we all ended at the demo, via different routes. From the tales we gathered back at the camp at the end of the day, some of the kids and grown-ups ended up in a tea house annexed to a church, some ended up having a picnic two metres away from the riot police, while others invaded the commons next to the red zone. Overall, it had been a fine day, and we all returned to the camp safely and ready for a good night's sleep.

IV

When our friends read this account, they said, 'Hey, that is all fine and great, but we think it maybe needs a concluding paragraph or two, in which you relate your story of the action(s) back to the question of the construction of new-world(s) and the three notions of time.' So, we sat down and thought. Should we end this with a moral of the story which, if followed in its linearity, would make the readers live happily ever after in their revolutionary certainties? Better not. Or should we make our activist readers hesitant, and remind them that the circular time of children's reproduction teaches us that 'struggle' is not only about wearing big boots and shouting big words, but is also about eating breakfast safely and resting our bodies in an environment we have helped to construct? Or perhaps we should end with an emphasis on phase time, and remind ourselves that as we entered the different time dimension in the camp, so upon our return to London, we travelled back to an old dimension of time.

But when we travelled back, the delirium hit us full blast. Indeed, what a return that was! Bombs on buses and the Tube, dead people on the streets and subways of London, scared bus drivers and commuters, trains into London stopped and roads closed... no, this was not the type of phase time we found at the eco-village. Quite the opposite. Here it is then, our friends should be happy now, the story of our actions is related to the question of the construction of a new world in a very simple way: the phase time of the Stirling camp was predicated on life exchanges, while the phase time brought by the bombs in London were part of death exchanges. It seems to us that from the perspective of children's safety they are very different, are they not?

19

GLENEAGLES, ACTIVISM AND ORDINARY REBELLIOUSNESS

Ben Trott

We are quite ordinary women and men, children and old people, that is, rebellious, non-conformist, uncomfortable, dreamers.

Subcomandante Insurgent Marcos[1]

We would live according to the ideas of others; we would live an imaginary life, and to this end we cultivate appearances. Yet in striving to beautify and preserve this imaginary being we neglect everything authentic.

Pascal[2]

On June 18 1999 ('J18'), over 10,000 people took to the streets in the City of London, storming the London International Financial Futures Exchange (Liffe). This 'Carnival Against Capital' was just one of many international actions held in the world's financial centres, timed to coincide with the opening day of that year's G8 summit in Cologne, Germany. Shortly after the day of action, an excellent article entitled 'Give up Activism' appeared in *Reflections on J18*, a collection of texts which attempted to assess the current strengths and weaknesses of the movement in the light of the events which had just unfolded, and to suggest ways in which it could move forward.[3] 'Give up Activism' was well received: it was widely discussed within the movement in the UK, reprinted in several other publications and has been translated into at least four other languages.[4] But despite this favourable reception, the article's impact, in terms of its stated intent – to provoke amongst activists a critical reflection on their mode of behaviour – has been negligible. To a great extent, the Dissent! mobilisation to Gleneagles was a case in point of this.

To briefly summarise, 'Give up Activism' argued, six years ago, that despite all good intentions, those who identify themselves as political activists frequently adopt a mentality which hinders the kind of radical social change of which we so often talk. Specifically, in the absence of an overt, generalised struggle, the activist identifies herself as a specialist in social change.

> To think of yourself as being an activist means to think of yourself as being somehow privileged or more advanced than others in your appreciation of the need for social change, in the knowledge of how to achieve it and as leading or being in the forefront of practical struggle to achieve this change.[5]

As with all expert roles, activism has its basis in the division of labour, the fundamental basis of class society. So just as the division of labour ensures that medicine and education becomes the sole domain of 'specialists' (doctors and teachers, for example) who jealously guard and mystify the skills they have, rather than common knowledge and tools possessed by us all, the activist becomes the 'expert' in bringing about social change.

> A division of labour implies that one person takes on a role on behalf of many others who relinquish this responsibility... The activist, being an expert in social change, assumes that other people aren't doing anything to change their lives and so feels a duty or a responsibility to do it on their behalf. Activists think they are compensating for the lack of activity by others. Defining ourselves as activists means defining our actions as the ones which will bring about social change, thus disregarding the activity of thousands upon thousands of other non-activists. Activism is based on this misconception that it is only activists who do social change – whereas of course class struggle is happening all the time.[6]

That struggle is taking place all around us continues to this day to be largely overlooked by many of those who identify themselves as political activists. More often than not, struggle is understood as 'activism' and activism alone.

Whilst the Zapatistas have been an enormous inspiration to many activists in the UK and elsewhere (the influence of their rhetoric, for example, is clearly identifiable in much of the propaganda produced in the run-up to the Gleneagles summit), their argument that they are ordinary *exactly because they are rebels* has been almost entirely ignored. Class struggle is not some kind of specialist activity performed by 'revolutionaries' alone, it is an antagonistic relation, in which all of us involved in the act of producing (whether we are waged labourers or not) resist capital's efforts to enclose an ever increasing proportion of social life. We do not only struggle in those moments during which we behave like activists – blockading the road to a summit or pulling up genetically modified crops, for example – but whenever we attempt to resist capital's effort to appropriate more and more of our daily activity. We struggle whenever we phone in sick; when-

ever we resist pressure to work harder, faster and longer; whenever we surf the internet instead of inputting data. And when we bunk the train or steal stationery from work or paint graffiti or tags on walls, again we are refusing capital's logic and its rule. This too is struggle. It is only when we begin to conceive of struggle in this broader sense that we can begin to make connections between our own resistance (as 'activists' or otherwise) with that of others.

'Give up Activism' made a similar argument. It explained that the day of action on June 18, which brought together environmentalists, peace campaigners, people who had been involved in the anarchist movement in the 1980s, animal rights activists and so on, made much of the importance of 'making connections'. The problem was, however, that these connections were almost entirely connections between 'activists'. The same, it must be said, was the case with the Gleneagles mobilisation. Again, important links were certainly made throughout the mobilisation and many 'activist' groups and individuals throughout the UK and beyond are now far more interconnected than they were two years ago. That such connections have been achieved was no small feat and should not be dismissed. As 'Give up Activism' argued, this sort of link-making is 'an essential prerequisite for further action.' It must, however, be recognised for the extremely limited form of making links that it is.

> It is not enough to merely seek to link together all the activists in the world, neither is it enough to seek to transform more people into activists. Contrary to what some

people think, we will not be any closer to revolution if lots and lots of people become activists... To work to escalate the struggle it will be necessary to break with the role of activists to whatever extent it is possible.[7]

The author of 'Give up Activism' concluded by remarking that he had no clearer insight than anyone else into the means by which a way of operating, adequate to putting our radical ideas into action, could be achieved. Neither, of course, does the author of this article. There are no hard and fast answers to the problems with which we are confronted today.

There were, however, a number of opportunities which presented themselves, both in the run-up to and during the G8 summit, which we, as a movement, could have made far more of than we did. First and foremost, we squandered many an opportunity to present a radical, anti-capitalist critique of the summit which could have made the mobilisation relevant to the lives of those with the greatest possibility of getting involved – the inhabitants of the region around Gleneagles specifically, and the population of the UK more generally. Dissent!'s propaganda and the image it projected through engagements with the mainstream media – not to mention the majority of the actions it carried out – failed to 'make the links' between the G8 and the way in which we experience our lives on a daily basis here in the UK.[8] Whilst we often made reference to the means by which the neoliberal policies imposed by the G8 on 'developing' economies have had devastating social and ecological consequences, little or no reference was made by Dissent! to the impact which twenty-odd years of neoliberal reform has had in the UK domestically, or throughout 'developed' countries more generally. I'm not implying for a moment that the expression of international solidarity, or a commitment to defending the Earth's ecosystems, should not remain key focuses for our movement. However, there are very real limits to the potential of any movement which does not organise, to a large extent, around the immediate needs and desires of those directly involved within it.

This is not to suggest, as has so often been argued following events such as the G8 summit, that we need to turn away from 'mass' mobilisations and towards localised struggles, organising in our workplaces and neighbourhoods. Of course, organising on a local level – around issues which can appear mundane in the face of spectacular, international mobilisations – has always been worthwhile. In this sense, discussions of the importance of 'local' relative to 'global' issues, events and struggles have always been premised upon a false dichotomy. As most of us who have experienced them are well aware, 'moments of excess', in which inspiring, mass, collective moments of rebellion (the 1990 poll tax riots, the events of Seattle in 1999 and so on) appear to open up spaces in which anything – briefly – appears possible, provide us with a glimpse of another possible world: a world in which we begin to relate to one another, and indeed to ourselves, in a very different way.[9] Such events often provide us with the energy and the conviction to continue struggling on a more day-to-day basis with a renewed sense of possibility.

In other words, the challenge with which we are presented is not one of deciding between the local or the global, but of developing a way in which we can organise around those issues relevant to our own lives, and the lives of those around us, whilst *at the same time* constructing global structures into which a multitude of singular struggles can be woven into one which never loses its multiplicity.

GLOCALISE RESISTANCE[10]

As I have already explained, throughout the Dissent! mobilisation, much was made of the ills of the neoliberal agenda being pursued by the G8. Nobody involved with Dissent! was under any illusion that the policies being forwarded by the Blair/Brown camp at Gleneagles (with the tacit support of Geldof and co.) were anything other than a cynical attempt to impose upon so-called 'developing' economies, under the guise of poverty alleviation, the very same policies against which the 'anti-capitalist' and 'global justice' movements had brought tens of thousands onto the streets of Seattle, Prague and Genoa.[11] What Dissent!, along with much of the rest of the movement in the UK, not to mention the other mobilisations against the G8, failed to do, however, was to 'render political' (i.e. to problematise, call into question, or suggest an alternative to) the means by which we experience work and life under neoliberalism here in the UK.

The period which immediately preceded the formation of the Group of Seven (G7) in 1976 was characterised by a deep economic crisis and a generalised upsurge in struggle. It was a period in which, to cite but a few examples, united action had been taken by students and workers in Paris in May 1968; the Italian 'Hot Autumn' of 1969 had overflowed into the decade-long movement known as *autonomia*; uprisings had erupted in a number of US cities such as Newark, Detroit and Los Angeles; and resistance to US military intervention in Vietnam had grown alongside a whole number of anti-imperialist and anti-colonial movements worldwide. In Britain, industrial action had brought about the collapse of two governments, and seen the 'three-day week' and the 'winter of discontent', eventually creating a fiscal crisis forcing the government to go cap-in-hand to the IMF. The G7 (which later, as we know, became the G8), was to play a key role in the period of intense political and economic restructuring which followed.

This process of restructuring involved a number of significant transformations within both the mode of production and of political and economic regulation. These developments were to have serious implications in terms of: (i) the recomposition of the working class which they brought about; (ii) the means by which they transformed working practices (and, in fact, the nature of social life itself); and (iii) the possibilities which existed for working class (self-)organisation and anti-capitalist practice. The shift has generally been described as one from 'Fordism' to 'post-Fordism'.

The so-called 'Fordist' era is generally understood as referring to the period

of capitalist development, spanning from the 1930s to the 1970s, in which workers tended to be organised within large industrial processes, producing standardised commodities for mass markets. The name derives from Henry Ford (of Ford Motors), one of the principal proponents of this form of social organisation. Within the Fordist era, jobs were reasonably secure and wage levels relatively high – the idea was that workers should also provide the market for the commodities that they produced.

Fordism is associated with the 'Taylorist' organisation of workers within the productive process, which generally involved workers being required to perform repetitive, monotonous tasks. It was based on the notion that the deskilling of workers would not only lead to an increase in productivity (the more frequently one is required to repeat a simple task, the quicker one is able to do it, or so the theory went) but that it would also remove from workers the bargaining power which had assured their collective power in previous eras (strike action, or the threat thereof, is far more effective when carried out by workers who can not be easily replaced).

However, the bringing together of large numbers of workers within one plant or factory, upon which Fordist production processes tended to be premised, provided favourable conditions in which workers were able to organise amongst themselves, either within trade unions or autonomously. Communication amongst workers, many of whom spent upwards of eight hours a day, five days a week, standing next to each other on an assembly line, was relatively easy, and the common condition within which workers found themselves was far more obvious than it is today. A widespread refusal of work (expressed in terms of strike action, absenteeism, sabotage and so on) became common to an extent which was unimaginable in previous eras in which skilled 'professional workers' were able, to a far greater degree, to take pride in the work that they performed.[12] By the mid- to late-1970s, Fordism/Taylorism had reached its limits. Capital needed a new strategy.

The tendency away from Fordist/Taylorist production processes and towards 'post-Fordist' (smaller scale, more decentralised, networked and flexible) forms of production which followed had a dual purpose. It allowed for capital to respond far more readily to fluctuations in demand and the changing market conditions, whilst simultaneously removing, or at least reducing, the need for large numbers of workers to be gathered in one place, and hence decreasing their ability to share grievances, develop a sense of collective identity and, ultimately, organise themselves into a force able to act in their own class interest.

It was during the time that this shift was taking place that a neoliberal politics began to emerge within a number of dominant economies, most notably the US and UK. The welfare state began to come under attack, legislative restrictions began to be placed upon the power of trade unions (in the UK, for example, so-called 'secondary picketing' became illegal), and state-run industries were privatised. It was only after Britain and the US had gone some way along this process of restructuring that the Washington Consensus,[13] of which Reagan and Thatcher were the principal proponents, began to usher in a period of more global restructuring.

The result of all this has been a radical transformation, over the past twenty years or so, of the way in which we work here in the UK.[14] This has largely corresponded, albeit to varying degrees, to similar developments in most other European countries, as well as North America. Across the board, jobs have tended to become increasingly *mobile* (we now move between jobs far more quickly than in the past), *flexible* (the work that we do requires us to perform a much wider range of tasks than in the Fordist era), and *precarious* (jobs are becoming increasingly 'casualised' with employment contracts becoming rare and stable, long-term employment increasingly uncommon). Furthermore, as capital increasingly attempts to capture the 'general intellect' (the combined intellectual and creative capacities) of society, the distinction between work and life itself is becoming blurred.

By this I mean that, today, every aspect of social life is tending to be rendered directly productive of capital. To cite but one example of this, in her book *No Logo*, Naomi Klein describes the 'cool hunters' commissioned by big name brands (Levi's, Absolut Vodka, Reebok and so on) to search out pockets of cutting-edge lifestyle and street trends which are then captured, transformed into marketable commodities and sold back to the youth cultures from which they were first appropriated.[15] The end effect of capital's effort towards capturing ever more of our daily activity – both within and beyond the realm of waged labour – has been the opening up of the whole of society as a potential site of struggle.

The mobilisation against the G8 summit, however, failed to draw attention, in any meaningful way, to the consequences of this neoliberal restructuring of the domestic political economies of most (if not all) of the G8 member states over the past few decades. Likewise, there was a similar failure to highlight existing resistance to the increasingly common (insecure/precarious) condition in which we find ourselves today, or to begin developing and experimenting with new collective forms of struggle adequate to our current post-Fordist reality.

To make the same argument another way, the neoliberal policies against which millions have revolted in the subordinated regions of the globe, mirror policies developed, and still being developed, here in the UK and other 'advanced capitalist' economies.[16] But the current global 'movement of movements', particularly in the UK and particularly in terms of the autonomous area of the movement to which Dissent! belongs, has largely failed to recognise and draw attention to the common basis of our mutual struggles. As such, the potential so often discussed as the global movement of today began to emerge – of creating a global network of resistance in which the various nodes developed and articulated forms of resistance relevant to the way in which they experienced their own lives under capitalism – is beginning to fade away. Counter-summits, in the dominant areas of the globe, are increasingly tending towards becoming a movement which understands itself as acting (primarily) on behalf of, or at least in solidarity with, an oppressed 'other'. Amongst other things, this has been a process in which the activist identity, mentality and mode of operation problematised at the beginning of this article has gradually been reinforced.

PREGUNTANDO CAMINAMOS – WALKING, WE ASK QUESTIONS

The purpose of this article, of course, is not simply to criticise the mobilisation against this year's G8 summit, within which the author of this article was himself involved, but to contribute to a discussion about the potential future(s) of the movement(s) on the basis of a critical reflection on our immediate past. If we accept that political 'activists' are not the only ones who resist the rule of capital and who seek to restore a sense of dignity to their own existence and that of others; and if we accept that the mobilisation against this year's G8 summit largely failed to connect the global 'movement against neoliberalism' to 'ordinary' people's daily lives, then what does this mean in practical terms? What is to be done?

The answer, of course, is that we do not exactly know. All that is certain is uncertainty. Moving forward, in other words, will require a process of experimentation. The phrase *preguntando caminamos* (walking, we ask questions) has been used by the Zapatistas to describe a new way of thinking about revolution. Whereas traditionally, Marxist-Leninists (and indeed, some anarchists) have presented a preconceived idea of revolution (normally, in the case of the Marxist-Leninists, defined in terms of the seizure of state power) as an *answer*, the Zapatistas have argued that revolution, in fact, should rather be understood as a *question* – one which can only be worked out collectively, through a process of struggle. In this sense, then, we need to look at the past and present action of ourselves, of those around us, and of those much further afield. We need to examine and study the current conditions in which we find ourselves today, and the tendencies and trends which hint towards the way in which things seem to be developing. And on the basis of this, we need to start working out, through constant, open and ongoing dialogue, a way of resisting which is adequate to today's reality. A mode of resistance which enables us to break down, rather than reinforce, the distinction between 'activist' and 'non-activist' so entrenched in both our own self-image and the way in which we are perceived by others.

One of the places from which we could, perhaps, attempt to draw inspiration is Italy and the attempt which has been made, over the last four years or so, to develop in the notion of the 'precariat' a social base for the movement of Seattle and Genoa.

ITALIAN LESSONS

In July 2001 over 300,000 people took to the streets of Genoa as the G8 met within a fortified and militarised 'red zone'. The demonstrators (both 'militant' and otherwise) were attacked with the utmost brutality by the full force of the Italian state (with the tacit support of the world leaders gathered in the Conference Centre). Hundreds were injured, dozens were tortured in police custody and one protester was shot dead. Genoa signalled a turning point in the Italian movement.

While some parts of the movement in Italy have retained a commitment to mass street mobilisations against the symbols of international power, an interesting process of experimentation with both a new political orientation and new organisational forms has been underway. In essence, this has been a process of attempting to identify (and, in part, thereby develop) the emerging subject of the neoliberal era. In other words, an effort has been made to explore the ways in which exploitation takes place within the 'post-Fordist', 'post-industrial', informational economy of today, and to develop forms of struggle adequate to this changing social reality.

Even in the years before Genoa, the term 'precariousness' (or, 'precarity') was used as a way of describing the generalised condition in which European workers were increasingly finding themselves. Precarity refers to the precarious (insecure, casualised, 'teetering on the edge'...) existence of an increasing number of workers involved in crucial reproductive and distributive services; in the media, knowledge and culture industries; and increasingly, throughout advanced capitalist economies in general.[17] Whilst capitalism, even in the heyday of Fordism, has always relied on precarious and insecure forms of labour – seasonal workers, 'hobos' migrating from job to job and city to city, apprentices and part-time workers – they are today an increasingly central feature of neoliberal accumulation. In most advanced capitalist countries, a substantial proportion of the workforce are now employed in part-time or temporary jobs (29.7% in the UK; 27.1% in Italy; 35.5% in Japan; 16.8% in the US; 46.1% in the Netherlands; 30.3% in Germany; 29.2% in France; 25.9% in Denmark). In other words, the condition of precarity is one in which a huge number of us exist today: Italy alone has 7 million 'flex-workers', plus an estimated 3 million paid 'under-the-counter.'[18] Amongst these millions are the vast majority of movement activists in the UK and elsewhere. Organising around the issue of precarity in Italy has allowed those involved in social movements to both render political the conditions of their own existence, and to begin making connections with the millions of others who experience a similar reality in their own daily lives.

Of course, there are a number of real and important differences between the UK and Italy (and, to a lesser extent, France and Spain where the notion of 'precariousness' has also been taken up by social movements). First of all, Italy, France and Spain have far stronger syndicalist traditions and strikes – even general strikes – remain reasonably commonplace, at least in comparison to the UK. Secondly, in many ways, the struggles which have emerged in these countries have, at least in part, been in response to a recent change in working conditions (and the conditions of life more generally). These conditions are, largely, the product of neoliberal polices developed in the US and the UK several decades ago and imported far more recently into the Mediterranean countries. That those of us living and working in the UK have become far more used to a precarious existence – juggling jobs, working flexible hours, finding only temporary work – presents a number of very real challenges to those wanting to organise around the notion of precariousness here in the UK. Nevertheless, the ingenuity of the recent struggles in Italy and elsewhere, and their apparent resonance with other issues, suggests that there is still much which could be learned from those already active around the issue.

MAYDAY, MAYDAY!

The largest, and perhaps best known, events organised by those involved in the movement of the precariat in Italy have been the May Day parades in Milan, the first of which took place in 2001. Here, 5,000 part-timers, freelancers, and others took part in a celebratory (but angry) expression of dissent which is said to have provided 'a horizontal method of cross-networking the Genoa movement with the radical sections of [trade] unionism – thereby enabling an alliance between two generations of conflict.'[19] By 2003, the event had grown to incorporate 50,000 people, and the following year a simultaneous event took place in Barcelona.

During this first so-called EuroMayDay event, 2–3,000 people joined a flying picket, succeeding in shutting down every major chainstore and retail outlet in central Milan, freeing up workers to take part in the parade or otherwise enjoy the day. The organisational process brought together people from collectives across Italy and Spain and included striking Parisian McDonalds workers who had occupied the franchise in which they worked, and the *Intermittents*, a group of stagehands, part-time actors and cultural workers from Paris who had been involved in blockading the Cannes Film Festival the previous year to draw attention to their precarious existence.[20]

In 2005, following a series of discussions at Beyond ESF, one of the autonomous spaces which were organised to coincide with the 2004 European Social Forum in London, events were held in around twenty European cities, including London.[21] In Milan, the parade grew in size once more with forty carnival floats and 150,000 people taking part.

Efforts to organise around the issue of precarity have not, however, been limited to the May Day parades and the subsequent EuroMayDay events. A huge number of actions, events and 'happenings' have been organised throughout Italy (and, gradually, further afield) with the aim of politicising the precarious existence of life in the age of high neoliberalism.

One such event was a 'proletarian shopping' trip to a supermarket in Rome. During a huge demonstration for a guaranteed income on November 6 2004, around 700 people entered a supermarket owned by Berlusconi to carry out an act of 'autoreduction' (an Italian term to describe imposing a discount from below!), chanting 'Everything costs too much!' Hundreds of people filled shopping trolleys and demanded a 70% discount. Before negotiations could be concluded, however, most of those inside the shop simply left – 'ordinary' shoppers, as well as 'activists' – taking what they needed/wanted with them.[22]

The Milanese group, Chainworkers, have been involved with the 'movement of the precariat' since its inception in the late-1990s. On their website they explain, 'Many in the ChainCreW have this strange profile of having a recent union past and a present working in Milano's media industry. Living in a country where commercial TV brought a dumb tycoon to power, we well understand the persuasive power of pop culture and advertising lexicon. Our intent is clearly to advertise a new brand of labor activism and revolt, i.e. subvertise, by using language and graphix geared to people who have no prior political experience other than the wear and toil of their bodies and minds in the giant outlets.'[23]

The creation by Chainworkers of *San Precario*, the Patron Saint of the Precariat, is an example of exactly such an attempt to use creativity, irony and subversion. *San Precario* first appeared in central Milan in February 2004 leading a mock procession and a series of surreal prayers in front of a newly opened supermarket to 'celebrate' the generalisation of Sunday work in Italy. During the EuroMayDay events in Milan, *San Precario* reappeared as an enormous statue, built and painted by Milanese theatre temps, leading the parade. Having caught the imagination of a number of people, manifestations of the Saint began to proliferate across Italy, performing miracles and holy deeds on behalf of the precariat. A 'counter-franchise', the San Precario Chain has recently been formed to provide legal information, practical advice and active solidarity to striking precari. Within a few months of the Saint's birth, the national media in Italy began referring to *San Precario* in reference to the radical unions and organised flex-workers. It had become the icon of nationwide conflict.

PRECARITY IS IN FASHION

A further brilliant example of the media-savvy of the Italian movement is the subversion of Milan's Fashion Week in February 2005. Early on in the week, a group of anti-precarity activists succeeding in carrying out a number of successful actions, disrupting a series of events, including a Prada catwalk show, and issuing statements about the precarious conditions of many of those employed within the fashion industry. The stage had been set for a more high-profile confrontation, and the activists declared that they would disrupt the *Serpica Naro* fashion show, organised by a famous Japanese designer, due to be held at the end of the week. Milan's police duly contacted *Serpica Naro*'s press agent and warned them of the threats which had been made. The agent in turn gave a number of press interviews about the prospect of disruption.

As the *Serpica Naro* team added the final touches to the set of their fashion show, which was to be held in a large marquee in a car park in the centre of the city which could only be accessed via a single bridge, anti-precarity activists began to gather in a nearby social centre. As they slowly made their way towards the event, the police gathered on the bridge were easily able to block their route (the location having been perfectly chosen to facilitate such protection). A stand-off soon commenced, but to the bewilderment of the police the activists were laughing rather than becoming aggressive or demoralised about being prevented from reaching their target. To add to the confusion, the protesters were accompanied by the *Serpica Naro* agent and a group of models. The protesters then produced a document showing that they had, in fact, officially booked the bridge for an event.

Eventually, the truth came out. There was no famous Japanese designer called *Serpica Naro*, the name is, of course, an anagram of *San Precario*. The whole event was an elaborate hoax which had been organised by the anti-precarity campaigners who were now set to turn the tables on the media and fashion industries with their own fashion show. With egg on their face, the police withdrew and allowed the growing crowd to cross the bridge. An hour or so later, the press, who were still largely unaware of the joke, began to assemble for the show. *Serpica Naro*'s press agent took the microphone and explained the situation to the gathered media. The spotlights then came on, traversed the catwalk and the show began.

Seven models took to the stage one after another in outfits designed to expose and poke fun at the issues surrounding the precarious nature of employment today. Cameras flashed and TV crews jostled for position. As the show drew to a close, the activists had succeeded once more in their attempt to step outside the confines of that which is traditionally perceived as activism (demonstrations, militant actions, blockades and so on) and to subvert an event with its roots firmly within popular culture. The following day, the media was full of reports from the action and a space had been opened up – not simply within the media itself, but throughout society more generally – in which the issue of our precarious existence within contemporary capitalism could be discussed.

FIRST TIME AS TRAGEDY, SECOND TIME AS FARCE

'Give up Activism' attempted to problematise the role of the activist within the anti-capitalist movement of today just as that movement was coming to fruition. Throughout the 1990s, numerous peace, environmental and animal rights activists had been radicalised through their experience of struggle in direct action campaigns (and in particular on anti-road and other camps); the experimentation with alternative forms of social organisation and the new sets of social relations which emerged amongst those involved; and the direct experience of repression. In addition, a concerted effort on the behalf of a number of people

involved in the movement, particularly those based around London Reclaim the Streets, succeeded in introducing a class-based anti-capitalist politics to the movement, perhaps most notably through the series of solidarity actions organised in support of the striking Liverpool dockers.[24] It was only really in the late-1990s that it began to make sense to talk about an anti-capitalist movement in the UK at all.

Of course, this process of radicalisation was by and large to be welcomed. But as 'Give up Activism' pointed out, the problem remained that although the *content* of activism had changed, its *form* had not. The limits of single-issue campaigning had been acknowledged: ecological destruction, for example, became recognised as a logical consequence of a capitalist society, and therefore it was capitalism – as opposed to any particular company, government or piece of legislation – which needed to be fought. But the mode of operation adopted by single-issue campaigners was carried over. Instead of going to Monsanto's headquarters to protest against genetically modified food, then, the early anti-capitalist movement found itself at the purported 'headquarters' of capitalism – the City of London.

Capitalism, however, is of course something quite different from a company, and with quite different vulnerabilities. As 'Give up Activism' explained, activists have often been successful in terms of dissuading companies from pursuing a particular course of action (building a road, testing cosmetics on animals, investing in genetic engineering, and so on) by threatening to make the venture unprofitable through consumer boycotts, sabotage or whatever. Other companies, such as Consort Beagles or Hillgrove Farm who were targeted by animal rights campaigners, have been shut down altogether. Capitalism, however, needs to be approached in an altogether different way. It would be utterly insufficient (and a doomed strategy) to simply attempt to extend the tactics deployed against specific companies to every business in every sector until 'capitalism' finally packed up and did something else instead. Yet, in a sense, this is what was attempted on June 18 (this was, at least, what the day of action was *perceived* by some as attempting to do), and it is on this basis that mobilisations against international summits have also often been criticised. As one critic of summit mobilisations has pointed out, capitalism does not have a general headquarters, or a centre, it is, after all, 'a social relationship and not a citadel of power.'[25]

However, whilst it is certainly the case that elements within the counter-globalisation movement have tended to identify international summits, institutions or certain multinational corporations as the embodiment of capitalism (a position which can, should and often has been criticised) what critics have often overlooked is the extent to which counter-summits (and other 'spectacular' mobilisations) have contributed to the development of new sets of social relations and commons. In other words, if we accept that capitalism is a social relation, and one which has escaped the confines of the factory wall and permeated every aspect of society at that, there is no particular reason as to why the cities, streets and golf greens surrounding international summits should not themselves become sites of struggle. The problem, of course, is not really that mobilisations take place around international summits, but that these mobilisations become reified and fetishised as the *de facto* form of anti-capitalist resistance today.

Summit mobilisations, then, should begin to be recognised (by both their proponents and their critics) not as an attempt to strike a blow to the very heart of capitalism, but as an opportunity to catch a glimpse of, experience and help build possible future worlds. This is, of course, not to suggest that life after capitalism would necessarily involve thousands of people living in fields together, taking every decision in interminable spokescouncil meetings and eating their evening meals from 350 litre saucepans. Rather, it is the transformations which take place in the way in which we relate to ourselves and one another which allow us to see the possibilities for a life beyond capitalism: a life outside and beyond exchange relations, based on solidarity, dignity and free association.[26] However, to realise their true potential, summit mobilisations – in the dominant areas of the globe – need to be made far more relevant not only to the lives of those in the area surrounding the summit but, importantly, to the lives of those involved. It is in this sense that the Gleneagles mobilisation failed to learn the lessons of June 18.

There are innumerable ways in which this could have been achieved. Our propaganda could, for example, have gone in to far more detail about the extent to which the simultaneous rebellion taking place on the streets of Bolivia was a response to the imposition of a set of policy prescriptions developed here in the UK.[27] A far greater effort could have been made to organise and promote events connected to EuroMayDay, which in turn could have been used as a springboard for further anti-capitalist activity around the G8. A conference, gathering or assembly could have been organised to discuss what it means to call ourselves anti-capitalists today, and what – if we reject the ideologies, structures and organisational forms of the 'old' left – we see as the problems, potentials and possibilities for developing a coherent anti-capitalist *strategy* today. In many ways, however, identifying the missed opportunities around the G8 is the least challenging aspect of the process of reflection through which our movement now needs to pass (which is not to say that it is not important – learning lessons for the next time around is essential). More challenging is to work out what needs to be done in the meantime.

GIVING UP ACTIVISM, WITHOUT GIVING UP

'Give up Activism' drew heavily on leading Situationist Raoul Vaneigem's critique of the leftist 'militant' of the '68 era.[28] It argued that today's anti-capitalist activists often fall into the same trap as the 'militant' of previous decades. It was this aspect of the article's argument which was singled out for the most criticism, and the author himself admitted later that the parallel was, perhaps, an inappropriate one to draw.[29] Whether or not this is the case, one parallel which certainly exists is the notion that 'consciousness' needs to be brought to the masses: 'If only people knew about the horrors of capitalism – about starvation and climate change – then they would join us!' The first step towards giving up activism (whilst, of course, maintaining a commitment to radical social transformation), then, would involve a rethinking of the way in which those of us who perceive ourselves as belonging to this movement relate to those perceived as 'outside'.

While it may well be the case that most people are largely unaware of the intricacies of the relationships between the G8, the IMF and the World Bank; or that 'aid' programmes have often been conditional upon the adoption of structural adjustment policies, this is perhaps not as important as some tend to think. The reason people do not get involved with social movements is not because they see nothing wrong with the world, but because they do not see much hope for changing things. Thatcher's famous maxim, 'There is No Alternative', appears in many ways to be true. Of course, not on an essential level, but certainly on a practical one. Our task, then, as individuals, collectives, groups and networks committed to the notion of another possible world is to work out a way of acting which allows us to organise around our own needs and desires, to demonstrate solidarity with our friends and neighbours as well as with movements and struggles elsewhere, and in the process develop structures which allow us to amplify this resistance.

Whilst the Old Left lament (or, at times, blindly deny) the passing of the Fordist era (a time in which unions appeared to offer a means of workers organising in their own collective self-interests and where a basic standard of living could, more or less, be assured) and the death of the Soviet Union (as a demonstrable 'alternative' to capitalism), the rest of us need to begin developing an understanding of the *possibilities* as well as the *problems* with which the neoliberal era presents us. To be sure, the highly fragmented, insecure and precarious world of today does not immediately appear to present us with favourable conditions within which a revolutionary movement could develop. But perhaps, as well as looking to contemporary Italy (or Spain, or France, or...) for inspiration, we need to look a little further afield and a little further back in history.

Exactly 100 years ago, in 1905, the Industrial Workers of the World (IWW) set out to organise a transient, mobile and largely immigrant American workforce.[30] Their intention was to organise all workers, of all industries into One Big Union. IWW militants migrated between sites of struggle, agitating and offering political and material support to workers as and when it was needed. Through promoting direct action (including strikes, sabotage and 'go slows') at the point of production, they were enormously successful in winning improved living and working conditions and in fomenting both solidarity and a revolutionary spirit amongst workers.

In many ways, the IWW offer a model for a way in which we – as a movement – could begin to organise around issues related to the conditions in which we live and work, whilst building on the experience, resources and sense of possibility that we have developed through our involvement in social movements. A French group calling themselves the Solidarity Collective (*Collectif de Solidarité*) have had real successes in terms of the contribution that they have made to struggles in and around Paris over the last few years.[31] For example, when five McDonalds workers were sacked after being accused of stealing from the till, Collective members joined picket lines and carried out solidarity actions (such as occupying, blockading and shutting down various McDonalds outlets around the city) leading to the workers being rehired and others granted concessions. Similar successes were achieved when the Collective took part in the campaign to improve the working conditions of a group of Senegalese and Malian women working as cleaners for ACCOR, a multinational hotel chain. The group joined regular occupations of the hotel chain foyers, distributing leaflets to staff and customers letting them know about the conditions in which the striking workers were employed (most were hired on a week-to-week basis with little or no sense of job security, and many acquired work-related injuries for which they received no compensation) and calling for solidarity. Benefit concerts were arranged and material support given to the strikers who were eventually rehired, offered regular hours and paid 35% of their regular wages for the time in which they had been on strike.

The Industrial Workers of the World, as their name implies, recognised the necessity of organising on an international level. In reality, however, they never really existed, in any meaningful way, outside of North America. Today, as the circuits of production, distribution and exchange increasingly traverse the entire globe, the need to organise on a global level – for our resistance, in other words, to become as transnational as capital – is increasingly clear (and the possibility of this actually becoming the case is greater than ever before). Perhaps, then, we require something along the lines of a Post-Industrial Workers of the World in order to provide an open, horizontal structure within which a multitude of resistances can coordinate themselves; an organisational form which, as was the case with the original IWW, allows for all of those involved in acts of social production to 'plug in' to the network as and when they need, to draw upon resources, experience and the solidarity of others, whilst constructing basic democratic forms of organisation on both a local and a global level.

Of course, such an initiative would not necessarily involve entirely escaping the role of the activist (and thereby the limitations of that role). Neither does it appear that a complete transcendence of the role of the activist/militant has been achieved in the movements which have emerged around the notion of precariousness described above. As 'Give up Activism' pointed out,

> Activism is a form partly forced upon us by weakness... it may not even be within our power to break out of the role... It may be that in times of a downturn in struggle, those who continue to work for social revolution become marginalised

and come to be seen (and to see themselves) as a special separate group of people. It may be that this is only capable of being corrected by a general upsurge in struggle.[32]

Whether or not this is the case, any serious efforts towards radical and lasting change require that we attempt to push the boundaries of our current limitations and constraints. Whether or not another world is possible, then, may not be entirely down to us. In which case, our first priority should be breaking down the division between 'activist' and 'non-activist' so that we, at least, do not continue to reproduce the current one.

1   *La Journada, August 4 1999. Translated and cited by J. Holloway in* Ordinary People, that is, Rebels *(2005), available online at: http://spip.red.m2014.net/article.php3?id __ article=138.*

2   *Cited in R. Vaneigem,* The Revolution of Everyday Life *(London: Rebel Press, 2003).*

3   *For a detailed account of the 'Carnival Against Capital', see 'J18 1999: Our Resistance is as Transnational as Capital' in* Days of Dissent *(2004) (available at www.daysofdissent.org.uk), or 'Friday June 18th 1999: Confronting Capital and Smashing the State' in* Do or Die: Voices from the Ecological Resistance, 8 *(1999) (at http://www.eco-action.org/dod/no8/index.html). Reflections on J18 is available online at http://www.infoshop.org/octo/j18 __ reflections.html.*

4   *'Give up Activism' was published in French in* Je sais tout *and* Echanges,.93, *Spanish in* Ekintza Zuzena, *German (available online at http://www.nadir.org/nadir/initiativ/agp/new/givupact.htm) and Portugese in* N. Ludd, A Urgencia das Ruas: Reclaim the Streets!, o Black Bloc e os Dias de Acao Global *(2003), a Brazilian publication.*

5   *Anonymous, 'Give up Activism', in* Do or Die: Voices from the Ecological Resistance, 9 *(2001). Also available at http://www.eco-action.org/dod/no9/activism.htm*

6   ibid.

7   ibid.

8   *There were, of course, a number of attempts made by people involved with Dissent! to make these connections. The Carnival for Full Enjoyment, held in Edinburgh on Monday July 4, was exactly such an attempt. It was, however, an event to which a relatively small number of resources were devoted by Dissent! and with which a small number of people were involved with organising. For more on this, see L. Molyneaux 'The carnival continues...' in this book (p.109–118).*

9   *The phrase 'moments of excess' was coined by Leeds May Day Group. See http://www.nadir.org.uk/Moments%20of%20Excess.html*

10 *The term 'glocal' has been adopted by a number of counter-globalisation groups to describe a way of organising, and of acting, which attempts to engage in local struggles whilst connecting them to regional, inter-regional, international and global processes. The import role that summit mobilisations play in facilitating international collaboration between locally-based groups and struggles has been set out by Glocal Group Hanau in* Gipfelperspektiven: Gipfelmobilisierung als ein Teil transnationaler Organisierung und Kooperation *(February 2005) (at http://libcom.org/forums/viewtopic.php?t=7031).*

11 *To be sure, Dissent! were far from alone in making this recognition. Many of those involved with G8Alternatives and some of the smaller NGOs involved in the Make Poverty History coalition made a similar argument, as did a number of left/liberal journalists and commentators. See, for example, G. Monbiot's 'A Truck Load of Nonsense' in* The Guardian Tuesday June 14 2005 (at*
http://www.guardian.co.uk/Columnists/Column/0,5673,1505927,00.html). *On the tensions and contradiction within Make Poverty History, see S. Hodkinson's 'Make the G8 History'* published in Red Pepper *(July 2005) (at www.redpepper.org.uk).*

12 *The term 'professional workers' has been used by a number of political theorists to describe the class of well trained workers (primarily craftsmen (they were, generally, men) and skilled machine operators) who, at the beginning of the twentieth century, were able to use their privileged position to achieve a degree of autonomy and authority. It was the professional workers of this era who largely formed the vanguard of the workers councils and soviets which sprang up in Germany, Russia and elsewhere.*

13 *The Washington Consensus is the name given to the set of neoliberal policy prescriptions imposed, first of all, upon a number of Latin American countries via a series of IMF and World Bank structural adjustment programmes.*

14 *The means by which working practices in the UK have been transformed is documented in, amongst other places, A. Gray 'Flexibilisation of Labour and the Attack on Workers' Living Standards' in* Common Sense, *18 (1995) (at* http://www.geocities.com/CapitolHill/3843/gray1.html).

15 N. Klein, No Logo *(London: Flamingo, 2000), pp.72-73.*

16 *G. Caffentzis and S. Federici's* A Brief History of Resistance to Structural Adjustment *(2001) presents a detailed account of resistance to neoliberalism in the subordinated regions of the globe. The text is available online at* http://www.thirdworldtraveler.com/Globalization/Brief__Hx__StrucAdj__DGE.html.

17 *For a good introduction to the concept of 'precarity' and the struggles which have emerged around the issue see:* Greenpepper Magazine: Precarity 2004 *(2004) (at www.greenpeppermagazine.org);* Mute: Precarious Reader *(2005) (at www.metamute.com); or the* Precarity *(2004) DVD-zine produced by P2P Fightsharing (more information at:* http://republicart.net/disc/precariat/dvdprecarity/).

18 *All figures cited in this section are from A. Foti 'Mayday, Mayday: Euro Flex Workers, Time to Get a Move on' in* Greenpepper Magazine: Precarity 2004 *(2004), p.23.*

19 *Foti, op. cit., p.21.*

20 *For more about the struggle of the* Intermittents, *see A. Capocci et al. (2004) 'Culture Clash: The Rise of the Flexworking Class in Europe' in* Greenpepper Magazine: Precarity 2004 *(2004; p.33-37).*

21 *For a report on the action in London, see www.precarity.info.*

22 *For more, see: Hydrachist, 'Disobbedienti Ciao' in* Mute: Culture and Politics After the Net, *Issue 29 (Winter/Spring 2005) (at www.metamute.com).*

23 http://www.chainworkers.org/dev/who.

24 *For an example of the argument made by some of those involved with London Reclaim the*

Streets as to the relation between workers' struggles and the radical ecological movement, see
'Why Reclaim the Streets and the Liverpool Dockers?' in Do or Die, 6 (1997) (available online at
http://www.eco-action.org/dod/no6/rts.htm). For a detailed account of the emergence and
development of the anti-roads and radical ecological movement in the UK, see 'Down with the
Empire! Up with the Spring!' in Do or Die: Voices from the Ecological Resistance, 10 (2003)
(available online at http://www.eco-action.org/dod/no10/empire.htm) or Aufheben, The
Politics of Anti-Roads Struggle and the Struggle of Anti-Roads Politics: The Case of the No
M11 Link Road Campaign (available online at
http://www.geocities.com/aufheben2/auf_mckay.html).

25 Some Roveretan Anarchists 'Notes on Summits & Counter-Summits' in Where is the Festival?:
    Notes on Summits and Counter-Summits (2003), p.18.

26 This is not to privilege summit mobilisations per se over other forms of struggle. There have,
    naturally, been counter-summits where repression, a low turn out or any number of other
    factors have prevented any effective action being carried out. In these cases, participants have
    often been left to feel powerless against the enemy with which they are confronted. Likewise,
    numerous other phases and periods of struggle – the British miners' strike of the 1980s, the
    anti-poll tax movement, the anti-road camps of the 1990s – have allowed strong communities
    of resistance to emerge. In the current era, with a downturn in struggle, summit mobilisations,
    however, appear as a rare opportunity in which another way of being can – briefly – be
    experienced.

27 In the weeks leading up to the summit, hundreds of thousands took to the streets of Bolivia,
    effectively shutting down La Paz, the country's capital, by blockading the only motorway
    leading into or out of the city. The rebellion had been sparked off by threatened privatisation of
    natural resources (water, gas and oil) as a result of the conditionalities attached to the Highly
    Indebted Poor Countries initiative, a 'debt relief' package designed and delivered by Gordon
    Brown. For more about the roots of the rebellion in Bolivia, see J. Whitney 'Bolivia's Laboratory
    of Dual Power' in Left Turn Magazine, 18 (2005) (available online at
    http://leftturn.org/Articles/Viewer.aspx?id=625&type=M).

28 Vaneigem's text to which 'Give up Activism' referred was The Revolution of Everyday Life,
    cited above.

29 The critique of 'Give up Activism' referred to here is 'The Necessity and Impossibility of Anti-
    Activism' which was originally published in The Bad Days Will End!, 3 and is available online
    at: http://www.geocities.com/kk_abacus/ioaa/necessity.html. The 'Postscript' to 'Give up
    Activism' was published alongside the original article in Do or Die: Voices from the
    Ecological Resistance, 9 (2001; p.166-170) (see: http://www.eco-
    action.org/dod/no9/activism_postscript.htm).

30 For an introduction to the IWW, see S. Bird et al. (eds) Solidarity Forever: The IWW – An Oral
    History of the Wobblies (Chicago: Lakeview Press, 1985).

31 For a detailed account of the activities of Collectif de Solidarité see L. Goldner 'Marx and
    Makhno Meet McDonald's: What does 'precarious' struggle look like in practice?' in Mute:
    Precarious Reader (2005).

32 Anonymous, 'Give up Activism', op cit.

20

CRE8 SUMMAT: PLANTING A GARDEN OF ACTIVISM

Leon Roman

Long before the G8 came to Scotland, a plan emerged for a creative action around the summit. The goals of the action were three-fold. First, to not only say that 'a better world is possible', but to build the foundations of that world in the here and now. Second, to use activism as a means of supporting and strengthening local issues and to empower those already involved with these issues. And third, to demonstrate that radical resistance can be part of our everyday lives.

The goals started lofty, and we continued to meet at each national Dissent! gathering to discuss these ideas. But how could they be put into practice? What should be our project? For months, we continued to discuss guerrilla gardening tactics, community murals, street performances and the like. However, one major thing was missing... we had no idea where we would focus our energies, or where our project would be based.

During a meeting at the Festival of Dissent!, a project finally emerged. One Glasgow-based activist explained that there was a derelict piece of land in the Southside of Glasgow that had been left unused for over twenty years. It was one of the sites for a pillar for the proposed M74, a raised motorway which would tear through that part of the city. Moreover, this land sat in between some of the city's most deprived communities. Slowly, the council had been disinvesting in the services for these communities in an attempt to push them out. Tensions between the city and the locals had recently reached boiling point when threats of closure for the local swimming pool ended in an occupation. There had been a recent upsurge in the campaign to stop the M74, and it was clear that the ongoing legal campaign could be effectively supported by a diversity of tactics. And so the idea to build a community garden on this land was hatched, and 'Cre8 Summat' was born as an idea.

We agreed that this project had huge potential and quickly abandoned the idea of organising further actions in Edinburgh as the enormity of our task began to dawn on us. Shortly after the Festival, we held meetings near the site where activists were able to familiarise themselves with the site and our possible courses of action. A core group of about a dozen organisers emerged as those who were going to be able to put in the planning and coordinating time over the next few months, yet we were also depending on a much larger number of interested activists joining in later.

As the format for the Cre8 Summat emerged, we were aiming at a complete community festival. For a week in the middle of June, we would start by building a community garden. However, we also wanted to hold workshops on a variety of topics from herbal medicine to tile mosaics and tenants' rights to Zapatista solidarity; to have music, entertainment, art and to create a space for social interaction. The week was planned early in the run-up to the G8 to allow activists who would be otherwise engaged in the following weeks to participate in the project, but we soon realised that by scheduling so early we had neglected to take into account the start of the school holidays. So it was also decided to hold a Family Festival in the gardens just before the summit started.

For the small group of dedicated organisers there was a huge list of things that had to be done to make this action a success, so each individual had to take on a separate role in the early planning. We had to cover the gardening aspects (making sure plants were propagated, that we had all the necessary materials and tools, etc.) and the workshop schedule; but we also needed to coordinate the entertainment (contacting and booking sound systems, organising power supplies and so on), and secure early participation from local people. Publicising the events to the local community was a high priority, along with the multiple days of dreaded litter removal from the site. As the start of the actual gardening got closer and closer, panic grew as we realised how much was still left to do. We had almost forgotten to consider how we were going to meet the needs of all the activists who planned on living on the site during our week-long occupation. Luckily, after a few calls, we managed to book marquees and the London-based Kaos Kafé said that they would be up for catering. And at extremely short notice, hundreds of plants were pledged by people as far away as Cardiff and Devon. But we still didn't know where we were going to get water from!

We organised a number of presentations about the Cre8 Summat with the aim of getting the local community involved in the early planning stages of the event, but the turn-out was always extremely low. Had we not done enough to

get the local communities involved? Were they even interested? Those who did come to the meetings and those we talked to during the days of the litter-pick offered a sense of hope as a counter-balance to our growing panic. People might have been a bit confused about the idea; how were a bunch of activists going to transform a derelict piece of land into a community garden? But even the sight of people removing all the rubbish from the site that had been used for fly-tipping for years brought kind remarks. And, as the final weeks counted down into days, it was possible to see the plans coming together, not least because the arrival of groups and individuals from all over the UK, and from further afield, meant that we could pass on some of the last minute jobs to others.

Around 5am on a damp and rainy Sunday morning, whilst most of Glasgow was still asleep, the vans of tools and plants pulled up to the site. Groups of people began shifting gear and soon our first marquee was in place. We had arrived, and for the next week this piece of land was to be not only our home but the place where our dreams would become reality. At this point we were still not sure what the reaction would be. How quickly would the police show up and what would they do? By the time we had set up our camp in the gardens and were ready to hold our workshop on creating a participatory design for the gardens, no one else had arrived. No locals, no police. So we went ahead and designed some ideas for the garden and work began on the first day's projects – a herb spiral, a willow entry arch and a circle of planted tyre seating.

Sometime during the afternoon, people started to show up. A bike ride of the Jam 74 campaign group ended their ride of the proposed M74 route in the gardens, community members were helping to build the herb spiral, and local kids were cutting out the bank with pick and shovel to create a new entrance to the land. Later in the afternoon, the first police arrived and, to our surprise, wished us luck with the project. By the second day, we had a liaison officer who was having a cup of tea with us each morning.

The work continued through the week at a tremendous pace, and after dinner each day it was quite rewarding to walk around the land taking stock of the recent additions – wood-chip lined paths, sensory gardens, new murals, a performance stage, a few more garden beds, a labyrinth, information signs, lots of tree planting, and a swing hanging from a tripod.

Throughout the week, there was a steady stream of wheelbarrows running to and fro, bringing all types of scrap materials for constructing garden beds – scrap wood, tyres, stones and bricks. However, one problem became evident: we needed soil and lots of it. Because the land we were working on was toxic, we had reluctantly decided to construct all planting areas as raised beds. By the second day we were buying in dump truck loads of soil, and almost every penny of our limited funds and donations went to the cause of non-toxic soil.

As Saturday came around, the land was looking full of life and vigour. The space was inspiring, and we were preparing for one hell of a celebration. There were, after all, plenty of reasons to celebrate! For a week, about thirty (maybe a total of about fifty or sixty weaved in and out) activists had organised in a cooperative and collective manner, with no hierarchy and no leaders, to create something that was well beyond what we had believed was possible.

Each individual could feel rewarded in the fact that a part of these gardens was defined by their labour, their passion and their creativity. Uniqueness and beauty cried out from each corner of this garden. And as the bands began to play and the clowns began to display their red noses and floppy shoes, the people who had spent a week living on that land were continually greeted and thanked by so many of the friends we had made from the surrounding area. As the day grew on, so did the number of new faces who were joining the celebrations.

That night, the energy was amazing – people around a fire passing the guitar and singing songs, films and bands and a sound system – and it seemed quite odd to realise this was all happening against the backdrop of city lights and tower blocks. The gardens had become a place where you could lose yourself and forget the traffic or the hassles of the working day.

PUSHING THE BOUNDARIES

There is no way I could describe the Cre8 Summat as anything but an amazing success. However, there are still a lot of things we learned and a lot of things we would do better next time. The most important thing to acknowledge is that an action like this, that intends to create something and to leave something positive behind, takes a lot of time and energy to make happen. Protesting *against* something is, in a way, a simpler objective than protesting *for* something, but the rewards of the latter are well worth it. With a goal of empowering the local community and getting them involved in the action, we learned that the most effective thing was to just start the actual work. Talking to people beforehand wasn't enough to excite them. But being on the land, doing work, and enjoying ourselves was the most effective way to get people involved. It would have been nice to have had more input into how the gardens were designed, what types of needs and desires we were catering for, understanding how the local community wanted to use their garden, but ironically doing this before the gardens actually started seemed almost impossible. This isn't really an excuse for not making those attempts at pre-work participation. However, for those attempts to be meaningful, it would either take months and months of early interaction or some better methods than leafleting door-to-door and holding public meetings.

There are a couple of things we could clearly have handled better. First, for some reason, no local people attended the workshops we organised. They did come and get involved in working on a project that was essentially the idea of a workshop, but the workshop schedule that looked really good from an activist point of view didn't create any interest. Again, if we had been able to talk to people earlier, maybe we could have found out what they were interested in. However, in one way our experience showed us that it is better in terms of scheduling events to worry about the entertainment side and ensure that each day several interesting projects are going to be happening that people can get involved with. Second, media relations could have been smoother. Before we felt ready to communicate with the media, they were contacting us. Our plan had been to allow the media to visit the site while we were working on it, but when they contacted us we were still in panic mode trying to sort things out and we just didn't respond. By the time we did get back to them, they were no longer so interested. Luckily, we didn't have to deal with them as much as we feared we may have to, but part of the reason for carrying out a creative action such as the Cre8 Summat is to generate interest and the media could have been a tool in doing so.

On the positive side, there were three areas that worked really well. First, it was great to not have a 'project coordinator'. We had talked about having one person nominated as a 'jobs coordinator' each day, in case people turned up and wanted something to do. However, none of us were interested in taking on this formal leadership role and the project worked brilliantly without it. One of the first things people would ask when they wanted to get involved in the work was, 'Who's in charge?' And our answer of 'Nobody!' always shocked them: they were amazed that so much work could be happening without a leader. We would explain to them that they could get involved with any of the work happening by just asking someone what they were up to, or that they were welcome to start a new project if they desired. Most would choose the former rather than the latter, but a few people who spent many days working in the gardens were inspired to take on one of their own ideas.

Second, planning was crucial. Although at times we worried that we were never going to reach the level of 'organised chaos' to which we were aspiring, the degree of planning which went into the action was the key to its eventual success. To use a metaphor, if the garden could be thought of as a painting, the organisers saw their role as providing the canvas, paints and brushes and very little more. We provided the tools and the plants with which the garden was built, and food and shelter for those who would take part. But the final product was the creation of all of those who got involved. Finally, celebration was a key theme throughout the project. Make sure you have as much fun as work; this is what really attracts people and draws them in. Besides, it's great to see something special form through your hard work but it is even more wonderful to see people enjoying what has been created.

There are five important things to consider for an action like this:
• *Start preparing early:* unlike lock-ons and banners, plants cannot be propagated at the last minute.
• *Diversify:* a one-dimensional action will appeal to a few, a multi-dimensional project will appeal to many.
• *Be friendly and fluffy:* just because it's fluffy doesn't mean it isn't radical. If you

put a friendly face on an idea like land reclamation, even the cops will start offering police horse manure for garden fertiliser!

• *Push the boundaries:* do not limit the possibilities to the easy things. Hearing local people comment that what we created was something they never would have dreamed possible (especially in one week) was really rewarding.

• *Let it go:* prepare the action as much as possible (get the venue ready, provide the materials, feed people, etc), but once it starts, let go – let the project become a mixture of everyone's input, time and labour.

The Cre8 Summat was a powerful experience to be part of. It was inspiring to see so many activists coming together to create and being joined by so many interested local people. And there was something really special about not directing our energies towards just attacking the powers-that-be but using them to build an example of the positive world we believe is possible.

21

THE CLANDESTINE INSURGENT REBEL CLOWN ARMY GOES TO SCOTLAND VIA A FEW OTHER PLACES
Kolonel Klepto and Major Up Evil

...the clowns are organising... the clowns are organising – over and out...
Overheard on police radio, July 4 2004 action against Menwith Hill spy base, UK

PLAYING GAMES WITH AUTHORITY
Clowns always speak of the same thing, they speak of hunger; hunger for food, hunger for sex, but also hunger for dignity, hunger for identity, hunger for power. In fact, they introduce questions about who commands, who protests.
Dario Fo, Italian political playwright/fool

The early morning radio reports traffic disruption across central Scotland. 'Avoid the area if you can', says the presenter as she lists dozens of roads and railway lines that have been blocked by protesters during the opening of the G8 summit. Fresh from a little jaunt on the A9 motorway involving 60 rebel clowns in military uniforms, over 100 policemen in riot gear, several barking police dogs, a few delegates coaches and dozens of bright orange traffic cones, a small gaggle[1] of clowns is making its way to the G8Alternatives march.

They pass over a bridge above the motorway. Half a dozen policemen line up, they face the line of clowns and the two groups stare at each other. A pair of clowns dressed as cops, part of the hilarious Backwards Intelligence Team,[2] start to count down – 'Five, four, three, two, one – go!' The (real) police and clowns rush towards each other, their hands outstretched, faces grimacing and screaming 'Kazamm'. There is a floating moment of confusion and then they run into each other's open arms – clowns hug cops, cops hug clowns. Everyone is a bit surprised, there is a roar of celebratory cheers from the clowns and slightly sheepish and embarrassed applause from the police.

Somehow, this clown gaggle had managed to persuade the police to play a game with them. Known as 'Dwarfs, Wizards and Giants' it's a version of paper-scissors-stone, but played in teams with the whole body. One of the rules is that if both teams choose the same character, no one wins and they all have to hug. This is exactly what happened as clown and cop teams simultaneously chose to be 'wizards'.

Perhaps this is not behaviour one would expect from this motley crew of activists who had been ridiculed by Bob Geldof as a bunch of 'thuggish... losers' with 'white painted faces' come to 'wreck' his Live8 events.[3] But in many ways this brief moment on a bridge, less than a mile away from where the G8 were meeting behind their fences patrolled by 15,000 police, could be seen as a beautiful example and illustration of the tactics and theory of rebel clowning. Behind its white-faced facade of stupidity, it is a serious attempt to develop a form of civil disobed-ience that breaks down the binary and oppositional thinking that is still so inherent within protest movements.

Dichotomies between the personal and the political, the classic us and them, activist and non-activist, violence and non-violence and, of course, protesters and police, seem outmoded ways of thinking in a movement that has been inspired by numerous types of thinking (from post-modern, ecological, late feminism or anarchism) which emphasise processes, continuums, relationships, systems and networks.

Rebel clowns refuse all dichotomies: they are often neither male nor female, neither artist nor activist, neither clever nor stupid, neither mad nor sane, enter-tainment nor threat. They know that these clear oppositions are oppressive and, more importantly, that if we really are to win this fight for the survival of humanity and the earth's eco-systems, then one day we will have to convince the cops and soldiers to change sides.

PEELING OFF THE REBEL ARMOUR

...our behaviour is a function of our experience. We act according to the way we see things. If our experience is destroyed, our behaviour will be destructive. If our experience is destroyed we have lost our own selves.

R.D.Laing, The Politics of Experience

The Clandestine Insurgent Rebel Clown Army (CIRCA) was founded in November 2003 to 'celebrate' George Bush's visit to the UK.[4] On the surface it seemed to many that it was just another carnivalesque protest tactic, in the footsteps of Reclaim

the Streets and the Pink and Silver Samba bands, adding colour and pleasure to the grey tedium of marches and traditional forms of direct action.[5] In fact, it was meant to be a lot more than a tactic. The methodology of rebel clowning was developed as a way of trying to overcome what we perceived as some of the deeper problems in the way we behave as radicals towards each other, ourselves and our world.

To share and disseminate this form, that we termed 'rebel clowning', CIRCA initiated a series of trainings that mixed methodologies from clowning and civil disobedience. The former helps us rediscover an inner playful, childlike state of generosity and spontaneity, while the latter provides us with effective tools of resistance. To join CIRCA it was necessary to take part in a minimum two-day training.

Having worked for many years in direct action movements, we had come to a realisation that more groups and movements are destroyed by poor group dynamics and internal fights than any number of police.[6] The state knows only too well that the best way to disrupt radical groups is by seeding mistrust and conflict amongst them, and letting them destroy themselves. As the state violence in Genoa showed during the G8 meetings in 2001, too much visible police violence creates movement martyrs and bonds between the liberal left and radicals – things which tend to strengthen rather than weaken social movements. Obviously police repression against activists is still rife: mass arrests and beatings are still very much the tragic reality for too many of us, but the ancient 'divide and rule'

strategy seems to be as active as ever.[7] It is much more effective for the state to play with the cops in our own heads than to batter our heads with truncheons.

Unfortunately radicals are often vulnerable souls. Most of us became politically active because we felt something profoundly, such as injustice or ecological devastation. It is this emotion that triggers a change in our behaviour and gets us politicised. It is our ability to transform our feelings about the world into actions that propels us to radical struggle. But often, what seems to happen is that the more we learn about the issues that concern us, the more images of war we see, the more we experience climate chaos, poverty and the everyday violence of capitalism, the more we seem to harden ourselves from feeling too much. Although feeling can lead to action, we also know that feeling too much can lead to depression and paralysis. Combine this with the stress of repression and criminalisation by the state and many activists begin to grow a thick armour around themselves. Controlling our feelings becomes a mechanism of survival.[8]

Yet in such a controlled state of being, it becomes difficult to be open to others, to listen to oneself and each other. Often we cover up this loss with the illusion of bravery. We become fearless warriors for the planet, often making reckless decisions and putting ourselves or others into dangerous situations. But a warrior who is unable to really feel and perceive what is around her/himself will soon end up dead and ineffective. Fearlessness comes from escaping our bodies, forgetting we are made of flesh and blood and living in the pure abstraction of a mind. By working with the body, rebel clown trainings attempt to peel off this armour (or try to avoid it appearing), to reveal the soft skin again, to find the vulnerable human being who once felt everything deeply and to give them courage – which is about feeling fear and yet deciding to overcome it because your heart tells you it is the right thing to do.

A key aspect of the anti-capitalist direct action movement is our desire for what has been termed 'pre-figurative politics'. A politics that sees no separation between means and ends. To paraphrase Gandhi, we want to be the change we want to see in the world. The eco-village in Stirling, with its permaculture design and horizontal forms of decision-making, was a beautiful example of this. Yet our experience has been that despite these inspiring structures, our behaviours, emotional intelligence and relationship to power are sometimes not examples of the world we want to see. Meetings or actions often become cold hostile sites of competitive and even aggressive behaviours and we can be notoriously bad at warmly welcoming strangers into our midst.

With CIRCA, we wanted to challenge this and find a way to bring the personal back into the centre of radical political action. We wanted to change the way we think and feel as much as the way we fight. For us the psyche, the body and the street should be seen as equally important zones of struggle and areas in need of radical transformation. Simply replacing the structures of society with new ones, without changing our own deeper internal structures, will just repeat the mistakes of so many past revolutions, where the very vision of change we had in the first place was destroyed by the re-establishment of an unfeeling rotten order with the same power structures in place. We don't want people to adapt to a new established society, rather we want society to adapt to a new person. Mixing the ancient art of clowning with contemporary forms of civil disobedience, we developed a methodology that tries to provide tools for transforming and sustaining the inner emotional life of the activists as well as being an effective technique for taking direct action.

THE STRENGTH OF THE STUPID

... I saw the clown, Pierino, at the fountain ... I was moved and admired the poor man dressed as a funny man, whom I realised was a free, amazing being, needing very little to live on and able to survive the most incredible disasters, able to rise from the most frightful calamities, pass unharmed through mockery and contempt and to the very end maintain an unflagging optimism: amused and amusing as only one under heaven's protection could possibly be.

Federico Fellini, Fellini on Fellini

The clown is a figure whose history can be traced back to some of the earliest forms of performance in the world. Linked to the role of the shaman, the social healer and magician, the clown has in various guises throughout history been someone

who was given the liberty to confront all the taboos and truths of a culture, to critique the very core principles of society and yet get away with it. They are able to do this because they inhabit a special place, an in-between space, a weird social no-man's land. The clown manages to be at the centre and the margins of society simultaneously. S/he is a popular archetype seen everywhere, from the circus to the corporate advert, the public street to the private children's party, and is recognised for speaking a certain wisdom despite a surface of folly. Yet at the same time, the clown is an outsider, a freak, an object of ridicule. This threshold space that the clown inhabits is powerful. It confuses the categories that the system imposes on us and through her/his eternal mockery, the clown refuses to fall victim to any posturing pride and arrogance.

Clowning is a state of being rather than a technique. At its root, clowning is about letting go, learning to approach every situation with an openness and vulnerability that we all once had as children. It is a state where we begin to value the power of surrendering to experience and living without fixed expectation. It is a state of being that we all grew up with, the state of being that society stamped on and imprisoned in fairgrounds, theatres and circuses. It is the state that learns about the world through play and knows that the difference between imagination and reality is only a matter of opinion.

Like most states it is something that can be developed and taught but this takes an enormous amount of time and effort. It would be naïve to pretend that one can reach such a state of letting go, that one can peel off so many layers of inhibitions, inner fears and conditioning that capitalism teaches us in so many insidious ways throughout our lives in a two-day training. Moreover the concept of the need for 'training' is sometimes seen as authoritarian within the movements, and there are people who feel that they can just put on white face paint and a wig, act stupidly and join the ranks of CIRCA. In this we see a potential issue.

Many of us probably remember seeing an incredible clown, perhaps it was Charlie Chaplin, or Harpo Marx. Their stupidity comes from a deep place of dignity and of doing very little. They don't pretend to be clowns, they don't act, they just are themselves and this ability to do very little and yet say so much is something that doesn't come with a costume, but a radically reformed mind and body: a lifetime's work. We can all recognise a mediocre clown, one that makes us cringe with embarrassment, such as the kids' party clown, or the kitsch corporate event clown who is unable to make us laugh however much s/he tries and is certainly unable to make us contemplate profound social truths. An army of incredible clowns is what we dreamt about for CIRCA, and perhaps in its own clownish way this was a dream that had not really taken into account the realities of radical social movements and the fact that there is never time and space for such deep slow work. Herein lies the biggest challenge of rebel clowning and the future success or failure of CIRCA hinges on this.

THE RIDICULOUS RECRUITMENT TOUR

This isn't a normal travelling theatre company you know.
Scotland Yard, unsuccessfully trying to dissuade a local council from hosting the tour

Summit mobilisations are not only about the actions. More important are the opportunities to develop new processes, and out-reach projects and institutions in the run-up to the actions. Some of us who had been involved in the founding of CIRCA had also been part of setting up the Laboratory of Insurrectionary Imagination (Lab of ii), a space to bring artists and activists together.[9] For the lead-up to the G8 summit mobilisations we decided to take the Lab of ii on a tour of the UK, to introduce people to numerous forms of creative resistance, recruit for CIRCA and present people with a radical take on the G8.[10]

The tour took in nine cities snaking itself up from southern England to Aberdeen and then on to the G8. In each place we performed an outdoor show, did a two-day intensive rebel clown training and ended with an action in the local cathedrals of consumption, involving several dozen people simultaneously praying to products in department stores.[11] The lab toured in an old bus painted bright pink, silver and green, and filled with dozens of bizarre looking human-size puppets, whose grimacing faces could be seen pushed against the windows. The bus was powered by biodiesel (non-petroleum vegetable oil-based fuel), which some discerning noses could spot by the smell of chip fat that followed us everywhere. In tow was our beautiful caravan, painted a deep green, topped with solar panels and decorated with clownish go-faster flames that erupted from the spinning wheels. The caravan would become the central image and tool of the tour doubling up as information and resource centre, changing room, sleeping space, meeting space and back stage for the performances.[12]

At each stop we set up the encampment with the caravan on one end and the bus on the other. The caravan had its own stage that pulled out of the side, a sound system and solar powered cinema. A large awning would stretch from the caravan to the bus (in case of British weather). The audience would sit underneath the awning between the caravan and the bus on cushions and bolsters made especially for the tour. In the back of the bus a makeshift kitchen would be assembled, providing free organic chips to the audience during the interval, which would give us an opportunity to talk about alternatives to fossil fuels as the chip fat would later be recycled into biodiesel.

The show involved a series of performances including a re-enactment of the Fourth World War by a grotesque clown eating and choking on money, a spoof lecture on the history of civil disobedience, a CIRCA recruitment show with 18 life-size puppets, and artist activist 'the vacuum cleaner' who showed films of creative actions of resistance from around the world.

A key aim of the tour was to try and break out of the activist scene by using popular art forms in very public spaces. We set up camp in a wide diversity of places with extremely varied audiences. These ranged from a grotty gravel-filled car park in Newcastle to the main town square in Aberdeen, from a squatted community garden (the Cre8 Summat) on the route of a contested motorway in Glasgow to a peace festival in a Sheffield cemetery, from a friendly street next to a thriving local city farm in Bristol to outside a Barclays bank in Birmingham's High Street. Permission was sought to get access to these places, and this gave us interesting opportunities to talk to and communicate with local council officers about the issues, which often led to fascinating discussions about resistance and the G8.

By the end of the tour we had trained over 200 people of all ages and backgrounds, a number of whom were not activists. Many trainees set up their own clown gaggles when we left, in preparation for the G8 and continued to work together afterwards.

For those of us involved in the tour, we saw it as effective a political and pedagogic tool as the actions at the G8. By using popular forms of culture in public spaces we attempted to make our ideas and values visible, attractive, and hopefully irresistible! We felt that turning up in the middle of a city with free food, showing films and putting on performances that glorify civil disobedience, was a strategy that challenges a system which works so hard on demonising us and pushing us to the margins. We created an event that clearly spoke of the pleasure of resistance but somehow fell outside people's expectations of what radical politics looked or felt like. We looked like the circus coming to town, but were clearly

more about subversion than entertainment. By blurring the boundaries between culture and resistance we were able to engage and touch people who might otherwise not have got involved in radical resistance to the G8.

DAYS OF DISSENT

One of the worst mistakes any revolution can make is to become boring. It leads to rituals as opposed to games, cults as opposed to communities and the denial of human rights as opposed to freedom.

Abbie Hoffman, **Museum of the Streets**

We arrived in Edinburgh completely shattered and the thought of a week of actions ahead of us felt like an almost impossible task. But our spirits were completely turned around when we saw over 160 beautiful rebel clowns converging on a small car park in Edinburgh for the first clown council on the morning of the Make Poverty History march.

A briefing booklet had been sent out to the clown gaggles across the country, which explained details of the framework of mobilisations organised by Dissent!, and described the structures of spokes-councils that we would use to plan and organise the actions.

From across the country and abroad, rebel clowns converged, dressed in the most extraordinary costumes, all different and yet all united by the identity of the rebel clown. This sense of unity within diversity amongst the clowns was one of the most effective aspects of CIRCA. We all shared a common language that we had learnt during the trainings, including various manoeuvring tactics, games and marching. At any point during an action someone could call out 'let's fish', say, and everyone would know exactly what kind of manoeuvre to do. Such a strong sense of unity is often hard to get within autonomous movements with such healthy diversity and difference. But feeling part of an army, sharing aspects of uniform and language, whilst at the same time acting autonomously in gaggles and having our own very particular clown characters, gave us a strength and sense of solidarity that was extremely rare and valuable.

The first spokes-council, and many to follow, was inspiring. For many of us this was the first time we had experienced this profoundly democratic yet difficult way of making decisions. We ended the first council with a huge group hug and formed up ready to march in military rank and file through Edinburgh. In that magical moment all the trials and tribulations of the gruelling tour faded into the background, as a sea of rebel clowns flooded the streets ready for a week of resistance to the G8.

It was to be a week which saw so many beautiful acts of rebel clowning. There was the clown drawing smiley faces on police riot shields with lipstick and then kissing them with her bright pink lips. There were the cops who had encircled the black bloc, unable to keep straight faces as a small group of clowns mockingly

sang 'One banana, two banana, three banana, four...' to them. There were the dozen bright coloured clowns moving in unison through the knee-high green barley as the fences were being pulled down. There was the surreal moment when 70 bleary-eyed clowns woke up at 5am in a real bright yellow castle, 20-minutes' walk from Gleneagles, that had been magically and mysteriously provided for them as accommodation for the eve of blockades. There was the moment of ecstatic joy as a large determined clown battalion marched straight through a line of confused riot cops whilst chanting 'Love and respect!' and ran onto the A9. And there was the moment that we began with, on the bridge, when for a few seconds the police forgot which side they were on.

1   CIRCA organises itself in small groups based on affinity and/or location called 'gaggles'
2   The Backwards Intelligence Team (B.I.T.) was set up by people who had trained with CIRCA.
    B.I.T. is a fantastic parody of the Forward Intelligence Team, a police surveillance group that
    monitors British street activists with banks of intimidating cameras.
3   'You're a bunch of losers, Geldof tells violent protesters', Daily Telegraph, July 6 2005.
4   See communique number 1, www.clownarmy.org
5   For more on protest and the carnivalesque see Notes from Nowhere (eds.) We Are Everywhere:
    The irresistible rise of global anticapitalism (London/New York: Verso, 2002), pp. 173–183.
6   This point was made by Starhawk during her extraordinary Earth Activists Training Course, see
    www.earthactivisttraining.org

7　Policing in Scotland during the G8 was a striking example of this very British approach: it was generally really 'hands-off'. The emphasis seems to have been put on PR and communication, with the most obvious set-up for the media in Auchterarder near the fence (where a huge field of barley became the scene for confrontational games between cops and protesters pulling fences down just under judiciously placed cranes where TV crews were coincidentally waiting for their usual image of 'violence').

8　Of course this also applies to non-activists, as it is this very control of emotions that enables capitalism to get away with so much violence and injustice.

9　See www.labofii.net

10　There were discussions with the popular education collective Trapese on whether we should tour together or as separate units, as they too were planning what was to become a mammoth road show to raise awareness about the G8 and the Dissent! network. In the end we decided that rather than centralise our resources, doing more than one tour would be politically more effective, both reaching more people and giving the impression that a lot of different groups were preparing for the G8. In the end Trapese, Lab of ii and SchNEWS all did separate tours and during the Lab tour it was inspiring for us to imagine all these radical collectives criss-crossing the country.

11　The lab produced a DVD, 13 Experiments in Hope, that we distributed on the tour. It includes a video of prayers to products and is viewable at http://www.labofii.net/tour05/dvd/watch/

12　The caravan set-up was made in collaboration with Birmingham-based www.A2RT.org and is now a resource available to groups who would like to borrow it. Contact john@labofii.net for details.

22

OPERATION SPLISH SPLASH SPLOSH
Corporal Clutter of CIRCA

The Global Day of Action against Climate Change is a squelcher. Having outfitted bikes with feather boas, the well-trained buffoons of 21st squadron Glasgow Kiss pedal towards the Boogie on the Bridge. How many riot squad vans does it take to thwart one gaggle of clowns? At a red light, General Support (we are all privates, generals, fools) smiles into the tinted windows. 'Think you can fit in a few more, don't you? Consider a carpool.'

We wear black armbands, and General Strike has balanced on her handlebars a flap of cardboard bearing the day's message: Oil–War–Terror

We lose the cop cars and get to the bridge just in time to make an entrance. It's a slick party, but after failing figure-eight cycle formation we receive intelligence that the gaggles are converging. By the time we arrive, Operation Splish Splash Splosh is underway. Our comrades have commandeered a kiddie pool and three mermaids. The Shell station is awash with red-nosed sunbathers, pink fluff and swimming instructors urging drivers to prepare for the fishes. In high afternoon heat, clowns play on the premises of two petrol stations, transforming them into urban oases of the hallucinatory variety. We get on our knees to pray to the filling stations and flirt with the pumps ('Oh, it's soooo big'). We play tig and lay about. We charm workers into donating an application form for assistant manager. The media are loving it. The cops are bemused but amusingly impotent. Shutting down the oil industry has never been more fun. Mission accomplished.

23

ACTIVIST TRAUMA: MUTUAL SUPPORT IN THE FACE OF REPRESSION

Activist-Trauma Support

If we want to be effective as a movement, we need to be able to support each other in the face of repression. We need to be conscious that what we are doing might be harmful to ourselves, potentially even life-threatening. This is not meant to scare people off – quite the opposite; but we need to face reality, deal with our fears and sort out our support if we don't want to give state repression the means to be effective.

Activist-Trauma Support (ATS) was started in 2005 in order to provide support during and after the G8 mobilisations in Scotland. Previous experiences have shown that while self-organised medical support for victims of police violence was quite well organised, there was a serious lack of assistance on a psychological level. For some, the idea for ATS was born from experiences following the Aubonne bridge action against the G8 in Evian 2003. During that action one person was seriously physically injured – and got lots of support. But several others suffered from varying degrees of psychological trauma and didn't get the support they needed or deserved. This is when we realised the pressing need for organised awareness raising, information and support.

While 'post-traumatic stress' is now taken quite seriously in mainstream society (it is standard practice for the emergency services to be trained in identifying and coping with it, and treatment is finally available via the National Health Service), it is surprising that, as activists, we still think we can live through situations of police brutality, fear and powerlessness without showing any emotional response. The fact is that we can't.

Of course reactions to stress vary. Everybody has their own way of dealing with it, but this reaction can extend to dropping out, disappearing, or feeling excluded because we feel scared or are suffering from post-traumatic stress 'disorder' (PTS'D').[1] Inside our movements a deeper understanding of these processes is lacking. Even after terrible incidents such as those at the Diaz school in Genoa where sleeping activists were severely beaten by police during the 2001 G8 summit, not enough emotional support was available for the victims. It is crucial to understand that emotional wounds often continue to hurt and debilitate long after the physical wounds have healed, and that people who don't get physically hurt can still suffer serious psychological damage. In the long term, many of those in Genoa suffered more from the emotional consequences than the physical injuries.

This lack of support within the movement can exacerbate the trauma. If the police treat us badly, it's hardly a surprise; but it's really devastating to feel let down by our mates afterwards. It can cause 'secondary traumatisation', which is often worse than the initial experience because it shatters our fundamental assumptions. We're not asking for all of us to become 'experts' in healing trauma, but there is a clear need for understanding and support: solidarity is a fundamental part of our politics.[2] The police and prison 'service' specialise in consciously creating traumatising conditions, especially aimed at breaking resistance. Beatings, arrests, isolation custody, violation of rights, threats, lies... Their focus is on creating fear, getting inside our heads and stopping us from taking action again. Within our movements this 'internal censorship' has not really been addressed and talked about. What stops us from getting where we want to get? Sometimes it might be real obstacles; but a lot of the time it is our fear. The state's strategy is a psychological one – they beat one of us up and a hundred get scared and feel blocked. And maybe the person they beat up never goes back on the streets. This is how repression works. And this is why we need to start talking about it. The repressive organs are in their hands – the more effective we are in our struggle, the harder the repression. But how we deal with it is in our hands. What are we going to do with our fear, what are we going to do about our pain, how are we going to support each other through all this and how are we going to show our solidarity?

AN ACTIVE PART OF RESISTANCE

In preparation for Gleneagles, a six-day training course was organised with a professional from a charity focused on trauma care called ASSIST. Most participants, plus some new people, went on to form the Activist-Trauma Support group. As far as we knew, it was the first time active trauma support had been taken on board for a big mobilisation. We were breaking new ground, and with no earlier experience to fall back on, we spent a lot of time trying to figure out what would be needed and useful.

In the end the group split itself between the campsite in Stirling, where a big recovery dome was set up, and the Forest Café in Edinburgh, in the ground floor of the Indymedia Centre where the missing persons helpline and prisoner/friends support were also based. Both groups ran a 24-hour phone helpline.

The recovery dome saw a steady flow of people coming to find somebody to talk to about what they were going through, to get a massage (often fulfilling the same purpose), to find a quiet place to cry, to retreat or to just calm down with a cup of tea and a blanket. Some people came once, some several times. A lot of people seemed to know of our presence on site and it gave them some level of comfort even if they didn't use the facilities – rather like the assurance when you know there is a medical first aid tent.

At the office in Edinburgh, the main tasks were phone support and personal support, but these turned out to be in much less demand than at the campsite. So we started focusing on avoidance of trauma – doing prisoner support (sending cards, money, organising visits) and helping prisoners' friends (making phones available to call families, lawyers, police stations, embassies...). We hadn't intended this to be part of our work but it transpired to be very useful. We also think it proved effective in blurring the distinction between 'trauma support' (which sounds quite dramatic and off-putting), prisoner support and 'general welfare' – we want to normalise and destigmatise trauma.

We know that one of the first things people need after distressing experiences is to see their friends, but tracking down people can be hard and stressful in itself. That's why we had set up a missing persons helpline which was run in close connection with the legal team. It also had the bonus of taking pressure off the legal phonelines when people were just calling to find out about their mates. In addition we organised a secret 'safe space' some miles away from any action for people who really needed to get out of the area. Fortunately it proved not to be necessary this time (at least we hope this is true).

In terms of education, we set up *www.activist-trauma.net*, printed and distributed flyers about what we were offering and what to do after instances of brutality, as well as a six-page briefing about PTS'D'. We organised a few workshops, although we should have done more and advertised them better.

After the summit, the long-term support by phone, email and/or personal contact was less than expected. We're not sure if it wasn't needed, or if people felt reluctant to use it, or if we didn't do sufficient outreach work. On the other hand, the hits on our webpage after the G8 were really high. We had started setting up a public contact base for support which is accessible through the webpage – it's a place where people who need help can find people who offer to help in different ways.

LEARNING THE LESSONS

A month after Gleneagles we had a debriefing weekend with the aim of looking into group dynamics and evaluating our work in order to draw lessons for others.

The general consensus was that all of us enjoyed doing the work; it felt useful, it was appreciated and it was rewarding to feel that somebody actually feels better after talking to you.

Internal group dynamics are often complicated and this is especially true if people have been traumatised in the past – which applied to all of the people in the working group in one way or another. Summits are stressful situations at the best of times: they trigger people's memories and recall previous traumatic situations. Of course, it is not only police violence that causes trauma – statistics suggest that one in four women and one in six men have been sexually abused at some time, while thousands are hurt in car crashes, injured at work and so on. Trauma can result from any situation where the natural reaction to fight or flight is blocked. It is important to remember that a lot of us have gone through some of that and still carry old trauma around while being exposed to new ones. Added to this was that fact that we didn't all know each other beforehand and had very different personal and professional backgrounds and attitudes.

We concluded it would be better for a future trauma support group to really try and get to know each other beforehand, put effort into trust-building and group bonding, since we should be able to draw strength from the group rather than having to deal with internal conflict. It might have been a good idea to have an external 'supervisor' or counsellor on site, independent of the group, who could provide support for the supporters and facilitation if necessary.

From the beginning we had made it clear amongst ourselves that we were offering emotional first aid and not therapy or deep counselling, since a camp-site with police at the gate is not the right space for that, and therapy is a longer term project anyway. As it turned out, it wasn't always easy to make that distinction and opinions about where to draw the line differed due to our different backgrounds. For future work we think it would be important to have an in-depth discussion on this topic beforehand and to establish some ground rules.

We found out that trauma support is very narrowly focused and inevitably ended up doing other mental health work. We recognise the need for broader self-organised mental health support in our movements, but at the same time due to limited resources we could only focus mainly on trauma. It also became clear that trauma work in itself during big mobilisations can't be reduced to police brutality, because the repressive environment triggers all kinds of old trauma like child-hood sexual abuse, rape, and other previous experiences of brutality. When doing emotional first aid it's crucial to keep in mind that the person you are talking to might be carrying all kinds of old trauma with them. And different people need different things, so it's essential to be prepared to adapt to people's specific needs and ways of coping.

There is a definite need for general welfare work – cups of tea, massages, a quiet space and blankets can make an enormous difference, and can help prevent burn-out (on a really basic level, we underestimated the profound impact of a lack of sleep). This blurring of general welfare and trauma support proved to be very useful, especially since a lot of people feel uneasy about going to some kind of 'trauma tent'. We need a longer discussion to come up with ways of making trauma support 'mentally' accessible for as many people as possible. But in the short term, cooperation with prisoner and legal support, cooperation with general welfare, and cooperation with medics can all provide a range of entry points. In the end it's important to raise awareness about the topic and to make an effort to destigmatise it by integrating it within our wider support networks and making that support easy to access.

Overall, we feel we succeeded in putting the topic on the agenda. Hopefully it will be an intrinsic aspect of future activist work, similar to legal and medical support. However, it might take longer to change the culture in our movements to a more supportive environment, where we are not ashamed of what we feel and can be confident that we'll be respected and supported in what we are going through. Activist-Trauma Support was a first step in that direction: we hope that one day going to trauma support will be just as normal as going to the medics and that any stigma will be overcome – not just in terms of traumatic stress, but in the widest sense of mental health.

1   *The term 'disorder' is controversial. Reactions to traumatic experiences are not a disorder, but normal. We use it here to differentiate between post-traumatic stress reactions which heal in 4–6 weeks (PTS) and the condition where symptoms persist after that period (PTS'D').*

2   *In some ways, we think trauma support goes beyond solidarity, it's about just being human and caring for each other. Then again, perhaps all truly revolutionary action is about struggling to become more human!*

24

STRATHCLYDE POLICE SLUMBER PARTY

Major Hassles

On the weekend of July 8 through July 11, I was a very lucky clown as I was invited to the Strathclyde Police Slumber Party! I got the invitation because I hugged a fairy during a street parade. 'Oh what joy!', I thought to my little clown self, excitedly anticipating party food, party games and new friends!

We did indeed play many games. I think the favourite was 'Wake Up, Everybody! Wake Up!' We really liked that game so much that we played it about 70 times over the weekend... Every hour, on the hour: 'Wake Up Everybody!' It was great! Another game we played was called 'Please Sir, can I have some more?' We played that a lot too. Whenever we wanted a glass of water or a sheet of toilet paper we played this exciting game.

All weekend we played party games and we even played tricks on each other. They played a lot of tricks on me. One trick they liked to play was 'Dinner Time'. This trick involved telling me it was 'Dinner Time', but instead of bringing me dinner, they brought 'gloopy poopy'. A very clever trick I thought. Of course, I knew it was a party trick and I didn't eat it.

When I was a young clown I once played a trick on my clown friend: I hid my friend's clothes behind the washing machine while he was in the bath. My friend had to look for a whole ten minutes before he found his trousers!! I think the Strathclyde Police liked this trick too, because they took Dr. Kramer's clothes from him (all except his underwear). They hid his clothes so well that he didn't get to find them the whole time we were at the slumber party!

Speaking of hiding things, one of the favourite games at the slumber party was 'Hide and Seek'. Everyone played this game really well! In fact I didn't see any of the other guests for the whole three days I was there!

I must say, there were a couple of things that I didn't understand that are different from a normal slumber party. For example when my cousin had his party we all slept in the same room. But at Strathclyde Police slumber party we each had to sleep in our own room! They have a very big house you see... My room was called 'Isolation Unit C, Cell 5.'

Also, I wish they had told us to bring our own sheets and pillows because they didn't have any of their own but they did give me a feral duvet... Hmm, come to think of it, they didn't have any beds either. Hey, maybe they had furniture too, but I didn't see that either! Oh they do hide things ever so well.

It was a fun slumber party and I can still hear the policeman's voice saying 'Wake Up, Everybody! Wake Up!' ringing in my ears. I shall write to them and my solicitor friends and tell them about what a fun slumber party it was, and how they could make it more fun the next time.

Bye for now!

Disclaimer: I have tried to make light of our experience in Strathclyde Police cells but this in no way reflects the serious torment I and my fellow G8 protester detainees experienced. I wrote the above as my clown whilst actually in the cells, and the act of writing was therapeutic for me during an intensely dehumanising experience.

25

NOTES ON MOVEMENT AND UNCERTAINTY

Werner Bonefeld

Without movement there is certainty.

The certainty of a world where the drowning of the dispossessed, the miserable and the enslaved, the poor and the hungry, can be watched on television as a 'really existing' reality show. And when they try to get clean water they will be shot. Their desperate attempts to get clean water, food and clothing were deemed a criminal offence against the iron law of private property – they called it looting. New Orleans – the 'Big Easy' – is a symbol of a world where the exception has become the rule. Shoot to kill. And when everything is back to normal, to its civilian best, the poor and miserable who have survived the ordeal will find that the city, its neighbourhoods and dwellings, has been developed and that they are debarred from the development. The developers will have had a good day's taking.

The poor and miserable have been told that they too are citizens with equal rights and freedoms. Their status as citizens was always a precarious promise. Nevertheless, and however inhospitable the conditions of their sacred life, they do indeed partake on the labour market as equals in exchange where labour-power is sold and bought for a wage. It is their liberty and equality as citizens that allow them the freedom to sell their labour-power, and therewith themselves, into conditions that were once described as infernal and that are now celebrated for their flexibility. Flexibility is seen as a form of self-responsibility and self-responsibility is associated with freedom. Those who contract on flexible labour markets and work in flexible conditions know the traditional and lasting meaning of flexibility: to bend and bow, to comply and work.

Without movement, there is certainty: the certainty of great wealth in the face of poverty, the certainty of exploitation, and the certainty of an economic process where destruction is the accepted means of creation, and conversely, where creation is the accepted means of destruction – as a process of creative destruction. Without movement, the ongoing accumulation of 'human machines' on the pyramids of accumulation is certain. Without movement the blind eagerness for plunder and the use of organised coercive force to perpetuate economic progress on the basis of dispossession and misery is certain. Marx's old description of the state as the executive committee of the bourgeoisie has been born out by so-called globalisation. There are thus no more wars between sovereign states. Wars have become 'global' civil wars. Only these civil wars remain.

Without movement there is the certainty of an economic system that produces poverty in a world of plenty, of an economic system whose constituted irrationality requires for its profitable functioning the lengthening of the working day – and this in the face of mass unemployment. Without movement society will suddenly find itself put back into a state of momentary barbarism. Such barbarism will make it appear as if famine, a universal war of devastation had cut off the supply of every means of subsistence. Industry and commerce seem to be destroyed; and why? Without movement there is indeed certainty – the certainty of a bourgeois society that appears to choke itself up on its accumulated wealth. And how does bourgeois society get over these crises? On the one hand, by enforced destruction of a mass of productive forces; on the other, by the conquest of new markets, and by the more thorough exploitation of the old ones.

With movement there is uncertainty.
There is no reality outside capitalism. There are no free, autonomous spaces that, as it were, provide bases for anti-capitalist struggles. We criticise the state, demand its transfer into the museum of history, and yet depend on it for all sorts of things. We reject cuts in welfare, and deteriorating welfare provisions, and we demand that the unemployed are paid well by the state in the form of benefits: the unemployed are not really deemed inessential by capital (they are just treated that way). They perform in fact an important social function. As the board member of Toyota, Mr. Shiramizu, helpfully explained recently, 'in France there are many unemployed people and so [those with jobs] tend to work harder'.[1]

We depend on welfare services, health services, educational services, access to welfare benefits, public transport provision and employment: we do indeed exist through the state and we do indeed exist as a wage-labouring commodity. This is a miserable condition – one can indeed not live an honest life in capitalism. We exist in and through and depend upon those same conditions that we reject. Still, it is because of this dependency that we struggle for social autonomy. That

is, an honest and dignified life already begins in the struggle against capital and its state. Social autonomy starts with the struggle against capital and its state, and associated institutions of social integration and incorporation. The struggle for autonomy is the struggle against definitions and categorisations. It is a struggle for diversity in communality – a struggle through a diversity that is at the same time a collective. Like dignity, it is a general human value that only exists concretely in each individual and is recognised as a general human value only in the concrete individual. Dignity is not abstract and cannot be abstracted from the concrete being. Thus, collectivity through diversity, and vice versa, is a form of organisation that exists only in and through the concrete individual. This collective individual is the multitude. It cannot be defined, nor categorised. It can only move and can only move against the time, not with the time. It is the movement of human emancipation that moves against the time. A movement that does not move is not a movement. Its erstwhile dynamic appears now as stasis. Stasis is to a movement what death is to a person: nothing remains – except the memory, itself dimming and prone to be exploited in and through the nationalisation of its legend. Against the dimming of time, the past struggles of the oppressed have to be unfrozen in the struggles of today. The danger is our own stasis – and thus our transport into an historical exhibit, carefully reconstructed to look as real as all the other dead exhibits.

    Any attempt at categorising or defining the movement in its movement reduces it to canon fodder that, led by the Party and under its auspices, is stripped of its negative potential. Instead of melting what seemed solid into thin air, the Party provides the multitude with a programmatic definition that perverts the aim of organisation in the means of resistance. Instead of doing, and learning by doing, the Party cages the multitude and this is indeed what it needs to do – a Party that represents no discernible quantifiable interests and which thus has no captive constituency is not a Party. Thus the multitude of human dignitaries becomes instead commensurate to foot soldiers. Do not think. Do not show humanity. Do not blink. Comply! The Party always knows best. However, the doing has to be learned – it cannot be commandeered. Commandeered doing is not doing: it is slaving. Learning by doing creates a public sphere in distinction from and as an alternative to the well-ordered bourgeois public sphere. For the Party to be the Party, it has to expropriate, contain, and control this alternative public sphere – the sphere where the multitude determines itself in the course of its own democratic becoming. By expropriating this public sphere, by reducing it to a spectacle of Party-political organisation, by taking from it its carnivalistic spontaneity of doing and experimenting, the Party transforms the not-yet of social autonomy in action into a well ordered, thoughtlessly thinking voting bloc.

Capitalism has nothing to fear from this sort of Party. Dignity has. The Party might still accept Trotsky's wish to 'spill blood'. The multitude does not wish to spill blood – it wants the spilling of blood to stop, once and for all, here and now. The Party might no longer favour violence as a means of seizing power. The multitude does not wish to seize power. There is no need for the master of violence – the state – in a classless society. The multitude does not compete with capitalism. Its purpose is the creation of an alternative to capitalism. The multitude's struggle for social autonomy is not conceived as a competition with capitalism. The Party competes – for votes, for participation in the convents of power, for governing responsibility in the palace, for certitude and responsibility in recognition of its own organisational self-interest, which it wishes to preserve at all costs. It competes by incorporating the multitude into a programmatic definition that is at once also pragmatic. Herein lies its usefulness for a political and economic order that it ostensibly wishes to demolish. The purpose and thus usefulness of the Party is that it seeks to make certain what is in fact uncertain. Its declamation of certainty – be it the correctness of its programme, understanding of the so-called laws of history, or tactical manoeuvre – is a mere posture; at best it confuses the struggle for a human society with the humanisation of inhuman conditions – a laudable endeavour that however perpetuates what it wishes to humanise; at worst, it tries to better capitalism in the name and on behalf of labour, collectivity and solidarity! If there were no such Party, the bourgeoisie would have to invent it. And maybe it did.

The negative potential of the multitude cannot be absorbed by the Party –

it either engages in the struggle for social autonomy and thus shows its negative potential in the democracy of the living or it does not and thus sheds its negativity in favour of certainty. The line between struggle and incorporation, between negativity and responsible acceptance of the given, is a fine one. Class struggle exists in and against capital. We all live in bourgeois society. It can however not be left behind by merely living within it. The negation of bourgeois society moves in and against its constituted forms. This is the site of class antagonism and class struggle. Only organised negation is able to transform the existence of class struggle in and against bourgeois social relations into the beyond of human history. This organised negation has however to be a self-organised negation. It learns by doing. The statement that one cannot live an honest life in the falsehood of bourgeois society is therefore only partially correct. An honest and sincere life starts already with the struggle against the falsehood of bourgeois society.

UNCERTAINTY AND NEGATION
The achievement of the society of the free and equal will depend on the sincere and honest struggle against capital and its state. There is no certainty. To speak about the multitude is to embrace uncertainty. Certainty and predictability belong to capitalism's own self-image. The image has little to do with reality. Capitalism depends on making certain, as a resource, and predictable, as a factor of production, our living labour-power, and therewith us. Our struggle against capital and its state is the struggle against the constituted certainty of capitalism – 'there is no alternative'. Our struggle is a struggle of uncertainty. Uncertainty is unavoidable. Uncertainty and the struggle for social autonomy belong together. Uncertainty entails doubt and patience. Since we do not and cannot know what history there will be, we have to make it with critical consciousness, a consciousness that thinks on its feet with dignity and is not corrupted by the sirens of power. Doubt is subversive. And patience? Patience, too, is a revolutionary endeavour. Impatience seeks quick, certain, predictable results; impatience laments – it rejects learning by doing; and prefers definite outcomes. Impatient revolutionaries are bosses in disguise. Impatience knows of only one time, the time of command, and is thus driven by time – the time of the clock – this homogeneous, steady and repetitive tick-tock. Impatience has no conception of how the time of insurrection melts away the time of exploitation. Lastly, we cannot do without irony. Irony helps us to overcome set-backs, defends us against depression and privatisation – this return to the safety of the living room. Irony, doubt, patience: these are the protective means against a life that is indifferent to itself and that therefore accepts without question its capitalist existence as a mere human resource.

In the misery of our time wage levels and income guarantees – be it in terms of money, goods or services – have to be defended and improved conditions have to be demanded. Pressure needs to be asserted to liberate millions of people from conditions of poverty and deprivation. However, the concept of welfare is

not enough. The demand is for human dignity. Dignity entails the human need for time, as against a life consisting solely of labour-time. Dignity entails the need of relations of human integrity, as against the reduction of human existence to a mere resource. Dignity entails the need for collectivity and solidarity, against the isolation of and indifference between individuals. Dignity entails respect and mutual recognition of the human subjects, against a form of existence that reduces humanity to a mere agent of economic rationality. Dignity entails the need for public space, as against enclosure, privatisation and communicative systems driven by development as capitalist freedom. Dignity entails the need for education, pleasure, human significance and mutual recognition. Dignity, in short, entails the equality of individual human needs for food, shelter, clothing, love, affection, knowledge and human significance. Human beings have either a price or a dignity. Price belongs to commodities. Dignity belongs to subjects. For the subject to be a subject, it cannot have a price. It can only have dignity.

The anti-globalisation conceptions of cosmopolitan democratic renewals or the anti-capitalist call for the intensification of economic struggle and building on that struggle, the intensification of political struggle to achieve a shift in the balance of class forces, reduce the struggle for democracy to a struggle for political power. The former sets out to democratise global institutions such as the World Bank, the IMF, the WTO and the UN. The great virtue of democracy that is celebrated here is the peaceful way in which it circulates elites, namely by means of competitive elections between two rival sets of political managers, each campaigning on the basis of a programme that promises a more effective, efficient and economic use of resources. Then there is the demand for an intensification of struggle to shift the balance of class forces. The idea here it seems is that neo-liberalism is a form of capitalist hegemony and that a shift in the balance of class forces at the expense of capital will lead to a different form of hegemony. It is difficult to say what this hegemony might look like. What is the meaning, say, of a socialist hegemony in capitalism? Is socialist coercion preferable to capitalist coercion? Marx's judgement of similar proposals at his time still rings true: 'Poor dogs! They want to treat you like human beings!' Human emancipation cannot be achieved through coercive institutions. The realism of these conceptions of anti-globalisation lacks emancipatory contents and is, in fact, much more removed from social conditions than the concept of humanity that is based on the following imperative: act in such a way that you recognise humanity in your person and in all other persons always as a purpose, never as a means. Democracy, if taken seriously, entails this conception of humanity in action. It does not belong to coercive institutions. It belongs to subjects.

The struggle for social autonomy is therefore a struggle for the complete democratisation of all social relations. This struggle follows a completely different conception of time from that which says that time is money. In fact, the struggle for human autonomy is also, and fundamentally so, a struggle for different conceptions of time, liberating social time from its reduction to product and cash. Time as measure of social wealth and time as human social self-determination belong to different worlds. The first is the time of the human being as a mere agent or personification of economic categories – price, product, profit; the second is the time of the human being as a self-determining subject.

Self-determining subjects need time. Thus, the struggle for the shortening of the working day is the basic prerequisite of human emancipation. The capitalist form of wealth, and its reduction of time to cash and product, restricts the potential of society as every crisis shows. It is also shown in every commodity that cannot be sold for profit in the face of want; and that is defended by brute force in the face of thirst and hunger. Poverty of conditions is all-too evident in the so-called 'developing' countries, and remains hidden under the cloak of apparent prosperity in the so-called First World. New Orleans showed class politics in action, it showed what poverty and dispossession mean. How much labour-time was needed in 2005 to produce the same amount of commodities that was produced in 1995? Twenty per cent? Forty per cent or fifty per cent? Whatever the percentage might be, what is certain is that labour-time has not decreased. It has increased and it has done so in the face of mass unemployment. What is certain too is that the distribution of wealth is as unequal as never before. The contradiction between the forces and relations of production does seek resolution: destruction of productive forces, scrapping of labour through war and generalised poverty and misery, and all this against the background of an unprecedented accumulation of wealth.

Struggle for the democratic self-organisation of society entails the politicisation of social relations, and therewith the cancellation of the concentration of the political in the form of the state. Discussion of this issue is beyond the remit of this piece. Suffice to say that such politicisation does entail social conflict, which might succeed or bring to power 'well-meaning dictators... genuinely anxious to restore' the rule of law.[2] There is no certainty. Against the background of the contemporary transformation of the 'citizen' into a security risk, the democratic personality is a scandal and is thus treated as a subversive element – and rightly so.

1   Financial Times, *March 3 2003*.
2   *Hayek, praising Pinochet, quoted in R. Cristi*, Carl Schmitt and Authoritarian Liberalism *(Cardiff: University of Wales Press, 1998) p. 168*.

26

G8 SECRETS: WE ARE MORE POWERFUL THAN WE CAN POSSIBLY IMAGINE

Haley Burton

I moved back to Scotland wishing I hadn't committed myself to getting involved in the G8 resistance. I'd made that commitment a year beforehand when I was under a lot of stress at work and home. Since then, my life away from Scotland had improved. I didn't want to be here. I had been happy living with Rose and Maurice in their beautiful crumbling old house with its well-tended vegetable and fruit garden. I felt privileged to share the lives of these inspirational people who'd spent their time working for peace and justice. It was a welcome change living with independent people who respected my space. My colleagues' childcare duties had become less of an obstacle to their presence at work. Just before I planned to leave, I met a man who I fell for in a big way. And I felt very bad about leaving the local peace movement, a group so small that the departure of a fully committed activist could leave a gap that might not be filled. 'I don't want to do this' ran through my head constantly. My mind was focused on the middle of July when I'd be free to go back south and see my lover Marco again.

Alex had come to see me in March just before I moved back. He seemed to think I was one of the only people who could make a difference between stuff happening and not happening. It looked like there was a big gap that needed to be filled. I sensed a certain amount of desperation in him, which upset me. But I thought he was placing far too much faith in my abilities and I was sure I couldn't help that much. I didn't say so, although I thought so all along, right up to the morning of July 6 when I sat in the van listening to the traffic news. I thought so when he and Pat came to tell me about the secret blockades plan. And I couldn't honestly see how we'd get all the practical stuff together to make the plan work.

It seemed important not to voice my doubts, so as not to dent anyone's confidence, especially in meetings where I was the only person from Scotland present, and so had to put forward some kind of framework for other people's efforts. It was obvious that Pat and Alex were under huge pressure getting this plan to work; I didn't want to add to their stress by saying I thought it wouldn't. The fact that it did work is a huge testament to the trust that activists placed in each other, in themselves, and in people they never even got to meet. Lastly, Alex's admiration means a lot to me. I didn't want to disappoint him and risk losing that – no matter how misplaced I feel it is sometimes.

Despite my personal feelings, it was clear that this was our chance, all of us in Britain and beyond, to show some determined, concrete resistance to the machinery of capitalism. We had to take it!

Certain things kept me going through the weeks before July 6. The thought of going away afterwards. The thought that it would all be over. The possibility I might learn to drive the site crew truck. The steady flow of activists into Scotland as the weeks advanced. The morale-boosting effects of Dissent! gatherings, meetings and contact with other activists. It was a tough time, but there was never a moment when I was ready to walk away. I spent time getting fit and put some energy into the hillwalking action, encouraging Lesley to organise trips to the Ochils. This enabled me to explore some of the roads and terrain around Gleneagles. Pat, Alex and I met frequently, or talked in abbreviated phone calls, to refine the plan and work out how to get practical stuff done. They had the entire scenario worked out in an impressive way. Often I just acted as a sounding board to enable them to fine-tune the details.

The action was organised by what was effectively a spokes-council, which the initiators had gathered around them. Each spoke was a link to a different affinity group, or groups, which was to take on blockading a specific location on the roads around the summit. Some spokes were links to the public part of the blockades – the large numbers who would arrive a few days beforehand ready to take part in direct action but without a plan or knowledge of the area. The spokes met a few times, and communicated, with a good deal of secrecy and caution, and as far as we know these communications weren't infiltrated.

Gradually my part of the actions – blocking a road with a vehicle – started coming together. I chose a point to blockade and visited it several times to check visibility, traffic levels, and road width. Sally said she'd join me. Later she changed her mind, but by then she and Pat had put me in touch with George and Alan, who were keen to be involved. We had an affinity group! We had access to all the equipment we needed, except we didn't have a vehicle. I lay awake at night worrying about it. How was I going to obtain a vehicle with only a week or two

to go? By this stage I'd stopped caring about losing my driving licence, having found that Allie had done something far more dangerous and had only been banned for a year. I reckoned I could handle that.

Ironically after making the effort to get fit, thinking I'd be walking over the hills to storm the gates of Gleneagles, I did an action that involved driving and sitting still. However as Marco said later, racing drivers keep extremely fit. Most people assumed I was helping to organise the hillwalking action – sorry, Lesley. I might have coined the phrase 'Gore-Tex bloc', but I think the blockades idea was better.

Taking a calculated risk, I left buying a van until the last minute in the hope that the change of owner wouldn't register until after July 6. This may have worked, because I overheard the cops wondering whose it was. I'd had the *Evening Times* for a few days before ringing some adverts. The first one I contacted was exactly what I wanted – old, taxed and MoT'd, for £280. Only problem – it was about 40 miles away. Even luckier, the owner was going abroad shortly and had moved out of the address on the registration document, so there was less chance she'd get hassled. She agreed a £25 discount for cash, and I did a mammoth bus and train mission all next day to collect it. In the meantime I'd been at the convergence centre in Stirling helping build the site. I never got around to putting my tent up there, just slept in the car park in a site crew truck. The next few days were a nightmare of worrying if the van had been broken into, moving it to remain inconspicuous, insuring it, which cost a lot, but there's a 14-day cooling-off clause where you can get a full refund. Filling it with all the equipment we needed was another cause of panic – 'Road Closed' signs were too big to go in the back, and so had to be put in view covered in dog blankets. A volunteer unexpectedly turned up at George's workplace while we were modifying and loading the signs on a Sunday afternoon – luckily, preparation for building an extension was a good enough explanation.

Throughout the planning stage we kept everything secret, even from our friends. We couldn't talk openly among ourselves unless we were sure no one could hear. The secrecy was a huge strain, and we all wanted to be able to have a normal conversation again. Further paranoia was induced by a huge police presence, including a camera van in the same place all week from which a motorcyclist followed me one day. It seemed every time I went out a police car appeared behind me. I took to driving convoluted routes to avoid it.

We decided to stash the van north of the Forth Bridge a day or two before. At last it was ready to go. I drove around the outskirts of Edinburgh while the Carnival for Full Enjoyment was getting the crap beaten out of it by the Met. As I paid for some petrol several carloads of police pulled up, refuelling on their way off duty. There were police on the bridge. I parked under CCTV at a convenient station, still nervous the van would get stolen; that model was a prime target for break-ins. There were police on the trains and stations on the way back, fearful of a threat to the rail bridge.

That morning I'd had a visit from Jackie who had put me in contact with an affinity group which was ready to help with our action by meeting us the next morning and joining the blockade.

Writing about it brings back the nervousness I felt. If I hadn't been doing a lot of this alone, I'd have felt less scared. Having few people to talk to about it, and having to be careful of being overheard with those in on the plan, made it more frightening.

I spent the last day getting food and equipment together and worrying whether Alan had been arrested at the Carnival. Then it was time to go. More police were on the trains and cruising the small town where we met. There was confusion about which bus stop to meet at, and everyone was late. Finally we were all in the same spot – and Alan had recruited Kate to join us! I retrieved the van and circled a roundabout three times waiting for the others to catch up. They got in. We were off!

We had a lot of time to kill. We had a chilled-out picnic on a beach, thanks mainly to Kate who'd brought lots of nice food like hummus. We looked at maps and decided on our route, along minor roads. We talked about interesting things like the clown army. At last, I felt like this could work, buoyed up by the warmth and friendship of my fellow blockaders, who were all really up for it!

At nightfall, which is at around 11.30 this time of year in Scotland, we walked back to the car park. We tested both lock-ons inside the van and found the best places for them.

My prime concern for this action had been safety. I knew I was capable of safe driving. I'd picked the spot on the road we blocked where the traffic would be slowest and we'd be most visible. I wanted to make sure we could move once in place, if necessary, and that we could get out fast. So we had keys to our padlocks handy and we didn't superglue the locks or otherwise disable the vehicle. We had food and water. Although I felt nervous, I managed to drive calmly and safely. Alan and George did a fine job with the maps, navigating perfectly all the way.

We left the beach and headed inland, hoping to find somewhere to park up and sleep unnoticed. We found a lay-by on a secluded driveway and stopped there for a few hours, sleeping reasonably well in the circumstances. At dawn we set off, driving through villages, finding the most minor, remote road we could over the motorway in case of police patrols, and meandering gradually towards our destination. We drove down a forest track and stopped for a while, surprising a motorist who was probably off fishing. By this time George and Alan had their fluorescent jackets on, so I guess we just looked like a carload of forestry workers. Just before seven o'clock we reached the last B-road before our destination. I turned down it and saw a blue flashing light in the distance. My heart sank. Had we been sussed? I turned the car, intending to find another route, hoping that, as it had rained hard during the night, the police car was merely there to warn of a flood. I think I was right. We doubled back and took another road, turned onto the main road and passed the stationary police car at a respectable 50mph, the yellow jackets probably giving the impression of everyday travel to work. I slowed for the junction and turned onto our chosen road. I stopped the car, George and Alan jumped out in their hard hats, and everyone frantically unloaded road signs, cones and red triangles. As soon as enough cones were in place I turned the car to block the road. A handful of international activists leapt over the wall with lock-on tubes and attached themselves underneath the car. Kate and I clicked our padlocks shut and we waited to see what would happen. Alan and George had the difficult job of dealing with irate drivers. A few of them squeezed by on the pavement. We had never wanted to stop local residents going to work anyway.

Kate and I grinned at each other. I was elated. We'd done it! In spite of all my misgivings, we'd succeeded.

The police arrived soon afterwards. I spent the next five hours locked on inside the car, watching the queues of traffic slowly easing past us on the pavement. We were joined by more friends and supporters, thanks to the communications that others in the spokes-council had worked out. Some people, held up on their way to the G8Alternatives demo in Auchterarder, stopped and joined us for a while. Having the advantage of a car radio, we listened to Radio Scotland travel news at full volume so that people outside could hear. All roads leading to Gleneagles had been blockaded, apart from some minor roads; the railway had been

blocked in two places. Our blockade was now a crucial link in the plan. I heard later that we had caused a long tailback. Traffic reporters were warning motorists to avoid central Scotland. Crieff, Kinkell Bridge, the A9, M9 and M80 and Yetts o' Muckhart were all reported as being blocked, as was the railway. A minor road at Forteviot had also been blockaded.

It was as if all my training, all my learning and previous experience had led me to this point; as if it was all preparation for this one, decisive act of resistance to capitalism. This was the biggest, most important action I felt I'd ever been part of.

After five hours the cutting crew arrived to break our blockade. They had been prevented from reaching us by all the other blockades and it had taken them time to cut people out of steel lock-on tubes. They broke the window and opened the doors. After some investigation of gaffer tape and carpet, they easily cut through our bike locks and lifted Kate and me out. We both refused to walk, saying we had cramp. After dealing with us, they investigated the lock-ons underneath. Luigi and Monika had locked themselves together with a steel pipe, one on each side of the car, but not locked to the car itself. Very clever as they prevented the car being moved. They eventually unlocked themselves.

Kate avoided being charged. I was charged with Breach of the Peace. There was no evidence I had committed any driving offences. Alan, however, got arrested trying to lock onto the towing hook at the back of the car, and Dieter, a German who claimed to come from Legoland ('You mean Heligoland?' 'No, Legoland') was nicked trying to de-arrest him. Luigi and Monika were also charged with breach of the peace. Sally and Margaret had come to support us and kept track of where we were taken. I spent 34 hours in Perth police station, sleeping, talking to cell-mates and every so often jumping up saying 'We did it! We stopped the G8!'

The plan I'd been so doubtful about had succeeded beyond my wildest dreams. My feelings changed completely – I didn't need a holiday, I wasn't bothered about getting away to see Marco, I wasn't interested in learning to drive the truck – I just wanted to go back and do another action with the same amazing bunch of brave, clever, determined, inspiring activists. Alex kindly reminded me that I probably needed a break, though I'm sure he worked far harder than I did.

This almost unbelievable success has been a huge lesson to me. We are more powerful than we can possibly imagine. It's been a lesson in not being deflected from achieving my aims by fear; in not letting doubts get in the way of an obviously good plan; in not paying attention to feelings of discouragement when I know I'm doing the right thing; a lesson in trust, in love, in anarchy. Here's to our continued collaboration in creative resistance to capitalism – as anarchists, as accomplices, as conspirators, as friends.

I'm still experiencing the emotional repercussions of the G8 mobilisation. I didn't get beaten up by the police, witness violence or any other traumatic events. But I'm not completely in touch with how good it felt to succeed. If I could feel like that all the time I'd be walking about ten feet off the ground; I'd know we were powerful enough do anything; and I'd love everybody.

27

A KNOCK AT THE DOOR: SPECIAL AGENT PARANOIA AND THE G8 INFO-LINE

Anonymous

There's a knock at the door. We look at one another. Our replacements aren't supposed to be here for hours. We leap into action and follow our prearranged roles. I grab the phones and head for the toilet. Neil runs to wake up Pete. It's Pete's job to buzz in anyone who comes to the door and has the right password but he won't wake up. Neil shakes him and runs to put the maps away. None of this should concern me. I'm struggling with the backs of the phones: I need to get those sim cards out. If this is a raid they're going down the pan, flush. I perch on the edge of the bath, sim cards in hand, hand hovering over the toilet. I'm listening for sounds of a front door crashing in or the harsh shouts of a police raiding party. I look at my hand and a thought goes through my mind – these fuckers will just sit in the bowl and get retrieved, I need to make sure they get smashed to pieces...

Friendly voices filter under the bathroom door. A quick chuckle at the situation and I let myself out. It's the next shift turning up early because it's hard to get here at the right time in the middle of the night. They have no idea of the bowel movements they've just induced. When we take them through the routine, they're going to think that cabin fever has set in. Well, it all makes sense when you think it through.

We introduce ourselves to those of the next shift we don't know. It's a funny thing, we're in a potentially dicey situation and paranoia is running at full pitch, yet I feel fine about these people I don't directly know being able to place me here. It's a bit like *Goodfellas*, or *Six Degrees of Separation*. Something needs doing, there's a risk of arrest, and a friend approaches you. Do you know anyone who can be trusted and will be up for this job? Yeah, I'll ask so-and-so, they're sound, they're goodfellas, they're friends of ours. That's how affinity groups network for semi-clandestine stuff. You rely on the judgement of your friends about their friends.

Teas all around and then the phone rings. Good, this'll give them the chance to see how it works. We're running the Info-Line. A highly complex plan has been developed. Thousands of cards have been distributed around Glasgow, Edinburgh and Stirling asking people to phone information in to one of three mobile phone numbers or to get in touch if they need to find something out. (Each number is for a different network in case one goes down or has no coverage in certain areas around Gleneagles.) The cards also tell people to subscribe to a text messaging system. If the cops shut down the advertised numbers, we've got two sets of back-up numbers we can send out to try and keep the information flowing. The system works best during the morning of the blockades with people spread all over central Scotland wanting to know if they are the only ones blockading the road. If we start a barricade here will there be anyone to join us? But when you answer the phone you have to be careful. You need to consider everything you say. We work out that it's best to take the question, say 'Hold on, wait a sec,' put the phone against your chest and talk it over with the other people there.

Everything you say you've got to be prepared to justify to a judge. You can't be seen to direct people. You say: 'We've heard reports that there are blockades on such-and-such a road.' Or: 'The BBC is reporting a demonstration at this point.' Or: 'You are not the first person to ask if your group is alone in those woods, we've received five other calls from groups near your position waiting to blockade the road.' You have to talk a weird language. You come across a bit like a politician being interviewed. Some callers click on to what you're doing straight away while others continue on confused. Even worse, some people recognise your voice and blurt out 'Hey, is that —?'

These precautions may seem a little over the top for something so innocuous as running a phone line, but there's good reason for it. After the Gothenburg anti-EU summit protests of 2001, eight Swedish youths were sentenced to between one year four months and two years four months in jail for doing something very similar. They'd been less cautious, running their 'Information Central' from a tent at the convergence centre. They were openly collecting information and directing people to the most useful places. That precedent was enough to concentrate our minds.

Our info-line was run from a 'clean' flat and when travelling there you were supposed to use 'counter-surveillance techniques' to make sure you weren't being followed. That is, any counter-surveillance techniques you'd picked up from trashy spy films. The thing is, we needed to do it, or at least I think we did.

Take this example: I was walking through Edinburgh in the days directly before the protests when I thought I was being followed. This guy seemed to have stuck with me even when I'd started to walk aimlessly. I did what any good secret agent does and paid into a cinema, settling down to watch the film. He followed me in. Ten minutes later I grabbed my bags, headed for the toilets and then slipped out the exit. No one seemed to be following me, so I went to the station to rendezvous with the person I was supposed to be meeting. But as I came out of the station, there he was again! That same man walking back towards me. I stared at the fucker, but no sign of recognition showed on his face. He could have been a copper, a journalist out to track down the 'secret leadership' or some guy killing time before catching his train. Fuck knows.

It's not a healthy state of affairs playing James Bond, you can never quite work out what the fuck is going on, and if you did it too much, you'd soon lose track and live your whole life in a corrosive netherworld of suspicion. Still, I'm not denying it's fun for a bit, and I still have a little laugh when I think of my state of mind as I hovered over that toilet.

28

ANTI-G8 RESISTANCE AND THE STATE OF EXCEPTION

Stefan Skrimshire

Protesters recovering from the week of demonstrations, marches and blockades surrounding the Gleneagles summit will have come home to a wide spectrum of reactions to what they had been doing and what they thought they had achieved. This was a question too easily monopolised by cynicism and overshadowed in the haste to 'interpret' the latest wave of terrorist attacks. In considering a response, however, it should at least be acknowledged that what protesters *did* over the space of a week was all the more remarkable for their adaptation to, and resilience against, conditions that resembled the tactics of a police state. Everywhere 'unauthorised' protesters congregated, travelled, and demonstrated, they met with permanent surveillance, stopping and searching, numerous arrests, and Section 60 detainment by riot police. In a particularly symbolic instance, the eco-village in Stirling, containing up to four thousand people, was put under temporary siege by riot police following a day of coordinated disruption of the routes transporting delegates to Gleneagles and at the perimeter fence itself.

The pattern of such tactics cannot have truly surprised anyone who has been protesting in the UK during the past five years. Section 60 of the 1994 Criminal Justice and Public Order Act – the right to stop and search in anticipation of violence, ordered for up to 24 hours – has been used extensively to pen in protesters for several hours at a time, such as the 'exclusion zone' imposed on parts of central London on May Day 2000. The Terrorism Act 2000 also came into effect for the first time in Scotland for the G8 summit, allowing police to detain protesters for up to a week without charge. The July 4 Carnival for Full Enjoyment in Edinburgh also witnessed the use of automatic street barricades that fold out to create temporary cages to confine protests at a moment's notice. The policing of public demonstration, it seems, simply extends a much wider and culturally established notion of public space as the controlled environment, able to respond instantly to the threat of disorder. The police cordon has become a necessary piece of town planning itself, the barrier that aims to protect 'the public' from unauthorised political expression. And whilst the cordons and arrests in Scotland provoked outrage and panic, there was, on the other hand, a feeling that *we have seen this before*. The routine ascription of 'Designated Protest Zones' is now assimilated within the logic of pre-emptive strike, since the *threat* alone of protest outside the space designated to it has become, in the eyes of the state, intolerable.

POLITICS OF THE CAMP

The development of this style of public containment bears important consequences for the future of public protest in general, no matter how confrontational social movements intend to be. It therefore merits a closer look at its underlying logic. The Italian philosopher Giorgio Agamben provides some insight with his use of the concept of the 'state of exception' intrinsic to the European model of sovereignty.[1] Historically, a sovereign's mandated role is to be able to suspend the rights and guarantees of its citizens in the greater interest of security, and of law itself. The strong arm of liberal state sovereignty as much as dictatorship, therefore, must live in this contradiction of both being the law and suspending the law, in order to monopolise violence. The right of exception is '...the point of indistinction between violence and the law, the threshold on which violence passes over into law and law passes over into violence.'[2] Today, in the context of the increasing erosion of civil liberties under the rubric of the 'war on terror', it is becoming clear that such an exercise of extrajudicial authority has become unexceptional. We witness its most visible expressions in the creation of a new breed of Camp X-Rays, detention centres, *zones d'attentes*, exclusion zones, non-places for a new generation of terror suspects, asylum seekers and others suspended from the protection of the law. The camp, writes Agamben, is 'the space that opens up when the state of exception becomes the rule...the structure in which the state of exception is permanently realised.'[3] Whilst it began its constitutive definition with the concentration camps linked to colonial struggles 100 years ago (the term 'concentration camp' refers to those set up by the English to contain the Boers at the beginning of the twentieth century),[4] it is still materialised whenever people are reduced to 'bare life', stripped of any rights or values, 'a space in which power confronts nothing other than pure biological life without any mediation.'[5]

Such a condition is not far from the status given those terror 'suspects' caught within the military logic of a 'total war' or a 'state of emergency.' Without

wanting to confuse the experience of Camp X-Ray prisoners with that of protesters'
treatment by the police, we should suspect that the same blurring of distinctions
between criminal and suspect, terrorist and potential terrorist, is creeping into
the domain of public protest. The presence of the camp in the midst of 'democratic' societies is only one, albeit powerfully symbolic, tool to remind citizens that
we are all caught up in a state of war. As a consequence, the use of 'special powers'
by police such as the 2000 Terrorism Act is becoming the increasingly 'normal'
experience of public order situations, those, for instance, as far removed from
terrorist threat as street carnivals. As Magnus Hörnqvist has written recently, both
the macro level tactics of the war on terror and the micro level introduction of
public order tactics have eroded the distinction between criminality and the
creation of a 'perception of insecurity', leading to the ability for *norms of behaviour* – including the right to protest peacefully – to engender violent repression.
This shift from the language of *law* and *rights* to that of *security* and *protection* –
exacerbated by a climate of intense paranoia surrounding the language of 'terror'
and 'anarchy' – is also the new paradigm in which political protest must function.[6]
Politics, it seems, must be removed from the public eye for its own protection,
and so walls must be erected. And if the public wishes to *be* politics, to represent
an alternative democracy opposed to that of the G8, for instance (as opposed to
being 'history'...protesters were never advised to Make Poverty Political) then
they need to be protected from themselves.

The containment of dissent in this way parallels the hidden performances of global power. Forced to retreat to a remote hotel in Scotland surrounded by five miles of fencing, riot police and the army, the world's most powerful today bear witness to the new mode of sovereignty: out of sight, out of mind. Its secrecy represents the retreat of politics itself to an ivory tower removed from the public glare. What can be the remaining symbols of power and hierarchy to the growing dissatisfaction of the masses *apart* from those fences and barriers themselves, the illegality of borders and barriers? In a liberal, laissez-faire political culture in which public life is carefully kept away from political life, in which public debate and rationalisation is confined to spectatorship and media consumption, the Gleneagles protest in *all* its guises represented trespass in the eyes of neo-liberal government.

RECLAIM SPACES!

Against this backdrop of a culture of exclusion zones and sieges, the disappearance of both the dissenter and the centres of power from public interaction, what *can* be achieved, to return to the original question facing the protesters? For one, it must never be forgotten that the logic of this siege culture is already rippling through the rhetoric and practice of resistance itself, the imperative of *territory* directing its survival under repression. In the very language of 'direct action' protest, there is a popular awareness of the perpetual threat to mobility, an acceptance that today's political skirmishes are fundamentally a contestation of space. The idea that resistance has strength in numbers is well known to be relative to the ability for those numbers to scatter, to work autonomously, to resist enclosure. And in Scotland protests responded tactically simply by the fact that, spread as they were over so many actions and geographic locations, there was never one group to be contained and defeated. Blockades of various delegate routes into Gleneagles, as well as protests at the perimeter fence, were spread out around the surrounding area. Whether people chose to march, sit down, or break down physical barriers, the fundamental police tactic of containment, unsuited to the countryside, was stretched to the limit of its resources. Whatever conclusions people come to in assessing whether the protests around Gleneagles were 'successful', therefore, should at least acknowledge that a broad rejection of the principle of containment and disappearance was evident throughout. In a global order often described, in its financial and power flows, as 'deterritorialised',[7] this battle for space is a powerfully symbolic as well as practical one. The palpable desperation of protest that wants to 'reclaim the streets' and 'reclaim the commons', is a significant reminder that even if global capitalist power has transcended geography, the popular consensus upon which it is founded still *lives* and works in those spaces. And what people are beginning to see in those spaces is an increasingly paranoid and violent erosion of the freedoms they were instituted to protect.

Global protest movements *are* waking up to the disembodied reality of global politics, through an exploration of mobility and fluidity of bodies. And if this is true, it is surely what invites a greater dialogue between the desires of more mainstream demonstrations such as the Make Poverty History march, the left-wing coalitions like G8Alternatives, and the more confrontational attitudes of direct action groups like Dissent! For it is potentially not so much the desire to be *seen* and *heard* that constitutes the 'publicness' of public protest, but the constant promise to be present and evade disappearance, to make known its political desires wherever power meets. In this case, the desires latent to each movement might not be as alien to one another as some people assume. As Hardt and Negri put it, the 'multitude' is a source of constant antagonism to Empire precisely because of its fluidity of movement across boundaries, *and* of ideas across social identities.[8] This idea continues to express itself in the critique of borders and fences, the containment and separation of social subjects. Organisations such as the 'no borders' campaigns against asylum deportations, international solidarity actions, or symbolic protests like the Camp X-Ray reconstruction in Hulme, Manchester, are, in their own ways, attempts to expose the encroaching borders that are placing us all under siege, 'protecting' us from the space of politics. Not only can such actions uphold the moral outrage that is appropriate to it, they also contest the containment of dissent itself. Perhaps more than any other summit protests, the experience in Scotland took the popular anti-capitalist slogan 'We Are Everywhere' to its most practical application, an attempt to defy the confinement and dehumanisation of political action.

1   Giorgio Agamben, Homo Sacer *trans. Daniel Heller-Rozen (California: Stanford University Press, 1998), p.20. Agamben's interest in the 'state of exception' is derived principally from the German political scientist Carl Schmitt. Central to Schmitt's legal theory was the 'paradox' that the sovereign is 'at the same time outside and inside the juridical order' (ibid., p.15). It therefore resembles the notion of the state of siege or of emergency powers in the French and English traditions. See also, Michael Hardt and Antonio Negri*, Multitude *(New York: Penguin Press, 2004) pp. 7–10.*

2   Giorgio Agamben, Homo Sacer, *p. 38*

3   Giorgio Agamben, Means Without End, *trans. Vincenzo Binetti & Cesare Casarino (London: University of Minnesota Press, 2000) pp. 39, 40*

4   ibid., *p. 38*

5   ibid., *p.41*

6   Magnus Hörnqvist, 'The birth of public order policy', Race & *Class, 46 (2004) p. 37*

7   See, for example, Gilles Deleuze & Felix Guattari, Anti-Oedipus: Capitalism and Schizophrenia *(London: The Athlone Press, 1984).*

8   Hardt and Negri, *Multitude.*

29

GINGER TAKES ON THE G8
The Ginger

SATURDAY

Complete darkness. He was trapped on all sides. His ginger hair nostrils quivered as the odour of stale urine reminded him of where he was and, more importantly, his purpose. He had to get out and he had to get out fast. The rumble of the tracks below indicated that the train on which he was travelling was slowing down. Now was his chance, his chance for freedom. It was now or never, 'HELP!!! Can you help me? I'm trapped in the toilet,' the Ginger screamed, 'I've been trapped in here for twenty minutes, it's so hot I'm going to faint and the floor is yellow and sticky.' Then slowly a shaft of light appeared in the eternal night of the train toilet and the Ginger's knight in shining Scottish Railways uniform pulled the door slowly back revealing a small and offensively ugly group of Liverpool activists laughing at the Ginger's misfortune and filming his ordeal on a hand-held camera.

'Morons.' It was only Saturday, the first day of a week of anti-G8 protests in Scotland and the Ginger had got himself trapped in the Stirling–Edinburgh train toilet. If this was the extent of the competence of the activists, then even the British police were going to have a comically easy week. It was embarrassing, and it smelt of urine. Undeterred the Ginger battled on through the adversity of a privatised public transport system and into a very large demonstration around a sunny and beautiful Edinburgh.

The day itself however had a strange mood to it; people were not angry

with the G8 but almost thankful for it. The G8 were here as saviours of the world, pure examples of great and good people happy to drop a few crumbs back to Africa after raping the continent for the last three hundred years. Well the Ginger wasn't happy with it and neither were many others who felt the day (partly overshadowed by Madonna, etc. 'Making Poverty History' through the power of song and Nokia sponsorship with a little help from Bill Gates) was de-politicised.

However the day was an amazingly diverse gathering. Everyone from nuns to the black bloc people had made the effort to get out on the streets and protest. The Ginger could see the clashes of ideology and it made him smile. The day protested on, and the sun had worn the Ginger and his friend Dave down, so they slipped inside a church, hoping the high ceilings and stone would cool them off. Only after sitting in the pews for twenty minutes did the Ginger realise that Dave had scrawled 'F*ck The Fences' on his back, and though he wasn't over familiar with the Bible, he was pretty sure that a blatant anti-borders attitude had not been expressed in such a succinct way within its pages, and so they left. The Christians, bless them, were forgiving.

The eco-village
A special place for vertically-challenged people, who live in neighbourhoods named after kitchens, to come together to plot, debate and celebrate; love the earth and treat it well; despise the G8 and all it stands for; volunteer their time and energy to help create a beautiful experiment in how life could be; and by existing, surviving, and succeeding, create a headache for the greedy rich. A living proof that cooperation can create a thriving, throbbing and beautiful place.

MONDAY

In the early hours of Monday morning the Ginger sat chatting to a charming American girl on the gate of the eco-village. They were the thin unwashed line between the ugly and the beautiful; welcoming the tired activist to the site and keeping an eye out in case the ever-friendly police decide to play 'Hit the Crusty' at 2am on a rainy cold morning.

Out of the gloom of a Stirlingshire morning two yellow glows menaced towards the Ginger and the CAG (Charming American Girl). The CAG froze, but the Ginger leapt forward ready to defend the campsite with his life. The car slowed, realising that a battle with such a formidable foe would be suicide. The Ginger strode towards the car armed only with a crap torch and his ninja skills. The door of the car opened slowly and out of the darkness emerged, with eyes blazing, a tri-headed beast from the pits of hell: three Canadian tourists. Eager to pose, because at heart the Ginger loves the attention, he agrees along with the CAG to let the Canadians get a picture of 'the protesters' and then drive off into the night. Sleep sound, eco-village, crisis averted.

By this time the sun was rising and the Ginger had to leave his sentinel duties and make his way towards Faslane nuclear base, along with three hundred very tired others from the eco-village, if they were to arrive in time for the shift change. By the time the Ginger had arrived at the first gate it was already successfully blocked with locked-on activists, massive blocks of concrete and dancers a-dancing. The police looked bemused. Walking round to the second gate there were even more protesters, food and cups of tea, and a small contingent of the Clandestine Insurgent Rebel Clown Army making even the most stony-faced police mouth smile.

By this time the sun was out and warming the ground and it was time for the Ginger to lie at the feet of the police line. However the Ginger was tired. He had made the stupid decision to stay up all night,and despite all attempts to stay awake, soon found himself fast asleep dreaming of a day when governments stop building killing machines and start building a fairer world. Then he got woken up by a man with a bicycle-powered PA singing songs about the benefits of pot.

Consensus decision-making
A system which can be amazingly rewarding when compromise leads to general happiness, frustrating when decisions need to be made quickly, beautiful when everyone feels included, disgusting when used to alienate people, rewarding when people understand each other, pointless when people ignore whatever decisions are made, funny when everyone waves their hands in delight and tragic when it takes four hours to decide upon whether or not to make a decision at all.

TUESDAY

Name? 'I don't have to technically tell you my name under any law.' *If you want to go down this road then you'll have to give me your name and be searched.* 'Why?' *Because we said so.* 'But I might just be going for a walk in the lovely Scottish countryside.' *We don't believe you.* 'Why are you breaking the law?' *Listen, it's up to you. Either give us your name and let us search you or you will not be let down this road.*

The Ginger begins to comply…

Stop. What's this? 'A red handkerchief.' *Why have you got that?* 'In case you gas us.' *Don't be stupid. Bring the camera here and film him with this red thing.* 'Why are you doing that?' *Because we know that you belong to different groups by your colours.* 'You police are really dumb.' *Watch it or you'll be going nowhere.*

The Ginger continues to comply…

Stop. Why is the address you have given different than the one on your driving licence? 'Because I've moved house in the last five years.' *Wait a minute, I know this address, I used to go to school on this road.* 'No way…wait a minute, I didn't think the police went to school.'

The Ginger finally makes it through the thousands of police with the rest of the beautiful Pakora Kollective from Liverpool and heads up to meet a disgusting prison which houses asylum seekers 364 days of the year. But not today as the police have evacuated them all, fearing what everyone wanted to happen, that

everyone turn the words 'no one is illegal' into action, break down the walls of the 'detention centre' and free everyone inside. Alas there were three police to every protester and there was a 20-metre high metal fence with razor wire at the top. But the Ginger did love the tunes of the ever-wonderful David Rovics, who was happily singing away on the stage interrupting the monotony of the speeches. Everyone cheered their support *en masse* via phone to a Zimbabwean asylum seeker on hunger strike, laughed at the police getting eaten by the obviously progressive-minded midges and realised that the further south the policemen came from, the uglier and meaner they were.

WEDNESDAY

The Ginger found himself trapped down a dead end in an industrial estate with a rapidly-advancing police line. He was wearing two jumpers, a jacket, a shirt and a vest. They were all soaked through and had begun to feel like a medieval suit of armour made a metre thick, so he moved at a similar speed to the Southport Bingo Players Over 60s Relay Team. The Ginger turned his head to his companions: a middle-aged couple from Newcastle on their first ever protest and looking as confused, soaked and miserable as himself. Realising defeat they walked towards the police line slowly, were searched, filmed, had their details taken and sent on their merry way. Then walked fifty metres and were stopped, searched, filmed and sent on their merry way. Then walked another fifty metres and were stopped searched and sent on their miserable GET ME TO A BED NOW way. (By 'bed' the Ginger meant a bumpy field and a cold damp tent).

Alas! It had started so well! Over a thousand activists had left the eco-village at 2.45am and marched towards the M9 ready to blockade the main artery to Gleneagles. Moving in three separate groups, with over three hundred in each bloc, the body of progressive change had made swift progress through the deserted rain-sodden streets, until from nowhere tens of police vans and hundreds of police appeared out of the night and stood blocking the road ahead, armed with riot gear and a mean look in their eyes.

The Ginger was in the 'safety' affinity group with the slightly odd job of making it to the motorway first and laying out signs to slow down traffic before the blockade. This group of beautiful individuals hung about in between the first and second blocs and prepared for their task. A group who later dubbed themselves 'the suicide squad' took the Ginger by surprise by charging at the lines of police despite being massively out-numbered, and the two groups proceeded to hit each other for a while. Meanwhile the Ginger and many others ran in various directions, everyone following each other and no one really knowing where they were going. Some rocks got thrown at a bank, some tables got smashed up outside a locally owned pub and the Ginger thought to himself how moronic and backwards it was, whilst others loved the ecstasy of destruction.

The Ginger stayed with the main body, a little confused about where his non-violent ideology stood in relation to the main protest. Some of his affinity group had already gone home. The Ginger was desperate to do some political good, but disliked the attitude of the overall group. The numbers had shrunk from over a thousand to fewer than two hundred and as the Ginger was chased down a street deeper into the industrial estate, he decided to split from the group. Partly because he thought they were running into a dead end and partly because the spasms of political debate had temporarily demobilised his under-slept ginger brain. He went a different way, got stuck, trapped by the police and was left feeling a little confused and miserable...

...however as all good things are about what is achieved and not about the individual, the Ginger was in a glorious mood by the evening hearing about the blockades which had taken place throughout the area surrounding Gleneagles and the fence being torn down by the sea of protesters and all the wonderful people doing all the wonderful things all over Scotland...

THURSDAY

The Ginger was all prepared to help coordinate a party outside the gate of a hotel where part of the American delegation was staying. However, the police had arrived at 2.30am in 30-odd riot vans, scared everyone dreadless and proceeded to block the entire campsite on and off for the next two days. Which was very rubbish. And illegal.

The Ginger attended meetings to help with the running of the campsite, gathered and deposited sawdust for the compost toilets and took in the beautifulness of the village. The place was starting to feel like home.

However, the Ginger did escape the blockade to a brilliant reconciliation meeting with local Stirling residents and was amazed at the local support for the actions. He met possibly the nicest lady in existence, the sort of lovely, soft spoken, middle-aged, long-term peace-lover who would, after being beaten, robbed and humiliated, offer her aggressor some crackers and cheese and, most probably, melt their angry little heart. Despite being kept from getting back in by a crazy police over-reaction to a candlelit vigil to remember those killed in London that morning, the Ginger made it to bed. As he lay down he had with him a warm feeling in his head thanks to some drum and bass in a field, a bit of wine and a campfire sing song.

FRIDAY

On the way home in the lovely red bus the Ginger realised a few things: the week had taught him more about important stuff than all of the years of formal education had managed, the week had confused him more than various chemical-induced nights he'd had had had yup yup and he'd made some lovely friends, all of whom needed a wash.

The End

30

NOTHING IS WHAT DEMOCRACY LOOKS LIKE
OPENNESS, HORIZONTALITY AND THE MOVEMENT OF MOVEMENTS

Rodrigo Nunes

Networked, horizontal forms have been at the centre of many of the political debates of the last ten years, and have often been treated alternatively as the limit (by their enemies) or the solution (by their proponents) to the problems of organisation of resistance to global capitalism. This has unfortunately meant that critiques carried out 'from the inside' – i.e. by those who have experienced and share a general belief in them – have been much rarer than those carried out by partisans of other forms of organisation. The result has been much back-patting and triumphalism, but few discussions of anxieties and frustrations that seem widely shared, a problem that is only enhanced by the fact that so often it is felt that horizontality must be defended from its detractors.[1]

It is this kind of internal critique that this paper attempts to carry out. In order to do so, it envisages a demystification of openness and horizontality, showing how it is often presented in complete absence of context and pointing to its inherent contradictions and dead ends. The point of doing this is not to engage in another debate along the lines of 'less' or 'more' horizontality, or horizontality versus verticality. Rather, the idea is to render these very notions problematic, and by affirming their problematic nature, to argue for a democratic practice that tackles this nature head on.

1. BEFORE OPENNESS AND HORIZONTALITY, THERE WAS OPENNESS AND HORIZONTALITY

One can start by asking the question why openness and horizontality have become so central recently. Two answers seem possible. The first one concerns the growing disappointment with 'real existing socialism' that erupted in the events of 1968 and was very present (and increasingly outspoken) in progressive movements all over the world, culminating in a strange aftertaste of consternation and indifference when those regimes crumbled *circa* 1989. In this narrative we have a learning process where the lessons of Eastern Europe – whose mistakes were universalised, in either their practical or theoretical form, to almost everywhere through the work of Communist and Socialist parties of all shades – made subsequent waves of people struggling for social transformation wise enough to know what not to do, though still in the dark, and in some cases frankly disillusioned, as to what could be done. While this process is undeniable, it is clear that it alone cannot account for the move towards the open and horizontal organisation of struggles seen in recent years. In fact, one could say it is more capable of explaining the rise of identity politics, single-issue campaigns, NGOs and/or the sheer surrender of many people to the idea of an inevitability of the world as it is/was, and the neoliberal stance taken by many Left parties and trade unions.

What is relevant about the 'rise' of openness and horizontality is not that it means a substitution of one total theory of organisation by another – that could maybe explain why people would value them highly – but the fact that something like 'network' has a place today in the vocabulary and practice of organisations and companies that remain hierarchical. In other words, what is relevant is not that these ideas have become important, but that they have become *practised*. Even if we say that openness and horizontality are the new ideology – and an across-the-board one at that – the ideology as such only exists because it has become (or is perceived as in the process of becoming) materially possible on a large scale.

The bulk of the answer therefore has to lie in a material process. One current narrative of this process identifies it with a restructuring in the most 'advanced' sectors of capitalism (which, it is argued, exerts a hegemony that re-structures all other sectors), commonly called the passage from Fordism to post-Fordism. This passage can be initially characterised by two processes. First, the transformation in the relation between the productive process, on the one hand, and what is supposedly outside it, on the other, namely: consumption, market-research, 'market-making', 'customer relations'. Second, the 'singularisation' of the product:

> We are witnessing today not really a growth of services, but rather a development of the 'relations of service'. The move beyond the Taylorist organisation of services is characterised by the integration of the relationship between production and consumption, where in fact the consumer intervenes in an active way in the

composition of the product. The product 'service' becomes a social construction
and a social process of 'conception' and innovation. (...) The change in this
relationship between production and consumption has direct consequences for
the organisation of the Taylorist labor of production of services, because it draws
into question both the contents of labor and the division of labor (and thus the
relationship between conception and execution loses its unilateral character).[2]

This transformation is in turn only possible through the socialisation of the
material means through which this new relation between production and
consumption can be established, i.e. means of communication. The internet adds
another layer to this process, since it is a multipolar (many-to-many) means of
production and circulation of content, as opposed to a one-to-many medium
such as television (even though TV channels establish their own many-to-one
media, through surveys, polls, mechanisms to observe the audience's behaviour,
etc.). The large scale massification of these media, and a multipolar medium like
the internet in particular, is thus the chief material cause behind the 'renais-
sance' of openness and horizontality. It is only within the horizon of a social life
that has become networked that a politics of networking as such can appear. And
it is only in a politics of networking that openness and horizontality can appear
as a goal.

'Networks' and 'open spaces', therefore, are ambiguous by nature. On the
one hand, they are what we perceive as the conditions of possibility of horizontality, the means by which it can be achieved. On the other, they are only partial
actualisations of the idea they make possible – and make possible not only as their
instantiation, but also as idea, since it is only within the horizon of a politics of
networks and open spaces that horizontality becomes a means and a goal.[3]

This is not to deny that many social and political groups in the past have
practised open and horizontal ways of organising. While this is obviously true,
they were always faced with the practical impossibility of extending this internal
relation to the whole of society, or even to large numbers of people, because of
the lack of material means through which to do that. Such groups could only
propose this as a desirable future by means of some kind of eschatological argu-
mentative device, such as an 'end of history' in the classless society of communism.
Faced with its material limits, horizontality had to 'stay small', and could only
'think big' in a 'march of history'. What is important about horizontality today is
that the material conditions for its existence are perceived as being given, at least
in potential, *in the present*. This explains the emphasis on horizontality as means
and goal: through working horizontally, we are developing horizontal forms of
cooperation. In other words, we are developing both the very social fabric that
we want to produce and the means through which it can be produced. Organisation and politics coincide. In the past, the non-separation of means and ends
has been a point of principle or ideology. Now it is a simple matter of practice.
And since large-scale media of communication, and the internet – by virtue of

its multipolarity – in particular, seem to provide the conditions under which this process is possible, it is no wonder that the models of networking, openness and horizontality we work with are largely derived from them. It is common to point to the practice of free and open source software communities as the 'vanguard' of this democracy-to-come.[4]

2. OPENNESS AND HORIZONTALITY – AND THEIR CONTRADICTIONS

This, it must be said, is the *ideology* of openness and horizontality. It is a way of charting the present and perceiving lines along which the future can be constructed. The ideology is thus secondary in existence to the present itself, i.e. to the existing practices of horizontality and openness, and their condition now. The distinction is important: it highlights the fact that it is the concrete practices that create the conditions of possibility in which the ideology is produced. Therefore the ideology can only be a theoretical production that shares the same situation, and limits, as the practices.

> In this sense theory does not express, translate, or serve to apply practice: it is practice. But it is local and regional ... and not totalising. ... A theory is exactly like a box of tools. It has nothing to do with the signifier. It must be useful. It must function. And not for itself.[5]

2.1. FIRST CONTRADICTION: ONE OR MANY HORIZONTALITIES? DEPENDENCE ON MATERIAL CONTEXT

Again, the point here is not to say 'horizontality is something that happens to people with internet access', but to highlight the difference between a model that springs from certain practices and models that spring from different ones.[6] In other words, there can be many horizontalities.

This is why the universalisation of certain ideas of openness and horizontality suffers precisely from the problem of abstracting these ideas from their material contexts. What kind of horizontality can we speak of when referring to a social movement such as the Brazilian Landless Workers' Movement (MST)? This has over a million members, many of whom are illiterate (despite efforts in popular education), has little access to any means of communication, has no territorial autonomy (unlike the Zapatistas) and is under a constant campaign of criminalisation from the media and the danger of attacks from landowners' henchmen. It is true that it is a movement with a strong Marxist-Leninist influence; but that does not stop us from asking what form of horizontality it does or could have. The problems of applying a model become clear if we look at the five 'ways in which the kind of openness identified' in free and open source software communities 'practically correspond to specific moments of organisation in the social movement', listed by Jamie King: the organisation of meetings and discussions; their documentation; decision-making; the organisation of demonstrations; the organisation of actions.[7]

The MST as a movement (i.e. through its leadership) does take part in global networking through *Via Campesina* and the World Social Forum. Many of the material conditions that make networked politics possible in Europe, however, are absent from the realm of possibilities of the vast majority of their membership: time-flexibility; high mobility; language skills; technological literacy; the access to means of communication, particularly the internet. Inversely, the frustration many people sense in attending something like a social forum (or many of them in succession) is the realisation of the existence of a restricted number of 'hyperactivists' who can attend all these networking spaces. (Of course, as soon as one has this first-hand realisation, it means that one is already part of this group!) This is the moment where real-existing networking runs against the real-existing differences in material conditions of its 'wider environment'.[8] And by fetishising one model of horizontality, one will incur in the need for the same distinction made in liberal democracy, between 'formal' and 'material' democracy or access.

2.2. SECOND CONTRADICTION: SUPERNODALITY

A ghost haunts networked politics: the ghost of the supernode. If networked politics is based on communication flows, the supernode can be seen as 'not only routing more than their "fair share" of traffic, but actively determining the "content" that traverses them.'[9] The definition already points to one attribute of the supernode: hyperconnectivity. In other words, some individuals are 'more networked' than others, a quality that can be derived from material conditions such as the ones described above (high mobility, time-flexibility, etc.) and others that are more contingent, such as knowing the people who are particularly relevant in a situation, 'having been around longer', being friends with other individuals or whatever. To these one might add personal attributes, such as being a good speaker, charisma, and so on.

In all networks, these characteristics – which are, so to speak, external to the network itself – will apply in different ways to different individuals, and contingence will distribute others in an equally random fashion. Therefore, it is safe to say there is no given way of preventing the occurrence of supernodes. Also, it is clear that it is not a matter of 'a malicious will to power',[10] but a function of the way networks (and groups generally) work. For example, one may become a supernode as a result of a temporary group or task-related need or by being active in periods of hypoconnectivity of a network. And of course, since there are no formal structures to be seen, the possibility of these informal hierarchies becoming sedimented is high.

Of course, this is only the network-age variation of the process described in Jo Freeman's classic text about informal structures within the American feminist movement, *The Tyranny of Structurelessness*.[11] But her final conclusion is not that the way to counter these tendencies is a return to democratic centralism or the Leninist party. She proposes instead 'a few principles we can keep in mind that are essential to democratic structuring and are politically effective also'. These include: 'diffusion of information to everyone as frequently as possible'; 'equal access to resources needed by the group'; and 'rotation of tasks among individuals'. All of these are common practices of groups who profess openness and horizontality today. We could say, then, that she does not have anything to say to those who, even using these principles, keep on coming across the same problems she identifies. But maybe we are asking the wrong question.

2.3. THIRD AND FOURTH CONTRADICTIONS: NO SUCH THING AS AN OPEN SPACE; DETERMINATION AND INDETERMINATION

If networks are the 'permanent' structures of our model of horizontality, 'open spaces' are the temporary coming together of these structures. But how open is an open space? Many of them are based on hallmarks (Peoples' Global Action, Dissent!) or charters of principles (World Social Forum) which define an inside and an outside. They work, therefore, by exclusion. Others (such as the *Caracol Intergalactika* – one of the 'barrios' within the International Youth Camp at the World Social Forum), without having anything of the kind, allow the identity of the groups organising it or the process by which it is organised to exercise a 'soft power' of exclusion. Before the *Caracol Intergalactika* of 2005, for example, a chat discussion took place where one participant raised the question about the possibility of the youth wing of a Communist Party wishing to take part in it. There was consensus, however, that there was no need to create a distinction, because the identity of the space itself created it. The very idea of an 'open space' is contradictory – for it to be opened, it must be opened by someone, for some purpose and with some people in mind. No matter how open this first determination is, it always already creates an exclusion.

This leads to a larger problem: the fact that every determination is a closure – every saying 'this is the problem', 'this is where we stand', 'this is what we have to do now' narrows down the terms of a debate and therefore (at least in thesis) excludes people who think differently, in the same way that hallmarks, for example, do. As a consequence, any determination of a goal, position, analysis, etc. beyond the constitutive terms of the open space is perceived as negative, because it reduces diversity. Discussions of this kind are considered only possible within smaller affinity groups, which means that more defined positions and strategies are the properties of small groups and/or individuals, and do not belong in the debate of larger networks or spaces. In this way, horizontality always posits its own limit: while it can produce decisions in small groups, the possibility of doing so in larger groups is very limited, and even – since having overarching goals, positions, etc. is a potential danger to diversity – something to be avoided.

2.4. FIFTH AND SIXTH CONTRADICTIONS: DEPENDENCE ON PRACTICAL CONTEXT; DIVERSITY OF TACTICS VERSUS CONSENSUS DECISION-MAKING

The movement that became visible on a world scale for the first time in Seattle has, from there to here, found various solutions to the problem of how it relates internally when networks come together. Seattle was a surprise not only because of the 'coming together' that took place, but also because of the nature of that coming together: a broad coalition of very loosely related groups, some with interests considered contradictory, coming together through a process of open, horizontal networking – without a previous conference, the debate of a ten-point programme or anything of the kind. That was not only this movement's first show of strength, it was also the first time a networked politics was affirmed loud and clear on such a scale.

This capacity to come together in an *ad hoc* fashion, with very little other determinations besides a common objective, has been described as 'swarming'. Swarming occurs when the dispersed units of a network of small (and perhaps some large) forces converge on a target from multiple directions. The overall aim is *sustainable pulsing* – swarm networks must be able to coalesce rapidly and stealthily on a target, then dissever and redisperse, immediately ready to recombine for a new pulse.[12]

While activists widely celebrated this definition – and the irony of a think-tank specialising in military studies being the first to pin them down – one part of it is often overlooked: 'on a target'. At a summit protest, of course, the target is given – the whole point of the summit protest is precisely finding something which can, for a few days, physically represent capitalism to the world. Once the summit is over, however, the question of what being 'anti-capitalist' means opens up again.

The lynchpin of swarming is the principle of diversity of tactics. The goal (or target) being given in advance, the most effective way to go about arriving at it, and the only way of respecting the diversity of approaches of the groups involved, is agreeing that each group is entitled to follow its own approach. The problem is that this principle was arrived at as a solution to the question of swarming, i.e. situations where the objective is already given, such as summit protests. When a commonality has to be produced, where some sort of agreement has to take place, there is very little that diversity of tactics can do. That most of the swarming moments of this movement have been summit protests cannot obscure this. In fact, it could be that it is the automatism of the ready-made solution that explains the persistence of the summit protest as the tactics by which this movement is recognised.

We could go as far as saying that a too-automatic application of the principle of diversity of tactics is in contradiction with the principle of consensus decision-making. It is always possible not to come to any conclusion by applying the former, and simply decide to 'agree to disagree'. The latter implies that differences cannot be approached as absolutes, consensus being precisely the method of working through them and coming up with new syntheses. Perhaps this last contradiction is simply the practical extension of the fourth one, between determination and indetermination.

3. ANTI-GLOBALISATION AND ITS DISCONTENTS

The first three contradictions show that horizontality is a practical and logical failure: (i) the opening of spaces proceeds by exclusion; (ii) all forms of external factors, including but not only material conditions, distort horizontal networks from the outside, creating differences between nodes; and (iii) these differences reintroduce through the backdoor hierarchies and informal structures that we desire to be free of. The three last contradictions point to the fact that, if swarming and the principle of diversity of tactics was the great victory of networked politics, it may have been a self-defeating one. Because diversity of tactics points to a larger contradiction between decision-making and diversity – every time something is decided, diversity is reduced.

These points probably sum up people's frustrations with openness and horizontality in their practical experiences. On the one hand, horizontality in practice does not live up to itself as an ideal, and always ends up creating exclusions and/or informal structures and hierarchies. In the email discussions on the future of Dissent! following the G8 summit, some of the positions expressed that feeling:

Dissent! should not go on, because it has served its purpose (creating the political and material conditions for the swarming in Scotland), and any attempt to move beyond that is bound to degenerate into some sort of proto-Leninist group, with a small clique of people moving it behind the scenes and defining agendas for the movement. Or, it has served the purpose of facilitating the summit mobilisation, but it has already failed the purpose of being horizontal, and therefore should not move beyond.

On the other hand (which might exist as either opposition or complement to the first point), horizontality does not seem effective: it is impossible to make decisions, it is impossible to see the whole picture, and the only thing it's useful for is facilitating moments of swarming, where lots of single-issue (or single-minded) small groups can come together without any problems, precisely because there is very little to be decided. This could be seen in other moments of the same email debate: some people supported the idea of taking Dissent! forward and made their proposals as to what the next things to focus on were; others replied that this would be the problem with continuing to use Dissent!, because everyone would try to impose their pet issue on everyone else as soon as there was no more G8 summit to unify people's attention.

Two great sources of frustration and dissatisfaction are two of the oldest practical debates – and this is probably because they are really two great *non*-debates that always take place, but never really happen – namely, our relationship with the media and the use of physical force. The two issues, despite being always discussed, are almost always solved by some form of application of the principle of diversity of tactics or some sort of interpretation of consensus decision-making. Practically, this means that 'pacifists' in the 'violence' debate are defeated, since their goal is to stop 'violence' from happening. And, in the 'media' debate, there is the outcome that, 'since we do not have consensus on whether to talk to the media, we cannot talk to the media', which in turn facilitates the emergence of groups and individuals who, by being alone in talking to the media, become *de facto* representatives. But since from the start the whole point is couched in terms of diversity of *positions*, this ends up meaning a fetishisation of what positions *are* – i.e. general maxims of behaviour that compose some kind of overarching theory of what politics, social change, 'revolution', etc. is – and hardly ever what the positions can be in that situation, that is, how the general maxims that individuals and groups have applied to that particular practical context. This is where the feeling of the debate never actually happening comes from: positions are taken from the start to be absolutes that do not suffer any inflection according to practical, situational contexts – and in fact are absolutely impervious to any debate and can never be changed. Therefore, it becomes a question of one position winning and the other one losing, but this winning/losing can never be acknowledged since making such decisions is bad, because it reduces diversity, and so on...

> In the wake of Seattle, debates around tactics often took on an abstract tone. The question of what constitutes 'violence' was posed, and while dogmatic pacifists moralistically condemned property destruction, others imbued it with a veneer of liberatory significance of its own. As the ACME Collective argued in their communiqué on the Seattle Black Bloc, 'When we smash a window, we aim to destroy the thin veneer of legitimacy that surrounds private property rights. At the same time, we exorcise that set of violent and destructive social relationships which has been imbued in almost everything around us.'
>
> Insofar as these debates proceeded on a terrain of absolutes, the discussions skirted the question of context. Those arguing for the enforcement of nonviolent guidelines were faced with a context in which nonviolent discipline could no longer be enforced and reacted with condemnation and differentiation. 'The revolution we are trying to create didn't and doesn't need these parasites,' argued one activist in a Seattle Weekly article. On the other hand, property destruction was often conflated with revolutionary anti-capitalism. It provided a way to seemingly distinguish 'reformist' from 'revolutionary' tactics. The strategic question of when and where property destruction could be effectively utilised was often left unanswered.[13]

Opinions and grand theories become defined as the private property of individuals and small affinity groups, but not desirable on larger levels. Since no substantive larger-level agreement is desired, this means that groups and individuals hardly ever get a chance to challenge and be challenged in a practical debate on what it means to be doing something there and then. At its best, debate actually takes place (often because something really needs to be decided), and some will have a feeling of 'why can we not have this more often?' At its worst, it can feel like attending a convention of tiny communist groupuscules (each with their theory of revolution, manifestos, literature) who are different only because they are capable of working together once a year under the only agreement that they all should 'be different together'.

To these two internal problems – the feeling that horizontality always fails in practice and the feeling that it promotes immobility of ideas and decisions – can be added to an external problem: how do horizontal groups relate to what is viewed as 'non-horizontal'? This is the horizontal dilemma – if I place horizontality and openness as political means and ends, how can I relate to those who do not? If I reject them, I am closed and sectarian; if I work with them, I am indirectly supporting hierarchical, vertical practices.

Like every false problem, it only exists in absolute terms. If you turn 'political parties' or 'universities' or anything else into a concept that is defined by certain features, such as having a hierarchical structure – and this feature excludes that concept from participating in the concept of horizontality, defined in opposition to 'verticality' and hierarchy – then you create a conceptual problem of difficult resolution. But if these things are not fetishised and turned into concepts, but rather treated in the particular context in which the relation may or may not happen, then what kinds of relationships can be established in this situation? What is the nature of the work they are doing? Who are the people they are working with? What goals can be achieved? What strings are attached? The question then ceases being about an idea, and becomes instead a practical problem which requires more information (rather than a theory of organisation and revolution) and eventually a practical solution.

Fetishisation, of course, works both ways: it is also possible to fetishise horizontality. The problem is that it becomes a word – like 'anarchism', 'socialism', etc. – with a normative value that is abstracted from all the actual practices and social contexts it is drawn from. The problem of this 'identification with oneself' – turning a self-image into a norm – is that this restricts one's capacity to transform oneself, congealing into an ideal that not only (for a social movement) is restrictive to its capacity to act and enter into relation with what is different, but also becomes blind to its own cultural, class, gender, etc. context.

The reverse side of this 'self-identification' is that, once one realises oneself as a minority against a majority that is either non-mobilised or identifies with control (or minorities that propose alternatives of control, such as communist parties) – that is, once one sees that there is very little in the immediate environment to relate to – the concrete, immediate other is substituted by an abstract other that is either absent by definition ('this is a middle class movement; if only

we had the working class with us...') or by distance (the 'beautiful resistance' of movements in the global South, many of which are often hierarchical themselves). What is immediate and near is devalued in favour of an ideal.[14]

4. BENEATH THE NETWORK THERE IS A NETWORK

The source of this idea was a natural reaction against the overstructured society in which most of us found ourselves, the inevitable control this gave others over our lives, and the continual elitism of the Left ... The idea of structurelessness, however, has moved from a healthy counter to these tendencies to becoming a goddess in its own right.[15]

Hopefully the point of painting the disheartening picture of horizontality above will by now become clear. If the concept is, as shown above, contradictory and unworkable, there is only one way to go: decide this is a false problem and ditch the concept. *Nothing* is what democracy looks like – horizontality is not a model (or a property that can be predicated of things) but a practice. And as a practice, it remains permanently open to the future and to difference. As soon as one says 'this is what it looks like', one is closing the door to all future and different things that might come under that name. The point here is not that horizontality is problematic, but that democracy as such is problematic. And problematic means just that: permanently open.

By deciding upon an ideal model of what it should be like, all we are doing is creating a transcendent image that hovers above actual practices. Because it is cleansed of the 'impurities' of this world, it will serve all sorts of purposes – ideological propaganda; eschatological device ('when everyone is horizontal, horizontality will reign'); rhetorical device (as when a group accuses another of not being horizontal); absolute indeterminacy ('the more is decided, the less open it is'); and being that thing in comparison to which everything always falls short. Meanwhile, back in the immanence of the only world that actually exists, we will keep on suffering with its limits. By becoming this transcendent ideal, horizontality and openness – themselves not unfamiliar to business and management discourses – can become very similar to liberalism. The dream of 'absolute openness' means that openness is only possible if we abstract all concrete differences. Also, nothing can ever be affirmed, for that would contradict openness.

Jo Freeman criticised structurelessness on these two accounts: how it informally allowed for the differences it formally excluded; and how it made feminist groups less rather than more effective. We have seen that what she had to propose back then had little to tell us about our impasses today, since her proposals were all more or less incorporated in the current repertoire of horizontal practices. If the other models available today – liberal, representative democracy and different shades of Leninism – do not seem to solve any of these problems (and create others of their own) and are rejected in principle, what are we left with?

Freeman cannot answer because she is looking for principles, for mechanisms. Since we more or less have those, and are still not happy with them, we should look for something else. If horizontality and democracy are problematic by nature because they refer to practices and not mechanisms, what we are looking for is an ethos – a 'becoming open'.

This does not mean the absolute indeterminacy of never producing any principles or mechanisms. On the contrary, they have to be produced, reproduced and deconstructed according to needs. Dissent!, for example, came up with a very good solution to the eternal non-debate on media. The CounterSpin Collective was, perhaps, another contradictory application of the principle of diversity of tactics ('if there's no consensus on not talking to the media, then it is possible to talk to the media'), but it was a workable, practical solution to the age old problem that did not place anyone in charge of 'representing' the network, while at the same time creating a channel for people who wanted to give interviews, or simply to divulge press releases.[16]

What it does not mean either is the fetishisation of diversity and differences. In fact, the whole attitude that constrains debates because 'diversity must be left alone' and which so often squanders good opportunities for the better understanding of positions, the collective development of syntheses and the overcoming of contradictions dealt with as insurmountable smacks of liberalism. Not only because it takes differences as givens, but also because it reduces them to individual property, be it of a person or of a group.

This accepts two of the tenets of liberalism: first, an irresolvable distinction between individual and collective good; and second, the liberal concept of individuality. It ignores that, beneath and before every political network or group, individuals are always already part of the larger network of communication, meaning, narratives and power relations of life. Therefore, there cannot be a private opinion, as much as there cannot be a private individual. Michelangelo's *David* is only a particular actualisation of a web of themes, models, techniques, materials, tools, etc. that stretch far beyond the man who sculpted it. This also puts the lie to any ideas of 'individual revolution': 'revolution in one person' is an impossibility because there is no action that is not always already social. 'Localism' has to mean more than living up to one's ideal of communal living in a house with friends while the world outside, along with the neighbours, goes up in flames.

Nothing here is calling for an ethics of sacrifice or normalisation. On the contrary, an ethos of openness would be one of plasticity: ceasing to be an individual does not mean becoming like everyone else, but maximising one's capacity to perceive how one has become what one is now, and what is contingent in that – and therefore one's capacity to adapt and change. Giving up on ideas of authorship and ownership of collective processes, giving up one's proper name (in a deeper sense than just by having a web persona), while never being afraid to affirm things, and then revise them again; sensing when is the right moment for an intervention, and when it is time to let things move even if one does not agree; being able to deal with supernodality in a way that is capable of bypassing it without burning anyone out. Nothing can be either absolute indetermination or total determination: the art lies in learning how to move between the two. It is between absolute openness (as indetermination) and total closure that a political practice of openness-as-a-problematic may happen.

> [S]uch intentions demand constant development of new organisational models adaptable to constantly changing situations. The issue is no longer to express a common way of struggle, nor a unified picture or one-dimensional solidarity, neither an ostentatious unity nor a secretly unifying sub-culture, but the profound understanding and the absolute will, to recognise the internal differences and create flexible groups, where different approaches connect with each other reasonably and for mutual benefit.
>
> It's about political communication in the best sense: networking understood as situational negotiations that are based on the possibility of changing one's own standpoint as well as the standpoint of the other. Rather than being based on some spurious qualifications of good versus evil, this approach instead seeks out the basics of a reasonable and practical temporal togetherness.[17]

The work of networking social movements and groups has already been going on for a while: if we keep coming back to the same discussions and they sound like they never happened, this is cause for thought. The first step in movement-building is believing one is in a movement, that is, in something that moves with a movement of its own. This means that both the individual sense of time has to be relativised in favour of the larger time of this movement, which stretches indefinitely between past and future, and the individual sense of space has to be relativised in favour of all the different positions that are or can be occupied in the larger spatiality of this movement. It is an ethos of the networked individual that is necessary. The latter must be simultaneously aware of and transformed by everything that happens in this larger network, and ready to sense what spaces in the network could and should be occupied.

The problem with traditional Marxist groups is the transformation of an analysis into a philosophy of history that grounds a practice. This means that everything will always have to be absorbed within the larger totality of this theory. There are objective laws of the development of history, and the task is to interpret them correctly and, through that, to identify what the right practice for the moment is. It is no wonder that, with such a regime of truth, all political applications of Marxism became known by proper names – Leninism, Stalinism, Trotskyism, etc. – the oracular task of correct interpretation is not one that can be shared. Surely networking moves beyond that; but it cannot be simply to 'devolve' the power of 'correct interpretation' to individuals, by banning any large-scale agreements while fostering a fetishised 'diversity'. A networked sensibility demands both the openness to sense the non-totalisable whole of the network, and to be transformed by it, and the determination to act upon that whole in the way that seems the most effective for the network. It is like becoming a Lenin and a proletarian, all at the same time.

5. THIS REVOLUTION, AND THE NEXT ONE

A black balloon drifts across the dusty cement floor, pushed by an invisible draught. Printed on it in small, white letters are the words, 'Everything is connected to everything else'.[18]

But beneath the network there is always a network.[19] And before the internet, mobile phones, radio and digital TV there was one already. To say that is both to put the lie to a transcendent ideal of absolute openness, where all relations of power are dissolved, and to refer to perhaps the largest impasse of all the open, horizontal political networks today: that of effectivity.

The point of these networks cannot be simply their enlargement; even though there is a lot of work to be done in bringing more groups across the globe together. Achieving that – in itself an utopian goal – would only ensure that all mobilised groups of the world would know more about each other and would be more capable of working together, supporting each other and swarming every now and then. The network that exists 'underneath' these political networks is the web of social relations that at once reproduce and always transform themselves slightly everyday. This is a web of relations of power, in the sense of 'actions upon actions', of creating fields of possible actions by excluding the possibility of others;

'domination' is just a species in the larger genus of 'power relations'.[20] Neighbours, parents, workmates, employers, bus drivers, policemen; everyone belongs in it, including political networks. All work for its reproduction in one way or another, and no one is necessarily good or bad for that reason.

This reinforces the point made above about individuality. If every relation is an 'action upon an action', there is no individuality in the classic sense; an individual is the plastic reconfiguration of its outside. The difference between networked politics and previous forms of political organisation is that it places *non-linear connection* above *linear accumulation*; and two things never connect, never enter in relation, without becoming a third thing.

A politics of linear accumulation has much simpler goals: the point is to expand, bring more people into the cause, until there are enough of them to storm the Winter Palace. Swarming has played in the past and is going to play in the years to come an important role, but it seems highly unlikely that it is ever going to achieve its 'anti-capitalist' objective of, well, putting an end to 'capitalism'. Even if it did, the immediate results probably would not differ much from what came after the Winter Palace. It is crucial to notice that when the authors of *Networks and Netwars* described the 'war of the future', the kind of political organisations they saw as the most successful were single-issue campaigns that could have great achievements through networking and swarming.[21] Anti-capitalist counter-summits are obviously not a campaign in the same sense, as they in and for themselves have no goal that can be delivered; neither getting a law passed, nor storming a palace, nor winning the elections. The conclusion is that there is only so much that swarming can do, and much still to be invented.[22]

What was given up with the idea of linear accumulation was the idea that there is a goal. Once you have a goal that can be identified with achieving an action – taking the state apparatus and using it to promote the 'transition to communism' – and this goal is identified as the completion of the entire process, you enter the realm of linearity: history marches towards an end, and the role of the 'revolutionary' is to speed it up. One of the central problems of Western thought from the Enlightenment to today is that of the 'next revolution'. The first was the one that created the conditions for what we have today: the nation-state, property relations and liberal democracy. Identifying the point of the next one, the one that would change this particular configuration, has been the problem ever since. In this period, the linear solution – the one that identifies one point as the end, and identifies this end with itself – has been largely discredited because all 'ends of history' always had to be enforced, and history stubbornly went on.

This is why the problematic nature of horizontality is its openness towards the future, and why its non-linearity will always move beyond any closure of the 'this is what it looks like' kind. If horizontal movements today try to produce this closure, they will just be left behind. Even though we call the moment where the configurations of power came to be the way they are now the 'first revolution',

this cannot be identified with any singular point in history. It was the result of an open development, which went through the Enlightenment and the bourgeois revolutions and has not stopped transforming itself ever since. This is the problem with 'capitalism': it is a name given *a posteriori* to an historical development that is still in movement, not – like 'communism' or 'anarchism' – the description of a desirable place where history comes to an end.

We do not even know what capitalism is, how could we know what its overcoming is? This is why any particular understanding of what openness and horizontality are cannot be allowed to simply become the new dogma. It is clear that enlarging the political networks that already exist is not an end in itself. These can only be effective – beyond swarming-effectiveness – by grounding themselves in a thorough politicisation of social relations. This might entail employing (both as 'going back to' and 'reinventing') other, older forms of political action: house visits, neighbourhood organising, community projects. These will, in turn, entail practices that might be looked down upon by 'horizontal' activists, such as campaigning to have laws passed, lobbying councils, collaborating with religious groups, trade unions, etc. Examples of this in the preparations for the G8 in Scotland can be found in the Trapese collective working within and across academic institutions, the negotiations with local councils in Stirling and Edinburgh, which made possible the rural convergence space and the urban camping area respectively. It is in the network inhabited by parents, neigh-

bours, bus drivers, migrants, mental patients, even policemen (who are people with employers, parents, neighbours...) and of course 'activists', in all the different subject-positions they may occupy here – that horizontal movements may find the *transversalities* that cut across it and are capable of bringing about change.

While the question of what this can mean has to remain a practical, problematic (and therefore open) one, it is possible to say here what this does *not* mean.

This does not mean a mystical appeal to 'a working class politics'. As argued above, this kind of reification of 'the workers' is not only just the reverse side of a lack of clarity in the politics of horizontal movements ('the rage of Caliban seeing his face in a glass'),[23] but also empirically inaccurate, given that these movements are not deprived of a social base (chiefly that of the new productive subjects created by the processes of restructuring described in the beginning). What it means is that issues that are very much at stake in both the productive and political practices of these individuals – such as the struggle against intellectual property – are relevant for myriad other areas (genetically modified organisms, pharmaceutics, education), and commonalities must be built between these struggles that go beyond the automatic, 'rent-a-swarm' model of the 'solidarity action'. In creating concrete relations, subjectivities are produced that are much more than a reified idea of 'worker' or 'activist'.

This does not mean 'localism', if that is understood as creating local spaces by and for 'activists', be they social centres, newspapers, etc. While these initiatives have undeniable value, they are tools, not ends, and must be considered in their capacity to create interfaces between struggles and subjectivities – not in a quantifiable capacity of making people 'join the club'.[24]

Finally, this does not mean abandoning any of the horizontal practices that exist today, but pushing them forward, exposing them to new situations, creating and recreating them, even by making mistakes. It is in the word 'transversality' that we find the reason why resorting to practices that are 'older' does not necessarily mean going back in history and returning to old, Marxist-type linearity. The point is finding the contexts in which horizontal practices can enter or open new spaces, meet new situations, establish different relations by identifying in the present lines of conflict, points of leverage and conjunctural possibilities that link different struggles and create commonalities between what is different. If horizontality means putting connectivity above accumulation, there is one answer to the age-old 'what is to be done': connect.

1   Four 'insider' critiques which I have referred to throughout the writing of this article are:
     C. Hurl, 'Anti-globalization and "diversity of tactics"'. At
     http://auto__sol.tao.ca/node/view/1334?PHPSESSID=b1f39f9f3af6c81b80a12ceb2b01a75d;
     J.J. King, 'The packet gang', Mute (Winter/Spring 2004). At
     http://www.metamute.com/look/article.tpl?IdLanguage=1&IdPublication=1&NrIssue=27&Nr
     Section=10&NrArticle=962&ST__max=0; S. Lang and F. Schneider, 'The dark side of camping',
     at http://makeworlds.org/node/44; R. Nunes, 'Networks, open spaces, horizontality:
     instantiations', ephemera: theory and politics in organization, vol. 5, no. 2 (May 2005). At
     http://www.ephemeraweb.org/journal/5-2/5-2nunes2.pdf.)

2   M. Lazzarato, 'Immaterial labour'. Archived at http://www.generation-
     online.org/c/fcimmateriallabour3.htm.

3   R. Nunes, op. cit.

4   The fact that openness and horizontality are present in management techniques and even
     some strains of liberal democratic thought today show even more clearly how these ideologies
     are all derived from the existence of the material conditions found, above all, in the internet.

5   G. Deleuze and M. Foucault, 'The intellectuals and power', at
     http://info.interactivist.net/print.pl?sid=03/01/13/0056200.

6   For example, the way of organising of the Zapatistas is often attributed to Indigenous practices;
     and they do not seem to see the coexistence of horizontal organising and the EZLN's more
     hierarchical structure as an insurmountable problem.

7   J. King, op. cit.

8   Jamie King extends this insight to free and open source software communities, 'the most open
     system theoretically imaginable': 'limitations to those who can access and alter source code are
     formally removed. But what then comes to define such access, and the software that is
     produced, are underlying determinants such as education, social opportunity, social
     connections and affiliations.' ibid.

9   ibid.

10 ibid.

11 At http://www.anarres.org.au/essays/amtos.htm.

12 J. Arquilla and D. Ronfeldt (eds), Networks and netwars. The future of terror, crime, and militancy. Santa Monica, Ca.: RAND Publications, p. 12. At http://www.rand.org/publications/MR/MR1382/MR1382.ch1.pdf.

13 C. Hurl. 'Anti-globalization and "diversity of tactics"'.

14 Another recurrent source of frustration for activists is, of course, the feeling that these movements can be self-referential and subcultural, and that a good deal of 'closedness' is brought about by their being limited to certain social and cultural profiles. Susanne Lang and Florian Schneider also point out how the incapacity to move from swarming to an actual debate may be solved by attracting state repression and thus, by conjuring a 'bad other', creating a fictitious unity of 'being on the right side of oppression' that substitutes a real, problematic unity that cannot be created in practice. Cf. S. Lang and F. Schneider, op. cit.

15 J. Freeman, op. cit.

16 There was a discussion on the night when the police surrounded the rural convergence centre in Stirling on whether to collectively write a statement and submit it to the assembly in the morning, and, there being consensus, issuing it as a statement on behalf of the camp. In the end it was decided against it, but it opens a debate for the future: in what moments can the mandate of the working group be extended, under what conditions and through what process?

17 S. Lang and F. Schneider, op. cit.

18 Notes from Nowhere (eds), We are everywhere. The irresistible rise of global anticapitalism (London: Verso, 2003) p. 63.

19 Referring to the web of social relations as being 'beneath' activist networks is, of course, entirely metaphorical: there can be no separation between 'us' and 'society', as we are all involved in relations where we are employers, employees, parents, sons, neighbours, etc. This separation is, however, created by ourselves when we speak in terms of 'us' and 'the others', 'activists' and 'passives'; we ask ourselves how we can communicate with these people, and yet this communication takes place everyday as a precondition of our social existence. When we speak of our horizontal activist networks as if they were the rightful space of this ideal, transcendent horizontality in society, we are paradoxically placing ourselves in a vertical place above the web of social relations. The term 'beneath' here should be then understood as describing this false dichotomy to question it – which becomes a real practical problem, however, by being posed – rather than accepting its existence. For a development of these themes, see 'Give up Activism', at http://www.eco-action.org/dod/n09/activism.htm; B. Trott, 'Gleneagles, Activism and Ordinary Rebelliousness', this book, pp. 213–233.

20 M. Foucault, 'Le sujet et le pouvoir', in, Dits et ecrits (Paris: Gallimard, 2001) vol. II, pp. 1041–1062.

21 J. Arquilla and D. Ronfeldt (eds), op. cit. In fact, distinguishing these from the 'dark side' of the netwar – terrorist networks, hooligans and organised crime – they welcome their potential 'liberalising effects' (p. 7). Their appreciation of Seattle lies somewhere between 'hooliganism' and 'extremist single-issue campaign'.

22 *A good example of what swarming can do, of course, is to be found in the blockades of the first day of the G8 summit. Small groups with little coordination among each other were a lot more effective (as well as more impervious to police infiltration) than a large mass of people gathering in one place. As I have pointed out, however, this is a case where the goal is given from the outside (blockading the roads, stopping traffic, shutting the summit down) rather than having to be constructed through political debate.*

23 *O. Wilde. The picture of Dorian Gray. Archived at http://www.worldwideschool.org/library/books/lit/horror/ThePictureofDorianGray/Chap0.html.*

24 *'The activist role is a self-imposed isolation from all the people we should be connecting to. Taking on the role of an activist separates you from the rest of the human race as someone special and different. People tend to think of their own first person plural (who are you referring to when you say 'we'?) as referring to some community of activists, rather than a class. For example, for some time now in the activist milieu it has been popular to argue for 'no more single issues' and for the importance of 'making links'. However, many people's conception of what this involved was to 'make links' with other activists and other campaign groups. June 18 demonstrated this quite well, the whole idea being to get all the representatives of all the various different causes or issues in one place at one time, voluntarily relegating ourselves to the ghetto of good causes.' In: 'Give up Activism', op. cit. This is a classic text in arguing that social change does not require 'more activists' as in a process of linear accumulation.*

31

MEDIA, MOVEMENT(S) AND PUBLIC IMAGE(S): COUNTERSPINNING IN SCOTLAND

CounterSpin Collective[1]

One of the key achievements of the last ten years has been the establishment and development of our[2] own forms of media. The global Indymedia network, *SchNEWS*, wiki-based websites,[3] independent films and local papers are all examples of attempts to create multiple spaces for debate, and for sharing information about our activities and politics with each other and with the wider world. More than mere sources of 'news', these media have provided vital inspiration, helping to build a real sense of solidarity amongst our many diverse (and diversely located) struggles.

The notion that we can directly speak, write and create, without having to struggle to have our voices heard and our stories told undistorted within the mainstream media, has been central to this development, as have issues of access to information. Seeking to directly challenge the idea that we should have to appeal to higher authorities for acceptance, legitimacy or mediation, this enormously important movement to reclaim forms of media (and create new ones) continues, offering a growing radical alternative to corporate news sources.

However, we need to look critically at how the vast majority of the population in the UK and beyond rely on the mainstream/corporate media for information about current affairs. This is not something we can simply wish away: it is something we need to confront. For these purposes, we should understand mainstream media itself as a site of struggle where we must challenge the kinds of political practices, policies and processes we are critical of. Moreover, we should question the content and form of 'news' production itself and the opinion-shaping that goes with it, at the sites where this actually takes place, and not just reflect on it within our own spaces.[4]

The CounterSpin Collective (CSC) emerged from within the Dissent! network as part of a collective attempt to work through this problem with particular reference to the G8 summit protest in 2005. The idea was to try and struggle for a space for 'our' critiques within the mainstream media, whilst also counteracting the polemical, at times hysterical, ways many of us are often portrayed in the mainstream media when we organise direct actions, especially at international summits like the G8.

It's not surprising that some activists oppose all dealings with the mainstream media. Whether this refusal is founded on having been personally misrepresented by journalists in the past, or on the fact that media coverage can and has been used against activists in courts and by the police; or whether it stems from a sense of futility in engaging with The Media[5] at all, because of the way that news in general is so distorted – these experiences have made us tread with caution. Having said that, all too often our debates about The Media become polarised,[6] as if there were fixed ideological positions of either rejecting any engagement with the mainstream media, because of its role as part of the establishment and the system of global capitalism, therefore structurally unable to further any critique of the system it is a product of, or of naïvely befriending anyone with a notepad, camera or microphone and hoping for the best.

The situation is more complex than this. Of course, no one involved with the CSC harboured any illusions about the structural role of The Media within global capitalism. We all understood that it doesn't exist as a 'neutral'/objective news service, always to critically hold politicians and other 'leaders' to account. Furthermore, we were well aware of some of the political and ideological barriers we would face in our attempts to engage with this media, and that the outcomes of our efforts would necessarily be a compromise. At the same time, many of us felt that it was a mistake to reject the possibility of strategically using mainstream media outlets to promote our ideas and tackle head on the discourses of politicians, corporations and political commentators we disagree with in ways that were also accessible to the public. And in doing this, we felt it would also challenge consumers/recipients of such media coverage to think differently outside of their own comfort zones. Many of us saw self-imposed isolation as a luxury that we collectively could not afford. How can we fight for a better world if we don't share our ideas and activities with those around us who live outside of our activist circles? What chance do we have if the vast majority of the 'general public' either don't hear about our activities at all, or only from perspectives other than our own?

BIRTH OF A NOTION

In February 2005, the semblance of a media response group emerged and began to look at ways of engaging with the mainstream media. Activists who had organised around the European Union summit in Dublin on May Day 2004 offered support and advice, giving our fledgling group much-needed confidence. Their workshops helped enormously in building the practical knowledge of people intending to facilitate mainstream media engagement. We set up an email list where refreshingly reflective discussions took place, as we tried to look at concerns regarding representation: what or who any notion of 'we' might constitute and what kinds of messages, if any, 'we' wanted to get across. This actually triggered much needed self-reflection, which went beyond discussions around mainstream media engagement. For example, what were we actually trying to achieve in organising actions against a summit like the G8? And how did this relate to questions of mediation and representation within a movement that holds dear its political diversity and its critiques of leadership and representation?

At a Dissent! gathering in Leeds in March 2005, some participants proposed that a media response group be set up for the Festival of Dissent!, taking place the following month. There had already been a flurry of journalists contacting the various email addresses listed on the Dissent! website, with sensationalist stories appearing in the tabloids about 'anarchist training camps' and the like. Moreover, the Glasgow Reshape! group had specifically requested help responding to interview requests. A press release was issued, and after much debate, a number of stringent rules for dealing with the press were agreed upon. These related in particular to the degree of access that journalists would be granted to the Festival site and the nature of acceptable filming and photography.

The Festival of Dissent! attracted significant mainstream media coverage. There were a few irritating 'exposés' in the *Daily Record* and *The Times* about our inability to put up marquees, and two individuals were inaccurately named as 'ringleaders'. However, we did meet a few journalists face-to-face and felt that we had enough control over the interviews we gave, experiences which set a constructive precedent for the next few months. A number of journalists consistently reported in what we thought was a fair way – at least always giving us the option of commenting. For a first foray into mainstream media engagement, it had been a decidedly positive experience.

After the Festival of Dissent!, The Media[7] continued to call looking for interviews and responses to police statements, or to find out about the myriad groups (such as the Clown Army, the People's Golfing Association and so on) who were planning actions as part of the summit protests, as well as plans for how activists were intending to travel up to Scotland. Discussions during the Festival of Dissent! helped form a vague plan for further media work which solidified during the following months. At the end of the Festival, a number of people from local, working and action groups gave us their names and contact details. If and when journalists approached us, we would put them in touch with these people. At the expense of having no coverage at all, we operated on the basis that if no one came forward from the various autonomous groups, then there would be no response – although some groups did ask for our direct assistance in communicating with journalists.

Things gained a little more structure at the Dissent! gathering in Nottingham in May 2005, where the media group took on the name 'Counter-Spin Collective'. Our main efforts here and throughout the subsequent mobil-isation were always to *facilitate* media relations for all those groups within the Dissent! network who wanted our help, like a sort of 'dating service' for journalists and activists (to schmooze with each other, one may quip!). A comprehensive list of global press contacts was built up, and we put together a network of translators, so that press releases could be distributed in multiple languages beyond the UK, often within as little as 24 hours. For a number of working and action groups this method proved effective. Individuals also wrote letters and personal responses to mainstream media, contradicting the positions articulated by police spokes-people and government officials. In two cases that we considered slanderous/libel-lous, formal written complaints were made to the newspaper concerned as well as to the Press Complaints Commission. In another case, a journalist was specif-ically challenged about unfair coverage of certain activists. The resulting conver-sation might have been the motivation for their second article the following week, this time about police violence against activists (or it may just have been that the latter made the better story the following week).

ON-SITE AND OFF-SITE

As the summit approached, the fact that 5,000 protesters were going to be camping in Stirling meant that it became a hub of mainstream media activity. A few days before the Hori-Zone (the eco-village in Stirling) officially opened, consensus was reached at an evening convergence meeting to allow accompanied journal-ists on site for a period of one hour. This limited period was agreed out of respect for those who did not want to be subjected to any coverage, and in order to control mainstream media access to the site on our own terms. This way, such media coverage could be better contained in an environment where there were such differing opinions on the matter.

We produced a press release announcing the 'open hour', and collated a press pack containing past press releases from Convergence 2005 (the working group responsible for the Hori-Zone), along with press releases from action or local groups. At 11am the next day, the corporate media arrived at the gates. Journal-ists were taken in groups of four and five onto the site for a tour and to meet people for interviews. An hour later they were escorted out again. Another benefit of chan-nelling the media engagement through a facilitation group was that people with interview experience were able to share the skills they had acquired with other

new interviewees. Consequently, people were not thrown by ambiguous questions as much as they might have been, and were able to stick to a few key points about why they had come to Scotland. The event ran smoothly, increasing confidence within the CSC.

While tabloid coverage ranged from rants about blood-sucking anarchists to happy hippies intent on saving the world, some papers (such as *The Guardian* and *The Independent*) along with the Scottish TV channels produced acceptable reports, where comments made by activists were not grossly distorted, and where there seemed to be hints of critical reflection offered in the coverage. This was definitely better than much of what had gone before and many stories carried the idea that Hori-Zone was aiming to be a model of a different type of social organisation: inspiring, ecologically sound and organised non-hierarchically in an inclusive way. Again, this experience reinforced our belief that our ideas could be spread via the mass media in a more positive way on specific organised occasions.

Soon after the Hori-Zone opened, the media response group erected a 'media gazebo' outside the site perimeter, near the entrance. It was set up off-site and clearly marked so that it was an obvious point of first contact for journalists and photographers. Here we explained to Media visitors that no journalists or photographers were allowed onto the site. Some journalists were upset by this and would argue one of two positions. They would either demand their right of access to a public space, or they would try and cajole us by asking us how they could provide fair coverage under such restrictions. In such cases, we would reiterate the consensus of the Dissent! network on the matter and proceed to brief them on further particulars, most importantly that they should not refer to any interviewees as spokespeople for Dissent! or photograph anyone without their consent. People from the CSC would then offer to find interviewees for them, which most journalists were actually pleasantly surprised about, as they saw this as us doing their legwork for them! Interviewees were usually selected at random (asking passers-by inside Hori-Zone whether they were up for giving an interview), or were arranged to suit the language requirements of the media outlet in question, or based on prior consent by willing individuals, who we would call on the phone.

Having followed most of the press coverage about Dissent! in the lead-up to the summit, we were able to build up a list of journalists that we regarded as 'supportive' or 'unsupportive', with degrees of cooperation offered accordingly. Consequently, journalists who had a good record of reporting favourably were granted interview opportunities, while others were asked to leave or were directly confronted about the nature of their journalism. This was a deliberate attempt to go beyond any false dichotomies in which all mainstream journalists are seen as necessarily having politically 'bad' intentions, or for that matter, all indy journalists as necessarily above criticism.

By July 5, the media reception tent was full and the phones constantly ringing. In this hectic environment, it dawned on us that we had not yet thought concretely enough about a media response plan for the following day of action. Out of this worry, an *ad hoc*, two-fold 'strategy' emerged: on the one hand, we would try and facilitate dialogue between activists and journalists during the day of action and gave the CSC mobile number to both parties; on the other, we counted on the presence of mainstream media being useful as a defence tactic in the event of the eco-village site being surrounded or raided by the police. When the police did eventually surround the camp at 2am on Thursday morning, and fear was spreading as to the possibilities of a full-scale raid, the CSC contacted some trusted journalists,[8] an action which had been agreed on at a site-wide meeting that afternoon – only to find that the police press office had already alerted all of the main media outlets to their plans.

During that night, the limitations of the CSC became apparent once again. As TV crews gathered behind the police line, the idea emerged of giving some sort of statement to the press. This statement would put into context our political motivations for protesting against the summit and relate it to the nature of the repression we were currently facing from the police. Whilst some set to the task of putting a short text together, others felt uneasy about it, fearing hostile criticism from within the Dissent! network for being seen to be acting as spokespeople without consulting others inside the eco-village at the time, i.e. the community of people affected by the situation at hand. The action was abandoned in the end because we could not agree, but the uneasy question has to be asked: was this a

lost political opportunity for engaging with the public through The Media,[9] to get our point across at a time when they were most interested in us? If it was, how could this moment have been used more effectively?

At 8am on Thursday morning, two activists were allowed through the police lines to speak to the 20 or so journalists camped on the roundabout, at the request of those who had spent most of the night out there negotiating with the police. At around 10.30am the news spread through the eco-village that bombs had exploded in London and an eerie silence descended upon the Hori-Zone: from this point onwards, the mainstream media interest in us dropped dramatically and the police line drew a little thinner before being disbanded later that day (although not until a full-scale forensic sweep of the eco-village was agreed to).

But our moment in the spotlight wasn't quite over. As the summit drew to a close, a couple of people gave an interview to Radio 5. They explained that the G8 summit had been successfully disrupted, and why this had been a necessary thing to do; they illustrated how civil disobedience was a legitimate form of protest and argued that the issues of climate change and poverty could never be solved by institutions such as the G8, whose very existence is tied up with the kinds of exploitation of people and of the environment which exacerbate poverty and ecological destruction. This was an articulate and timely interview that, juxtaposed with the G8's weak communiqué officially released around the same time, served to highlight the shortcomings and failures of global capitalism and its institutions.

Another political moment that was perhaps lost, not by the CSC *per se*, but by our movement(s) more generally, was in relation to the July 7 London bombings. Despite the fact that a paralysis of shock and worry swept the Hori-Zone at the news, we could have thought about how to publicly (and again through The Media as one channel) articulate our concerns and our politics at this time.

SOME LESSONS LEARNT

The pro-active media stance taken by those working within the CSC meant that journalists had a point of contact with people from within the Dissent! network. Even if not all media coverage of the protests was as we might have wanted it,[10] what we were able to do was actively push for space within the mainstream media spheres for our politics to be made visible, as well as respond, albeit not always completely successfully, to where de-politicisation, de-legitimisation and criminalisation of our actions occurred in the public domain. It was alleged, for example, that weapons were being found on people leaving the convergence centre site – camping knives and tent poles hardly constitute weapons – but the police were determined to place the camp in the worst light possible. When we challenged this, the BBC and ITN both changed their online reports to include unedited comments by activists explaining the ridiculous police accusations.[11]

Working within the CSC, we were constantly aware of the problems with the nature of our work, but we were still disheartened at the level of hostility we faced from within the Dissent! network, where the people who were in support of our work seemed to be either in a minority, or were maybe just less vocal. We experienced repeated hostility and encountered inaccurate gossip about what we were doing. In one instance at the Hori-Zone, activists speaking to journalists were screamed at and threatened with physical violence and then had bottles thrown at them from inside the site. This hostility was cumulatively very demoralising and some were concerned that they would face the sort of political crucifixion experienced by those who had engaged with The Media during previous mobilisations of this sort.

A number of questions arise here. When our aim is to avoid recreating the kinds of oppressive power structures we are critical of within our own networks, is it simply a matter of trusting that those who want to engage with the corporate media will do so in good faith with regard to their fellow activists? Is this good faith any different to that which we show individuals who choose to be street medics, legal observers, police negotiators, cooks or compost toilet-builders? Obviously, engaging with the mainstream media involves engaging with an entity that is 'external' to our movement(s), and is bound up with all the issues to do with the politics of representation in a way that being a cook, street medic or legal observer[12] might not be. But at the same time, how can we learn to trust each other and share our skills with others? How can we find comfortable degrees of specialisation within our movement(s), enabling people to take on specific tasks and be held accountable for them? How do we resolve the kinds of conflicts we have around such issues before, during and after mobilisations? Can we go beyond agreeing to disagree?

Further to these arising questions, there were our own shortcomings as the CSC. We were inevitably limited by time, energy and resources, and too often we were forced to fire-fight issues as they arose. Once the Hori-Zone was open, we lacked a coordinated link with its decision-making processes. We could have been more effective if we had been able to attend logistics, barrio, and site meetings much more frequently than we managed to do, or if barrios had sent representatives to the twice daily CSC meetings.

Moreover, the CSC could have been more pro-active, as opposed to reactive. We could, for example, have attended police press conferences to counteract misinformation on the spot; we could have visited and/or come up with some sort of creative direct action at the G8 summit's own press centre; we could have facilitated much more provocative press releases to highlight political issues, been more available for interviews, engaged more with local media, especially local radio, and written even more articles for the mainstream papers. Additionally, we could have released a Dissent! press release/communiqué on July 6, explaining why so many people felt so passionately about shutting down the G8. Whether (and then, how) to do these sorts of things collectively remains an issue for us all and we need to reclaim the space (from ourselves!) to talk politics within our movement(s). Unfortunately, it often seems like we get too het up with the practicalities of organising, thus forgetting the wider politics at stake, or we end up making politics and practicalities synonymous, whereby the way we organise practically becomes the be all and end all of our politics.

But, when we're out on the streets, or in the Scottish hills, what is it that we're actually trying to do? Are we trying to get a message across? Are we trying to galvanise support for our politics and/or 'convince' people beyond our own activist circles? Do we need to worry about things like 'public image'? Is a summit protest a spectacle? If so, who explains or represents that spectacle to the world, and should it need 'explaining' or 'representing'? Is protest something that is limited to a person's experience of it, those energising 'moments of excess', of putting oneself, in all sort of ways, on the line for what one believes in? And perhaps more provocatively: to what extent can a disdain for the mainstream media be another way of remaining firmly locked in the inside-outside dichotomy of counter-culture/sub-culture versus the mainstream, not wanting to engage with anything that's considered 'mainstream' because of being beholden to an existence as 'anti', as 'indy', as 'alternative', as 'pure', thereby reproducing precisely the kinds of static identity positions which capitalism thrives on as it continuously commodifies identities?[13]

These and other related questions have been asked by many others many times before. Nevertheless, these are questions that are still bubbling away under

the surface of our actions, and will need to be addressed continuously as our contexts and compositions change. But maybe this is why we should shift from struggling with the question of *whether* to engage with The Media, to the question of *how*. In this spirit, this piece is a reflective contribution to that proposed shift as much as it is an account of 'CounterSpinning' in Scotland.

1   *This text has not been collectively written or endorsed by the CounterSpin Collective, but is an attempt by some of the individuals who were involved with this collective to reflect upon key events and arising questions.*

2   *Throughout this text, notions of 'we' have been used in a three-fold way. First, we refer to 'us' to talk about the people involved with the CounterSpin Collective. Second, we have used a notion of 'we' to refer to the groups, networks and individuals who came together around the G8 summit protest in 2005, the Dissent! network and the eco-village 'Hori-Zone' in Stirling. Finally when we ask some broader reflective, political questions, the 'we' includes those people who were not necessarily at the summit protests but who consider themselves to be part of or sympathetic to the politics of these networks and/or spaces. We have chosen the first person plural because we want these reflections on media work to be read as coming from within this movement.*

3   *'Wiki' is a piece of server software that 'allows users to freely create and edit web page content using any web browser', see http://wiki.org/ for more info.*

4   *Which are also, of course, never 'neutral' spaces devoid of normative assumptions or power relations.*

5   This term is capitalised in this text to refer to 'mainstream' or 'corporate' media.

6   Although it seemed too often like the situation was not so much polarised, as one in which a few individuals or one or two collectives within the network, who felt very strongly that we should under no circumstances engage with the media, would block any collective media work, thereby creating a deadlock around the issue of media engagement, which raises the issue of how we work through conflict, rather than remain paralysed by stalemate when we use certain kinds of consensus-decision-making methods in our networks.

7   Before and during the mobilisation, we had contact with UK-based and some foreign press across the globe. The organisations that maintained the most frequent dialogue with us were The Guardian, The Independent, The Scotsman, BBC, Channel 4 and the Associated Press.

8   We also communicated with Indymedia activists who were not at the eco-village.

9   As one particular site of struggle.

10 Whatever that may mean!

11 It is perhaps also relevant here to mention that Stirling Council remained publicly supportive of the eco-village throughout the protests.

12 We might point out that legal work involves an implicit recognition of the state's juridical system and that, at one time, legal volunteers were subjected to opprobrium from certain sections within social movements.

13 For interesting arguments on this notion, see Nato Thompson, The Flipside to Commodification of Revolution: A Critique of the Activist Scene, archived at http://www.journalofaestheticsandprotest.org/4/issue4.php?page=nato.

32

FROM GLENEAGLES TO HEILIGENDAMM
Some people from the No G8 Coordination Berlin

People's impressions of the events in Scotland are very different. Our personal impressions are rather positive: we had good fun, met great people, got to know other cultures of resistance, were too smart and too fast for the British police and took part in some inspiring actions.

Having come back from walking in the Highlands, we feel various issues still require collective discussion. Was it a political success? Were the blockades successful? What did the actions achieve? What did we manage to get across to the 'public'? Critics say these discussions have hardly taken place. Neither in Scotland, nor before or after.

The main focus of this text, however, is an examination of the network that formed in the German-speaking countries – Austria, Switzerland and Germany – against the summit in Gleneagles. What did it achieve, what failed, what could we do in the future?

It all began at the European Social Forum in London, back in 2004, when some people from Germany and Switzerland attended the Day of Dissent. A mailing list was set up soon afterwards and we all kept in touch. Our goals were to spread awareness about the G8 meeting, encouraging people to take action either in Scotland or elsewhere, and to support the Dissent! network where possible. Beyond Scotland, the idea was to form a network which could facilitate resistance to the 2007 G8 summit in Germany.

Our networking remained primarily internet based, with all the advantages and disandvantes of this. Besides the mailinglists, a website was set up and people started using a wiki – a website whose content can be edited easily by anyone. We also met a few times in 'real life', at an international networking meeting in Tübingen and at the 'Bundeskoordination Internationalismus' (BUKO) conference in Hamburg. On top of this, there was a meeting of the German-speaking network in Mannheim.

We tried to use the wiki to share out the jobs that kept being left; we hoped that people would take on these tasks, and make sure what needed to be done got done. But the lack of people with time and energy often meant that nobody took responsibility. You can't criticise a wiki for being lazy, so we resigned ourselves to the fact that it simply wouldn't be possible to do all the things that we had hoped.

The fact that not everyone is familiar with using technologies such as wikis and email encryption created further problems – but at least we managed to spread knowledge about these things a little further within our own networks.

In general, however, the internet was a useful medium for communication for the sort of work that we were doing – which was mainly producing and distributing publicity and coordinating info-nights. All of this went fairly well. As well as in Berlin, there were well attended info-nights in cities across Germany and Switzerland, and some ten thousand stickers, posters and leaflets were designed, printed, sent out and distributed. It was exciting to see how quickly our publicity spread – our stickers encouraging people to 'Form Autonomous Highland Gangs!' could be found in toilets across Europe. On the other hand, none of us really know how many Highland gangs were actually formed (in toilets). But at the very least, people got to hear about the G8.

SUMMIT PERSPECTIVES

As we mentioned at the beginning of this article, the political debate about the goals of the G8 mobilisation – from a radical-left perspective – hardly took place at all in Germany, leading to heavy criticism. In Berlin, for example, there was only one public discussion about the question as to whether summit mobilisations still make sense. Apart from that, the 'Glocal Group Hanau' were the only ones to articulate their political strategies by discussing the pros and cons of big mobilisations in a discussion document. According to their text, international mobilisations like Gleneagles have empowering outcomes rarely seen in 'ordinary' campaign work. Other international gatherings (like caravans, 'no borders' camps, conferences and so on) have to complement confrontational events, but can't replace them, as some experiences are only made possible through common action. So they propose a balance between local and international activities.

Their attempt to start a debate was welcomed by many, but there was little response from within the German-speaking network. Mainly this was because people were focused on structural debates and getting things done. We think these strategic questions should be discussed more, including on an international level, but perhaps not during the summit when time is short.

At our first meetings in Berlin, we agreed to approach people outside the radical-left. We wanted an open anti-G8 network, in dialogue with churches, environmental groups and trade unions. However, we didn't really succeed in stepping outside of our own circles. Monthly open meetings didn't really help either, as we found that only people from a very similar background to us ended up coming along.

It was difficult to get people on board who didn't see the relevance of an event so geographically distant and it was hard to explain what they would get in return for their international solidarity. The problem was further compounded by the fact that the majority of people here had not heard about the Gleneagles summit – or, in some cases, the G8 at all – until Geldof announced the Live8 concerts in June.

WHERE TO GO FROM HERE?

The 2007 G8 summit will take place in Eastern Germany, in the health resort Heiligendamm, close to Rostock, right on the Baltic Sea. The Berlin group is focusing on the mobilisation against this summit. The group is already far bigger than before, although there is still a need to inspire and involve a broader range of groups and individuals. We are continuing to organise within the Peoples' Global Action hallmarks, although this will be up for discussion later on. And we helped organise the first 2007 preparation meeting in Hamburg in October 2005 where over 200 people discussed strategies for radical resistance to the Heiligendamm summit.

People hope the campaign will have a positive impact on the left-wing movement in Germany which will last well beyond 2007. The initial focuses of the campaign will be the 2006 G8 summit in St. Petersburg, and the international resistance camp in 2006, just after the summit in Russia. This camp will be set up close to Heiligendamm.

The Initiative for an Interventionist Left (IL) has been set up independently from, but parallel to this mobilisation, and also comes from the radical-left. The IL hopes to use the summit as a focus for setting up a broad, movement orientated, horizontal grassroots alliance.

They write: 'The overall project of the G8 mobilisation in 2007 is so big and ambitious, that a single movement or organisation would be overstretched. Every solo attempt, or the domination by one tendency, would restrict the possibility to act and the political charisma of the actions at large... We therefore call for the forming of a broad alliance that takes on the organisation and coordination of the common tasks that can't be performed by a single group. Here initiatives from the whole range of left-wing struggle should unite: the local social forums, unemployed and social initiatives, antifascist and refugees groups, anarchist groups and other radicals of the movement, 3rd world solidarity- and church groups, Attac and the no-global networks, traditional communist and trotskyist organisations, trade union groups, youth organisations, Linkspartei/PDS [the socialist party], etc."[1]

The IL suggest that the groups they list agree upon a minimum consensus of four points around which they could organise. First of all, a definitive 'delegitimation' of the G8. Secondly, the mutual acceptance of different forms of actions and resistance. Thirdly, a cooperation in solidarity and reliability. And finally, a clear and offensive separation from right populist and right-wing forces. The IL are planning on organising, around these proposed principles, a large conference in spring 2006.

At present, then, there are two approaches being taken to resisting the 2007 G8 summit: on the one hand, a broad alliance, and on the other, a radical network. The two approaches are not, of course, mutually exclusive and will hopefully complement each other. Whether or not the network will become part of the alliance remains to be seen in the coming months. All that is certain now is that the summit will not pass by unnoticed. International campaigns and networks will be built, actions planned and productive political arguments put forward. We hope to meet you there!

1   More information about the alliance can be found on their website: www.g8-2007.de

33

AFTER GLENEAGLES: WHERE NEXT?

Simon Tormey

As with any major event for which activists have been planning, deliberating and organising for many months, the 'after' of Gleneagles has been difficult for many to come to terms with. The meeting of the G8 gave focus to activist efforts after the London European Social Forum, serving as limit horizon against which to measure the degree to which the 'alter-globalist-movement' (AGM) could match or even – hope upon hope – exceed the protests elsewhere. The protests duly came and went. Global big-wigs were momentarily reminded of the existence of the 'little people' whilst the 'big people', the Geldofs and Bonos, had their day in the media sun. There was a flurry of interest, and then nothing. The media gaze moves on to some other pressing issue: Hurricane Katrina, Islamist 'fanaticism', the Ashes, Sven-Goran's preposterous team tactics.

It would no doubt be easy for DIY and non-affiliated activists to be depressed about the G8 protests and what they herald as far as the state of UK activism is concerned, particularly as gauged on the basis of media coverage. So many hopes and expectations are built up in preparing for major summit protests that the realisation that the world remains almost exactly the same once the protests have finished can be difficult to bear – it *should* be difficult to bear given the effort that goes into them. Not much of any tangible note was achieved – so it seems. It would be entirely reasonable to slump into gloom and to wonder whether all the effort was really worth it. It is evidently time (once again) to confront the big questions.

What was Gleneagles for? What is radical disaffiliated activism for? Where are we going after Gleneagles?

On these occasions a healthy dose of context is usually needed. I want to use this space to try to put Gleneagles in a larger perspective so as to provoke some reflection on the larger aims and causes of which the protests are, arguably, a part.

Firstly, if we measured the success or failure of summit protests by their ability to influence directly or even indirectly what is going on inside, then we need to disabuse ourselves of the notion quickly if we are to avoid slumping individually and collectively into depression. Summits are not crucial to the business of global elites. They could quite easily do without them, and do so through the use of video-conferencing and alternative forms of interaction. Most of the business at such summits is already decided at mini-summits of flunkies and functionaries, in the ongoing and permanent negotiations of inter-governmental and supra-national bodies, sometimes meeting in session, but largely in the constant bureaucratic business of paper-swapping, diplomacy, business meetings and so forth. Summits are set-piece shows where what has already largely been decided is signed off by leaders who are themselves mere representatives of much larger and complex aggregate interests. Protests don't influence summits, and summits rarely influence global elites.

On the other hand, the idea that summits do matter in some tangible, measurable fashion is perhaps the key fallacy of 'summitism' (the view that summits are major occasions for elite deliberation and governance and hence that shutting down summits represents a substantive and meaningful blow to global elites). One of the more glaring examples of 'summitism' was the TV drama, scripted by Richard Curtis, *The Girl in the Café* shown on BBC just before the launch of the G8. It painted the participants of such summits as real-live decision-makers with the fate of the world almost literally in their hands. Watching the drama unfold we have the impression that an impassioned plea or a voice of reason in this world of madness could make a difference. We should know otherwise. Not only are decisions arrived at well in advance of the summit. They are arrived at less by the interplay of distinct moral or ethical positions, than by a rather cruder combination of perceived national interest, elite perceptions of necessity and the fear of the backlash unleashed by global forces beyond the reach of the participants (transnational corporations, global media barons such as Murdoch, party donors and so on).

This is not to say that decisions are wholly immune to ethical and moral considerations. Clearly the 'climate of opinion' is an important, if not determining, influence on the business of summits. Can we suppose that Blair and Brown would be quite so excited about the fate of the 'developing' world in general and Africa in particular were it not for the fact that ordinary men and women, opinion-formers, newspaper columnists and such like had been hammering away at the topic for some time?

Politicians are pragmatic individuals. They like to address issues that matter to constituents. This is particularly the case if it comes at zero or near-zero cost to themselves. (Banning fox hunting is the now classic example of a zero-cost measure that mattered to large swathes of the electorate but about which politicians were famously indifferent.) Politicians don't like to be thought of as immoral or unethical, even if they recognise in Machiavellian fashion that necessity is at the heart of the political. They would prefer to be doing things that are 'right and good'. They become uncomfortable if what they are doing is seen as 'wrong and bad'. But this alone will not stop them doing wrong and bad things, as the example of Britain's support for the US invasion of Iraq makes clear. However, continuing to act in ways that are widely perceived to be wrong and bad will lose politicians elections.

To move back to the point, summit protests are not merely symbolic but also substantive forms of protest – but the 'substance' here is what is contested. Stopping summits, making them expensive to police and putting elites in discomfort, has never and will never have direct impact either on the ability of elites to agree measures or on the decisions themselves. Even the Seattle protests, which at one level are still the most successful of the large-scale protests of recent years, had an only marginal impact on the proceedings of the WTO. Business that would otherwise have been attended to at the Seattle meeting was picked up and dealt with electronically and at subsequent mini-meetings and summits.

The notion that global elites are anything more than momentarily inconvenienced by summit protests is one that has to be dispensed with – and quickly. This is not the same as saying that summit protests are unimportant and that the energies that go into protests against them are wasted. Far from it. Protests are absolutely crucial, but for reasons that one rarely hears articulated, not least by activists themselves, perhaps because many are inclined (still) to think that summits are literally or figuratively centres of power and influence. They are not, and activist actions will not make a difference at this level at all. How then can summit protests make a difference? How more generally can DIY and disaffiliated activism come to matter – as it does?

A number of points come to mind here:

Summit protests help disaffiliated activists to connect and act together. Summits get activists to focus on something that requires collective mobilisation. They get activists to talk amongst themselves. People who might be busy with other projects will drop those things to join with others, thereby enlarging the scope for cooperation. People meet, they discuss, they interact, they plan actions, they work together. They might not have met if it were not for the fact that a big summit was coming to town. Without summits DIY activism is more difficult to coordinate. Coordination against something concrete like a summit is more immediately practical and focused than coordination against 'neoliberal governance' or 'global poverty'. Whilst these larger campaigns are absolutely crucial, they are ongoing, continual aspects of the present and the future of the present. A summit is an event which draws activists together, making the otherwise disaffiliated conjoined to something larger than themselves and to their particular causes and concerns.

Summits are one of the key moments when what is otherwise disaggregated crystallises. It is the moment when what otherwise appears to be multiple, heterogeneous, fuzzy becomes singular, distinct, unified. Summit protests are moments when the 'multitude' – Hardt and Negri's otherwise preposterously metaphysical notion – gains a measure of validity. The idea of a movement moves from the virtual to the actual; from conjecture to reality.

Summits produce a kind of agent – the 'alter-globalisation movement of movements'. There are not that many moments when the movement is made present to itself (social forums are another, certain festivals and carnivals have been in the past). Such moments are therefore important reminders that the movement can become an agent, can matter, can act, can coalesce. Summits are moments when what is otherwise molecular becomes molar – and in turn when the molar, the sense of the movement is affirmed as molecular – as composed of a multitude of different groups, causes, activisms, passions.

Summit protests can radicalise participants. Such protests already involve many who are radical, who oppose the system and everything that it represents. Many who attend protests are not very radical, but they often become so in the course of the protest. This is so for a variety of reasons.

The first of these is that protests can radicalise individuals who might otherwise be unreceptive to engaging with the nature of global rule, poverty and powerlessness. People are exposed to new ideas, new analyses, connections are made, examples multiplied, oppressions exposed. Protests are moments when the sheer scale of the misery inflicted on the world is the stuff of discussion and interrogation. To attend a major protest is to encounter that which for many is hidden, outside of normal experience, only momentarily glimpsed.

Protesters become a kind of proxy for those who cannot be there, cannot be heard. Of course this produces its own danger; one that is all too well known in the history of radical movements. This is thinking that at one level one can represent these multiple oppressions, can somehow embody them. It is to imagine that one transcends the contingent and bounded existence of who we are, to embrace the multiple oppressions of others. One cannot escape who and what we are, thus involvement evokes a responsibility as well as mode of participation. We can and should listen and learn from others.

We should not presume to know, but rather, should use protests as a means of finding out more. But protests provoke a 'becoming radical' in ways that cannot be imitated elsewhere – and certainly not in the confines of a student bedroom or stripped pine suburbia. Protests are a kind of active learning, a pedagogical moment, for those who might otherwise be locked into the media blackout against reality.

Protests are often the first taste of what it means to be confronted by state power in its most immediately concrete, direct and unmediated form. The idea of the police or the state as being an agent of the power of the ruling class is laughable to many who have not attended a major protest. Yet the sheer intimidatory power of the police is on these occasions startling, even for the most obdurate supporter of the status quo. Participants at recent pro-hunting and Countryside Alliance events have spoken about having been made to feel like an antagonist, an outsider, an enemy of law and order. And of course such protesters are treated with kid gloves compared with anti-capitalist protesters at major summits.

To be photographed, videoed, ridiculed, humiliated, herded into human pens, trampled on, barged into, charged, detained is to enter a different world. A world where the police and the state appear not as the neutral, benevolent guardian of our eternal interests, but agents of elite rule. State power is revealed for what the honest apologists of capitalist rule always asserted it should be: a harsh 'nightwatchman' whose job it is to beat back the feckless, indolent mob. To activists nothing is new here. Activists know from bitter experience about the nature of state power. However to those who are just starting down the road of activism, such experiences are often revelatory moments of radicalisation. The world is turned upside down and we begin to see that the Thatcherite rhetoric of 'enemies within' is not just rhetoric: they mean it.

Summit protests are the most visible reminder of the conflict and antagonism at the heart of contemporary globalisation. It was pretty easy for Francis Fukuyama to present his claim in 1989 that we had reached 'the end of history', that fundamental antagonisms and arguments had disappeared from contemporary politics, that liberal-democracy (aka liberal-capitalism) had won and that we could settle down in our 'air conditioned comfort'. There were few major protests concerning the state of the world. His claim had the veneer of empirical respectability. Of course radical activists knew this claim was nonsense and that beneath the surface of the administered world of transnational brands and corporations lay something much less edifying and much less easily controlled.

But people's view of the world is heavily mediated by an elite-controlled media spectacle that covers events as opposed to analysing issues. Anger, disillusion and alienation are channelled into affirmative actions or at least in ways that do not disrupt the normal functioning of the machine. The media controls 'bad news' by focusing on human interest stories and of course on 'events' such as elections, accidents, disasters and the like. Summits conform to the logic of a media agenda in that they are events – time-limited with leaders, and thus photo and interview opportunities, gravitas, and the impression that something is 'happening'. Globalisation, global poverty, exploitation, degradation of the environment do not 'happen' in this sense and thus can be safely ignored by most parts of the media, until and unless they intrude as events (as with Hurricane

Katrina). But summits happen and so do summit protests – they intrude in the order of things. They need to be covered and some explanation has to be given for why there are protests. Most of the time these 'explanations' are pithy, incomplete, wrong or misguided, and any opportunity to present protests in a negative light is usually grabbed with both hands. But protests are visible reminders that the 'everything is right with the world' rhetoric that marked elite discourse between 1989 and 1999 is fragile, incomplete and questionable. Summits induce some reflection, if not necessarily action on the part of many 'ordinary' men and women. But reflecting is a prelude to acting.

Needless to say, the mediatisation of summit protests produces its own problems and dilemmas. One of these is that some are attracted by the prospect of the 'protest as spectacle', ignoring the substantive political message that most activists wish to project in favour of behaviour that will fall straight into the hands of a hostile or uncomprehending media. This is the stance of what Vaneigem aptly terms the 'active nihilist', the individual who is attracted to the image of himself (it is usually a him) as 'protester', 'militant', 'outsider'. One of the successes of recent summit protests in this country is the degree to which such 'activists' have been side-lined, leaving the media scratching around forlornly looking for the 'action'. More generally, however, there would be even less mainstream coverage of the kinds of issues that matter to activists had it not been for the summit protests.

Summit protests embody the hope for something better. Related to the above, summit protests are suggestive in non-conformist, idealistic and utopian ways. They embody the impossible hope for something better. Utopianism used to be laughed at by activists of all shapes and forms, and in particular by those busily 'building' the po-faced Party-movement. As the Party-movement form receded into the sepia-tinted gloom, so something was needed to punctuate the present and to remind us that Tomorrow does not have to be like Today; that there are values, beliefs, ways of living, modes of thought and action that are radically at odds with 'common sense' and 'received wisdom'. Summit protests involve the creation of spaces in which people can experience a different ethic or way of doing things directly – from the convergence spaces and hubs involved with the organisation of protests and action, to the conferences and workshops that accompany them, to the eco-villages, camps and settlements that spring up to sustain them. To DIY activists it is a no doubt banal point that such spaces represent something outside the commodified, routinised exterior world. Some activists might know little of this 'exterior', such is their facility to move between activist spaces and places without having to encounter the ever-increasingly one-dimensional world in which the 'muggles' live. Yet for initiates, first-timers, the curious, to interested on-lookers, neophytes, unaffiliated students, even journalists and those covering protests, such spaces are reminders that protests are not just protests – they are not just events. They are moments where such experiments in living and working can be approached directly. This matters to those who might otherwise be put off by media reports of violent protesters, black bloc 'fanatics' and lawless activists. The ability to enter spaces, interact with activists, learn about campaigns, protests, the cause of poverty, be different, think different is key. They are little suggestive islands in a sea of 'normality', in turn part of an archipelago of hope.

My suggestion is thus that summit protests matter, but not for the reasons that many activists and commentators offer. The G8 met and it deliberated. It decided matters that had already been decided, give or take some details on aid. The existence of protests made little direct difference to the proceedings of the summit at all – nor could they have. Power does not lie in the summits themselves and summits are not arenas of contingency or unmediated choice, except in a very marginal sense. If protesters managed to close down every summit from the Gleneagles G8 meet onwards, it would make little difference to the ability of elites to impose their vision of the world on the global majority. It would inconvenience them, it would make the business of creating consensus around certain decisions perhaps more demanding to achieve, it would deny the global media the chance to look at and examine global issues against the backdrop of important people and important buildings. It would not change global politics. It would not make the lives of the poorest easier. It would not undermine global capitalism.

Where however the summit protests did make a difference and continue to make a difference, is to the much more nebulous and difficult battle for the hearts and minds of those without whom real and fundamental change to the structure of global capitalism cannot take place: ordinary men and women. Lasting change will not be effected by challenging global elites in some literal battle for the space of power. Storming Gleneagles and taking Bush and Blair hostage might have made for an entertaining Eisenstein-type distraction, but the notion that storming parliaments and disrupting global media events will deliver power to the masses is a gloriously antique notion that we can dispense with in short order. Whether one likes it or not, we are in the current conjuncture engaged in what in another part of the radical jungle is called the battle for 'hegemony' – a 'war of position' as opposed to a 'war of manoeuvre'. This is to say, we are in the midst of a struggle to transform the thoughts, ideals and beliefs of our fellow human beings so that substantive change to the structures, institutions and processes of power can be contemplated on terms that are dictated by us as opposed to global elites.

Here, however, we tread on the toes of a number of orthodoxies concerning the future of the AGM. For most radicals, the place of power is still vital to the movement and to effecting change to global politics. We need to capture power. In order to do that we need to build the Party-movement that will enable those with the needs and interests of the global majority at heart to change the global balance of power. Summit protests are on this view a decorative form of resistance, at best an occasion to summon the masses behind a ringing message of revolt, at worst, a case of 'hysterical' or spectacular politics whose results are meagre to say the least. The 'real' business of radical activism should (of course) be building a revolutionary Party – or, even more grotesquely, taking back ownership of the Labour Party so that it can be the vehicle for a radical transformation of British society. Hence the critique – so often aired by Marxist groups, radical democrats and fashionable neo-Leninists such as Slavoj Zizek – of 'summitism', 'spontaneity', 'movementism' and other crimes besides.

As my account above indicates, summit protests and the forms of activism and engagement that underpin them should not be regarded as 'second-best'. They are not gestural, ineffective or impotent sideshows in the real battles that confront us. Summit protests are the product of a kind of activism that prefigures and embodies a wholly different kind of politics, a politics of 'everyday life', one that seeks to transform the way we envisage power and relate to it. This is a hidden, subterranean politics when compared with the muscular revolutionism of Trotsky and friends, but it is one that gives shape and substance to what can indeed seem an apparently random and sporadic set of revolts against the system. In theoretical terms it is a praxis of the kind analysed by Max Stirner, Deleuze and Guattari, Vaneigem, James Scott, Foucault, Piven and Cloward, de Certeau, Hakim Bey and most latterly John Holloway, in short by those whose vision is one informed by the necessity of real and far-reaching change in the way we think about power. What kind of politics is this?

One that challenges, undercuts and supplants the idea that the task of the politically radical is to capture power as a macro-social 'thing'. What disaffiliated activism has sought is the transformation of power, not the creation of a machine that imitates the very exclusionary dynamic of the world we are seeking to change. This involves empowering ourselves and others. It is to take power back from those who would annex it in institutions and processes that are removed from those who are subject to them. It is to generate micro-social resources – a praxis in which proposals, legislations, plans and projects are generated immanently, rather than imposed by virtue of office, hierarchical positioning, celebrity, strength, wealth or any other transcendent quality. It is to generate micro-communities, micro-spaces in which people are heard, react, learn, speak, listen, take decisions, participate and above all create power through their own interactions, solidarity and collective desire to do something, achieve something, run something.

One that seeks to resist incorporation into an ideology of liberation/emancipation/universal good. As DIY activism has long demonstrated, it is enough to have a sense of what one is against to effect a mobilisation, whether that is against human rights abuses, racism, imperialism, war or neoliberalism. 'Being against' is not weaker than 'being for', whether that 'for' is anarchism, socialism, communism or Moonyism – it is the condition that allows anarchists, socialists, communists, and indeed Moonies to act together in the name of a commonly perceived injustice.

Such forms of action may be temporary, contingent, fragile, but they are also inclusive, open, and negotiable – qualities distinctly lacking in traditional ideological crusades. They also necessitate or make desirable a dialogue of a tactical kind. People need to discuss, come together, formulate plans. They have to enter into a dialogue with each other, to listen to each other as opposed to listening to the One who will tell us what to believe, what the line is, where we are expected to line up. It necessitates spaces of negotiation, learning and listening. Being against is a step towards something else: becoming radical – desiring change, desiring a reappropriation of the world for the world.

Radicalism is not necessarily an *ideological* stance of opposition. One doesn't need to have read Marx, nor Bakunin for that matter. One needs to desire change, and desire is not the preserve of the well-read, the theorist or the 'strategist'. It is the quality of those who have seen and heard enough. As Subcomandante Marcos puts it, this encompasses everyone who believes in as simple a value as human dignity. Dignity and respect for what is distinct, particular, idiosyncratic – not just the 'working class'. No analysis or special training is required. What is required is a willingness to open one's eyes to the state of the world, at the simple causes of misery and powelessness, and the desire to do something about it.

One that seeks to nurture and promote the movement through alliance, affinity and association – not Party-movement building. Protests are the most visible reminder that at the core of a disaffiliated politics is the sense of impermanency and contingency of contemporary activism. Activists come together for this event, this moment, this summit. This is of course a source of huge frustration for the 'vertical' wing of the AGM which argues that without the permanent and institutional crystallisation of activist demands in the Party form the movement cannot build and conquer power. Verticalists are confusing problem with cure. The problem is the lack of voice, the lack of participation and opportunities to act – the cure is not to close off these feelings of powerlessness and exclusion, but the opposite: to recognise that no amount of Party-building will substitute for forms of interaction that fully meet the need to be included, to count and be heard. What is required is rather the generalisation of inclusive forms of activism so that they are not isolated moments, as the (media) focus on summits can sometimes make them appear to be.

In the UK context, there are already many ways in which such a process of generalisation is taking place: through social centres, squatting, the creation of Indymedia, disaffiliated yet conjoined protests across a range of issues from animal rights to welfare reform and protection of immigrants and asylum seekers. A web of interactions already exists that facilitates and encourages coordinated responses to a dazzling array of matters of pressing concern. Of course the results are uneven and can seem depressingly minor when compared with actions elsewhere.

Yet we know there is something linking the various efforts of radical activists across the 'developed' and 'developing' world – whether or not they attain head-

line-grabbing status. It is the generalisation of forms of radical inclusivity, one that moves from the site of protest to the site of economic power and communal governance. The autonomous social centres of Leeds and London are not the autonomous zones of Chiapas, and the various experiments at collective and communal economic activity scattered around the country are not the same as the large-scale reappropriations of economic power of the kind found in Latin America. Yet they manifest the same *desire*: to take control, to make power everyday, to make democracy something immediately lived and experienced as opposed to a form of 'governance' to which we are subject. It is the transformation of power as something held by distant elites, to something that is creative, immanent, subservient. It is to make power a collective-communal resource as opposed to a distant Leviathan that looms over us. Those of us who think such a characterisation of the aims and goals of the AGM is valid are not alone. Far from it. As the title of the book says, 'We are Everywhere'.

In view of the above it would be quite wrong in my opinion to regard the hegemonic battle both within the AGM and between the AGM and the wider public, as something that disaffiliated activism is struggling unsuccessfully to influence let alone win. On the contrary, as I think is evident, the last decade has seen an enormous upsurge in efforts to resist not only neoliberalism, but also those ideologies that promise to *overcome* neoliberalism and implant some monotone blueprint of human happiness on activist efforts ('the counter-empire').

This is a revolt against power as macro-social sledgehammer, as something that is captured and used for 'our' benefit, leaving us as powerless as we were before. If this is what protests are supposed to build, then we have to reject building in this arid, alienating and uninteresting way. We need instead to continue to generalise, nurture and promote forms of self-activity and self-creation.

This is not, of course, an easy task nor, in the context of advanced industrial society, is it one that is easily imagined or envisaged as creating the conditions for a reappropriation of what is rightfully ours: our own power of individual and collective invention. It is one that confirms that the widespread pessimism concerning the possibility of radical activism is misplaced. But the conditions that gave rise to the expectation of the Party-builders are exhausted. Class-consciousness, ready-made practices of collective production, clear and demarcated group identities have collapsed under pressure of individualisation, atomisation and differentiation. Of course whereas some theorists draw notoriously conservative conclusions from such developments, telling us that all we can hope for is some sort of half-baked semi-contractual welfarism, it is possible for us to construct a quite different account of the potentials contained within such otherwise bleak sounding prognoses.

Individualisation means an escape from the inherited mantle of received roles and subservient identities. Atomisation means the end of traditional and usually submissive sectionalisation of society under conditions of extreme division of labour. Differentiation means a greater desire to be heard for what one is and what one wants to become as opposed to the subject of group or class representation. Such tendencies are at the very heart of the problem which animates the AGM and yet which seems curiously ignored by those who imagine that barking out a correct analysis to the hapless masses will enable the coalescence of identity, interest and consciousness needed to create the Party. It will not, and such efforts are likely to go to waste or to become the basis for authoritarian-populism.

The point is that the AGM is itself multiplying, diversifying, fractalising and becoming *more* not less 'chaotic'. One only has to recall 2004's World Social Forum in Mumbai and the incredible diversity of aims, demands, groups, needs, interests and voices to remind us that a genuinely inclusive politics means going beyond the passive acceptance of the denumerable, the already known and established. Inclusivity means being open to the new, the unpredictable and yet-to-become. This in turn implies that the stance of the AGM should be less one of building in the name of some fixed future (communism, anarchy, 'another world' in the singular) – but a task of proliferation and multiplication of the networks, actions and resistances and experiments that are already being generated, spawned, nurtured so that other *worlds* become possible.

Summit protests are thus to be differentiated from Party-building by an acknowledgement that the time to act is not tomorrow or at some point to be decided by the central committee. The future is already here; the future is the future of the present, the future of the myriad molecular projects, plans and experiments we see developing in force and influence across the world. Protests are part of that present, and we can use protests to remind ourselves and the rest of the AGM that we have outworn a *strategy* – whether Trotskyite or radical democratic – in favour of a *practice* of resistance in the here and now. We have moved beyond being told what to do and how to do it – whether by elites, vanguards, theorists, or 'strategists'. There is a movement, there is a network, there are protests and many opportunities for making voices heard. We don't need to change the tune; we need to turn up the volume.

34

THE END OF THE WORLD AS WE KNOW IT
Kay Summer and Harry Halpin

I. WHAT NEXT FOR THE WORLD?

All empires fall, yet they do not do so by accident. Complex systems, be they rainforests or global capitalism, prosper precisely because they are adapted to the circumstances of the world around them, and the systems themselves shape the environment within which they prosper. Tropical rainforests, in part, create the rainfall that maintains them as rainforests. Capitalism expands when buying and selling occurs: as ever more products, processes and people are measured on the same single monetary scale, they become commodities, and capitalism creates the wider enclosures necessary for its continued existence.

Any complex system, whether capitalism or rainforests, has a few basic organisational principles that keep the system operating. When the environment changes, these complex systems must adapt to survive. In the rainforest, over a run of dry years, more drought-tolerant trees would be winners, less drought-tolerant trees losers, but the forest would remain a forest. Neoliberal capitalism destroyed the 'job-for-life', industrial employment of the late 20th century and is replacing it with short-term, contract jobs. Is this a victory *for* people who rejected industrial employment and attempted to live differently, or a victory *against* labour struggles for a 'just' and social wage? In a fundamental sense it doesn't matter: the accumulation of capital continues, the inhumanity of selling our own lives remains, capitalism survives. However, if the basic assumptions that keep the system operating are rendered obsolete by social or physical environmental changes, the system faces a crisis and may collapse.

The key feature of complex systems is that when their elasticity is stretched to breaking point, unlike in 'normal' times, small changes can have large and long-lasting effects. Yet, which changes will have such impacts cannot be precisely stated: any looming collapse can itself only be predicted in broad terms. Furthermore, if a system collapses, there is no way of knowing in advance what any new system (or systems) that replaced it would look like. The final feature is that such a change is fundamental – there is no going back.

In rainforests, a run of dry years may occur such that, at a certain point, no trees survive: trees will be wholly replaced by bushes or grasses – a fundamentally different system. Even if wet years returned, the lack of seeds and the lack of animals and other systems that disperse them would mean that a return to the previous forest is impossible. In Europe, the transition from feudalism to the capitalist mode of production was one such moment of crisis, which led to irreversible transformation.

Today, we are at another historical moment of crisis, a fork or turning point where anything can happen. Capitalism assumes that the supply of resources which can be converted into capital is infinite. To these ends, capitalism consumes the resources of the world in its never-ending search for greater cycles of production and consumption. But in direct contradiction to this most basic premise of capitalism, our planet is no more than a small spheroid and its resources are finite. A key organisational principle of capitalism – its expansion – is being breached on multiple fronts. This is a problem with no solution and obvious symptoms are present: climate change and the irrevocable decline of oil, to name but two. Collapse and transformation are around the corner.

Broadly, two sets of arguments attempt to counter any claim to the demise of capitalism on ecological grounds. The first concerns the capitalist system itself, while the second is about resistance to capitalism's inhumanity. Economists argue that there is such a thing as 'resource substitutability': as one resource begins to run out, it becomes more expensive, giving an incentive to find either more of it or, ultimately, to find another resource that will do the job. In one example of resource substitutability, synthetic medical drug production now counters the difficulties in harvesting increasingly rare wild plants and animals. However, not everything is readily substitutable.

Oil has been the fuel of capitalism for a century and it cannot last forever. Whoever has control of oil has power and wealth. If someone could find or invent an alternative to oil, untold wealth and power would flow their way. This incentive has been around for a century. Nothing has turned up. When important environmental problems are identified, such as carbon emissions and climate change, the usual answer is to fix the problem through technology: an increased role for nuclear power, for example. Yet the estimated amount of uranium required

to switch today's global energy use to nuclear power is far more than all the known and predicted deposits of uranium across the Earth's surface. The use of uranium in nuclear weapons means its whereabouts have been fairly extensively mapped, although figures are subject to the same secrecy and volume-inflation as oil reserve figures.

More worryingly, there is no substitute possible for the chemical elements required for high-yield crop production, some of which are fast running out (notably phosphorus). More broadly, where are the substitutes for land and water, the demand for which will always expand with economic expansion? The so-called 'knowledge economy' is not free from these two precious resources: it takes 71 litres of freshwater to produce a single 2-gram, low-specification computer chip. Or more than 20 million litres daily for a single chip factory. The environmental impact of replacing a computer every two years (their current average lifespan) is roughly equivalent to that of replacing a new car every ten years.

The second set of arguments countering claims of capitalism's inevitable demise on ecological grounds revolve around the purported 'failure' of previous social change movements. The analysis of capitalism by the Left is that, given enough time, capitalism would plunge the majority of the world into such misery that people would revolt, precipitating a revolution that would cause the emergence of another social system based on more humane principles. So far, capitalism has managed to avert this crisis through dividing people along lines of privilege, 'race', nation, gender, and so on *ad infinitum*, through control and manipulation of information through the mass media, through minor modifications to the system and through the use of extreme violence.

Capitalism's strategists believe they can use similar techniques to avert problems caused by our planet's environmental limits being breached. One good example of this is the attempt to create a market in carbon emissions, which actually seeks to make money out of climate change through enclosing or privatising the atmospheric commons. This tactic has been coupled with the manipulation of information about the threat of climate change. But there are major differences between human beings and carbon dioxide molecules. Humans may resist or rebel, and they may be pacified with threatened or actual job losses, starvation, torture or prison. But a carbon dioxide molecule is immune to such attempts at control. Nothing that is said, written or done will change the amount of energy (heat) it reflects back to Earth, so further warming up the planet. Journalists can report what they like, but the temperature will still rise. An anthropocentric world-view, as is common on the Left, leads to looking at the environment as one of many similar problems created by capitalism, rather than understanding the intrinsic differences. Capitalism is immensely resilient, but it cannot, like some latter-day god, alter the physical limits of the planet.

We are not considering some grim future. The crisis is already present today, although few connect the disparate dots. The Red Cross charity already estimates that there are more environmental refugees than those displaced by war. Resource wars (the occupation of Iraq and fighting in the Congo), land and freshwater scarcity (in part fuelling the war around Darfur in Sudan), climate change-induced hurricanes (Katrina and 20 others) and other natural disasters on varying scales (the East Asian Tsunami, the 2003 European heatwave causing 30,000 deaths), new infectious diseases (Sars, 'bird flu' and Ebola) all mean the social fabric of the world is being stretched towards, and beyond, its limits. Moreover, most of the world's population is highly dependent upon the infrastructure of global capitalism. When the food does not arrive at the supermarket, truly dangerous times begin.

Ecological collapse is spelling the end of the world as we know it. This currently slow and chronic collapse is caused by global capitalism, as its search for infinite resources to fuel its infinite pursuit of profit is coming up against the finite bounds of the environment, causing nearly irreparable damage to global life-support systems in the process. The finite amount of world resources directly contradicts a founding principle of global capitalism.

II. WHAT NEXT FOR SOCIAL MOVEMENTS?

The very danger of our situation gives us hope that fundamental social change is possible. When systems are relatively well-adapted to their environment, fundamental change is nearly impossible. But in times of crisis, when the social and physical environment is changing rapidly, the system itself teeters and it is immensely susceptible to change: indeed, revolutionary transformation may be the only way to survive. However, in desperation to retain the certainties of the current system, strange adaptations of previous social forms once thought long-dead can re-appear, such as authoritarianism and medieval religious fund-amentalism, as exemplified by the rise of the neoconservatives in the USA and political Islam in the Middle East. These signals indicate the potential scale of changes on the horizon.

The fundamental point for those who want a much more humane future, is that it is necessary to incorporate an understanding of the imminence of ecolog-ical collapse, and how to halt it, into our analyses of the world. Our very survival is not guaranteed. We simply do not have time for endless sectarian debates over ideology. Nor do we have the luxury of patiently waiting for the 'correct moment' to strike.

Belief in the old two-step strategy for social change, to take state power and then transform the world, is through bitter experience no longer widely held. The ideological Party that patiently waits for either the next election or the correct conditions for 'armed struggle' has evaporated. And the (male) First-World industrial worker has lost his privileged position as the only (perceived) agent of change. A different form of struggle has emerged in many places across the world. The emphasis is on creating our own worlds, not on seeking state power. We demand nothing from the state, but instead prefer to 'do our own thing'. We excavate capital's power by exercising our own power here and now. This is attrac-tive, in part, because many no longer see the world and its workings as a linear machine, to be confronted on these terms, with ever larger political parties, or more unity within the working class, or more people becoming activists. Instead many see the world as inherently non-linear, and best confronted by expanding on multiple fronts (as capitalism does), yet with different social relations. This form of politics leads to a rejection of the centralised Party as an organisational form, and has meant instead the revival of the affinity group, the council and the assembly. We have seen all these forms reemerge over the past decade or so, and both affinity groups and assemblies were utilised productively over the period of the Gleneagles counter-mobilisation.

Affinity groups, councils and assemblies relate to each other in networks. Networks provide the space for people to develop connections between each other. Instead of homogenising its participants into an obedient mass, a network preserves and facilitates self-organisation by maximising the flow of information and potential connections between its members. While a hierarchy takes power away from individuals to a distant leader, a network respects the concerns of every participant, keeping consensual decisions to a minimum. Hierarchies tend to demand that everyone adopts the same worldview. Networks thrive on a diver-sity of viewpoints that may never agree, and merely provide the means for the

many voices of their participants to communicate, allowing people with differing beliefs to change and to discover common ground, while preserving their own unique perspective.

Networks are primarily for communication between relatively autonomous groups, and have been strengthened immensely by the proliferation of information technology such as the web, email and mobile phones, giving groups quick reaction times and the ability to coordinate globally. On the streets these networks encourage a diversity of tactics and thrive off swarming and creativity.

Dissent! is a good example of such a network. The focus on local groups, mostly having a physical presence in social centres, meant that the counter-mobilisation against the G8 was grounded in the unique conditions of every group in Britain. The continual growth of these social centres will provide the physical points of contact and information for a sustainable way of life beyond capitalism. The network had distinctly minimal foundation that comprised just five 'hallmarks' from Peoples' Global Action. This potentially allowed people from a wide diversity of backgrounds to weave together multiple ecological and social struggles into a generalised movement against their root cause: capitalism itself.

In action, the network tied local struggles against the M74 motorway in Glasgow to global struggles against climate change through the 'Boogie on the Bridge' street party and demonstrated alternatives to unlimited growth in the form of the Cre8 Summat community garden. Struggles in Edinburgh against 'precarity' were connected to the universal need of humans for dignity and joy through the Carnival for Full Enjoyment, while the Indymedia Centre provided a dense communications network, broadcasting these examples of both resistance and alternatives across the world. As the G8 summit itself approached, the Dissent! network provided the infrastructure to demonstrate alternatives in action on a large scale: low-impact living in the Stirling eco-village and the decentralised road and rail blockades which shut the summit down on its opening morning, all organised on the basis of consensus.

Dissent! understood capitalism as an entire social system to be confronted and transformed and, in response, developed a mix of living and demonstrating alternatives, taking direct action against both the symbols and practical institutions of capitalism, while keeping the environment, broadly termed, centre stage.

This is not to say that the Dissent! network and anti-G8 mobilisation did not both have numerous problems – they did. Here we are concerned with making some general points. While we broadly agree with the approach of building other worlds, living life despite capitalism, there is a central issue that troubles us. How do we build a new world upon the blasted ruins of the current one? And how do we do so on the urgent time-scale forced upon us by the massive ecological crisis facing humanity? In short, you can't have a revolution on a dead planet.

The lack of interest in taking power means conflict is down-graded. It no longer occupies centre-stage in revolutionary politics, as it previously has done for many from both Marxist and anarchist backgrounds. Of course, by attempting to take what we need to 'build a world in which many worlds are possible' – land, buildings and the like – we are brought back into conflict, but it is a reluctant conflict. This is epitomised by the Zapatista Army, an army constantly questioning the use of armed conflict, and more interested in community assemblies and poetry than 'armed struggle'.

Our fear is that in wealthy areas of the world where we are well plugged into the infrastructure of global capitalism, it is certainly possible to have cosy, parallel 'alternative worlds', which pose no real threat to capitalist social relations. The legalised squatting scene in parts of continental Europe or New Age 'drop-out' culture across the world are busy perfecting non-hierarchical meeting skills while the planet burns. It is entirely possible that the social centres and Dissent! generally could follow this pattern. Such contradictions between not contesting power, yet confronting governments and corporations to secure what any future society will need – a stable climate, freshwater, clean air, unpolluted and undeveloped land – need to be made explicit.

So what's the plan? As there is no certainty in these immensely unstable times, there can be no master strategy. However, some tactics obviously appear to make more sense than others. Broadly speaking, we need to be action-focused to gain and defend the resources that humanity and life in general need. We must keep a focus on protecting our life support systems for the future. To do this, we need lots and lots of people to be involved, and so our actions need to resonate with people who are more and more diverse – people who are, apparently, different from ourselves! – allowing them to fuse with networks of resistance. This can only happen if we ground our actions in the concrete reality of people's lives, not any abstract belief system cooked up in revolutionary journals or universities. Taking action that builds a foundation for further action is a major incentive for people's involvement.

Let's be honest: our ability to avert ecological collapse and the deaths of millions of people is, at present, minimal. Yet we live in extraordinary times: a historical turning point where anything can happen. As shown by Indymedia and the internet in general, ideas and information can today spread with unprecedented speed, and news of social unrest in one place often inspires revolts in a thousand others. As the system shifts further and further into collapse, we have a fighting chance of surviving capitalism and healing the ecological crisis.

We write from the UK, so what about something specific? We know that the coming together of different elements can bring about a socially explosive crisis. How about an all-out campaign to stop the new nuclear power stations we are told are needed to meet the shortfall in the UK's energy needs? There is the potential to halt a hugely destructive 'development project' – one which would leave a damaging legacy for thousands of years – to critique the entire system and to bring talk of alternatives centre-stage, while piling the pressure on the government. Electricity blackouts would focus everyone's minds. Mutual aid and solidarity between local communities, anti-war, anti-roads, anti-capitalist and climate change groups, could transform us, all those groups, the Dissent! network, and the UK as a whole.

III. WHAT NEXT FOR ME?

We have presented a terrifying spectre of collapse, but also of hope. Yet the hope rests with us. As individuals, we often feel dwarfed by powers seemingly beyond our control. But let us not forget that it is ordinary people who fuel this system, both figuratively when we go to work every day and literally when we pump our car full of petrol. It is people like you and me who built the pyramids and the skyscrapers. Despite the immense power accorded by the media to the G8 and other so-called 'leaders', it is people like you and me who have the power to transform the world.

To survive this turmoil and thrive, we will need to look after ourselves. We will need resilient social networks of friends and political allies: the wider and deeper they are, the better we will fare. We will need to take and defend the resources we need for any future society: water, buildings, land. We will need to be smart, understanding how the current world (dys)functions, so as not to repeat the mistakes of the past. Importantly, our ideas – how to live the world differently – need to be well-known, easy to take on board, easy to join in with, and open to be adapted. We will need changes at every scale, from the tiny, individual 'everyday' things, up to more intermittent, massive surges of collective energy.

The essence of action is to get involved now to change the immediate social and physical environment around you to reflect the world you want to live in. This can sometimes be difficult and daunting at first, but it is possible, and it leads to a more enjoyable life in the here and now. There are things we can do as individuals: instead of shopping at a supermarket, try instead to purchase locally-grown food from small farmers near you, or even grow your own food in an allotment. Most importantly, find other people. No one can change the world by themselves. There are almost certainly like-minded people nearby who want to live in a better world. Search the web, talk to people in pubs, find like-minded groups that make you feel less lonely and isolated. Find different groups whose viewpoints may expand your own. There may be an anti-capitalist social centre near you that doubtless needs your help. If you live in the UK there might be a local group that participates in Dissent! If there isn't one, there are always local community centres, or why not start your own group with friends and plug into wider networks across the world?

Remaining open and transparent – building groups and networks on the solid basis of trust is critical. This is frequently difficult. Most people will be there for the long-haul: genuinely committed to changing the world around them into a freer and more humane place. However, a few will be there solely to develop their careers, one or two might be spies for the police; some will have personal grudges, others you may just find hard to work with. Assemblies and the ubiquitous email lists will sometimes be chaotic and seemingly far from being 'another world'. But resist the temptation to say 'fuck it': you *must* deal with all of this in order to keep on expanding and deepening these networks of struggles and experiments in living. A further obstacle is the tendency to label. Calling ourselves or our groups 'activists' or 'anarchists', for example, both limits our potential and excludes others, making change much more difficult. Remember, this is deadly serious – nothing less than the fate of the world is in your hands. Your viewpoint on life is unique and your perspective and imagination is needed by the world. In concert with others, your action or inaction can determine the future of life on this planet. In times like these, the smallest of actions can have global effects.

Other worlds are certainly possible. No social system has lasted forever, and this empire too will fall. But these other worlds are going to exist as part of this physical world, which we must fight for. It will take all the strength and creativity of the multitudes of people underneath the heel of capitalism to formulate the strategies and tactics to fight the current system and so create the space for sustainable alternatives to flourish. To escape the intrinsic depravity of capitalism and its so-called leaders like the G8, we must shut them down, anywhere and everywhere. While simultaneously, amongst the ruins of this world, our networks are already sending up the tender shoots of better futures.

35

COWS ARE SCARIER THAN PIGS
Anonymous

when we left the eco-village at 2.45 in the morning on July 6, my friends and i walked at the front. sometimes in front of the rubber rings. eager to act. i remember looking back and seeing a sea of hundreds of us and it filled me with a sense of pride and of confidence, the feeling that we could achieve anything. at the first police line i ran to the front and was crushed between pushing protesters and baton-wielding pigs. they hit me in the face and then broke my thumb, the bastards. we fell back and re-grouped. after this a sense of defeat and of fear spread through us as panic set in. most of us were not accustomed to violence, unlike the desensitised pig-robots. we ran through lines, we ran over, under and around them. i can't remember how many. then a group of a hundred or so of us split and headed into the fields. long grass, crop fields (single file!), railway lines (not sure if they were in use or not), a stream or two, embankments. we didn't all know the way, but we had a few black bloc with us and they showed us. thank you to them!

gathering sticks and stones. helicopters – cover your faces if you don't want to be photographed! lines of pig vans everywhere. keep going! exhausted, i'd been at the gate all night with a young guy from holland, too excited and wired to sleep. a phone call, some had already made it to the M9! cheers, elation, heart jumps a beat, pride restored. we have to get there and help them. up that hill, over there. we look down from the top to see the M9 empty of traffic, lots of stationary blue lights, queues of traffic. cheers all round. we will make it. fields of cows! don't run! i'm from a city. cows are scarier than pigs.

WE REACHED THE M9!!!!!! kiss the ground, lay the blockade. fuck the pigs. we take the slip road.

not for long though, by now our numbers are down to 50. we have to get out of here. they are riot pigs, they have dogs. the helicopters and the exhaustion. we have walked miles, and all are drenched from rain and long wet grass. i decide to make a break. we had achieved our goal and i had to go. not wanting to be caught, remembering Burger King and the shopping trolleys. i ran, they were chasing us through a field, and many were left behind. an abandoned farmhouse with no roof. 2 hours freezing, shaking, crying, burying my maps. hiding under mud and grass. ALONE. dogs barking all round me, helicopters overhead. FEAR. finally, i decided to break for it, across more fields, woods and 2 motorways. met up with 2 guys. the best people i ever met. walked back. 32 mile round trip cross-country, in holey old trainers. soaking, scared, injured, bleeding, aching, blisters. TRAUMA!!!! got back to camp at about 2 or 3 in the afternoon. collapsed in med tent, taken to trauma tent. cup o' tea. wish i'd brought some weed, dyin for a spliff.

6 hours crying, jibbering, the aloneness in the farmhouse will remain with me forever. it contrasted so starkly with the group dynamic i had had just moments before.

mission accomplished, now to get the fuck out of the eco-village before the fuckers block us in. bus to stirling station, pigs at station proudly taunt that they are nazis.

we were fluid and dynamic, and without preordained hierarchy. they were rigid and immobile and locked to their orders and to their training. we ran rings around them. fleeting hierarchies of experience and knowledge, or of sheer confidence developed naturally as each situation presented itself to us. heroes emerged. we kept each other going. anarchy was proven before my eyes.

contacts

21	Isabelle Fremeaux: isa@labofii.net;
	John Jordan: john@labofii.net
22	kristina.nellweaver@gmail.com
23	activist_trauma@riseup.net; www.activist-trauma.net/
24	sean@paganarchy.net; www.clownarmy.org
25	wb3@york.ac.uk
26	haleyburton@hotmail.co.uk
27	—
28	stef@fish.co.uk
29	—
30	rgnunes@riseup.net
31	—
32	g8-2007@riseup.net; http://de.dissent.org.uk
33	simon.tormey@ntlworld.com;
	simon.tormey@nottingham.ac.uk
34	kaysmmr@yahoo.co.uk; harry@j12.org
35	—

credits

The publication of this book was funded primarily by the Dissent! network (*www.dissent.org.uk*). However, it would not have been possible without the additional financial support of Active Distribution (*www.activedistribution.org*), and the help of a number of other friends. Any money raised will go back into supporting Dissent! or similar projects. The Editors would like to thank all those, too numerous to mention, who contributed articles, images, ideas, time and inspiration to making this book possible.

Photo credits

© All photographs are **copyright** of the photographers and may not be reproduced without permission, except for those marked below with an asterisk which fall under the **Creative Commons Attribution Non-commercial Share Alike Licence**.

Paul Mattsson
(*paulmattsson@btopenworld.com*)
3, 7, 81, 126, 158, 310, 363

Guy Smallman (*www.guysmallman.com*)
11, 14, 16, 21, 54, 57, 59, 67, 89, 93, 98, 105, 106, 111, 113, 114, 115, 120, 123, 131, 134, 137, 143, 144, 147, 150, 152, 155, 179, 182, 215, 218, 223, 226, 229, 253, 256, 262, 267, 270, 275, 278, 280, 284, 287, 288, 292, 295, 298, 303, 307, 315, 316, 325, 327, 330, 332, 339, 342, 347, 350, 353, 356, 360

****Erin Siegal** (*www.erinsiegal.com*)
24, 28, 31, 32, 36, 85

****Fergus Ray Murray** (*www.oolong.co.uk*)
38, 70, 108, 174, 320

thomblower
45 (top left, top right & bottom left)

South Bristol anarchists
45 (bottom right)

Bristle **magazine** *46, 48*

Leon Roman (*cre8summit@riseup.net*)
62, 75, 189, 206, 234, 237, 238, 241

Eleanor Hoad *129*

Starhawk (*http://starhawk.org*)
184, 190, 195, 198, 202

kartoonkate (*www.kartoonkate.co.uk*)
205, 209

Ian Teh *242, 245, 246, 251*

Steve *248*

Unattributed *50, 79, 140*

171 advanced to Belgium, 181 Holland, 191 safe after
Victory in Europe, 198 war leave, 199 final Victory –
anxiety relieved, 203 hoping for demobilisation, 210
– 212 Palestine, Egypt, 235 wedding preparations, 239
marriage to Joan Easton
Tolson, George, 2, 17, 20, 29, 30, 56, 71, 77, 83, 89, 90, 94,
104, 179
Tolson, Joan, see Easton
Tolson, John, 2, 13, 19, 43, 71, 77, 104
Truman, Harry, President USA, 232

Upton, 78

War: views on and events
       possibility, 13
       Munich Crisis, 14 - 16
       Hitler's designs on Prague, 17
       Views on Huns, 20
       posting possible, 24
       tank exercises, 30
       Imminent, 31
       Recommends Churchill, 32
       Poland invaded, 46
       Italy threatens war, 55
       Hitler invades Belgium and Netherlands, 57
       Italy declares war, 62
       Future course of, 90
       D-Day, 147
       Comparison 1940/1944, 149
       Victory over Japan, 199
Watts, 118
Webb, 38
Wilkes, Michael, 63
Winant, Mr., Ambassador, 232

Yeo, 27
Yately, 20